Financial Analytics with R

Building a Laptop Laboratory for Data Science

Are you innately curious about dynamically inter-operating financial markets? Since the crisis of 2008, there is a need for professionals with more understanding about statistics and data analysis, who can discuss the various risk metrics, particularly those involving extreme events.

By providing a resource for training students and professionals in basic and sophisticated analytics, this book meets that need. It offers both the intuition and basic vocabulary as a step toward the financial, statistical, and algorithmic knowledge required to resolve the industry problems, and it depicts a systematic way of developing analytical programs for finance in the statistical language R. Build a hands-on laboratory and run many simulations. Explore the analytical fringes of investments and risk management.

Bennett and Hugen help profit-seeking investors and data science students sharpen their skills in many areas, including time-series, forecasting, portfolio selection, covariance clustering, prediction, and derivative securities.

Mark J. Bennett is a senior data scientist with a major investment bank and a lecturer in the University of Chicago's Master's program in Analytics. He has held software positions at Argonne National Laboratory, Unisys Corporation, AT&T Bell Laboratories, Northrop Grumman, and XR Trading Securities.

Dirk L. Hugen is a graduate student in the Department of Statistics and Actuarial Science at the University of Iowa. He previously worked as a signal processing engineer.

Financial Analytics with R

Building a Laptop Laboratory for Data Science

MARK J. BENNETT
University of Chicago

DIRK L. HUGEN
University of Iowa

CAMBRIDGE
UNIVERSITY PRESS

CAMBRIDGE
UNIVERSITY PRESS

University Printing House, Cambridge CB2 8BS, United Kingdom

Cambridge University Press is part of the University of Cambridge.

It furthers the University's mission by disseminating knowledge in the pursuit of
education, learning, and research at the highest international levels of excellence.

www.cambridge.org
Information on this title: www.cambridge.org/9781107150751

First published 2016

Printed in the United Kingdom by Clays, St Ives plc

A catalogue record for this publication is available from the British Library.

Library of Congress Cataloging-in-Publication Data
Names: Bennett, Mark J. (Mark Joseph), 1959– author. | Hugen, Dirk L., author.
Title: Financial analytics with R : building a laptop laboratory for data
    science / Mark J. Bennett, University of Chicago, Dirk L. Hugen,
    University of Iowa.
Description: Cambridge, UK : Cambridge University Press, 2016.
Identifiers: LCCN 2016026635 | ISBN 9781107150751
Subjects: LCSH: Finance–Mathematical models–Data processing. |
    Finance–Databases. | R (Computer program language)
Classification: LCC HG104 .B46 2016 | DDC 332.0285/513--dc23
LC record available at https://lccn.loc.gov/2016026635

ISBN 978-1-107-15075-1 Hardback

To our parents:
Mary and Herb and Patricia and Bernard

and family:
Rachel, Austin, and Cheryl
for all their kindness, love, and support

Contents

Preface

In 1994 the Channel Tunnel opened between England and France, allowing high-speed Eurostar trains to whisk passengers from the continent to the United Kingdom and back on a grand scale. What an amazing engineering feat it was for the time (beyond many people's earlier imaginations), yet we take it for granted today. In 1994, Grumman Aerospace Corporation, the chief contractor on the Apollo Lunar Module, was acquired by Northrop Corporation to form the new aerospace giant, Northrop Grumman. It was the prime contractor of the newly deployed advanced technology B-2 Stealth Bomber. On a much more mundane and personal scale, also in 1994, in a townhouse just outside the City of Chicago, I was performing a tedious daily exercise: looking up daily closing prices each evening in a stack of *Investor's Business Daily* newspapers for the two stock investments that were about to be purchased. This was not only to find out their running rate of return but also to find out their historical volatility relative to other stocks before entering into the positions. Doing this manual calculation was slow and tedious. The World Wide Web was introduced in the form of the Mosaic browser the next year. It was not long before Yahoo! was posting stock quotes and historical price charts, as well as technical indicators on the charts, available on demand for free in just a few seconds via the new web browsers.

The advent of spreadsheet software took analysts to a new level of analytical thinking. No longer were live, human-operated calculations limited to a single dimension. Each row or column could present a time dimension, a production category, a business scenario. And the automated dependency feature made revisions quite easy. Now spreadsheets can be used for a prototype for a more sophisticated and permanent analytical product: the large-scale, analytical computer program.

With modern programming languages like R and Python®, a skilled analyst can now design their analytic logic with significantly less effort than before, using resources such as Yahoo! or other free services for historical quotes. It has been said that Python's terse syntax allows for programs with the same functionality as their Java equivalents, yet four times smaller, and we suspect that R is similar. A small financial laboratory can be built on a laptop costing less than $200 in a matter of weeks, simulating multiple market variables as required. Or, by obtaining a higher-end laptop model with more drive space, the entire market can be loaded with 10 to 20 years' worth of historical data on a scale never before possible.

Once that laboratory is built, one can start to gain insights. Knowledge discovery was once a term for a human process. Now we're talking about computer automation.

Knowledge discovery seems like a bold term, a little too ambitious for anything a computer program could create. For example, the computer science professional society, the Association for Computing Machinery (ACM), has a special interest group called Knowledge Discovery and Data Mining (KDD). Hardly anyone would challenge the "data mining" part of that. After all, statisticians and computer scientists having at it with data is what they do. But discovering knowledge with a machine? Really? Automatically? Now that seems a little too exaggerated to be true. Then again, experiencing firsthand the algorithms that will be described in this book, we soon realized that the programs, using data science techniques, can not only automate very tedious calculations but then very positively yield insights into the human thinking level: insights that would otherwise not be found.

Perhaps one can view the experience with a sports analogy. In many sports we have defense to protect our current position and prevent the opponents from scoring further points. Offense is the ability to piece together athletic feats sequentially to put more points on the scoreboard. The data mining portion of KDD can be thought of as defense: the more disciplined, regimented side of the sport. Single achievements can be effective: thrusting up one's hand to block a pass, throwing a curve ball to prevent a hitter from connecting on the pitch. On the other hand, knowledge discovery is the offensive skill set, going beyond the required and expected data analysis and into the creative side. On offense, an entire series of events needs to be successful to yield progress: a full-field soccer scoring drive or a series of three successive baseball base hits before three outs to score a run. The likelihood of a success on offense is less.

So in the KDD model and sports analogy, data mining is the defense and knowledge discovery is the offense. Achieving knowledge discovery is a rare event with amazing impact. The discovery can be as powerful as human-made ideas, and can certainly enhance them. For example, we may discover that there is a publicly traded stock with uniquely desirable properties. The KDD domain touches the limits of what these machines can do with all the advancements in computer science.

In 1968, a Hollywood movie and novel by author Arthur C. Clarke, *2001: A Space Odyssey*, predicted automated reasoning, natural language speech recognition, video calls, and face recognition. The HAL9000 computer controls the flight to Jupiter while conversing and playing chess with astronaut Dr. Frank Poole and monitoring life conditions of over 300 astronauts. Since then, computer science, specifically simulation, has greatly impacted the research and discovery process in many fields and effectively achieved many of these science fiction goals now. Among others, there are fields of computational biology, computational cosmology, and computational linguistics. Images from these fields are shown in Figure 1.

Throughout this book we are concerned with computer simulation. Computer simulation has become so successful that it is now widely accepted that, after theory and physical experimentation, it is a third scientific method. As the subtitle says, this book can be used to build a simulation laboratory for finance. The book was developed as study material for the graduate Financial Analytics course in the Graham School at the University of Chicago Master of Science in Analytics program and from the undergraduate Investments course in the Department of Finance in the Tippie College of Business

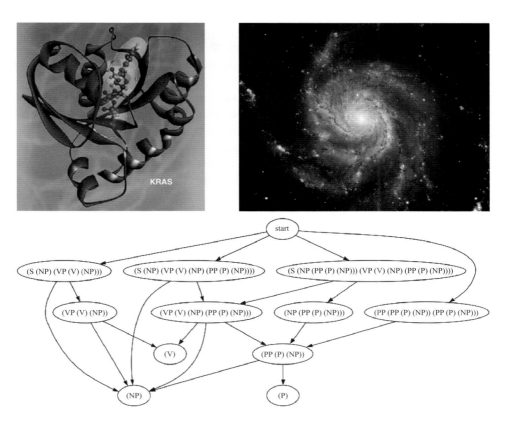

Figure 1   Sample images from computational biology, computational cosmology, and computational linguistics.

at the University of Iowa. It is recommended as a graduate textbook when used at a college or university. With the proper mathematical and computer science background, it could also be used at the advanced undergraduate level.

It is best to have taken a course in statistical analysis, probability and statistics, or, ideally, mathematical statistics for the material in the book, but much of the required material is introduced within the main text and the Appendix. It is best to have an undergraduate-level background in calculus, linear algebra, and enough computer science to be familiar with array manipulation with one or more scientifically based programming languages such as C, C++, Java, C#, Python, or Matlab®. A finance background is not necessary. Any experience with R is, of course, useful.

Financial computer simulation in the R language can be more intricate and challenging than building a spreadsheet. A quantitative optimizer can be better controlled and tailored when its logic is immediately apparent from the surrounding program code. More computer science knowledge is required by our reader to build more robust and sophisticated platforms, and more goes into the compiler and run-time system behind the scenes. But as the pieces are completed, the builder, or operator, or student of financial analytics begins to realize the benefits of simulation performed in a language designed for statistical simulation. The insights that can be gained from building simulators and from observing the simulations will help deepen understanding for upcoming professional venues. Just as it is now for machines, for people it has always been about learning.

Regarding the exercises at the end of each chapter, data science involves the study of statistical and computational models. In this book, that means that we are unlocking the economic value which exists in the financial markets. Data engineering is the process of implementing models on computers as applied to large datasets, using files, program logic, testing, and continuous improvement. With these exercises, we take advantage of the data science principles of the prior chapters to build and engineer our financial laboratory.

As the reader performs these exercises, they may need to install various R packages from time to time. Various pages found by internet searching will steer the reader to proper instructions for loading R packages and troubleshooting any failed attempts. There are too many packages, conditions, and cases to repeat those instructions here.

The exercises focus individually on the various components so that we obtain an understanding of the logic and data. Each new component builds upon prior components in order to provide the level of sophistication required to answer our financial analytics inquiries.

Acknowledgments

Through our careers we are influenced greatly by people who are special to us. We can never pay them back for the gifts they have bestowed upon us: conversation, insight, opportunity, knowledge, and companionship.

Mark would like to thank Ron Krupp and Barry Finkel at Argonne; Phil Ridinger, Pat Baldwin, Howard Seckler, David Rouse, Bill Neidfelt, and Tom Bishop at Bell Labs; Christopher Marlin and Adrienne Critcher at the University of Iowa; Per Brinch-Hansen and Orna Berry at the University of Southern California; Dave Martin, Milos Ercegovac, Stott Parker, and Dan Berry at the University of California, Los Angeles; Bob Mac-Gregor at System Development; Mark Christensen, Paul Schmitz, Tim Bancroft, Clare Morgan, Margaret Lakins, and Joe Dvorak at Northrop; Shelly Reis, Greg Brim, Brian Ostrow, Ron Netzel, David Joffe, Mack Amin, Thayer Allison, Dilip Nair, Gregg Berger, Haider Sajjad, Yuri Salnikov, Jim Bohmbach, Dante Lomibao, Paul Lee, Li Chen, Steve Zhu, Mario Konrad, Brian Philpott, Nancy Goldberg, Laura Lang, Raja Afandi, Ashish Batra, Krishna Bhamidi, and Chris Leakeas at Nationsbanc-CRT; Harry Georgakopoulos and YeeMan Bergstrom at XR Trading; and Adam Ginensky, Yuri Balasanov, and Sema Barlas at the University of Chicago and Marc Tempkin at the Chicago ACM for being tremendous mentors and colleagues over the years. Inspiration for this effort was provided at these wonderful locales: the bohemian Wolverine Farm book store in Fort Collins, the stately Pentacrest at the University of Iowa campus, and the Crerar Library of the gothic University of Chicago campus.

Dirk would like to thank his advisor Joseph Lang for all his help as well as Luke Tierney, Kate Cowles, Joyee Ghosh, Dale Zimmerman, Rhonda DeCook, Kung-Sik Chan, Erik Lie, David Bates, Ashish Tiwari, Wei Li, and Paul Weller for the excellent statistics and finance coursework at the University of Iowa. Thanks also to Kung-Sik Chan, Brian Ripley, Dirk Eddelbuettel, Hadley Wickham, David A. James, Seth Falcon, Winston Chang, Romain Francois, J.J. Allaire, Kevin Ushey, Qiang Kou, Douglas Bates, Jeffrey A. Ryan, Joshua M. Ulrich, Wouter Thielen, and John Chambers for development of the R packages used in the book.

The authors would particularly like to thank managing editor David Tranah for insightful comments based upon his vast experience, Clare Dennison for the timely content decisions, and Austin Bennett for the creative data scientist caricature on the cover.

1 Analytical Thinking

As an investor, there is no more immediate feeling of excitement than a stock split during a bull market or an acquisition that can bid one's stock up by 20 percent in a day. Maybe it is something like the feeling a soccer forward gets after completing a kick into the goal. Even though semi-random events can risk the desired outcome (specifically, actions by the defenders between the goal and the forward), all of the practice and preparation for the offense is being applied quickly, and the result of success is appreciated by the fans. In a nutshell, when faced with risks, preparation makes success more probable.

This book is all about that preparation. Being one step closer to paying for one's child's college education, or replacing one's employment income as the prospect of retirement looms, makes us feel more financially secure. Financial analytics involves, among other analysis, the creation of forecasted scenarios based upon historical data using simulations. When amateur investors talk about stocks in a qualitative sense – for example, "Hey, Qualcomm is really rocking lately, bud!" or "Hey, I bought some Intuitive Surgical and it's really on a roll!" – this is the way we naturally interact: informal advice. We are human and need to feel our way through many situations. But the question to ask one's self quietly is: "Sure, that sounds like a good investment that you are telling me about, but is there an alternative investment that will do better than that based on historical evidence?" What would a financial analytics approach tell us from a purely objective perspective? As we practice financial analytics, like the soccer forward practicing goal kicking, we are trained, informed, and more prepared for unexpected situations.

Along with robust and accurate data, designing models is a key component of the professional practice of analytics. This book focuses on mastering some of the most important applied models so that they can be adapted, relied upon, and expanded. Models are presented using hand-written code in the R language, using historical market datasets to gain a deeper understanding of the behavior.

Coined from "Big Science," "Big Data" is a term used to describe datasets that are too large to fit into common memory and disk hardware and traditional files and relational databases. Sophisticated algorithms and processing are often required to analyze Big Data. Analytics are applied to Big Data in order to take advantage of the large sample sizes. Insights and discovery are simply more realistically possible with large datasets. This book is intended to foster an individual and classroom software laboratory for performing financial analytics. It serves as a resource for models, program logic, and datasets for stocks and other common securities as we tackle Big Data.

1.1   What Is Financial Analytics?

Since the 2008 financial crisis, market practitioners are realizing that reliance on models which are mathematically pure but fundamentally inaccurate is no longer acceptable. A more practical approach is needed. The markets where the instruments reside have many more tail events than most of the market models of the 2000 decade would acknowledge. These tail events have contributed to the flash crash, tech bubble, and mortgage-based crisis with more to come. Practitioners are in need of tools for quick discovery and simulation to complement and calibrate the mathematics.

Meanwhile, the emerging new field of Analytics, also known as Data Science, is providing computational intelligence to businesses in ways many had never envisioned. Analytical computer programs are recommending everything from medical diagnoses to automobile routes to entertainment contents. Analytics is a practical and pragmatic approach where statistical rules and discrete structures are automated on the datasets as outcomes are observed in the laboratory and in the business world. Corporations are able to mine transactional data and predict future consumer buying patterns. Health professionals can mine health records to help with decision analysis for diagnosing diseases.

In today's world, businesses as well as consumers are affected by fluctuations in consumer prices, industrial production, interest rates, and the price of natural gas. These changes let us know that risk is ever-present. Now that large datasets are widely available, market practitioners are stepping up their efforts to use algorithms to measure econometric patterns and examine their expected trends.

Analytics has become the term used for describing the iterative process of proposing models and finding how well the data fit the models, and how to predict future outcomes from the models. Financial analytics describes our subject: a domain where contributions have been made by scholars and industry professionals for decades, and where the latest technology advancements have made recent discoveries possible. Financial analytics involves applying classic statistical models and computerized algorithms to the financial market data and investment portfolios. Analytics applied in this area address relationships that occur in practice every day in time-critical fashion as investors, speculators, and producers of valued securities and commodities trade across the country and the globe.

Investment firms like PIMCO and Vanguard have helped investors meet retirement goals or send their children to college by carefully delivering positive market exposure. This book will provide the tools for being able to understand better what firms like these and other financial entities do.

While many business intelligence books have been written to describe *what* is happening in Big Data, this book is specifically focused on *how* to achieve detailed results. The book is multidisciplinary in its combining of statistics, finance, and computer science.

Businesses are looking for profitability and financial risk reduction. Optimization is an important aspect of financial analytics. Any business intelligence approach makes appropriate use of data to attempt to optimize outcomes.

These are the kinds of issues to be tackled by financial analytical simulations. What is the optimized return and what is the level of risk assumed? What kinds of financial metrics can become good random variables and how are they distributed? What datasets are available to sample these random variables analytically? Which financial metrics are highly correlated? Which are relatively independent? Can analytical thinking give an algorithm an edge over a simple holding strategy when generating transactions? These are questions we explore in this book.

1.2 What Is the Laptop Laboratory for Data Science?

Professional data scientists are not purely statisticians. Yes, applied statistical skills are important, but they must also possess practical software engineering skills and be able to build reliable and testable models that run rapidly, repeatably. They must understand data types in order to implement analytical algorithms, so that their employers and clients will gain a competitive advantage from the robust models they produce. Our aim here is not to treat one financial instrument at a time, but rather in mass. In essence, clusters and structures of instruments are needed so that comparisons can be made. Investing is a matter of decision-making, and the more stock candidates, the better the chances of success.

Regarding the subtitle, "Building a Laptop Laboratory for Data Science," this book guides the reader on how to build a software simulation laboratory on which significant-sized working modules can answer analytics inquiries. Laptops are fast becoming pervasive. When using the R language, any operating system will do. As evidence of how inexpensive powerful computing has become, the laptop on which all of the book's simulations were run can be found for less than $200. After installing Crouton, a variant of Ubuntu Linux® found for free online, and RStudio, an analyst can soon be downloading datasets and analyzing away with millions of rows from freely available financial datasets.

Our own laptop computer is called AL, short for Analytics Laboratory. (In some families, cars are given names: Betsy, Handsome, Chester, Venom, and Myles are typical. If cars can be named, why not name a device that is at one's side most days?) AL's hardware and operating system was purchased from a Groupon coupon for the nominal price of $139. Your version of AL could run on an Apple or Windows PC: any computer that can run RStudio and hold a large set of flat files and a small portion of a database will do.

For the flat files, one of the coded modules downloads and caches six million rows of prices for subsequent analysis. While many books have included code, in this book, when we include the code, the pieces build upon each other, providing an increasing level of sophistication as readers follow along with the option to try running the code on their own computers. The reader can use R on any type of computer operating system for which R is available, which covers most of them. When running the Analytics Library on a higher-performance Apple or Windows laptop with a large internal hard drive, one can literally load the "whole market" and perform queries at will.

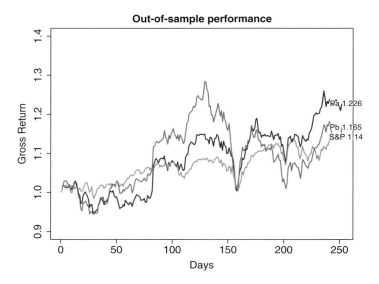

Figure 1.1   An out-of-sample calibration (2014 to 2015) of the S&P benchmark portfolio (green) and two optimized portfolios of NASDAQ and NYSE stocks (purple and red).

It has been a successful year for AL, the laptop laboratory for data science. On the data mining side of things, through the analytical programs presented herein, AL was able to find choice stock candidates for the portfolio optimizer. By using classic mean–variance optimization, the R program was able to deliver a stock portfolio that beat the S&P 500 Index return: not in sample in the laboratory, but in the actual stock market. This was accomplished by putting together a portfolio that had higher volatility than the S&P 500 Index, but not substantially higher. In fact, when measuring the return over risk of the portfolio from AL compared to the Index, it was better. This means more return for the amount of risk we are taking. Figure 1.1 shows the in-sample performance of two optimized portfolios against this benchmark.

```
> logRetPortf = diff(log(indexRecentPrices1))
> mean(logRetPortf)/(sd(logRetPortf)*sqrt(252))
[1] 0.006083248
> logRetBench = diff(log(benchPrices/benchPrices[1]))
> mean(logRetBench)/(sd(logRetBench)*sqrt(252))
[1] 0.00497942
```

You may ask why we think the recommendations of AL were successful. Well, by making use of R's functional and vectored expressive notation and packages, AL gives us an ability to process hundreds or even thousands of possible stocks and select the best one based upon the most consistent past performance. With R this can be done more correctly and with less code than with many other platforms.

Those of us who invest often receive emails from investment advisors, web sites and might pick stocks qualitatively. SeekingAlpha.com is one such web site we can read for information in decision-making. MotleyFool.com is another. These are good sites. They focus on a particular stock in the articles, and they can be quite entertaining when reading about why they think that the Google CFO resigned, or why they think a travel web site company is overvalued. Of course, AL does not need to be entertained; in fact, AL *cannot* be entertained, and it therefore does not get distracted with pieces of qualitative information. Unlike people who brag about certain winning picks they found by conversing with the right folks, AL is a system and can only look at datasets and statistics. Using AL with R enforces a rigorously quantitative decision approach which is worth considering.

1.3   What Is R and How Can It Be Used in the Professional Analytics World?

Since the financial crisis of 2008 there has been a need for professionals in the banking, insurance, fund management, and corporate treasury sectors who are more knowledge-able about statistics and data analysis and can discuss and measure the various risk metrics, especially those involving extreme events. While quantitative finance programs appeared at various universities in the 1990s, these programs are more mathematical in nature and students spend more of their time constructing proofs and deriving formulas and less of their time with datasets from the markets. While deriving the formulas helps the understanding of the models, on an opportunity cost basis, that time could be used building an operating data analysis platform.

People can enter the financial analytics profession through a combination of experience and education. Professionals with an extensive math background can find it easier to make the transition to the field. Those with a less formal math background, and those lacking some financial vocabulary, will find this book quite helpful in making the transition. This book provides the intuition and basic vocabulary as a step toward the financial, statistical, and algorithmic knowledge needed to resolve the industry problems and issues. For more experienced readers, the book presents the latest techniques, leveraging new packages which meld traditional finance metrics with modern data mining and optimization subjects. Professionals who are making the transition to analytics, professional quantitative finance analysts, and students who want to supplement their background with financial analytics, would find this book of interest.

This book presents a systematic way of developing analytical programs for finance in the statistical language R. R has become the language of choice for use in academic analytics circles because of its sophisticated expressibility for statistical algorithms. It is open source and freely available via download for all common computer operating systems. And thousands of previously contributed and available packages eliminate the need for redeveloping common algorithms from scratch.

Since financial analytics is the application of statistical and economic rules with computational logic in ways that can solve problems, the role of the analytical computer program is expanding: to tie together models which would previously have been isolated. These computer programs can be constructed more efficiently using specialized programming languages.

This book presents the reader, both the practitioner and the scholar, with many solutions in financial analytics. For individual investors and investment firm analysts, as shown in this book, the results can be obtained by a reference model and a manageable-sized R program. The book begins with a background in probability and statistics for markets, basic algorithms in R for finding price vector characteristics, including returns, split adjustments for quotes, and also comparing performance of securities, measuring volatility and risk, direction, skew, and market tail weight with examples. Finding optimal portfolios and using unsupervised machine learning techniques using graphs and clustering algorithms to connect related securities within portfolios are ways to gain insight. The acceleration of the speed of the financial markets means that quantitative analysis and financial engineering are no longer exclusively focused on minute details of a single instrument but on the big picture of thousands of prices and transactions happening nearly simultaneously. This book presents a new step in this direction.

1.4   Exercises

1.1. Examine Figure 1.1. What is the return of the S&P 500 Index in percent for the 252-day or one-year period, assuming it is adjusted so that it begins the period at 1.0, as in the figure?

2 The R Language for Statistical Computing

Like so many innovations in computing, including the Unix operating system and the C and C++ languages, the R language has its roots at AT&T Bell Laboratories during the 1970s and 1980s in the S language project (Becker, Chambers, and Wilks, 1988). People think that the S language would not have been designed in the way it was if it had been designed by computer scientists (Morandat, Hill, Osvald, and Vitek, 2012). It was designed by statisticians in order to link together calls to FORTRAN packages, which were well known and trusted, and it flourished in the newly developed Unix and C environment. R is an open source variant of S developed at the University of Auckland by Ross Ihaka and Robert Gentleman, first appearing in 1993 (Ihaka, 1998). The chosen rules for scoping of variables and parameter passing make it hard for interpreter and compiler writers to make R run fast. In order to remedy this, packages such as Rcpp have been developed for R, allowing R programs to call pre-compiled C++ programs to optimize sections of the algorithms which are bottlenecks in terms of speed (Eddelbuettel and Sanderson, 2014). We discuss the Rcpp package toward the end of the book.

Clearly the recent popularity of R, fueled by its open source availability and the need for statistical and analytical computing tools, shows that the benefits of R far outweigh the negatives. Overall, R is based upon the vector as a first class item in the language. R shares this attribute with LISP, Scheme, Python, and Matlab. This and the prevalence of over 4,000 publicly available packages are two of the many strengths of R. In this book, we will focus on R packages that revolve around financial analytics.

It is our intention to introduce R at this point for those readers who need or are interested in a summary. Feel free to skip this chapter if you are experienced in R. For those who are not, many of the examples are worth trying out in an R environment to get a feel for the language. By including this section, this book is self-contained and we make no assumption that the reader arrives at this book having an R background. Covering this chapter as an introduction to R or as an R refresher will position the reader for the upcoming analytical programs which will slice and dice market datasets to uncover what is happening.

2.1 Getting Started with R

One of the great things about R is how easy it is to install. In your browser, head to the web site for the Comprehensive R Archive Network (CRAN), `http://cran.r-project.org` and, whether running an Apple Mac, a Linux system, or a Windows

PC, the basic R interpreter is available for download. R began as a command line interface (CLI), but, once downloaded and installed, there is a basic graphical user interface (GUI) available via the

```
R --gui=Tk
```

command on an Apple or Linux operating system, and that will display a GUI window as shown in Figure 2.1. For Windows, this same R GUI can be launched from an icon.

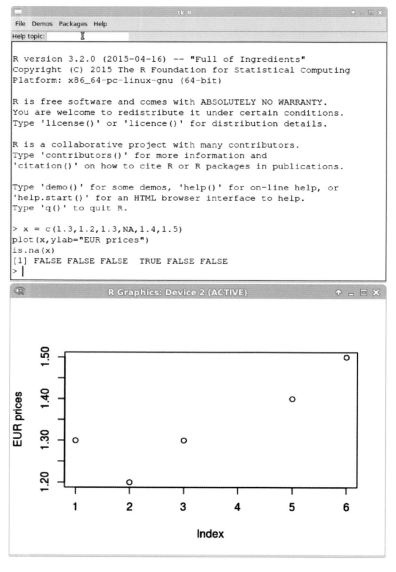

Figure 2.1   The basic R user interface window and a second pop-up window showing the result of the *plot*() command.

Just as a basic test, we can create a vector of prices and plot it with this block of code:

```
> x = c(1.3,1.2,1.3,NA,1.4,1.5)
> plot(x,ylab="EUR prices")
> is.na(x)
[1] FALSE FALSE FALSE  TRUE FALSE FALSE
```

The *c()* operator creates a vector of elements. This is the basic vector operator in R. Note the "not available" (NA) element appearing as the fourth item of the vector. R's ability to handle NAs, infinite values (Inf), and not a number (NaN) is one of its many strengths. Three Boolean-valued functions can be used to interrogate a variable for these respective values: *is.na()*, *is.infinite()*, and *is.nan()*. In data science, we certainly do encounter these erroneous values as inputs or results from algorithms.

Back on the subject of R interpreters, a later development is the RStudio GUI available from the web site www.rstudio.com. RStudio is a commercially developed GUI allowing management of plot windows, variable contents, and better debugging than the basic R interpreter. Figure 2.2 shows how the plotting window, variable contents, and workbench are all integrated into one view. People have spent years being productive in the basic R interpreter from CRAN, but those who have used interactive development environments for C++ or Java will find that the syntax highlighting, options for execution, and multiple source file handling of RStudio are more like what they are used to. Projects like RStudio and the Oracle Big Data Appliance are evidence of the growing popularity and commercialization of R (Ora, 2011).

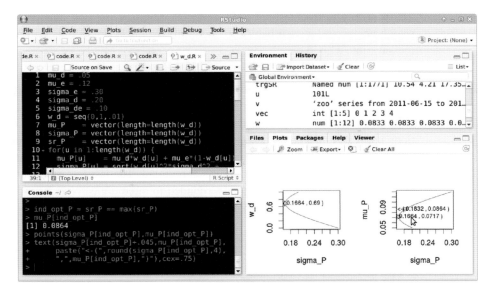

Figure 2.2 RStudio is a second-generation R user interface with integrated code, execution, variable inspection, and plotting windows, and expression completion.

A very important initial task in order to use the code from this book with an R language tool is to be sure to always have the current directory path defined by setting the *homeuser* variable. We reserve this variable to set the base directory where all the code for the book will reside. If, every time we use R, we set the *homeuser* variable as follows:

```
homeuser="<basedir>"
```

where <basedir> is something such as /home/<myuserid> or c:/Users/<myuserid>, which is specific to your computer system, then <basedir>/FinAnalytics/<dir> is where the input and output will occur from the R code. <dir> is typically ChapII for this chapter or another working directory name and is stored in the R variable *dir*. The publisher's web site for this book, www.cambridge.org/financialanalytics, contains a downloadable archive file with the code and datasets set up in directories so that FinAnalytics/<dir> will be ready once unpacked. The file is called FinAnalytics.zip. Download it and unpack it to obtain the book code, and remember to define the *homeuser* each time you use it.

Any time a *library* statement is encountered, R will check that the package is available. If not, it must be downloaded. As an example, to download the ggplot2 package, use the following command:

```
update.packages()
install.packages("ggplot2",dependencies=TRUE)
library(ggplot2)
```

Packages can be dependent upon other packages: hence the "dependencies=TRUE" setting. This flag is very important in order to avoid chasing down all the dependent packages and loading them one-by-one. Packages do not always succeed in loading. The best way to troubleshoot package installation is using your favorite browser and search engine to locate a helpful page on the World Wide Web by entering the error message into a good search engine.

2.2   Language Features: Functions, Assignment, Arguments, and Types

For many use cases, R provides a computational statistics platform. Mathematical functions are readily available. The basic log() function provides a natural logarithm. Of course, executing log() on a vector, x, results in a vector of natural logarithms, y. Unlike many imperative languages, no looping is required. The last line computes the simple expression, y, and prints its contents, rounded to three digits. Note how the NA value was preserved. The computation of log() on NA is NA as expected.

```
> #Filter prices:
> x[x > 1.3]
[1]   NA 1.4 1.5
> #Keeps the NA intact:
> y <- diff(log(x))
> round(y,3)
[1] -0.080  0.080     NA      NA 0.069
```

In R, not only vectors but also functions are first-class objects. It shares this attribute with the functional languages LISP and Scheme. Assigning a function to a variable is the usual way to define it. If g is assigned to the function definition, then $g(4)$ will evaluate it and g, without parentheses, will return its definition. Arguments can be matched positionally and by name. Defaults for arguments can be specified. In the case below, matching the arguments by name allows the arguments to be supplied in a different order than that in the definition.

```
> #g(x,y) is a power function:
> g <-function(x,y=5) { return(x^y) }
> g(4)
[1]  1024
> g(4,6)
[1]  4096
> g(4,y=7)
[1]  16384
> g(y=8,x=4)
[1]  65536
> g
function(x,y=5) { return(x^y) }
```

R has four assignment operators. The most basic operator is "<-". This is the one we use in the first assignment in the code block below. R's functional nature is so strong that even this can be replaced by the function call *assign("x",1)*. The arrow assignment operator of R came from the APL language. Over time, because people were used to other languages that use "=" instead, and even though "=" was used to assign parameter values in function calls ($g(x, y = 7)$, for example), it was also made available for assignment in R. So using "<-" or "=" is now really a matter of preference. Each of these three ways of assignment is for local assignment: they do not affect other variables with the same name which are in the outer layer of scope. To see this, the following R output shows how x being assigned a value of 3 is not affected by the assignment of 4 to x in the function $f()$.

```
> x <- 1
> assign("x",2)
> x
[1]  2
> x = 3
> x
[1]  3
> f <-function(x)
+ {
+ x = 4
+ x
+ }
> f(x)
[1]  4
> x
[1]  3
```

R's fourth assignment operator, with two "<"s, is known as the "super-assignment" operator. Executing it will look outside the current frame for *x*, which is global to the function *f*, and assign to that *x*. If there is no *x* in the global environment, it will create one and assign the value to it. Since arguments to functions are passed *by value*, the super-assignment operator is a way to get results back to the calling environment.

```
> #The fourth type is "<<-"
> x = 3
> x
[1] 3
> f <-function(x)
+ {
+ x <<- 4
+ x
+ }
> f(x)
[1] 4
> x
[1] 4
> typeof(f)
[1] "closure"
> typeof(x)
[1] "double"
```

We can see that the result in the above output with super-assignment is different from the result in the earlier code output using assignment. There are two "*x*"s: one outside the function and one within it. The super-assignment operator looks outside the function and side-affects the *x* declared outside the function.

R is dynamically typed so that variables do not have types. Instead, values have types. So we can see that the type of a variable is determined by the type of its current value. The function *typeof()* can be used to return the type of the value assigned to a variable. We can see its use in the output block above: *typeof(f)* is a "closure" for a function while *typeof(x)* is a "double."

In keeping with R's dynamic nature, evaluation can occur dynamically using the *eval()* function. Let's look at an example of using *eval()* to execute one of two possible functions. In order to evaluate strings as R expressions or programs, the *parse()* function is used in conjunction with *eval()*.

```
> #Classic if-else:
> call_type = 2
> if(call_type == 1) {
+ str = "f(2)"
+ } else {
+ str = "g(2)"
+ }
> eval(parse(text=str))
[1] 32
```

As long as we are also discussing **if–else**, there is also an *ifelse()* function which takes three arguments, evaluates the first one, and then supplies either the second in the TRUE case or the third in the FALSE case.

```
> #Not so classic if-else function:
> call_type = 2
> ifelse(call_type == 1,
+     eval(parse(text="f(2)")),
+     eval(parse(text="g(2)")))
[1] 32
```

In Chapter 9, we make the case for needing this language feature. For more details on this feature, the reader can consult R Development Core Team (2011).

If it can be deduced how to apply a function to a vector or matrix, R will do that. For example, if *vec = c(1:3)*, then *sqrt(vec)* is the three-element vector (1.000000,1.414214,1.732051). Another feature of R is the functional programming primitive known as *apply()*.

```
> #Functional nature:
> set.seed(1)
> vec = c(1:3)
> sapply(vec,rnorm)
[[1]]
[1] -0.6264538

[[2]]
[1]   0.1836433 -0.8356286

[[3]]
[1]   1.5952808   0.3295078 -0.8204684
```

The first line contains the *set.seed()* function, which is described in Section 2.5. In one of its simplest forms, we can see above that *sapply()* can be used to imply iteration, avoiding a **for** loop to iterate, over a vector and apply a function: *rnorm()* in this case, the normal variate generator. The result is a list of vectors. We discuss lists in more detail in Section 2.7.

2.3 Language Features: Binding and Arrays

Binding scalars or vectors together is one way to return aggregate results from functions. (Another way, introduced in Section 2.3, is by side-affecting new variables submitted back to the environment outside the function with the super-assignment operator.) For binding, *cbind()* binds items into two columns and *rbind()* binds items into two rows. If the two items are scalars then the two operations are equivalent. *rep()* is a very common function to create a vector of repeated items. For example, $rep(4, 5) == c(4, 4, 4, 4, 4)$ is TRUE and states to repeat 4 five times. We illustrate the use of these functions below.

```
> #Create two column matrix:
> A = cbind(rep(x,length(y)),y)
> A
              y
[1,] 4 -0.08004271
[2,] 4  0.08004271
[3,] 4         NA
[4,] 4         NA
[5,] 4  0.06899287
> B = rbind(rep(x,length(y)),y)
> B
          [,1]        [,2] [,3] [,4]       [,5]
   4.00000000  4.00000000    4    4 4.00000000
y -0.08004271  0.08004271   NA   NA 0.06899287
> t(A) == B
   [,1] [,2] [,3] [,4] [,5]
   TRUE TRUE TRUE TRUE TRUE
y  TRUE TRUE   NA   NA TRUE
> sum(t(A) == B)
[1] NA
```

In the output frame above, *rep()* forms five instances of the scalar *x* before binding into two columns and then two rows. *A* and *B* have now become arrays or matrices. The common matrix operator to transpose a matrix, *t()*, is then used to make *A* have the shape of *B* (2 by 5). Comparing them with "==" reveals how R determines that the results of two 2 by 5 arrays are being compared with the equality operator. The resulting 2 by 5 array is almost all Boolean TRUE except for the NA values, originally from the *y* vector, which, when compared to anything, returns NA.

R is very powerful when it comes to shorthand array notation. If we want just the fourth column of *B*, we can write that as *B*[, 4]. This provides an array slice of *B* with two values:

```
> #Subscripting: positive and negative
> B[,4]
   y
 4 NA
> B[,-4]
          [,1]        [,2] [,3]       [,4]
   4.00000000  4.00000000    4 4.00000000
y -0.08004271  0.08004271   NA 0.06899287
> t(A)[,-4] == B[,-4]
   [,1] [,2] [,3] [,4]
   TRUE TRUE TRUE TRUE
y  TRUE TRUE   NA TRUE
> sum(t(A)[-2,-4] == B[-2,-4])
[1] 4
```

We can also take away the fourth column by the expression to include all other columns by preceeding the column index by the negative sign (−). So we take away the fourth column for both matrices and check how many of the items match in the last line of code above.

Ranges in R can be created independently or as part of a *for* loop. A range is indicated with the ":" operator and evaluates to a vector as seen below.

```
> #Ranges and looping:
> n <- 12
> z <- 1:n
> z
 [1]  1  2  3  4  5  6  7  8  9 10 11 12
> z <- c(1:n)
> z
 [1]  1  2  3  4  5  6  7  8  9 10 11 12
> z <- vector(length=n)
> for(i in 1:n)
+ z[i] <- i
> z
 [1]  1  2  3  4  5  6  7  8  9 10 11 12
```

While vectors are one-dimensional, matrices in R are two-dimensional, and arrays have two or more dimensions. Matrices use the *nrow* and *ncol* arguments to set the bounds.

```
> #Matrices and arrays:
> mat2by4 <- matrix(1:8, nrow=2, ncol=4)
> mat2by4
     [,1] [,2] [,3] [,4]
[1,]    1    3    5    7
[2,]    2    4    6    8
```

Arrays use the *dim* parameter as seen in this second example, a three-dimensional array.

```
> arr3by4by2 <- array(1:24, dim=c(2,4,3))
> arr3by4by2
, , 1

     [,1] [,2] [,3] [,4]
[1,]    1    3    5    7
[2,]    2    4    6    8

...

, , 3

     [,1] [,2] [,3] [,4]
[1,]   17   19   21   23
[2,]   18   20   22   24
```

One of the handiest features of R is the negative subscript. Historically, many computer programming languages forbade negative subscripts. In R, they are used to form the vector, matrix, or array with the positive version of those negative subscript values removed. If *arr3by4by2* is our three-dimensional array from before, the *arr2by4by3*[1, ,] is a 4 by 3 matrix fixed at first dimension element 1. Using a negative subscript, such as -4 in the second dimension in the second line of code below, eliminates the fourth element.

```
> arr2by4by3[1,,]
     [,1] [,2] [,3]
[1,]    1    9   17
[2,]    3   11   19
[3,]    5   13   21
[4,]    7   15   23
> arr2by4by3[1,-4,]
     [,1] [,2] [,3]
[1,]    1    9   17
[2,]    3   11   19
[3,]    5   13   21
> arr2by4by3[1,c(-3,-4),]
     [,1] [,2] [,3]
[1,]    1    9   17
[2,]    3   11   19
```

An even better R feature is that including a vector of negative subscripts, $c(-3, -4)$ above, eliminates an entire set of elements from a dimension. In this case, the last matrix above shows this vector of negative subscripts feature eliminates two rows.

Length and dimensions are important for vectors, matrices, and arrays. The *length()* and *dim()* functions are seen being used below.

```
> length(c(-3,-4))
[1] 2
> dim(arr2by4by3[1,c(-3,-4),])
[1] 2 3
```

Matrix multiplication is important in the optimization material of Chapter 8. This can be accomplished in R using the *%*%* operator. We assign a matrix A first. Then we find its transpose matrix A^T and multiply A and A^T.

```
> A <- arr2by4by3[1,c(-3,-4),]
> t(A)
     [,1] [,2]
[1,]    1    3
[2,]    9   11
[3,]   17   19
> A <- arr2by4by3[1,c(-3,-4),]
> A
     [,1] [,2] [,3]
[1,]    1    9   17
[2,]    3   11   19
> t(A)
     [,1] [,2]
[1,]    1    3
[2,]    9   11
[3,]   17   19
> A%*%t(A)
```

```
       [,1] [,2]
[1,]   371  425
[2,]   425  491
> 1+9*9+17*17
[1] 371
```

In our last step above we check the element at [1, 1].

2.4   Error Handling

Error handling is an important part of data science, in order to keep erroneous data from making its way into the variables and to keep the dataset as clean as possible. When calling certain packages, it is common to have errors returned. R has a *tryCatch()* feature which is implemented as a function. There is the original main block expression, followed by an argument which is the code for the handling of warnings, followed by the code for the handling of errors, followed by any common clean-up code. In this example, we use division by zero as the type of error handled.

```
#Exception handling:
fh <- 0
tryCatch({
  #main block
  fh <<- file("file1.txt", open="r")
}, warning = function(w) {
  #warning-handler-code
  print(w)
  fh <<- NA
}, error = function(e) {
  #error-handler-code
  print(e)
  fh <<- NA
}, finally = {
  #cleanup-code
})
if(!is.na(fh)) readLines(fh)
```

Running the code block above detects the lack of *file1.txt* in the current directory and produces this following warning message:

```
<simpleWarning in file("file1.txt", open = "r"):
cannot open file 'file1.txt': No such file or directory>
> fh
[1] NA
```

As we obtain market data from the R series package in upcoming chapters, not having the requested market data is common outcome, so *tryCatch()* is utilized.

2.5   Numeric, Statistical, and Character Functions

To set the mode of calculations, *options(digits = n)* sets the number of digits to round to in calculations.

```
> #Setting precision:
> options(digits=10)
> pi = 3.1415926535897932384626
> pi
[1] 3.141592654
```

Distributions of random variates are available readily within the language with *runif()* for the Uniform Distribution, *rnorm()* for the Normal Distribution, and *rbinom()* for the Binomial Distribution, to name just three. Histograms and density plots are also native to the language with *hist()* and *density()*. Inspecting the density of the variates from the Binomial distribution can be done by plotting the *density()* function results as shown in Figure 2.3 as follows:

```
#Random sampling:
plot(density(rbinom(50,50,1/2)))
```

Setting the random seed is supported by the *set.seed()* function. When this is used, the subsequent calls the statistical functions will produce the same results in different runs. A related statistical function is called *sample()*. It returns a vector of random integers which can be used directly or as indexes. Sampling with and without replacement is possible.

```
> options(digits=6)
> set.seed(99)
> sample(10, replace = TRUE)
 [1]  6  2  7 10  6 10  7  3  4  2
```

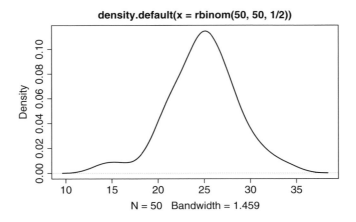

Figure 2.3   R plot window containing a density plot for the Binomial distribution.

Character strings are supported via a set of utility functions. One of the most common is the *paste( )* function, which performs concatenation. Setting the current directory can be accomplished by pasting together the pieces of the path. The parameter *sep* is used to determine the separator, which defaults to a space.

```
> #String concatenation:
> print(paste("PCLN","UNP","IBM","MCD","PFE",sep=","))
[1] "PCLN,UNP,IBM,MCD,PFE"
```

The common *substr( )* function takes as arguments the string variable and the beginning and end position of the substring.

```
> #Date and string functions:
> date <- as.Date("2014-02-01")
> substr(date,9,11)
[1] "01"
```

The *match( )* function works on a character string array and returns the position of the key in the array.

```
> #String array:
> tickers <- c("PCLN","UNP","IBM","MCD","PFE")
> match('MCD',tickers)
[1] 4
```

2.6 Data Frames and Input–Output

Data frames are one of R's more unusual and handy features. A data frame is a sequence of rows where the columns are heterogeneously typed. A common way of loading data frames is from the Excel .csv files. There are several R packages that use data frames as the primary mechanism to transmit data to the primary algorithm, especially in the case of the machine learning packages. The *$* operator is used to reference columns of a data frame as depicted in the last line of code below.

```
> #Data frame:
> L3 <- LETTERS[1:3]
> fac <- sample(L3, 10, replace = TRUE)
> d <- data.frame(x = 1, y = 1:10, fac = fac)
> d[1:4,]
> d[1:4,]
  x y fac
1 1 1   B
2 1 2   B
3 1 3   A
4 1 4   B
> d$fac
 [1] B B A B C B B A A A
Levels: A B C
```

Now that this data frame has been created, we can use the *write.csv()* utility to write it to a file.

```
> #Input-ouput:
> write.csv(d,file="d.txt",row.names=FALSE)
> e <- read.csv("d.txt",header=TRUE)
> e[1:4,]
  x y fac
1 1 1   B
2 1 2   B
3 1 3   A
4 1 4   B
```

Data frame columns can be displayed and modified. Below, we keep the first two column names of the data frame *e*, but reassign the third column name to "factor."

```
> names(e)
[1] "x"       "y"       "factor"
> names(e) <- c(names(e)[1:2],"factor")
> e[-c(2:dim(e)[1]),]
  x y factor
1 1 1      B
> typeof(e)
[1] "list"
```

We can also see that a data frame is considered a list by *typeof()*.

Setting the proper directory in the file system is important for reading and writing with success. R must be in the proper directory when running the code in the book, and we use R's *setwd()* and *getwd()* as required. Typically we always prepend the *homeuser* portion of the file path so that *setwd()* succeeds.

```
setwd(paste(homeuser,"/FinAnalytics/ChapXI",sep=""))
```

If you encounter an error such as

```
Error in file(file, "rt") : cannot open the connection
```

that error often occurs because *homeuser* is not set for your R session. Use *getwd()* at the R command prompt to discover the current directory path.

2.7   Lists

Lists are ordered aggregates like vectors, which are constructed by *c(...)*. However, lists differ from the basic vectors, in that they are recursively formed, using *list(...)*. Lists can contain lists. We can see the difference in the code output sequence below.

```
> #Lists:
> c(1,c(1,2),3,"A",c(4,5))
[1] "1" "1" "2" "3" "A" "4" "5"
> list(1,c(1,2),3,"A",list(4,5))
[[1]]
[1] 1

[[2]]
[1] 1 2

[[3]]
[1] 3

[[4]]
[1] "A"

[[5]]
[[5]][[1]]
[1] 4

[[5]][[2]]
[1] 5
```

If *l* is assigned to our list above, referencing elements can be done in two ways. *l*[2] yields a list of the vector $c(1, 2)$, whereas *l*[[2]] yields just the vector $c(1, 2)$ itself.

```
> l <- list(1,c(1,2),3,"A",list(4,5))
> l[2]
[[1]]
[1] 1 2

> l[[2]]
[1] 1 2
```

We can see that our data frame, *e*, from earlier can be treated as a list in the following sequence.

```
> e[[1]]
 [1] 1 1 1 1 1 1 1 1 1 1
> e[[2]]
 [1]  1  2  3  4  5  6  7  8  9 10
> e[[3]]
 [1] B A B A C C B B B C
Levels: A B C
```

In this book, our main use of lists is to help us return a structure of items from a function. Unlike forming a vector with the *c( )* operator, using the *list( )* operator to construct the return value for a function keeps all the list items of differing types separated and ready to be indexed by the calling routine with the *[[ ]]* list indexing operator. Lists are very handy in this case.

If we have a vector *A* of symbols and a corresponding vector *B* of their current prices, we may want to return both of these to the calling code sequence.

```
> obtainPrices <- function() {
+ A <- matrix(c("VRSN","UNP","HPQ","NSC"),nrow=1)
+ B <- matrix(c(37.61,125.62,50.48,50.44),nrow=1)
+ list(A,B)
+ }
> res <- obtainPrices()
> res[[1]]
      [,1]   [,2]  [,3]  [,4]
[1,] "VRSN" "UNP" "HPQ" "NSC"
> res[[2]]
      [,1]    [,2]   [,3]  [,4]
[1,] 37.61 125.62 50.48 50.44
```

Note that if we try to use the vector constructor, *c()*, or the *rbind()* or the *cbind()* operators, we quickly run into limitations. For example, if we are binding together two vectors which are not of the same length, the calling program code needs to unpack the items and figure out the length of each one separately. It gets rather tedious quickly. Fortunately, lists take care of things automatically, as each element can be of a different dimension and a different length.

This concludes our brief introduction to and survey of R.

2.8   Exercises

2.1. Run all the code presented in Chapter 2 to gain familiarity with, and as a test of, your R environment.

2.2. Use *seq(−2,2,.1)* to obtain a range of *x* values for input to the probability function *f(x)* which is defined as

$$f(x) = \begin{cases} 2x & \text{for } 0 \le x \le 1 \\ 0 & \text{elsewhere.} \end{cases} \qquad (2.1)$$

Write R code to define *f(x)* and code to apply *f(x)* to the vector of *x* values and code to plot the results of *f(x)* against the *x* values.

2.3. Write R code to find the squares of the numbers from 1 to 25 and plot the numbers on the *x* axis and their squares on the *y* axis. Hint: you can use the *c()* operator to append an element to a vector.

3 Financial Statistics

Statistics is a mathematical science which is concerned with collecting and organizing data and conducting experiments involving random variables which represent the data. These random variables can represent natural or simulated events. The amazing attribute of statistics is its ability to explain the organization of the data we observe. In this chapter we will cover some basic formulas that will lay a foundation for the subsequent analytics framework.

A discussion of statistics is necessary for any treatment of financial analytics. In order to discuss investments in financial instruments from a quantitative perspective, a certain amount of preliminary background is needed. This will provide a higher level of accuracy. We will not be able to do our job well without it. This background will be conveniently stated in terms of formulas, beginning here and continuing throughout the book. Formulas provide crisp specifications for the computer instructions in R.

We begin with probability with discrete outcomes. After completing the first three sections, the reader is invited to visit the Appendix for a review of the many potential probability distributions and statistical analysis concepts that are used in analytics.

3.1 Probability

In probability we are concerned with the likelihood of events. An event A is defined such that $\emptyset \subseteq A \subseteq S$, where $\emptyset$ is defined as the *null space* or empty set and S is defined as the *sample space* or set of all possible outcomes. We also set that the probability of event A occurring as $0 \leq P(A) \leq 1$, where the probability of the null space is $P(\emptyset) = 0$ and the probability of the sample space is $P(S) = 1$. We define the complement A^c as the set satisfying 1) $A \cup A^c = S$ and 2) $A \cap A^c = \emptyset$. While they might seem superfluous, these two conditions simply make mathematically rigorous the requirement that (1) an event must either happen or not happen, and (2) an event may not both happen and not happen.

Let us now consider two events A and B. We define the joint probability as the probability of the intersection of the two events, i.e. the probability that both events happen: $P(A \cap B)$. We also define the union probability as the probability that either event happens: $P(A \cup B)$. We often write $P(A, B)$ as a shorthand for $P(A \cap B)$. We relate the probability of the union of the two events to the probability of intersection of the two events as

$$P(A \cup B) = P(A) + P(B) - P(A \cap B).$$

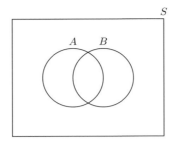

Figure 3.1   The four regions for the event sets A and B.

Bayes' Rule

We define the conditional probability of A given B as the joint probability of A and B divided by the probability of A:

$$P(B|A) = \frac{P(A|B)P(B)}{P(A)} = \frac{P(A \cap B)}{P(A)}. \tag{3.1}$$

Similar to the partitioning of the sample space, above, we may also partition events: $P(A) = P(A, B) + P(A, B^c)$. This is to say that if we have two events A and B, then A must happen either with B or without B as shown in Figure 3.1. Dividing through by $P(A)$ states the same result in the language of conditional probabilities, specifically that given event A has happened, then event B has either happened or not happened:

$$P(A) = P(A, B) + P(A, B^c) \tag{3.2}$$

$$1 = \frac{P(A, B)}{P(A)} + \frac{P(A, B^c)}{P(A)} \tag{3.3}$$

$$1 = P(B|A) + P(B^c|A). \tag{3.4}$$

Extending Bayes' Rule

Bayes' Rule of Equation 3.1 can be extended to many events that depend upon event A:

$$P(B_i|A) = \frac{P(A|B_i)P(B_i)}{\sum_{j=1}^{n} P(A|B_j)P(B_j)}. \tag{3.5}$$

3.2   Combinatorics

In discrete (i.e. finite state) probability we must often count outcomes to arrive at probabilities. The probability of the sum of the roll of two fair dice, for example, can be solved by counting. The probablility of a full house in poker can also be solved by counting. We need two tools: permutation and combination.

Permutation

Say we have a set of n distinct objects and wish to calculate the number of all possible orderings. There are n objects from which we can choose to fill the first slot, $n - 1$

objects from which we can choose the second slot, $n - 2$ objects from which we can choose to fill the third slot, and so on until there is only one object to choose to fill the last slot. The number of possible orderings is then

$$n! = n \times (n - 1) \times (n - 2) \times \cdots \times 2 \times 1. \tag{3.6}$$

Consider the case where we want to count the number of possible orderings of r objects from a set of n distinct objects. Similar to the above reasoning, there are n objects from which we can choose to fill the first slot, $n - 1$ objects from which we can choose the second slot, $n - 2$ objects from which we can choose to fill the third slot, and so on until there are $n - r + 1$ objects from which to fill the rth slot. This is denoted as $P(n, r)$ and is defined as

$$P(n, r) = \frac{n!}{(n - r)!}. \tag{3.7}$$

Combination

Now consider the case where we are interested in the number of possible sets of size r objects from a set of n distinct objects. In permutation we are interested in the order of the objects in the set, whereas in combination we are not interested in the order. Back to the poker example: the presence of the cards in the hand is what defines the hand. The order in which the cards were dealt is irrelevant. Accounting for this reduction we simply divide the number of permutations by $r!$ to arrive at the definition of combination. This quantity is so often used that it has its own shorthand name: "n choose r":

$$C(n, r) = \binom{n}{r} = \frac{n!}{r!(n - r)!}. \tag{3.8}$$

This makes sense because, to arrive at the number of sets of size r, we need only to account for the permutation of set size r for each unique set. Hence, we have the number of permutations of size r divided by the permutation of each set of size r. Seen another way,

$$P(n, r) = C(n, r)r!. \tag{3.9}$$

that is, if we multiply the number of unique sets of size r by the number of permutations of each of those sets, we arrive again at the number of permutations of r objects drawn from a set of n unique objects.

Example

Poker Let's look at some examples from poker to get familiar with the logic behind discrete probability. To calculate the probability of any given poker hand we must know how many poker hands there are. The deck has 52 cards, and a player is dealt a hand of five cards. Since the order of the cards dealt in the hand does not matter, we calculate the number of unique poker hands as 52 choose 5:

$$N = \binom{52}{5} = \frac{52!}{5!(52 - 5)!} = 2,598,960. \tag{3.10}$$

Now that we know the total number of poker hands, we can calculate the probability of a given hand. Let's calculate the probability of four aces. Since the four aces account for four out of the five cards in the deck, we have $52 - 4 = 48$ cards left in the deck to deal, any of which will result in a four-ace hand:

$$P(\text{four aces}) = \frac{48}{2,598,960}. \tag{3.11}$$

Let's now calculate the probability of a four-of-a-kind. In this case we are interested not only in the four aces, but in four of any single face. There are 13 faces and one way to get any of the 13. After the four equal face cards are dealt, we have 48 leftover cards from which to choose the fifth card for the hand.

$$P(\text{four of a kind}) = \frac{(13)(48)}{2,598,960}. \tag{3.12}$$

With a basic intuition developed, we can turn toward to the calculation of more complex hands; say, a hand with a single pair. Now, for a hand to have a single pair it must have one pair and only one pair: we have the pair face and the other three cards must be of different faces and not the pair face. So it follows that we have 13 possibilities for the pair face, $\binom{4}{2}$ ways of choosing the pair, $\binom{12}{3}$ ways of choosing the non-pair faces, and 4^3 ways of choosing those three cards from the non-pair faces. This gives the probability of a pair hand as

$$P(\text{one pair}) = \frac{13\binom{4}{2}\binom{12}{3}4^3}{\binom{52}{5}}, \tag{3.13}$$

and we can calculate the probability of a hand having a single pair as

```
> 13*choose(4,2)*choose(12,3)*4^3 / choose(52,5)
[1] 0.422569
```

So the chance of a player getting a pair is pretty high: 42.26%. A two-pair occurs when we observe two pairs of two different face cards. There are $\binom{13}{2}$ possibilities for the two-pair faces, $\binom{4}{2}^2$ ways of choosing the two pairs, 11 ways of choosing the last non-two-pair face, and four ways of choosing the suit of the non-two-pair faces. This gives the probability of a two-pair as

$$P(\text{two-pair}) = \frac{\binom{13}{2}\binom{4}{2}^2(11)(4)}{\binom{52}{5}}, \tag{3.14}$$

which can be calculated as

```
> choose(13,2)*choose(4,2)^2*11*4 / choose(52,5)
[1] 0.04753902
```

A three-of-a-kind has three of a single face with the last two card faces not matching the three faces and not matching each other. So there are 13 possibilities for the pair face, $\binom{4}{3}$ ways of choosing the pair, $\binom{12}{2}$ ways of choosing the non-pair faces, and 4^2

ways of choosing those two cards from the non-three faces. This gives the probability of a three-of-a-kind as

$$P(\text{triple}) = \frac{13\binom{4}{3}\binom{12}{2}4^2}{\binom{52}{5}}. \tag{3.15}$$

Building on the pair and three-of-a-kind, let's calculate the probability of a full house. A full house is a hand with three matching faces of one suit and two matching faces of another suit. There are 13 possibilities for the three face, $\binom{4}{3}$ ways of choosing the three, 12 ways of choosing the pair face, and $\binom{4}{2}$ ways of choosing those two cards from the pair. This gives the probability of a four of a kind as

$$P(\text{full house}) = \frac{13\binom{4}{3}12\binom{4}{2}}{\binom{52}{5}}. \tag{3.16}$$

While we have already the probability of a four-of-a-kind, we include it here for completeness. A four-of-a-kind has four of a single face with the last card face not matching the four face. We have 13 possibilities for the pair face, $\binom{4}{4}$ ways of choosing the pair, $\binom{12}{1}$ ways of choosing the non-pair faces, and 4^1 ways of choosing those two cards from the non-four faces. This gives the probability of a four-of-a-kind as

$$P(\text{four}) = \frac{13\binom{4}{4}\binom{12}{1}4}{\binom{52}{5}}. \tag{3.17}$$

In a straight we have five faces in order, of any suit. There are 10 ways to pick the sequence of faces and 4^5 ways of picking the suits of the straight. From $(10)4^5$ we must subtract the number of straight flushes to prevent double counting:

$$P(\text{straight}) = \frac{(10)4^5 - (4)(10)}{\binom{52}{5}}. \tag{3.18}$$

A flush has all five cards of the same suit. There are four suits to choose from, and for each suit there are $\binom{13}{5}$ possible combinations. From $4\binom{13}{5}$ we must subtract the number of straight flushes to prevent double counting:

$$P(\text{flush}) = \frac{4\binom{13}{5} - (4)(10)}{\binom{52}{5}}. \tag{3.19}$$

In a straight flush we have a sequence of face cards all of the same suit. There are ten such sequences for a given suit, and four suits, which yields the probability of a straight flush. Again, from $(4)(10)$ we must subtract the number of royal flushes to prevent double counting:

$$P(\text{straight flush}) = \frac{(4)(10) - 4}{\binom{52}{5}}. \tag{3.20}$$

A royal flush is a straight with face cards of 10, J, Q, K, A. There only four such hands: one for each suit. This gives us the probability of a royal flush as

$$P(\text{royal flush}) = \frac{4}{\binom{52}{5}}. \tag{3.21}$$

No hand:

$$P(\text{no hand}) = \frac{\left[\binom{13}{5} - 10\right](4^5 - 4)}{\binom{52}{5}}. \tag{3.22}$$

Conditional aces:

$$P(4 \text{ aces in 4 cards}|i \text{ aces in } i \text{ cards}) = \frac{P(\{4 \text{ aces in 4 cards}\} \cap \{i \text{ aces in } i \text{ cards}\})}{P(i \text{ aces in } i \text{ cards})} \tag{3.23}$$

$$= \frac{P(\{4 \text{ aces in 4 cards}\})}{P(i \text{ aces in } i \text{ cards})}. \tag{3.24}$$

$$P(i \text{ aces in } i \text{ cards}) = \frac{\binom{4}{i}}{\binom{52}{i}}. \tag{3.25}$$

$$P(4 \text{ aces in 4 cards}|i \text{ aces in } i \text{ cards}) \tag{3.26}$$

$$= \frac{1}{\binom{52}{4}\frac{\binom{4}{i}}{\binom{52}{i}}} = \frac{\binom{52}{i}}{\binom{52}{4}\binom{4}{i}} \tag{3.27}$$

$$= \frac{(4-i)48!}{(52-i)!} = \frac{1}{\binom{52-i}{4-i}}. \tag{3.28}$$

Example
Independence Want to show for two events A and B

$$P(A|B) = P(A|B^c)$$

if and only if A and B are independent? First some intuition. Say event A is "I get hit by a truck" and event B is "I am wearing khakis." If we can show that the probability that I get hit by a truck given I am wearing khakis is equal to the probability that I get hit by a truck given I am not wearing khakis, then it follows that getting hit by a truck has nothing to do with wearing khakis, both intuitively and statistically (independence). Conversely, say the events are independent; then it must follow that the probability of getting hit by a truck is the same regardless of whether or not I am wearing khakis.

To demonstrate this more formally, we must first recall the law of conditional probability, namely that

$$P(A|B) = \frac{P(A, B)}{P(B)}.$$

Also, recall that events A and B are defined to be (statistically) independent if

$$P(A, B) = P(A)P(B).$$

From basic probability we know that

$$P(B^c) = 1 - P(B),$$

which says that the probability that I am not wearing khakis is one minus the probability that I am wearing khakis.

We also know from basic probability that

$$P(A) = P(A, B) + P(A, B^c),$$

which says that if hit by a truck, then either I am wearing khakis or I am not wearing khakis.

So back to our problem. By hypothesis we know that

$$P(A|B) = P(A|B^c).$$

By conditional probabilities we have

$$\frac{P(A, B)}{P(B)} = \frac{P(A, B^c)}{P(B^c)},$$

so then by cross multiplying

$$P(A, B)P(B^c) = P(A, B^c)P(B)$$

and substituting

$$P(A, B)[1 - P(B)] = [P(A) - P(A, B)]P(B)$$

we have

$$P(A, B) - P(A, B)P(B) = P(A)P(B) - P(A, B)P(B)$$

with cancellation yielding

$$P(A, B) = P(A)P(B),$$

which is the definition of independence.

Example

Birthday Paradox Question: How large must a group be to have a 50 percent chance of *at least* one birthday match? Recall that

$$P(\text{at least one match}) + P(\text{no matches}) = 1,$$

which then implies

$$P(\text{at least one match}) = 1 - P(\text{no matches}),$$

so we are interested in the group size n such that

$$P(\text{no matches}) = 0.5,$$

since $P(\text{no matches}) = 0.5$ is easier to calculate.

Recall that since

$$P(A, B, C) = P(C|A, B) \cdot P(A, B)$$
$$= P(C|A, B) \cdot P(B|A) \cdot P(A)$$

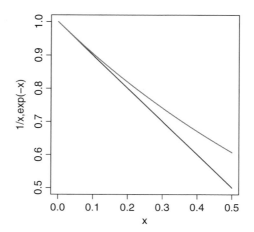

Figure 3.2 Approximating e^{-x} with $1 - x$.

we have

$$P(\text{no matches}) = P(\text{no match in two}) \cdot P(\text{no match in three}|\text{no match in two}),$$

and since there are 365 days in the year, the above becomes

$$= \frac{365}{365} \cdot \frac{365 - 1}{365} \cdot \frac{365 - 2}{365} \cdots$$
$$= (1) \cdot (1 - 1/365) \cdot (1 - 2/365) \cdots .$$

Now recall the Taylor expansion of e^x:

$$e^x = \sum_{n=0}^{\infty} \frac{1}{n!} x^n$$
$$= 1 + x + \frac{1}{2} x^2 + \frac{1}{3 \cdot 2} x^3 + \cdots$$

so that for small x:

$$e^{-x} \approx 1 - x.$$

We can see that this is true in Figure 3.2.

So then

$$P(\text{no match}) \approx e^0 \cdot e^{-\frac{1}{365}} \cdot e^{-\frac{2}{365}} \cdots$$
$$= e^{-\frac{1}{365} \sum_{i=1}^{n} i} = e^{-\frac{1}{365} \cdot \frac{n(n+1)}{2}} = 0.5,$$

since

$$\sum_{i=1}^{n} i = \frac{n(n + 1)}{2},$$

which in turn is true since

$$\sum_{i=1}^{n} i = \text{Area} = \frac{n^2}{2} + \frac{n}{2} = \frac{n^2 + n}{2} = \frac{n(n+1)}{2}.$$

So we have

$$P(\text{no matches}) = e^{-\frac{n(n-1)}{2 \cdot 365}}.$$

Set equal to $\frac{1}{2}$:

$$e^{-\frac{n(n-1)}{2 \cdot 365}} = \frac{1}{2}$$

and solve for n:

$$n^2 - n = -2 \cdot 365 \cdot \ln\left(\frac{1}{2}\right)$$

using the quadratic formula.

Solving for n gives us 23. That is, a group size of only 23 gives a 50 percent chance of having at least one birthday match in the group. This is much lower than most people expect. Most think 100 to 200. Why is this? I myopically imagine the probability of someone in the group having a birthday match *with me*, and ignore the outcomes in which other group members have matches *among themselves*. This myopia is common in how we perceive and react to probabilities and risk in general.

3.3   Mathematical Expectation

Expected value is one of the most fundamental concepts in statistics. We can come up with an expected value of a series of events that have not happened by combining their probabilities, $p(x)$, with their outcome values, x. X is the random variable and x are its possible outcomes.

In the discrete case, where the outcomes are enumerable, we define the mean and variance as

$$E(X) = \sum_{x \in S} xp(x) = \mu$$

and

$$Var(X) = E[(X - E(X))^2] = \sum_{x \in S} (x - E(X))^2 = \sigma^2.$$

In the continuous case, we define the mean and variance as

$$E(X) = \int xp(x)dx = \mu$$

and

$$Var(X) = E[(X - E(X))^2] = \int (x - \mu)^2 p(x)dx = \sigma^2.$$

The *standard deviation* is defined to be the square root of the variance

$$\sigma_r = \sqrt{Var(r)}.$$

Two more moments of interest also involve expectation. The *skewness* is defined to be

$$Skew(X) = E\left[\left(\frac{X - \mu}{\sigma}\right)^3\right].$$

The *kurtosis* is defined to be

$$Kurt(X) = E\left[\left(\frac{X - \mu}{\sigma}\right)^4\right].$$

The covariance of two random variables is an indication of how likely they are to occur together:

$$Cov(X, Y) = E[(X - E(X))(Y - E(Y))] = E(XY) - E(X)E(Y)$$
$$Cor(X, Y) = \frac{E[(X - E(X))(Y - E(Y))]}{E(X)E(Y)} = \frac{E(XY) - E(X)E(Y)}{\sigma_X \sigma_Y}.$$

The mean is a location parameter which places the distribution at a particular place on a the horizontal axis. For example, moving μ from 0 to 1 will reposition the entire distribution over to the right by one unit. The variance and its square root, the standard deviation, are scale parameters determining how wide the distribution will be. For example, if the standard deviation is tripled, it will widen out the distribution by a factor of 3. The skewness and kurtosis are shape parameters. The skewness tells us the amount of symmetry. When zero, there is perfect symmetry. When negative, there is left-skewness, where the tail on the left is elongated. When positive, there is right-skewness, where the tail on the right is elongated. Like the mean, the skewness is an odd-numbered moment, so the value can be positive or negative. The kurtosis tells us how heavy the tails of the distribution are. A higher value means a heavier tail. Interestingly enough, all normal distributions have the same kurtosis, and that value is 3.

Example

St Petersburg Paradox Imagine the following game. You flip a coin until you get "heads." The payoff for the game is 2^n where n is the number of flips *before* the first "heads." What are you willing to pay to play this game? Or equivalently, if you had a ticket to play the game, what would you sell it for?

Let's calculate the expected payout of the game.

$$E(\text{payout}) = \sum_n \text{payout}(n)p(n) = \sum_{n=0}^{\infty} 2^n P(N = n),$$

which in this case is

$$= 1 \cdot \frac{1}{2} + 2 \cdot \frac{1}{4} + 4 \cdot \frac{1}{8} + \cdots,$$

which is

$$= \frac{1}{2} + \frac{1}{2} + \frac{1}{2} + \cdots = \infty.$$

So the game's value is infinite, but what are we *willing to pay* to play it? Assume again the log utility of wealth: $U(W) = \ln W$. Now, instead of expected wealth, let's calculate expected utility of wealth:

$$E(U(W)) = \sum_n \ln(W(n))p(n)$$

$$= \sum_n \left(\frac{1}{2}\right)^{n+1} \ln(2^n)$$

$$= \ln 2 \sum_n \left(\frac{1}{2}\right)^{n+1} n$$

$$= 0.693.$$

Since $\ln(2) = 0.693$ and under certainty equivalence,

$$E(U(W)) = E(\ln(W))$$

implies that

$$W_{ce} = 2.$$

This is quite close to what the average person is willing to pay to play this game. So we can conclude that the assumption of log-utility is not perfect, but it is a good approximation.

Note that the game's value is infinite, but we are willing to pay only a very small amount to play. This opens up an arbitrage opportunity. Let's say there was a firm that was willing to buy your ticket and play for you. There are such firms, of course, and they are called insurance companies. Let's say a company bought the tickets from the entire class; say 16 for the sake of discussion. What would the expected payout be? What about the 90th percentile payoff? The 95th percentile payoff? The 99th percentile payoff?

Example

Risk Aversion and Insurance As an application of the discrete expected value calculation, let us assume that you have a total wealth of 250,000, of which your house is worth 200,000. You are considering fire insurance for your house. The probability of fire in a given year is 0.001, in which case the value of your house is reduced to zero. Your liquid wealth is invested at the risk-free rate of 6 percent. Assuming you have log utility of wealth, how much are you willing to pay for fire insurance?

Well, recall that 200,000 of your wealth is invested in your house, and 50,000 is invested in the risk-free asset. Without insurance, the probability distribution of your end-of-year wealth is

	Probability	Wealth
No fire	0.999	253,000
Fire	0.001	53,000

since in the risk-free asset we will have: $50,000 \cdot 1.06 = 53,000$.

Now find the expected utility, assuming $U(W) = \ln(W)$:

$$E(U(W)) = \sum_s p(s)U(W(s))$$

$$= p(\text{no fire})U(W(\text{no fire})) + p(\text{fire})U(W(\text{fire}))$$

$$= 0.999 \cdot U(253,000) + 0.001 \cdot U(53,000)$$

$$= 0.999 \cdot \ln 253,000 + 0.001 \cdot \ln 53,000$$

$$= 12.439582.$$

The (wealth) certainty equivalent of this expected utility is

$$e^{12.439582} = 252,604.85,$$

since $U = \ln W$ is equivalent to $W = e^U$.

With insurance, we can have certain year-end wealth, but we need to pay an insurance premium P. We pay P out of liquid wealth at the *beginning* of the year. So we have $50,000 - P$ to invest in the risk-free asset at the beginning of the year. Since we are insured, end-of-year certain wealth is

$$(50,000 - P) \cdot (1.06) + 200,000.$$

To find the indifference premium, set end-of-year insured wealth equal to expected wealth certainty equivalent:

$$(50,000 - P) \cdot (1.06) + 200,000 = 252,604.85.$$

Now solve for the premium P:

$$50,000 - P = \frac{252,604.85 - 200,000}{1.06}$$

$$P = 50,000 - \frac{252,604.85 - 200,000}{1.06}$$

$$= 372.78.$$

Compare the premium a representative agent is willing to pay to protect his/her house to the insurance company's expected cost: $0.001 \cdot 200,000 = 200$. Note also that it is critical how high a percentage of my total wealth is in my house. The higher the percentage, the more I am willing to pay for insurance.

3.4   Sample Mean, Standard Deviation, and Variance

Going from the discrete to the continuous probabilities can be more challenging. For those readers who have not had (or who wish to review) major probability distributions and some statistical analysis, please see the Appendix.

All probability distributions have parameters which characterize them. For example, most have a mean. The mean is known as the first moment of the probability distribution. Each probability distribution can be sampled. There are sample moments corresponding to the moment of the probability distribution.

By using the sample moment which is the unbiased estimator of the moment of a probability distribution, we can estimate a key parameter from a sample (Hogg and Craig, 1978). For the sample mean, we can estimate the theoretical mean of a sample. In the case of log returns of prices, finding the mean can tell an investor whether the price trend is upward or downward. By finding the sample standard deviation, known in the markets as the historical volatility, an investor can tell whether an investment is too risky.

The most common estimator is the sample mean, which a very common estimator. Finding it involves summing the data points in the sample and dividing by the number of data points, N. We call random variables for the sample returns R_i where $R_i = \log(S_i/S_{i-1})$ for $N + 1$ values S:

$$\bar{R} = \frac{1}{N} \sum_{i=1}^{N} R_i, \tag{3.29}$$

and can be found with the R function *mean()*. This can be shown to be true as seen in the Appendix, Section A.14. The higher moments have sample estimators that use a $1/(N-1)$ factor rather than a $1/N$ factor.

The historical variance, s^2, and historical volatility, s, of a security, the standard deviation of the sample log returns, are important in forecasting the scale of the prices expected in the future. The latter of these two statistics is more commonly quoted in practice and is often used to compute risk measures or by itself as a simple risk measure. The historical volatility is the square root of the historical variance

$$s = \sqrt{\frac{1}{N-1} \sum_{i=1}^{N} (R_i - \bar{R})^2} \quad \text{where} \quad \bar{R} = \frac{1}{N} \sum_{i=1}^{N} R_i, \tag{3.30}$$

and daily log returns are used and $\bar{R}$ is the mean log return. This figure is usually discussed as an annualized amount in market circles, so the need to convert from daily to annualized is satisfied by multiplying the variance by 252 days per year or, equivalently, multiplying the volatility by the square root of 252:

$$s_{ann}^2 = s_d^2(252) \tag{3.31}$$

$$s_{ann} = s_d\sqrt{252}. \tag{3.32}$$

If the original prices for s were quoted weekly, then we use 52 instead of 252. And if they are quoted every day, not just Monday through Friday, then we use 365 instead of 252. As a financial analytics or risk professional, one of the more common tasks is to find the historical volatility of a security of interest in order to simulate the potential future market movements. It provides an objective measure of the security's market risk. Intuitively, if we know that the annual historical volatility for the Euro vs. US Dollar goes from 10 percent down to 7 percent then we know that the market has become quieter. If we know the existing annualized historical volatility, we know what to expect in terms of up and down movements. We can set trading limits by establishing stop limit orders based upon these expectations. We can also determine when those limits are exceeded.

Here is R code which will compute annual historical volatility from a time series one year long of daily or weekly prices.

```
> S = c(1.3,1.2,1.3,1.4,1.5,1.4,1.3,1.4,1.5)
> diffLogS = diff(log(S))
> diffLogSmean = mean(diffLogS)
> N = length(diffLogS)
> histVol = sqrt(1/(N-1)*sum((diffLogS-diffLogSmean)^2))
> annHistVol = histVol*sqrt(length(S))
> annHistVol
[1] 0.2296238
```

3.5   Sample Skewness and Kurtosis

The *sample skewness* is computed from the dataset. It can be calculated as

$$Skew(R) = \frac{1}{N} \sum_{i=1}^{N} \left\{ \frac{(R_i - \bar{R})}{s} \right\}^3. \tag{3.33}$$

In R, the *skewness(x)* function from the *moments* library will use the *moment* method above to compute the sample skewness.

The *sample kurtosis* is also computed from the dataset. It can be calculated as

$$Kurt(R) = \frac{1}{N} \sum_{i=1}^{N} \left\{ \frac{(R_i - \bar{R})}{s} \right\}^4. \tag{3.34}$$

In R, the *kurtosis(x)* function from the *moments* library will use the *moment* method above to compute the sample kurtosis. Examples of the use of the *skewness()* and *kurtosis()* function will appear in Chapter 5.

3.6   Sample Covariance and Correlation

Correlation among securities in different times series becomes important when designing portfolios. Just like in an athletic team, different securities in the portfolio "team" are expected to do their part and "pick up" the portfolio return at different times. Since each security will have a peak and valley at different times, studies have shown that lower correlation is best. For example, we do not want the valleys to occur at the same time, otherwise a large drawdown in the portfolio value will occur. When one security is bottoming, the goal is to have another security pick up the portfolio value.

The R language plotting utilities have the advantage of allowing users to visualize equities markets' random variables in any number of dimensions at once with the plotting parameter command. The nine stock time series of Figure 3.3 from before are equities with a log-normal distribution.

The log returns for the same nine time series are depicted in Figure 3.3. These are the time series random variable that can be regarded as multivariate normal. In any case, measuring correlation of prices is best done with log returns. As we saw earlier, log returns are approximately normally distributed except for a higher frequency of extreme values. In this case, we have p time series of length N each, $(R_1, \ldots, R_p)$. Once again we assume that $R_{i,j} = \log(S_{ij}/S_{i-1,j})$. If we pick any two column series R_j and R_k, then covariance and correlation matrices are defined as

$$\Sigma = Cov(R_j, R_k) = E\left\{(R_j - \bar{R}_j)(R_k - \bar{R}_k)\right\} \tag{3.35}$$

$$Cor(R_j, R_k) = diag(\Sigma)^{\frac{1}{2}} \Sigma diag(\Sigma)^{\frac{1}{2}} \tag{3.36}$$

$$\text{where } \bar{R}_j = \frac{1}{N}\sum_{i=1}^{N} R_{i,j} \text{ and } \bar{R}_k = \frac{1}{N}\sum_{i=1}^{N} R_{i,k}. \tag{3.37}$$

R code to compute covariance uses the $cov()$ primitive. R is so statistically based that covariance is native to the language. In Figure 3.4, the x and y axes are the row and column values 1 through 9 for nine securities and the z value is the correlation coefficient for the security pairs (x, y), with value range -1 to 1, covered in an upcoming section. The "peak" green diagonal values appear to be in the foreground. Since the correlation of each variable x with itself is 1, these are the highest values in the matrix. The third random variable has the lowest correlation with the others, being close to zero, and this is seen as the deep blue and "valley" representation.

Example

The basic idea of a portfolio is to place a set of securities into a basket with weights representing the amount of investment in each. Each investment return is a random variable. In the case of two investment returns, X and Y, if a and b are the investment weights, we are interested in how the variance of the portfolio turns out.

Two random variables in a portfolio weighted by the factors a and b have the following variance:

$$\begin{aligned}
Var(aX + bY) &= E(aX + bY)^2 - E^2(aX + bY) \\
&= E(a^2X^2 + 2abXY + b^2Y^2) - E(aX + bY)E(aX + bY) \\
&= E(a^2X^2 + 2abXY + b^2Y^2) - [E(aX) + E(bY)][E(aX) + E(bY)] \\
&= a^2E(X^2) + 2abE(XY) + b^2E(Y^2) - a^2E^2(X) - 2abE(X)E(Y) + b^2E^2(Y) \\
&= a^2[E(X^2) - E^2(X)] + b^2[E(Y^2) - E^2(Y)] + 2ab[E(XY) - E(X)E(Y)] \\
&= a^2Var(X) + b^2Var(Y) + 2abCov(X, Y).
\end{aligned}$$

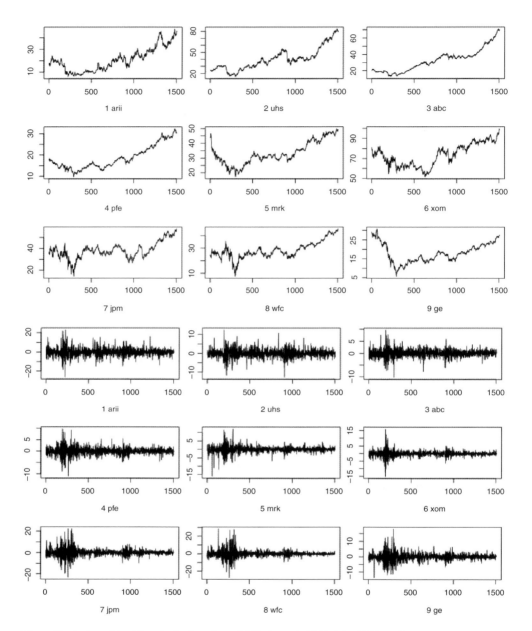

Figure 3.3   Typical equities historical prices from 2008 through 2013. The 2008 and 2009 market downturn in conjunction with the Great Recession is clearly seen, especially in the case of MRK, JPM, WFC, and GE. Next, log returns of the same set of daily closing stock prices.

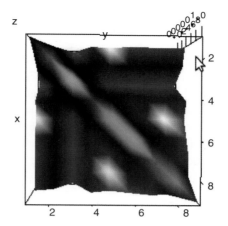

Figure 3.4   3D plot of the correlations of the stock log returns of Figure 3.3. Note the valley at the third row and column. It indicates the lowest correlation and lowest covariance of the ABC company with the other securities.

3.7   Financial Returns

In mathematical finance, the current price of an investment in a stock could be represented as

$$S(0), S(1), \ldots, S(t), \ldots$$

with initial value $S(0)$, which goes on into the future. Or the final value we are interested in could be labeled at time T as in Figure 4.2. In this figure, we are concerned with the value of $S(t)$ for t in the range 0 to 44, where the unit of t is days.

Returns are the amount of gain or loss we have in an investment as time progresses. When working with financial investments, measuring returns is critical. We would not think of driving a car without a speedometer. We need this vital piece of information for safety and planning our trip. Similarly, we need to objectively examine our current returns, returns of the past, and expected returns in the future. Let our Ss be random variables representing prices in our country's currency. The book by Ruppert has a quintessential definition for returns which we discuss here (Ruppert, 2011).

Gross returns are

$$R_g(t) = \frac{S(t)}{S(t-1)}.$$

Gross returns which represent gains are always greater than 1.

Net returns are

$$r(t) = \frac{S(t)}{S(t-1)} - 1.$$

Net returns which represent gains are always greater than 0.

Log returns are

$$R(t) = \log(1 + r(t)) = \log\left(\frac{S(t)}{S(t-1)}\right) = \log(S(t)) - \log(S(t-1)),$$

where log is natural logarithm. The log() function does not reorder values given to it. It is monotonically increasing in the sense that if $x > y$ then $\log(x) > \log(y)$. For log returns, if $S(t) = S(t-1)$ then $S(t)/S(t-1) = 1$. The log() function maps this 1 to 0 so, like net returns, zero is the threshold. For log returns, gains are always greater than 0. We will be using log returns for most of the automated processing in the R language, so we reserve the letter R for those.

3.8   Capital Asset Pricing Model

In the Capital Asset Pricing Model (CAPM), we assume the return on stock r_i takes the form

$$r_i = \alpha_i + \beta_i r_M + e_i,$$

where α_i is stock i's excess return when the market return is zero. It is the expected amount by which stock i is expected to "beat" the market. The parameter β_i is the sensitivity of stock i's return to the market return r_M, and e_i is the idiosyncratic component of stock i which is normally distributed with mean zero. Taking expectation of both sides gives

$$\begin{aligned}
E(r_i) &= E(\alpha_i + \beta_i r_M + e_i) \\
&= E(\alpha_i) + E(\beta_i r_M) + E(e_i) \\
&= \alpha_i + \beta_i E(r_M).
\end{aligned}$$

Calculating the variance of the return yields

$$\begin{aligned}
\sigma_i^2 &= Var(r_i) \\
&= Var(\alpha_i + \beta_i r_M + e_i) \\
&= Var(\alpha_i) + Var(\beta_i r_M) + Var(e_i) \\
&= \beta_i^2 Var(r_M) + Var(e_i) \\
&= \beta_i^2 \sigma_M^2 + \sigma^2(e_i).
\end{aligned}$$

Now let's find the covariance between the returns of two stocks i and j:

$$\begin{aligned}
Cov(r_i, r_j) &= Cov(\alpha_i + \beta_i r_M + e_i, \alpha_j + \beta_j r_M + e_j) \\
&= Cov(\alpha_i, \alpha_j) + Cov(\beta_i r_M, \alpha_j) + Cov(e_i, \alpha_j) \\
&\quad + Cov(\alpha_i, \beta_j r_M) + Cov(\beta_i r_M, \beta_j r_M) + Cov(e_i, \beta_j r_M) \\
&\quad + Cov(\alpha_i, e_j) + Cov(\beta_i r_M, e_j) + Cov(e_i, e_j) \\
&= \beta_i \beta_j Cov(r_M, r_M) \\
&= \beta_i \beta_j Var(r_M) \\
&= \beta_i \beta_j \sigma_M^2,
\end{aligned}$$

which says that the covariance of the returns of the two stocks is equal to the market variance times the two beta factors for each stock. We can carry out a CAPM calculation for Apple AAPL. Using the RSQLite package, after connecting to the database, we load monthly return data for Apple AAPL and the S&P 500 SPY. Then we extract returns AAPL to the variable x and S&P 500 returns to y.

```
> library(RSQLite)
> library(foreign)
> setwd(paste(homeuser,"/FinAnalytics/ChapXII",sep=""))
> funda <- read.dta("funda.dta")
> msf <- read.dta("msf.dta")
> con <- dbConnect(SQLite(),":memory:")
> dbWriteTable(con,"funda",funda,overwrite=TRUE)
> dbWriteTable(con,"msf",msf,overwrite=TRUE)
> command <- "SELECT tsymbol,ret
+            FROM msf
+            WHERE date BETWEEN '2005-01-01' AND '2013-12-31'
+               AND tsymbol IN ('AAPL','SPY')"
> result<-dbGetQuery(con,command)
> y<-result[result$tsymbol=='AAPL',]$ret
> x<-result[result$tsymbol=='SPY',]$ret
```

We can calculate β_{AAPL} both as a ratio of covariance to variance and then by noting the linear component of the linear fit. We will use the regression function from R, known as *lm( )*. The Appendix has more about regression.

```
> cov(x,y)/var(x)
[1] 1.219438
> summary(lm(y~x+1))
Call:
lm(formula = y ~ x + 1)

Residuals:
     Min       1Q    Median       3Q       Max
-0.267367 -0.057082  0.004689  0.051996  0.196984

Coefficients:
            Estimate Std. Error t value Pr(>|t|)
(Intercept)  0.02446    0.00857   2.853   0.0052 **
x            1.21944    0.19374   6.294 7.11e-09 ***
---
Signif. codes:  0 '***' 0.001 '**' 0.01 '*' 0.05 '.' 0.1 ' ' 1

Residual standard error: 0.08807 on 106 degrees of freedom
Multiple R-squared:  0.2721,	Adjusted R-squared:  0.2652
F-statistic: 39.62 on 1 and 106 DF,  p-value: 7.106e-09
```

Note also that we observe a statistically significantly positive α for Apple. This is rare. The CAPM claims that normally $\alpha = 0$.

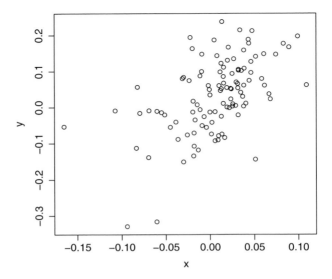

Figure 3.5   Relationship between the stock AAPL on the *y*-axis and the S&P 500 Index, SPY, on the *x*-axis.

```
> shapiro.test(x)

Shapiro-Wilk normality test

data:  x
W = 0.96002, p-value = 0.002527

> shapiro.test(y)

Shapiro-Wilk normality test

data:  y
W = 0.96924, p-value = 0.01323

> plot(x,y)
```

Above, we check for normality of monthly returns using the Shapiro–Wilk test. With the p-value less than 0.05, we will reject normality for both and plot to illustrate the positive return relationship in Figure 3.5.

3.9   Exercises

3.1. Sales of industrial earth movers X in a given month follow the probability function

$$p(x) = \begin{cases} 0.7 & \text{for } x = 0 \\ 0.2 & \text{for } x = 1 \\ 0.1 & \text{for } x = 2. \end{cases} \tag{3.38}$$

Calculate the expected value, variance, and standard deviation of monthly sales.

3.2. The proportion of time a server is operating during a given 24-hour day is given as

$$f(x) = \begin{cases} 2x & \text{for } 0 \le x \le 1 \\ 0 & \text{elsewhere.} \end{cases} \tag{3.39}$$

(a) Calculate the expected value and variance of X.

(b) Find the probability that the server is operating for less than six hours out of a given 24-hour day.

(c) The profit Y from operating the server is a function of the operating time such that $Y = 5X - 2$. Calculate the expected value and variance of the profit.

3.3. The time (in years) to failure of a brand of golf cart battery is described by the following probability density function

$$f(x) = \begin{cases} \frac{1}{2}e^{-2x} & \text{for } x \ge 0 \\ 0 & \text{elsewhere.} \end{cases} \tag{3.40}$$

(a) Calculate $E(X)$ and $E(X^2)$. Use the fact that $Var(X) = E(X^2) - E^2(X)$ to calculate the variance of X.

(b) Find the probability that the golf cart battery lasts for more than three years.

(c) Find the probability that the golf cart battery lasts for less than one year.

3.4. Refer to Section 3.6 for the variance of a weighted portfolio of two stock values. Now derive the formula for the variance of three stock values, weighted by constants a, b, and c. Use X, Y, and Z as your random variables.

4 Financial Securities

The benefit of studying securities along the lines of this chapter is a better understanding of the relationships between the various securities in the financial markets. We begin with some basic quantitative aspects of bonds and stocks and then move to a narrative about events from recent history. Many of us were impacted by these adverse events. If we were not affected, we probably know somebody, maybe a good friend or loved one, who was: they lost their retirement nest egg or their job. As we look back on these stories, we can see why having financial analytic skills in our background can help us. We need to understand the individual security statistical behaviors and their interrelationships: this is key in the complex world we live in. Indeed, just to manage our own portfolio toward our children's future school funding, budgeting for an aging relative or our own eventual retirement, requires this knowledge, especially in these days of minimal return on savings accounts.

There are many stories of fortunes made and lost in securities trading. From our personal experience, on a business trip from Chicago to New York, a Chicago-based taxi driver was asking questions about securities markets and seemed to know quite a bit about them. As the luggage was retrieved from the taxi cab trunk at the airport drop-off spot, he revealed that he busted some years back in the volatile Chicago commodities markets and needed to find a new way to make a living: from trader to taxi driver. This can happen.

In the past few decades, securities price discovery has gone from human conversations, often loud and dynamic, to quiet devices sending signals over a computer network. Securities are different from most products we encounter in that their prices fluctuate continuously during trading hours. Therefore, analyzing securities prices is a study of random processes. The mathematical study of randomness predates our modern investment banks and computerized exchanges.

We will distinguish between the most basic securities whose prices are quoted – underlying securities – and those securities whose value is derived from those basic securities – derivative securities. Basic securities include stocks, bonds, and spot commodities which are priced in the present. Their prices can be found directly without much in the way of special algorithms, but derivative security prices introduce another level of complexity since they move relative to the underlying security prices, volatility, and time to expiry.

The focus of this chapter will be on basic securities. A large portion of stock market transactions use basic securities, so establishing an analytical foundation with these is a priority.

The most basic financial instruments and the most common investment securities are bonds and stocks. With a bond, the purchaser of the bond – the bond holder – is holding a certain amount of debt of the bond issuer. The bond issuer owes the bond holder from the time of purchase until the time of maturity. The bond issuer can be a sovereign entity, such as a local or national government, or a corporation. The issuer may be obligated to pay the bond holder periodic payments, for example, semi-annually, which is a percentage of the overall or "notional" amount in addition to a full payment at maturity. This type of bond is called a *coupon bond*. A *zero-coupon bond*, however, involves no periodic payments; only a repayment at the time of the bond maturity. The idea, in either case, is that the purchaser is expecting to gain value through the income provided by the coupons and through the increase in the final bond value when compared to the original purchase price.

With a stock, the stock purchaser or owner is buying a small piece of the corporation, determined by the number of shares. Unlike the bond, there is an unlimited time period to hold the stock. There is no time of maturity. Since stocks are traded actively in the stock market, the price per share will fluctuate quite rapidly as buyers and sellers are trading shares and determining the price by the rules of supply and demand.

Both bonds and stocks also have what are known as *derivatives*. These are securities which always have a time of maturity, also known as their expiration date. Derivatives derive their value from the value of the underlying security on which they are based. The derivatives are contracts to buy or sell the bonds or stocks at a particular value by a certain date. Although there will be discussion of bonds, most of this book will concern itself with stock securities. Derivative securities will be discussed later in this book, beginning in Chapter 14.

4.1 Bond Investments

Having introduced bonds above, one question we would like to concern ourselves with is how to calculate a bond's value. If a bond's coupon payments are every six months, the interest rate, r, is typically fixed throughout the life of the bond. If one purchases and becomes the owner of a bond, we say they are *long the bond*. The bond seller is then *short the bond*. The bond has a limited period of coupon payments. In mathematical terms,

$$\text{Bond Value} = \text{Present value of coupons} + \text{Present value of par} \tag{4.1}$$

$$\text{BV}_{ann} = \sum_{t=1}^{T} \frac{\text{C}}{(1+r)^t} + \frac{\text{P}}{(1+r)^T} \tag{4.2}$$

$$\text{BV}_{semi} = \sum_{i=1}^{2T} \frac{\text{C}}{(1+\frac{r}{2})^i} + \frac{\text{P}}{(1+\frac{r}{2})^{2T}}. \tag{4.3}$$

Note that, of all the coupon payments, the coupon payment and the par amount, P, are the two quantities most discounted to today in that the interest rate $(1 + r)$ is raised all the way to the T. With *zero-coupon bonds*, there are no coupons in the Bond Value, which leaves only *Present value of par* to be paid to the bond holder by the bond issuer at maturity.

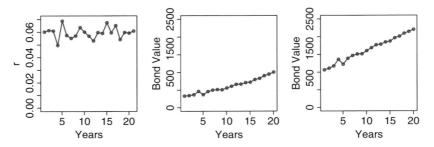

Figure 4.1   20-year position in a semi-annual floating rate bond with rate $r(t)$ which accrues value as coupons and the principles are paid over time. On the left is the rate fluctuating in the interest rates market. In the middle is the value of the zero coupon ($C = 0$) version of it. On the right is the coupon bond value accruing at a variable pace, depending upon discounting, determined by the rate.

A common type of bond is issued by the US Government treasury. Treasury-bills, or T-bills, are short-term bonds with $T \leq 1$ year. They do not pay interest before maturity. The interest is the difference between the purchase price and the price paid either at maturity (face value) or the price of the bill if sold prior to maturity. Treasury notes and bonds are securities that have a stated interest rate that is paid semi-annually until maturity. What makes notes and bonds different are the terms to maturity. Notes are issued in $T = 2$-, 3-, 5-, and 10-year terms. Bonds are long-term investments with terms of $T > 10$ years.

The value of a bond is a common application of *opportunity cost*. Once the bond holder has purchased a bond at rate r, and the bond market continues to move, if the prevailing rate goes up, the bond holder now holds a bond which is worth less. If the bond holder's rate $r = 2\%$ and the market moves to 3%, then we can calculate the value of the original and newer zero-coupon 30-year bonds as follows:

```
> 1000/(1.02)^30
[1] 552.0709
> 1000/(1.03)^30
[1] 411.9868
```

The already-purchased bond is paying less than the current market rate. The inverse relationship between a bond's interest rate r and the Bond Value is clear from this calculation. The interest rate went up, but the bond value went down.

This relationship can be seen graphically in Figure 4.1. Once again, the inverse relationship of the $r(t)$ and the bond value can be seen if we match up movements, up and down, in the left and right sides of the figure. The following R program simulates $r(t)$ the market rate fluctuating over time with a Gaussian distribution of N($\mu = 0.03$, $\sigma^2 = 0.0025^2$). In the program, the bond value defined in Formula 4.3 is extended to include coupon payments which have been paid in the past or accrued.

```
P<-1000
T<-20
r<-.06 #annual rate
C<-30
```

```
BV <- function(P,C,r,t,T) {
  #Finds coupon Bond Value at time t mat T
  tmat <- T-t
  acrued <- C*2*t #already paid
  if(tmat != 0) { #include interim coupons
    i <- seq(1,2*tmat)
    acrued + sum(C/(1+r/2)^i) +
      P/(1+r/2)^(2*tmat)
  } else #no coupons left
    acrued + P/(1+r/2)^(2*tmat)
}
```

Now that we have a function to find the bond value *BV()*, we can set our seed and simulate *r(t)* using the *rnorm()* function to obtain Gaussian variates. We then loop to simulate *t* from 0 to *T*. *BV()* implements our Formula 4.3 for BV_{semi}, the semi-annual version, by doubling the time to maturity.

```
set.seed(437)
par(mfrow=c(1,3))
#Simulate rates market for r
rvec <- round(c(r,r+
              rnorm(T)*.0050),4)
plot(rvec,type="l",ylim=c(0,.07),
     xlab="Years",ylab="r",col=4)
points(rvec,col=4)
#Simulate PV of Bond at time t
simBV <- function(P,C,rvec,T) {
  BVvec = rep(0,T)
  for(t in 0:T) {
    i = t+1
    BVvec[i] <- BV(P,C,rvec[i],t,T)
  }
  plot(BVvec,type="l",col=4,ylim=c(0,2500),
       xlab="Years",ylab="Bond Value")
  points(BVvec,col=4)
  BVvec
}
BV(P,C,r=.06,t=0,T=20)
BV(P,C,r=.06,t=1/2,T=20)
BV(P,C,r=.06,t=1,T=20)
BV(P,C,r=.07,t=1/2,T=20)
BV(P,C,r=.06,t=20,T=20)
BV(P,C,r=0,t=0,T=20)

C <- 0
simBV(P,C,rvec,T)
C <- 30
simBV(P,C,rvec,T)
```

While the prior code will simulate the interest rate and plot the bond value, the upcoming code corresponds to "unit test" cases for checking the results of the bond value. Unit testing involves a very small number of lines of code to demonstrate a basic expected property of a function. In many cases, these are one-liners as they are here. The function tester, which may very well be the author of the function, needs to gain confidence that basic elementary operation is correct.

```
> BV(P,C,r=.06,t=0,T=20)
[1] 1000
> BV(P,C,r=.06,t=1/2,T=20)
[1] 1030
> BV(P,C,r=.06,t=1,T=20)
[1] 1060
> BV(P,C,r=.07,t=1/2,T=20)
[1] 924.4875
> BV(P,C,r=.06,t=20,T=20)
[1] 2200
> BV(P,C,r=0,t=0,T=20)
[1] 2200
```

The final unit test case when time rates are zero ($r = 0$) illustrates what payments are present when there is no discounting. The value of 2200 comes from the 40 payments of 30 and the par value of 1000.

With bonds, there is one party who issues the bonds and is expected to make payments, the bond seller and bond issuer. The other party, the bond buyer and bond holder, expects to receive the payments until final maturity. Default risk arises from potential difficulties in making coupon payments or the final par value payment by the bond issuer. Default risk is reflected as a portion of the rate r expected by the bond holding investors. The rate is higher because of it.

4.2   Stock Investments

Unlike a bond, which is a loan to a company or government entity, a stock allows an investor to buy a portion of a company. The stock market is one of the most dynamic places to invest in terms of price movement, as the supply and demand for shares of the company fluctuates on a daily, second, or even sub-second basis. If one purchases one or more *shares of stock*, one becomes part owner of a company and is considered *long the stock*. If the stock appreciates in value, then the long stock owner stands to profit or gain if they decide to sell the stock.

It is also possible to sell a stock without owning it by borrowing the stock from a brokerage house. In this case, the investor is *short the stock*. This is not as common, and is considered a more risky investment than being long the stock.

In order to quantify stock prices as accurately as our methods will allow, securities prices can be modeled as random variables over time. We designate the price of a stock as being a random variable S, or more specifically, $S(t)$. At the beginning of a trade, time 0, the stock prices is $S(0)$, and at the end of the trade, time T, the stock price is $S(T)$. Our time increments here are days.

The stock trade for a *long position* of the security where the investor owns the security during the trade. With a long position the investor profits when $S(T) > S(0)$ by the

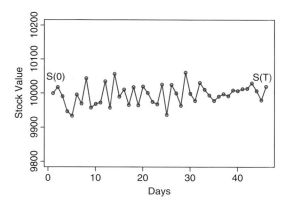

Figure 4.2 45-day-long position on security $S(t)$ with slight gain.

amount $S(T) - S(0)$. When $S(T) = S(0)$ there is no gain or loss. When $S(T) < S(0)$ the investor loses the amount $S(0) - S(T)$. As the stock appreciates or depreciates in value, as an investor, we have an *unrealized gain* or an unrealized loss, respectively. When the trade is complete, if the stock position has been settled for a profit or loss, we then have a *realized gain* or *realized loss*, respectively. In Figure 4.2, we have a $T = 45$-day trade where there is a realized gain at time T. If the stock began the period at 100 per share and we purchase, or "go long" 100 shares, then we have invested 10,000 at the outset. The following code will simulate a simple hypothetical long stock position using the *rnorm()* generator to yield Gaussian variates:

```
#Stock position:
par(mfrow=c(1,1))
#Simulate rates market for r
T <- 45 #days not years
Svec <- round(c(1,1+1.1*
                rnorm(T)*.0025),4)
SVvec <- 10000*Svec
plot(SVvec,type="l",col=4,ylim=c(9800,10200),
    xlab="Days",ylab="Stock Value")
points(SVvec,col=4)
text(c(1,T),c(10050,10050),c("S(0)","S(T)"))
```

The stock trade for a *short position* where the security is borrowed so that it can be sold to a buyer for the period of time 0 to T. With a short position the investor profits when $S(T) < S(0)$ by the amount $S(0) - S(T)$. When $S(T) = S(0)$ there is no gain or loss. When $S(T) > S(0)$ the investor loses the amount $S(T) - S(0)$. Short positions are rarer than long positions and are sometimes prohibited in investor accounts because they are more complex operationally.

4.3 The Housing Crisis

Now that we have introduced some details about bond and stock investments, let's consider some of the recent events that have affected their value. The housing crisis was a near perfect storm of unfortunate situations. Let's look at the historical set of events to see how securities across markets affect each other. Collapse of the tech bubble in 2000 and the post-9/11 collapse in consumer spending led the US Federal Reserve Bank to lower rates to near zero. This encourages a bubble in housing since a demand shock in loans is chasing a relatively constant supply of housing. Everyone wants a bigger home or to refinance their current home at the new lower rates. In addition, the government helps make housing loans available in the sub-prime category. Sub-prime loans are those with the highest chance of defaulting on payments.

Proliferation of sub-prime loans and demand from Wall Street for AAA securities (those rated as having the least chance of defaulting on payments) leads to securitization of loans. This is where agencies bundle together sub-prime loans into tranches. These are known as Mortgage Backed Securities (MBS). The higher tranches are assumed to have statistically AAA riskiness which means that the probability of default in one year's time is less, about 1 in 10,000.

Further down the line, investment banks are forced to keep some of the MBSs on their balance sheet to align interests. These are called "skin-in-the-game" requirements. Buy-back clauses are also used to force issuing banks to buy back the MBS if tranche performance falls below a certain level. The US Federal Reserve Bank starts raising rates, adjustable rate mortgages (ARM) reset to higher rates, and sub-prime mortgages start defaulting. The problem is that default rates were much higher than anyone thought, and, therefore, liabilities on investment banks' balance sheets, due to buyback and skin in game, grew faster and grew larger than anyone had anticipated.

How did this happen? Interest rates started to rise, leading to greater default rates as people could no longer pay their mortgages. MBSs, which are less valuable as underlying mortgages, then stopped performing. Investment bank balance sheets were being financed with short-term commercial loans, which also see rising rates. Banks assets started decreasing due to sub-prime mortgage under-performance. Liabilities are increasing due to higher financing costs, so equity gets squeezed. Because of all this, Lehman Brothers and Bear Stearns, two of the banks most involved with the MBS game, went bankrupt.

The US Federal Reserve Bank stepped in to stem losses. It then started the Troubled Asset Recovery Program or TARP. Banks, insurance companies, and others were able to post MBSs with the Federal Reserve in exchange for government debt. This stabilized banks' capital bases. It also stopped the free fall in MBSs due to the vicious cycle of margin calls, then wave of selling, then margin calls, then selling, and so forth. The Federal Reserve has lowered rates again since to near zero. During 2012 most markets showed signs of turning up after a five-year decline.

4.4   The Euro Crisis

The Euro currency was established in 1999 as the next step in European integration, begun in the 1950s. Currencies were frozen and linked to each other in 1999. Prices were dual-listed for a year and then the Euro rolled out in 2000. Citizens had a one-year window to turn in old currencies before those currencies were invalidated. This common currency led to conversion of risk premiums across Europe. No longer does an insurance policy need to consider currency risk when paying or collecting premiums. This resulted in a boom in real estate across southern Europe, especially in Spain. The thinking was that "convergence" would happen as Northern European capital flowed to Southern and Eastern European markets.

Wages and productivity rose, corruption fell, economies became more similar and interlinked within the common currency, and, in the story books, everyone lived happily ever after. Needless to say, things didn't work out this way. As happens many times in economic cycles, things go through periods of boom and bust. Southern Europe over-invested in housing, which is a non-productive asset. Total unit labor costs rose to the point where they were 15 percent to 30 percent above German levels, which led to much manufacturing being pushed out. The housing and financial crises hit, and growth in southern Europe fell to recession levels. Benefits and government spending held steady and so government deficits spiked.

In 2008 the housing crisis hit, and growth across the Mediterranean fell hard. From 2008 to 2010 Greece was in deep recession, social expenditures stayed high, and deficits skyrocketed. The critical point is when a 100 percent debt to GDP ratio is reached. Once over 100 percent, the economy needs to grow by at least the rate of interest or the ratio spirals out of control. As a part of the European Union (EU), countries cannot devalue their currency, which other countries can do; that is, print their way out.

Greek debt began to fall sharply as investors realized Greece would default. Spring 2010: markets start backing away from Greek debt. Let's have a look at bond values when considering Greek bonds and their present value, found by discounting:

- Initial yields of 7 percent produced a present value as follows: $1000/1.07^2 = 873.44$ where the squared rate is due to two years of discounting.
- May 2011: annual yields on two-year Greek debt hit 40 percent: $1000/1.4^2 = 510.20$.
- August 2011: annual yields on two-year Greek debt hit 60 percent: $1000/1.6^2 = 390.63$.
- September 2011: annual yields on two-year Greek debt hit 87 percent: $1000/1.87^2 = 285.97$.

We can see how the present value of bonds goes way, way down as the interest rate and yields are rising. This inverse relationship will be covered more in an upcoming section.

So, the question may arise: why was the Greece problem such a big deal? It was because of the structure of EU bailout funds and the composition of European bank balance sheets:

- Spanish and Italian banks were heavily exposed to Greek debt.
- If Greece goes bust then part of the bailout must be paid by Spain and Italy.
- Another problem is that Italian and especially Spanish debt is too high for those countries to pay their share of the Greece bailout *and* bail out their own banks.
- So the danger was that a Greek collapse would lead to a chain of events that would force most of southern Europe to break away from the Euro.

Now, if one were not a citizen of Greece, Spain, or Italy, and was, in fact, a citizen of northern Europe, then perhaps one would not particularly care about these troubles. Who cares? Just let them go, right? Well, not so fast:

- Germany's trade surplus as a percentage of GDP is among the highest in the world. Most economists attribute this to having a currency that is roughly 40 percent undervalued.
- If most of southern Europe broke away from the Euro, the value of the Euro against the dollar would shoot up.
- Having the US Dollar price of a BMW or Mercedes increase by 20 percent to 50 percent (depending on domestic labor proportion) over the course of a year is the last thing Germany wants.
- And so we have the impasse.

Spain is among the hardest hit, with a housing overhang of 1.5 million units at the height of the crisis. This was comparable to the US housing overhang, but the USA has $300M/40M \approx 7.5$ times Spain's population and $15T/1.477T \approx 10$ times Spain's GDP. Southern Europe could not devalue using Quantitative Easing (QE) to re-shore manufacturing and reflate home prices as the USA has. They were stuck in the Euro. So who benefits from the situation? Southern consumers and northern producers. Who loses? Southern producers and northern consumers. This leads to the current situation where, in Italy and Spain, industry is being hollowed out and youth unemployment is at extreme (50 percent plus) levels.

So where does the Euro crisis go from here? The situation with Greece was touch and go; now it is resolved. The Cyprus bailout was more ominous, with individual depositors at a failed bank losing part of their deposits over 150,000 Euros. This set a new precedent as it has never been done before. The elephant in the room is France. The French economy is in deep recession and not showing signs of improvement. French housing is looking at a significant fall. Economists predict a fall of 20 percent to 50 percent. France is too big to bail out, which means that the only thing left is QE, which Germany adamantly opposes. So this situation continues to develop and time marches on.

4.5   Securities Datasets and Visualization

With some discussion of these economic stories behind us, let us proceed into a very specific technique for analyzing stocks: charting. Charting is the most common form of visualization. Just like a geographical profile of a hillside or valley, one can easily perceive the stock price activity from looking at a two-dimensional chart with time on the horizontal axis and price on the vertical axis. In Figure 4.3, the Euro currency (EC) from the foreign exchange or "Forex" market is plotted on a one-minute interval for one month. These prices represent the number of US Dollars required to exchange for one Euro at that instant in time.

Using the chart, one can make observations about the price behavior. We can see that the price movement of EC can be quite erratic. There is a sudden 1 percent movement

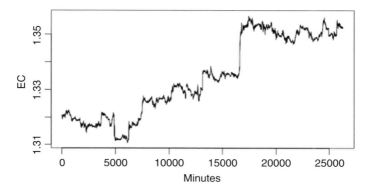

Figure 4.3 Actual one-minute prices of EUR/USD for September 2013.

which occurs where the Euro strengthens against the US Dollar, going from about 1.3360 to 1.3500. This 0.0140 change is the kind of bullish move that a foreign exchange speculator would appreciate if it has been forecasted and if they happen to be in the market holding a long position. On the other hand, the speculator would be frustrated if they had sold EC short or bought US Dollars and held on to that position through the move.

The following R routine takes a multivariate matrix of $n \times p$ prices and plots them in rectangular display array with the R command for parallel plots: *par(mfrow= c(nrow,ncol))*. It will be used frequently to help analysts visualize portfolios of securities prices and log returns. In terms of our time-based random variable $S(t)$, in this case, we have p of these which can be expressed as $(S_1(t), \ldots, S_p(t))$ and are named *prices*.

```
displayCharts <- function(prices,lab,nrow=3,ncol=4,sleepSecs=4) {
  Dims=length(prices[1,])
  for(chartGrp in (1:ceiling(Dims/(nrow*ncol)))) {
    print(chartGrp)
    par(mar=c(3.82,1.82,1.82,0.82))
    par(mfrow=c(nrow,ncol))
    for(i in 1:(nrow*ncol)) {
      j = ((chartGrp-1)*nrow*ncol+i)
      if(j <= Dims) {
        print(paste(j,lab[j]))
        plot(prices[,j],type="l",xlab=paste(j,lab[j]))
      }
    }
    Sys.sleep(sleepSecs)
  }
}
#unit test
prices <- matrix(rep(1,10),nrow=5,ncol=2)
prices[3,] <- c(6,6)
prices[4,2] <- 2
lab <- c("X","Y")
displayCharts(prices,lab)
```

In the *displayCharts()* function, the *nrow* and *ncol* refer to the plot display grid, not the price data. *lab* is a vector of ticker symbols. In the unit test code below the function definition, two dummy stocks X and Y make up this vector.

Often R packages contain embedded datasets for analysis. A package available for R for machine learning, Higher-dimensional Undirected Graph Estimation, called *huge*, contains a *stockdata* dataset which provides five years of daily closing prices for 452 stocks in the window January 1, 2003 to January 1, 2008 (Zhao, Liu, Roeder, Lafferty, and Wasserman, 2012).

The best way to discuss the *huge stockdata* dataset is in the context of adjusting the data for stock splits. We bring the *stockdata* into the R environment first.

```
library(huge)
data(stockdata)
D = length(stockdata$data[1,])
len = length(stockdata$data[,1])
prices = stockdata$data[,1:D]
lab = stockdata$info[1:D,1]
```

We may visualize the first ten stocks in the *stockdata* dataset by calling the *display-Charts()* function.

```
> displayCharts(prices[,1:12],lab[1:12],sleepSec=30)
```

By setting *sleepSec* to 30 seconds, we have time to physically capture the first display screen, pictured in Figure 4.4. Now we can see abrupt price movements, probably needing data adjustments, for the MMM, ADBE, and AET charts.

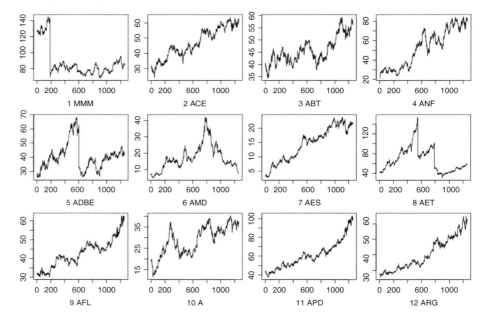

Figure 4.4   Daily charts: first 12 securities of stockdata on the same scale, unadjusted for splits.

4.6   Adjusting for Stock Splits

A stock split is an interesting event. When a stock's price has appreciated greatly, splitting the common stock makes the price of a share more affordable to new investors. The percentage ownership of the company does not change since the number of shares is multiplied by the reciprocal of the split ratio. So in a 2-to-1 split, for example, the price is cut in half while the investors are holding twice the number of shares. A forward split such as this makes the shares more attractive to new buyers for two reasons:

- the cost per share is more affordable;
- the commission per share is reduced since commission is based upon the number of shares involved rather than the share price.

When buying 100 shares or fewer, the commission is traditionally a fixed amount. Buying fewer than 100 shares increases the commission per share. If an investor can only afford to buy 50 shares, they still must pay the commission for 100 shares. If the stock undergoes a 2-for-1 split, however, then afterward the cost of 50 shares is for 100 shares as the cost per share was cut in half. This results in the commission per share being the lowest that the investor could expect to pay.

While this scenario has been generally true over the years, with commission costs declining in the last decade, the commission per share has become less important. For this reason, some companies no longer split their stock in order to avoid administrating the change. Companies like Priceline (PCLN) and Google (GOOG), which appreciated greatly in price during 2010 to 2015, have not split their stock very often and the price per share is in the multiple-hundred US Dollar range.

In any case, splits are still very common and so adjustments must be made to the market price data. Normally a split is in the forward direction, like our example where the split ratio is 2-for-1 or 3-for-2: a ratio greater than 1. However, a reverse split can occur, usually after a stock has depreciated in price. Citigroup, for example, went through a 1-for-10 reverse split in 2013 in order to reduce the number of outstanding shares that investor reports show. In a reverse split, the split ratio is less than 1.

A classic case of a reverse stock split is JDS Uniphase, a high-technology company involved in optical networking, in their 2006 announcement. The announcement explains the rationale for the split to investors (JDSU, 06):

```
JDSU Announces 1-For-8 Reverse Stock Split

Milpitas, California, September 21, 2006 - JDSU today announced that
its Board of Directors has approved a 1-for-8 reverse split of its
common stock, following approval by the Company's stock-
holders on December 1, 2005.  The reverse stock split will be
effective at 11:59 pm, Eastern Time, on Monday, October 16,
2006. JDSU's common stock will begin trading on the NASDAQ on
a split adjusted basis when the market opens on Tuesday, Octo-
ber 17, 2006, under the temporary trading symbol "JDSUD". The
```

trading symbol will revert to "JDSU" after approximately twenty
trading days.

JDSU's reverse stock split is intended to enhance investors'
visibility into the Company's profitability on a per share basis.
The Company also believes that a higher share price could broad-
en JDSU's appeal to investors, in addition to reducing per share
transaction fees and certain administrative costs.

The reverse split will reduce the number of shares of the Company's common stock outstanding from approximately 1.7 billion
to approximately 211 million. Furthermore, proportional adjustments will be made to JDSU stock options and other equity
incentive awards, equity compensation plans and convertible
notes. The number of authorized shares of common stock will be
reduced from 6 billion to 1 billion.

In this 1-for-8 reverse split, if the number of shares of common stocks becomes 211 million, then eight times that, or 1.688 billion, appears to be the original number of shares.

Often, only the prices are available in the time series and either the dates are provided or they are implied for each price. Data for announced stock splits and the split ratio are often not easily available. If the price data is not split-adjusted already in the freely available historical data, and there is no available source of split event information, one can use R's vector, matrix, and plotting features to inspect the dataset:

1. Monitoring time series: manually inspecting unexplained jumps;

2. Data adjustment: adjusting for stock splits by automatically detecting and correcting them.

The need to perform data cleaning becomes apparent by using one of R's strongest tools: its plotting capabilities. For the *huge stockdata*, an equity chart is displayed in Figure 4.4, and it becomes obvious that unexplained price changes are present in the data. These are not sudden price movement, but rather unadjusted stock splits, and they appear as jumps in the price charts.

Stock splits are the most common cause of such an event, but the effect of earnings announcements can look very similar on a chart. The key is to be able to discern between the two events as stock splits must be adjusted by smoothing the prices over the day of split for a consistent chart.

In large datasets, many stock split ratios are present, so transformation rules must be written. For example, a sudden jump in the chart for Comcast (ticker symbol CMCSA) in Figure 4.5 appeared to be an earnings announcement but, after further investigation via the internet, is was discovered that there was a 3-for-2 split event during the timeframe in question, resulting in a much smoother transformed second chart, depicted in Figure 4.6. Without adjustment, the initial chart results in incorrect return and volatility calculations. We discuss how to compute volatility in Chapter 3.

The following routine adjusts the *prices* vector by finding the multiplier and applying it:

```
splitAdjust <- function(prices,symbol) {
  len = length(prices)
  origFinalPrice = prices[len]
  for(j in 2:len) {
    split = 0
    #print(paste(prices[j-1],prices[j]))
    if(prices[j-1] >= 1.4*prices[j]) {
      split = +1.5 # a 3 for 2
      if(prices[j-1] >= 1.8*prices[j])
        split = +2 #At least a 2 for 1
      if(prices[j-1] >= 2.9*prices[j])
        split = +3 #Ah a 3 for 1
      if(prices[j-1] >= 3.9*prices[j])
        split = +4 #Ah a 3 for 1
      if(prices[j-1] >= 4.9*prices[j])
        stop(paste(symbol,'detected more than 4:1 split'))
      print(paste("split adjusting",symbol,split,
                  j,prices[j-1],prices[j]))
```

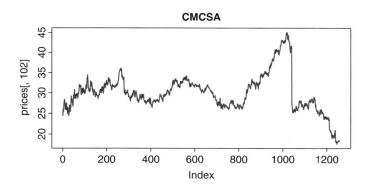

Figure 4.5   A chart for the Comcast security, CMCSA, unadjusted.

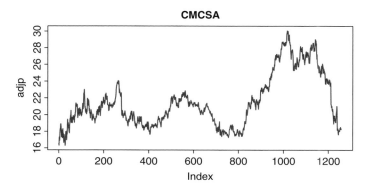

Figure 4.6   A chart for the Comcast security, CMCSA, adjusted after a 3-for-2 price split.

Our rules above handle the case that the stocks becomes worth less in value: a split. A reverse split is when the stock becomes worth more in value than before the day of the split. Common reverse splits that we have seen in our dataset form rules below:

```
} #reverse splits: price increases so divide
if(prices[j-1] <= prices[j]/1.4) {
  split = -1.5
  if(prices[j-1] <= prices[j]/1.9 &&
      prices[j-1] >= prices[j]/2.1)
    split = -2
  if(prices[j-1] <= prices[j]/2.9 &&
      prices[j-1] >= prices[j]/3.1)
    split = -3
  if(prices[j-1] <= prices[j]/5.8 &&
      prices[j-1] >= prices[j]/6.2)
    split = -6
  if((prices[j-1] <= prices[j]/7.7) &&
      (prices[j-1] >= prices[j]/8.3))
    split = -8
  if((prices[j-1] <= prices[j]/9.7) &&
      (prices[j-1] >= prices[j]/10.3))
    split = -10
  if((split == 0) && (prices[j-1] <= prices[j]/2.9))
    stop(paste(symbol,
                'detected more than double reverse split'))
  print(paste("reverse split adjusting",j,symbol,j,
                split,prices[j-1],prices[j]))
}
```

Now that the *split* amount has been determined, it can be applied to the *prices* vector; dataset form rules below:

```
if(split != 0) {
  for(k in j:len) { #adjust all prices to right from j:len
    if(symbol=="C")
      prices[k] = prices[k]/10 #hard coded for Citi
    else if(split == +1.5)
      prices[k] = 1.5*prices[k] # 3 for 2
    else if(split == +2)
      prices[k] = 2*prices[k] # 2 to 1
    else if(split == +3)
      prices[k] = 3*prices[k] # 3 to 1
    else if(split == +4)
      prices[k] = 4*prices[k] # 4 to 1
    else if(split == -1.5)
      prices[k] = prices[k]/1.5 # 2 to 3 rev
    else if(split == -2)
      prices[k] = prices[k]/2 # 1 to 2 rev
    else if(split == -3)
      prices[k] = prices[k]/3 # 1 to 2 rev
    else if(split == -6)
```

```
            prices[k] = prices[k]/6 # 1 to 8 rev
          else if(split == -8)
            prices[k] = prices[k]/8 # 1 to 8 rev
          else if(split == -10)
            prices[k] = prices[k]/10 # 1 to 10 rev
          else stop('splitAdjust internal error')
        }
      }
   }
   finalPrice = prices[len]
   return(prices*origFinalPrice/finalPrice)
}
#unit test:
p <- c(3.0,3.0,2.0,11.88,5.9,1.95,3.90,3.90,
         1.5,.75,1.00,1.2,1.4,1.8,2.1,1.05,1.30,1.31,1.32,.44,
         .43,.11,.12,.13)
sap <- splitAdjust(p,"SYM")
plot(p,type='l',ylim=c(0,15)); points(sap,col=4)
```

Now we can examine our example of a 1-to-8 reverse split, JDSU, and use *splitAdjust()* in a test:

```
> JDSUidx <- match('JDSU',lab)
> plot(prices[,JDSUidx],type='l',xlab='JDSU')
> adjp<-splitAdjust(prices[,JDSUidx],c('JDSU'))
[1] "reverse split adjusting 956 JDSU 956 -8 2.13 16.6"
> plot(adjp,type='l',xlab='JDSUadj')
```

which produces the before and after plots of Figures 4.7 and 4.8.

The code for *findR()* appears below. It finds the log returns for the D price series. We use the super-assignment operator to side-affect D in addition to returning the log return matrix, R:

```
findR <- function(prices,isSplitAdjusted=TRUE) {#Find R: logrets:
  len = dim(prices)[1]
  D <<- dim(prices)[2]
  R   = matrix(nrow=(len-1),ncol=D)
  for(i in 1:D) {
    #print(i)
    if(!isSplitAdjusted) prices[,i] <<- splitAdjust(prices[,i],lab[i])
    R[,i] = 100*diff(log(prices[,i])) ###log rets
  }
  R
}
```

Now that we have tested out our split adjustment utility to correct the non-adjusted stock time series, we can invoke it to correct those elements of the *prices* matrix. We use *findR()* with *isSplitAdjusted == FALSE* to invoke *splitAdjust()*:

```
> R <- findR(prices,isSplitAdjusted=FALSE)
[1] "split adjusting MMM 2 188 140.54 69.07"
[1] "split adjusting ADBE 2 603 62.72 32.42"
[1] "split adjusting AET 2 553 147.71 74.76"
[1] "split adjusting AET 2 790 202.5 99.42"
[1] "split adjusting AGN 2 1127 114.47 58"
[1] "split adjusting ABC 2 755 83.77 41.48"
...
[1] "reverse split adjusting 956 JDSU 956 -8 2.13 16.6"
...
[1] "reverse split adjusting 114 PCLN 114 -6 4.24 25.22"
...
[1] "split adjusting YHOO 2 343 53.53 27.08"
[1] "split adjusting YUM 2 1129 64.57 32.37"
> D <- dim(prices)[2]
> D
[1] 452
```

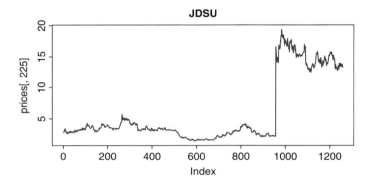

Figure 4.7   A chart for the JDS Uniphase security, JDSU, unadjusted. Clearly there is an extreme event before day 1,000 that should be investigated.

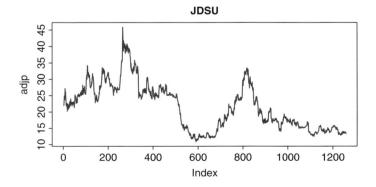

Figure 4.8   A chart for the JDS Uniphase security, JDSU, adjusted after a 1-for-8 reverse price split. When matched against Figure 4.7 we can see the similarity, after adjusting the scaling for the time of the split.

To build our confidence that the 1-for-6 split for PCLN really happened, we can scan the internet and find several references to this split. It occurred on May 6, 2003 according to the CNBC site (Spechler, 2011). In fact, the article focuses on a number of securities which did quite well from a common stock price point of view after undergoing a reverse split. As we will see in the charts of upcoming chapters, PCLN is no exception to this trend.

4.7 Adjusting for Mergers

Mergers and acquisitions occur continuously and affect our dataset. When one company buys another, typically one of the two ticker symbols is chosen to remain and the other has the effect of appearing to stop trading on the merger day or one day before. When we have a portfolio of stocks and are looking at the performance by obtaining prices, we can encounter errors: either a missing file or a quoting utility function cannot return accurate results. For example, here is a metals company merger or acquisition event from GoogleFinance.com (2014) for the symbol TIE that occurs in our desired dataset:

Titanium Metals Corporation (TIMET) is a producer of titanium melted and mill products. \ldots In January 2013, Precision Cast-parts Corp acquired TIMET.

Here is another example, but this time from the healthcare industry in Forbes.com for symbol CVH (Forbes.com, 2013):

Healthcare providers have also been hard at work trying to posi-tion for a rapid change to Medicare and Medicaid as 'Obamacare' kicks in over the next 12-to-18 months. At around the act's passage and affirmation by the Supreme Court, WellPoint (WLP) and Amerigroup (AGP) merged, followed shortly thereafter by a merger between Aetna (AET) and Coventry Healthcare (CVH).

When the flat file named resD26QP1Days1258.csv has these two symbols, we encounter errors; then edit rows for TIE and CVH out and write the new file called resD24Days1258.csv:

```
adjustForMergers <- function(dir,portFile) {
  #Take in symbols and their weights and emit a
  #rebalanced file summing close to 1.0
  setwd(paste(homeuser,"/FinAnalytics/",dir,"/",sep=""))
  df    <- read.csv(portFile)
  lab   <- df[,2]
  w     <- df[,3]
  if(abs(sum(w) - 1.0) < .002) {
    print('All weights sum to 1.0')
  } else {
    print(sum(w))
    amtToRealloc <- 1.0 - sum(w)
```

```
    wInc <- w*amtToRealloc
    print(sum(w+wInc))
    df[,3] <- w+wInc
    newFile = paste("rebal",portFile,sep="")
    write.csv(df,file=newFile,row.names = FALSE)
    print(paste("wrote file",newFile))
  }
}
adjustForMergers('huge','resD26QP1Days1258.csv')
adjustForMergers('huge','resD25Days1258woTIE.csv')
adjustForMergers('huge','resD24Days1258.csv')
```

Running the utility function *adjustForMergers()* we first find out that, for the first file, the weights sum close to 1.0, but these weights cannot be used because of ineligible TIE and CVH.

```
> adjustForMergers('huge','resD26QP1Days1258.csv')
[1] "All weights sum to 1.0"
> adjustForMergers('huge','resD25Days1258woTIE.csv')
[1] 0.9498
[1] 0.99748
[1] "wrote file rebalresD25Days1258woTIE.csv"
> adjustForMergers('huge','resD24Days1258.csv')
[1] 0.9918
[1] 0.9999328
[1] "wrote file rebalresD24Days1258.csv"
>
```

In the case of TIE, its new parent company, PCP, was already in the portfolio, so we decide to take the weight for TIE, $w_7 = 0.0491$, and the weight of PCP, $w_{15} = 0.0269$, and add them, replacing the weight of TIE with the new weight of PCP, $w_{PCP} = 0.0760$. In the case of CVH the parent company is not already in the portfolio so we eliminate it. Then we run the utility function on *resD24Days1258.csv*, and it produces a third file called rebalresD24Days1258.csv which has the rebalanced weights summing to 1.0.

4.8   Plotting Multiple Series

Another way to display the prices for the first few stocks of the dataset is using the *plotMultSeries()* function, which scales all prices to 1 unit of currency or 1 unit of gross return at the beginning of the time series. Figure 4.9 has this plot.

```
plotMultSeries <- function(prices,lab,w,D,cc="days",ret=NA,
                ylim=c(.2,15),isAlone=TRUE) {
  if(isAlone) plot.new()
  mapToCol <- function(d)
    if(d%%8==7) 1 else if(d==8)
      2 else if(d==15) 3 else if(d==23) 4 else d
  par(mar=c(4,2.82,1.82,1))
```

```
if(isAlone) par(mfrow=c(1,1))
tot <- 0; len <- dim(prices)[1]
first <- TRUE; D <- dim(prices)[2]
for(d in 1:D) {
  if(!is.na(prices[1,d]) && !is.na(w[d]) && w[d] > 0) {
    print(lab[d])
    tot <- tot + 1
    if(first) {
      first = FALSE
      plot(prices[,d]/prices[1,d],type="l",
           col=mapToCol(d),xlab=cc,
           ylim=ylim)
    } else
      lines(prices[,d]/prices[1,d],type="l",
            col=mapToCol(d))
    text(len,(prices[len,d]/prices[1,d]),lab[d],
         col=mapToCol(d),cex=.8)
  }
}
print(tot)
print(paste("density or non-zero weights (sparsity) is ",tot/D))
}
#unit test:
D2 <- 12
w <- rep(1/D2,D2)
plotMultSeries(prices,lab,w,D2,cc=
    paste(sum(w>0),"stocks"),ret="", ylim=c(.5,8))
```

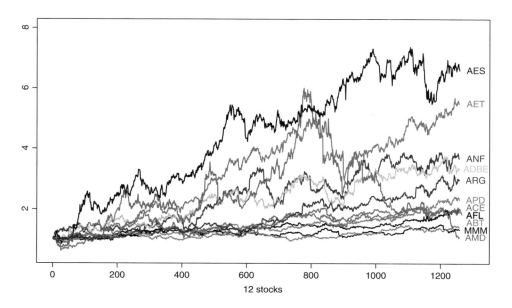

Figure 4.9   Replotting the first 12 securities of stockdata on the same scale of $1.

This scaling replaces the actual prices with relative prices so that securities returns can be compared.

4.9   Securities Data Importing

The *huge stockdata* dataset is a fairly robust place to start. However, there are a lot more traded equity securities than the 452 provided by it, and we want to be able to control our time frame rather than be limited to from 2003 to 2008. We especially want to get current quotes for today and immediately prior to today to see how a portfolio is performing lately.

To be able to measure historical return and even calibrate a chosen portfolio to the current market, we need software mechanisms. The *tseries* R package provides an extremely useful function called *get.hist.quote()* for obtaining Yahoo!-based historical prices:

```
library(tseries)
pv <- get.hist.quote('YHOO',quote="Adj",start="2011-02-09",
                     end="2015-02-09")
pv
```

This function can be used to manage our historical data retrieval and our caching of the data.

When the dataset is new there is no choice but to connect to an outside source. Often we need to repeat a simulation multiple times, changing logic in-between. Using an online data source is somewhat convenient, but caching it makes it available locally, without the need for a network connection. So we can connect to the internet using the *get.hist.quote()* when we require a new dataset and cache it into flat files as it streams in. Reading from the cache makes our simulation run faster and allows it to run offline, providing flexibility. Of course, we are limited to the same data from the same time horizon as long as we use the cache.

```
readExchSymbols <- function(fileName) {
  frame <- read.csv(fileName,header=TRUE,sep="\t")
  return(as.character(frame[,1]))
}
```

The above routine, *readExchSymbols()*, reads our desired stock quotes for our time horizon and caches the data into individual flat files in two directories: *NYSE* and *NAS-DAQ*. The following initialization R code makes use of routines *displayCharts()* and *splitAdjust()* to read from a directory of historical prices and display them in an array. *splitAdjust()* was introduced above.

There are two sub-directories: one for the NYSE stocks and another for NASDAQ stocks. Each directory contains approximately 2200 cache files, one per security. For example, for the NYSE security IBM, the file is named cacheIBM.csv and contains multiple years of prices arranged in a single-column format. The following routine, *createDirs()*, sets up a directory for storing stock prices for a test date range. Typically there is one sub-directory for NYSE and one for NASDAQ under the main directory. If *isSubDir*==TRUE, it assumes the two ticker files for the NYSE and NASDAQ need to be copied over into the sub-directories:

```
createDirs <- function(dir,isSubDir=TRUE) {
  #check for the two subdirs if isSubDir TRUE
  mainDir <- paste(homeuser,"/FinAnalytics/",sep="")
  destDir <- paste(mainDir,dir,sep="")
  if (!file.exists(destDir))
    dir.create(file.path(destDir))
  setwd(file.path(destDir))
  if(isSubDir) {
    f1 <- "NYSEclean.txt"
    f2 <- "NASDAQclean.txt"

    NYSEsubDir <- paste(destDir,"/NYSE",sep="")
    if (!file.exists(NYSEsubDir))
      dir.create(file.path(NYSEsubDir))
    if(!file.exists(paste(NYSEsubDir,"/NYSEclean.txt",sep="")))
      file.copy(paste(homeuser,"/FinAnalytics/",f1,sep=""),
                NYSEsubDir)
    NASDAQsubDir <- paste(destDir,"/NASDAQ",sep="")
    if (!file.exists(NASDAQsubDir))
      dir.create(file.path(NASDAQsubDir))
    if(!file.exists(paste(NASDAQsubDir,"/NASDAQclean.txt",sep="")))
      file.copy(paste(homeuser,"/FinAnalytics/",f2,sep=""),
                NASDAQsubDir)
  } else {
    f <- paste(dir,"clean.txt",sep="")
    if(!file.exists(paste(destDir,"/",f,sep="")))
      if(file.exists(paste(mainDir,"/",f,sep="")))
        file.copy(paste(homeuser,"/FinAnalytics/",f,sep=""),".")
  }
}
#unit test
createDirs("CDUT")
```

Try to define this routine in your R environment and run the unit test. The final line of code above creates a test directory called CDUT under the main FinAnalytics directory. After CDUT is created, inspect the directory contents on your computer. There should be two sub-directories, each with a file of ticker symbols when the unit test run completes.

```
readSubDirs <- function(dir,isSubDir=TRUE) {
  if(isSubDir) {
    #Case: 2 sub-dirs: NYSE and NASDAQ
    #Return 3 results, the last being a large vec
    setwd(paste(homeuser,"/FinAnalytics/",dir,"/NYSE",sep=""))
    lab <- readExchSymbols("NYSEclean.txt")
```

```
    D1 <- length(lab)
    print(D1)
    setwd(paste(homeuser,"/FinAnalytics/",dir,"/NASDAQ",sep=""))
    lab2 <- readExchSymbols("NASDAQclean.txt")
    lab <- append(lab,lab2)
    D2 <- length(lab2)
    print(D2)
    list(D1,D2,as.character(lab))
  } else {
    setwd(paste(homeuser,"/FinAnalytics/",dir,sep=""))
    lab <- readExchSymbols(paste(dir,"clean.txt",sep=""))
    D <- length(lab)
    print(D)
    list(D,as.character(lab))
  }
}
```

The function above, called *readSubDir()*, accounts for two primary cases:

- a directory with a sub-directory for the *NYSE* and the *NASDAQ* exchanges.
- a directory with no sub-directories.

acquirePrices() is our main routine for downloading and caching price quotes. Initially, *acquirePrices()* must download all prices for all the securities listed in the *lab* vector. As price vectors get acquired from R *tseries* utility *get.hist.quote()* for the required date range, they are cached in CSV files for later use. NYSE and NASDAQ quotes are kept in separate sub-directories.

As we look at the declaration of *acquirePrices()* below, we see the *start* = *start, end* = *end* portion. This indicates to set the initial values of the local variables *start* and *end* in *"YYYY-MM-DD"* format if they are provided as arguments positionally; otherwise the default values will be assigned. The default values, in this case, are the values of variables *start* and *end* global to the function.

```
acquirePrices <- function(prices,lab,len,D,D1,D2,dir,
                 start,end,isSubDir=TRUE) {
  isSuccessfulQuote <- FALSE
  for(d in 1:D) {
    if(d == 1 || (isSubDir && d == (D1+1)))
      if(d == 1 && isSubDir) {
        setwd(paste(homeuser,"/FinAnalytics/",dir,"/NYSE",sep=""))
        unlink('bad*')
        print(paste("NYSE=======:",d))
      } else if(d == (D1+1) && isSubDir) {
        setwd(paste(homeuser,"/FinAnalytics/",dir,"/NASDAQ",sep=""))
        unlink('bad*')
        print(paste("NASDAQ=======:",d))
      } else {
        setwd(paste(homeuser,"/FinAnalytics/",dir,sep=""))
        unlink('bad*')
        print(paste("ETF==========:",d))
```

```
  }
print(paste(d,lab[d]))
fileName = paste("cached",lab[d],".csv",sep="")
usingCacheThisFileName <- FALSE
if(file.exists(fileName)) {
  usingCacheThisFileName <- TRUE
  pricesForStock <- read.csv(fileName,header=TRUE,sep="")[,1]
  if(!is.na(pricesForStock[1]))
    isSuccessfulQuote <- TRUE
}
if(!usingCacheThisFileName ||
    (usingCacheThisFileName && length(pricesForStock) != len)) {
  usingCacheThisFileName <- FALSE
```

An interesting feature of R is the *tryCatch()* wrapper function, which encloses a block of code and attaches a warning, error and final block of code to each outcome. Our *tryCatch()* logic appears below:

```
tryCatch( {
  print(start);print(end)
  Sys.sleep(1)
  pricesForStock <- get.hist.quote(lab[d],quote="Adj",
                    start=start,end=end)
  if(!is.na(pricesForStock[1]))
    isSuccessfulQuote <- TRUE
}, error = function(err) {
  print(err);cat(lab[d],file="badsyms.txt",
                append=TRUE,sep="\n")
  isSuccessfulQuote <- FALSE
} )
}
```

The returned length must exactly match our requested *len*, otherwise we determine that the symbol cannot be quoted by *get.hist.quote()*:

```
if(length(pricesForStock) == len) {
  prices[,d] <- pricesForStock
  if(sum(is.na(prices[,d])) > 0 || (sum(is.na(prices[,d-1])) == 0 &&
      d > 1 && prices[1,d] == prices[1,d-1])) {
    print(paste(lab[d],'has NA prices'))
    cat(lab[d],file="badsyms.txt",
        append=TRUE,sep="\n")
    isSuccessfulQuote <- FALSE
  }
} else {
  cat(lab[d],file="badsyms.txt",append=TRUE,sep="\n")
}
if(!isSuccessfulQuote)
  cat(lab[d],file="badsyms.txt",append=TRUE,sep="\n")
if(isPlotInAdjCloses) {
```

```
    if(d == 1)
        plot(prices[,d]/prices[1,d],type="l",col="blue",ylim=c(.2,6))
    else
        lines(prices[,d]/prices[1,d],type="l",col="blue")
    text(len,(prices[len,d]/prices[1,d]),lab[d],cex=.6)
}
```

Above is the error-handling logic. When NA is returned in the *pricesForStock* vector, an entry is made into *badsyms.txt* file. Later, the *elimSyms()* routine will use this file to remove these entries from the *lab* vector and *prices[]* matrix. If we determine that caching is on and we have not used a cache for this item, the logic below will create a cache item for this symbol; that is, a flat file containing its prices.

The following block is the code sequence where the cache files are written:

```
    if(isCacheEnabled && !usingCacheThisFileName &&
        isSuccessfulQuote) {
      #save redundant re-write
      fileName = paste("cached",lab[d],".csv",sep="")
      print(fileName)
      write.csv(prices[,d],file=fileName,row.names = FALSE)
    }
    isSplitAdjusted = TRUE
  }
  prices
}
```

So that is our logic for acquiring prices from the internet repository using *get.hist.quote()*, which uses Yahoo! for stocks prices and Oanda for foreign exchange rates. This utility is quite a powerful tool for obtaining daily prices. For the case of our four thousand-some stockprice series, however, it takes a considerable amount of time to download these. The cache allows us to debug or rerun by reading the files locally, decreasing the time to obtain prices significantly after they have been initially downloaded.

Two key arguments to the *get.hist.quote()* utility are *start* and *end*. For a six-year daily price study, one of the main studies of Chapter 8, we set them as below:

```
start = "2008-02-14"
end   = "2014-02-14"
```

These key variables set the historical data range.

To set up a directory structure to start acquiring prices via the *get.hist.quote()* routine of *acquirePrices()*, we need a basic two-level setup. If *MVOx* is our first-level directory name under the *<homeuser>/FinAnalytics* directory, where <homeuser> is typically something such as *C:\Users\<userid>* or */home/<userid>* and where we use *x* to denote the number of years back we are collecting prices for (3, 4, 5, or 6 typically), then we need two files containing our desired ticker symbols under two sub-directories listed in Table 4.1. The flat files have a simple header line, which is ignored, followed by consecutive lines of a single ticker name per line.

Table 4.1 The names of simple flat files containing one ticker per line.

Directory path	File
<homeuser>/FinAnalytics/MVOx/NYSE	NYSEclean.txt
<homeuser>/FinAnalytics/MVOx/NASDAQ	NASDAQclean.txt

We discussed unit testing a bit when we introduced the bond value calculation in Section 4.1, above. Setting up our two-level directory structure, with one sub-directory for each exchange, NYSE and NASDAQ, and with flat files for the cleaned list of ticker symbols, *NYSEclean.txt* and *NASDAQclean.txt*, is a little tricky. In order to ensure that the components are there to support the stored prices, known as the cached files, a unit test script can be built in R. The following steps are needed:

- Initialize the NYSE and NASDAQ ticker symbols.
- Set up the top-level directory (APUT for Acquire Prices Unit Test) and two sub-directories.
- Set the $D1$ and $D2$ dimensions to the number of symbols.
- Merge the symbol vector into one vector and set $D = D1 + D2$.
- Acquire prices. These must be from the network as there are no cache files yet. Create the cache files: one for each symbol which has prices returned from *get.hist.quote()*.
- Test the use of the cache files by re-running the above step. This time the prices will be selected from the cache files, if they exist.
- Delete the top-level directory and sub-directories so that the unit test is rerunnable.

We chose to use 20 NYSE and 26 NASDAQ ticker symbols. Not all of the requested ticker symbols will succeed with successful price quotes.

```
library(tseries)
APUT <- function(isTestElimSyms=FALSE) {
  dir <- 'APUT'
  l1 <- c('A','AA','AAN','AAP','AAT','AAV','AB','ABB','ABC','ABG',
          'ABM','ABR','ABX','ACC','ACCO','ACE','ACG','ACH','ACI','ACM')
  l2 <- c('AAL','AAME','AAON','AAPL','AAWW','AAXJ','ABAX','ABCB',
          'ABCD','ABCO','ABIO','ABMD','ABTL','ACAD','ACAS',
          'ACAT','ACCL','ACET','ACFC','ACFN','ACGL','ACHC','ACHN',
          'ACIW','ACLS')
  topdir <- paste(homeuser,'/FinAnalytics/',dir,sep="")
  NYSEdir <- paste(topdir,'/NYSE',sep="")
  NASDAQdir <- paste(topdir,'/NASDAQ',sep="")
  if(!file.exists(topdir))
    dir.create(topdir)
  if(!file.exists(NYSEdir)) {
    dir.create(NYSEdir)
    setwd(NYSEdir)
    if(!file.exists("NYSEclean.txt"))
      write.csv(l1,file="NYSEclean.txt",
                quote=FALSE,row.names=FALSE)
  }
}
```

```
  if(!file.exists(NASDAQdir)) {
    dir.create(NASDAQdir)
    setwd(NASDAQdir)
    if(!file.exists("NASDAQclean.txt"))
      write.csv(l2,file="NASDAQclean.txt",
                quote=FALSE,row.names=FALSE)
  }
  D1 <- length(l1)
  D2 <- length(l2)
  l <- c(l1,l2)
  D <- D1 + D2
  len <- 1006
  p <- matrix(rep(NA,len*D),nrow=len,ncol=D)
  #acquirePrices assumes user knows proper
  #len, start and end
  isPlotInAdjCloses <<- FALSE
  isCacheEnabled <<- TRUE
  p <- acquirePrices(p,l,len,D,D1,D2,dir,
       start="2010-02-18",end="2014-02-14",isSubDir=TRUE)
  #Second time cached files exist.
  p <- acquirePrices(p,l,len,D,D1,D2,dir,
       start="2010-02-18",end="2014-02-14",isSubDir=TRUE)
  if(isTestElimSyms) {
    dim(p)
    D
    system(paste('sort ',paste(NYSEdir,'/bad*',sep="")))
    system(paste('sort ',paste(NASDAQdir,'/bad*',sep="")))
    saveD <- D
    res <- elimSyms(p,l,"APUT")
    p <- res[[1]]
    l <- res[[2]]
    print(paste("elimSyms returns",l))
    #print(p[1,])
  }
  unlink(topdir, recursive = TRUE)
}
#acquirePrices unit test (APUT):
APUT()
```

In our runs of this unit test sequence, all but two of the 46 ticker symbols produced a price vector.

```
> p[len,]
 [1]  38.954475  11.223343  29.747891 127.015142         NA   3.880000
 [7]  20.996400  23.711670  66.778435  49.259998  26.564400   6.129368
[13]  19.929171  34.144345   5.990000  94.616193   6.821497   9.250000
[19]  40.801209  30.000000  34.018565   3.879132  18.988840  75.606251
[25]  32.939999  56.436053  38.114603  19.883766   1.930000  61.419998
[31]  61.419998   1.790000  28.139999  18.049999  23.930000  14.820000
[37]  45.126448         NA  18.506554   3.990000   3.670000  55.259998
[43]  51.180000   3.570000  19.150000   2.190000
```

We can see this result in the preceding output. This is the contents of a time slice of the price vector after two runs of *acquirePrices()*: one to obtain prices over the network and cache them and one to read them back in the from the cache files.

4.10   Securities Data Cleansing

As we try to acquire prices for the two ticker lists and are not able to do so for all, we can edit the *NYSEclean.txt* and *NASDAQclean.txt* files to remove tickers that we will not be able to acquire prices for. In addition, *acquirePrices()* will emit rows into three types of error with "bad" in their names.

Data cleansing can be automated by using this set of files for each type of error:

- *badsyms.txt* for symbols with unavailable prices;
- *badsharpes.txt* for symbols with uncomputable Sharpe Ratios;
- *badcors.txt* for symbols with uncomputable covariances or correlations.

The *elimSyms()* routine takes the accumulated *badsyms.txt* files and removes them from the ticker set *lab[]* and *prices[]* matrix. For example, even though we have a candidate such as ACO, the routine *get.hist.quote()* cannot find prices for it. And, looking it up in Yahoo! or Google Finance, we do not find quotes, so we can eliminate this candidate by adding it to the *badsyms.txt* file:

```
elimSyms <- function(prices,lab,dir,isSubDir=TRUE) {
  len = dim(prices)[1]
  D = dim(prices)[2]
  #First find removal list in 3 files in each of NYSE and NASDAQ
  indInFile = as.vector(rep(FALSE,D))
  ifelse(isSubDir,subdirVec <- c("NYSE","NASDAQ"),subdirVec <- c(NA))
  for(subdir in subdirVec) {
    if(isSubDir)
      setwd(paste(homeuser,"/FinAnalytics/",dir,"/",subdir,sep=""))
    else
      setwd(paste(homeuser,"/FinAnalytics/",dir,sep=""))
    for(file in c("badsyms.txt","badcors.txt","badsharpes.txt")) {
      badlab = NA
      if(file.exists(file))
        badlab <- read.table(file) # badcors.txt badsharpes.txt")
      if(length(badlab)>1 || !is.na(badlab)) {
        for(l in badlab) {
          print(paste("elimSym",l))
          pos = match(l,lab)
          indInFile[pos] = TRUE
        }
      }
    }
  }
  indNAPrices = (is.na(prices[1,]))
```

```
indNALab = (is.na(lab[1:D]))
indTooBig = (prices[1,] > 1e5) | (prices[len,] > 1e5)
#missing price or lab is NA or too big
indUnion = indInFile | indNAPrices | indNALab | indTooBig
#Create new prices matrix smaller for only NonNAs
smallerSz = D - sum(indUnion)
print(smallerSz)
newPrices = matrix(rep(0,len*smallerSz),nrow=len,ncol=smallerSz)
newLab = vector(length=smallerSz)
e <- 1
for(d in 1:D) {
  if(!indUnion[d]) {
    #print(paste("e",e,lab))
    newPrices[,e] <- prices[,d]
    newLab[e] <- lab[d]
    e <- e + 1
  } else {print(d)}
}
list(newPrices[,1:smallerSz],newLab)
}
```

In *elimSyms()* we check three error files in each sub directory (if *isSubDir* is TRUE), for symbols with errors. At the end of the loop, we have a Boolean vector, *indInFile* per symbol to tell us if that symbol would be eliminated from the *lab* vector.

When it becomes necessary to unit test the routine, we can reuse the unit test for *acquirePrices()*, APUT. This time we invoke the inner block which tests *elimSyms()* by setting *isTestElimSyms* == TRUE.

```
#unit test:
APUT(TRUE)

isPlotInAdjCloses = FALSE
dir <- 'MVO4'
len <- 1006
createDirs(dir)
res <- readSubDirs(dir)
isCacheEnabled <- TRUE
D1 <- res[[1]]
D2 <- res[[2]]
lab <- res[[3]]
D <- D1 + D2
start = "2011-02-09"
end = "2015-02-09"

prices <- matrix(rep(NA,len*D),nrow=len,ncol=D)
prices <- acquirePrices(prices,lab,len,D,D1,D2,
                        start=start,end=end,dir,isSubDir=TRUE)

res    <- elimSyms(prices,lab,dir,isSubDir=TRUE)
prices <- res[[1]]
```

```
lab      <- res[[2]]
D        <- length(lab)
D
dim(prices)

R <- findR(prices)
D <- dim(prices)[2]
```

Now that we have *findR()* and its dependent routines defined, we can see and run the code sequence above to read the sub-directories, acquire the prices, and compute the *R* log return matrix.

findCovMat() finds the mean vector and the covariance matrix. It then uses the covariance matrix to find the vector of standard deviations. Next we turn to computing our statistics.

```
findCovMat <- function(R) {
  meanv <- apply(R,2,mean)
  cov_mat <- cov(R)
  diag_cov_mat <- diag(cov_mat)
  sdevv <- sqrt(diag(cov_mat))
  list(meanv,cov_mat,diag_cov_mat,sdevv)
}
#unit test:
res <- findCovMat(R)
meanv       <- res[[1]]
cov_mat     <- res[[2]]
diag_cov_mat <- res[[3]]
sdevv <- res[[4]]
```

The covariance matrix must be free of NAs for the process to proceed. In addition, if duplicate prices make their way into the process, the covariances will be duplicated as well and that can be detected here.

```
checkCovMat <- function(cov_mat) {
  #Check for duplicate covariances:
  D = dim(cov_mat)[1]
  for(d in 1:D)
    for(e in d:D) {
      print(paste(d,e,cov_mat[d,1],cov_mat[e,1]))
      if(d != e && !is.na(cov_mat[d,1]) &&
           !is.na(cov_mat[e,1]) && cov_mat[d,1] == cov_mat[e,1])
        stop(paste("dups in cov_mat",d,e))
    }
}
#unit test:
checkCovMat(cov_mat)
```

While preparing this book, for example, an unexpected failure of the *checkCovMat()* routine occurred. Darn it, why, after repeated runs of the packaged code, would it fail on our known set of tickers? Here is its output message:

```
...
[1] "16 291 1.35732246087691 1.93682271844313"
[1] "16 292 1.35732246087691 1.35732246087691"
Error in checkCovMat(cov_mat) : dups in cov_mat 16 292
> cov_mat[16,1:5]
[1] 1.3573225 1.3360865 0.8959254 0.7315397 0.8271826
> cov_mat[292,1:5]
[1] 1.3573225 1.3360865 0.8959254 0.7315397 0.8271826
> lab[c(16,292)]
[1] "ACE" "CB"
```

Well, looking on the internet the same day that *checkCovMat()* failed, it turned out that ACE acquired the Chubb Group (Chubb15), and so they became one and the same company as far as prices returned by *get.hist.quote()* are concerned. Chubb, ticker CB, is the surviving ticker symbol, so we removed ACE from the *NYSEclean.txt* file.

For the years 2008 through 2013, we can see the *displayCharts()* output in Figure 4.4. We can visualize several typical stocks in a 3 × 4 table and their price action over the same time period.

4.11   Securities Quoting

Having introduced our very useful utility *get.hist.quote()*, we can expand on it and the R plotting capabilities to create *getHistPrices()*. It loops through all the weighted tickers in the *lab* vector and finds historical prices:

```
library(tseries)
getHistPrices <- function(lab,w,len,start="2013-11-29",
                          end="2014-11-28",startBck1="2013-11-28",
                          startFwd1="2013-11-27",cached=NA) {
  #gather recent prices for all lab symbols
  D <- length(lab)
  recentPrices = matrix(rep(NA,len*D),nrow=len,ncol=D)
  for(d in 1:D) {
    if(w[d] > 0.0) {
      print(lab[d]) #Use cached list for now-obsolete tickers
      if(!is.na(cached) && !is.na(match(lab[d],cached))) {
        x <- read.csv(paste("cached",lab[d],".csv",sep=""))[,1]
        recentPrices[,d] <- x
      } else
        tryCatch({
          x <- get.hist.quote(lab[d],quote="Adj",start=start,end=end)
          if(length(x) != len) {
            x <- get.hist.quote(lab[d],quote="Adj",
```

```
                                    start=startBck1,end=end)
                if(length(x) != len) {
                  x <- get.hist.quote(lab[d],
                                    quote="Adj",start=startFwd1,end=end)
                } else { #partial quotes
                  recentPrices[1:length(x),d] <- x
                }
              } else {
                recentPrices[,d] <- x
              }
          #}, warning = function(w) {
            #warning-handler-code
            #print(w)
          #}, error = function(e) {
            #error-handler-code
            #print(e)
          })
      }
    }
    return(recentPrices)
}
#unit test: one good one bad
getHistPrices(c('PCLN','UA'),c(.5,.5),252)
```

By starting off with NA values in the *recentPrices* matrix, the warning and error-handling code can simply allow these values to persist. The NA values will be returned to the caller in columns corresponding to the tickers without valid price quotes for the date range *start* to *end*. The *cached* parameter is used to provide previously downloaded price files when ticker symbols become obsolete to *get.hist.quote()*.

4.12 Exercises

4.1. If $S = c(1.3, 1.2)$, two successive prices for the EUR quoted in term of USD, use R to compute the gross return, net return, and log return. What do you notice about the log return as compared to the net return?

4.2. Locate the code for the function *adjustForMergers()* along with the three test case files, resD26QP1Days1258.csv, resD25Days1258woTIE.csv, and resD24Days 1258.csv. Create the directory under *FinAnalytics* called *huge*. Write and run code to invoke the function once per file, three times, and explain the results for each test case.

4.3. Locate the code for the function *plotMultSeries()* and run the unit test, producing the multi-colored 12 stock chart of Chapter 4.

4.4. Use *par(mfrow=c(2,1))* to set up two plots:

(a) One should be the unadjusted prices for the AET stock in the first 12 of the 452 stocks in the *stockdata*.

(b) The second plot should be the split-adjusted prices for the AET stock.

(c) How many split adjustments are needed?

(d) What is the ratio for each split adjustment?

(e) Piece together a vector using the *c()* operator multiplying or dividing by proper constants in each segment. Match your vector to the result returned by *splitAdjust()*.

4.5. Locate the unit test code in Chapter 4 for the *acquirePrices()* utility. This test creates a directory called *APUT*, which stands for *acquirePrices Unit Test*, with two sub-directories. It removes them as the final step. Run the unit test and explain the behavior.

5 Dataset Analytics and Risk Measurement

When performing Monte Carlo simulation in finance, *mixture models* are probabilistic models that can be used to represent subpopulations within a population. In order to simulate extreme events which can occur in the various financial markets, the subpopulations can be jumps or crashes in the market. While applying a non-Gaussian distribution is common practice for introducing these jumps, it is also reasonable to use two or more single-variate Gaussian distributions and combine them into a mixture model. We apply it to simulations from the foreign exchange markets.

5.1   Generating Prices from Log Returns

Performing financial analytics is now easier than ever before due to the sophistication of open source toolkits such as RStudio and web-available market datasets. When forecasting and predicting future outcomes using such data, measuring the uncertainty and risk is important. We start with the most basic properties of mixture models and then work our way into actual market events.

Whether the log returns are Gaussian or normally distributed (the theoretical assumption), or not really normally distributed (the practical reality), simulating prices from log returns is important. Once we know the distribution of the log returns, simulating realistic prices allows one to go back and forth between simulated and actual market prices without losing much accuracy.

R has such convenient functional programming syntax that it can really save, at times, the analyst a lot of programming. The best trick in the book for quantitative finance is the idiom

```
Ylogrets = diff(log(Y))
```

Being able to apply the log() function to the vector and then feed the results into the *diff()* function is quite powerful. Imagine how unwieldy this is in a spreadsheet by comparison. Let's see: we must find the top and bottom of the row with the prices and create a column with the logs, now another column with the differences of the logs which is one row fewer in length. In any case, whether in a spreadsheet program or R, finding the inverse to the above equation is not quite so obvious! A little algebra will get us there, though.

For N original prices Y where $Y = (Y_1, \ldots, Y_N)$, the convention that $r_2 = \log(Y_2/Y_1), \ldots, r_N = \log(Y_N/Y_{N-1})$ will be used to name our log returns. If we accumulate the sum of the log returns increasingly, from 1 to N, in a vector,

$$\left(Y_1, Y_1 \exp(\sum_{j=2}^{2} r_j), \ldots, Y_1 \exp(\sum_{j=2}^{i} r_j), \ldots Y_1 \exp(\sum_{j=2}^{N} r_j) \right), \qquad (5.1)$$

which is multiplied by our initial value, Y_1, then this can be written, by the properties of the exp() function, as

$$\left(Y_1, Y_1 \prod_{j=2}^{2} \exp(r_j), \ldots, Y_1 \prod_{j=2}^{i} \exp(r_j), \ldots Y_1 \prod_{j=2}^{N} \exp(r_j) \right), \qquad (5.2)$$

which is a vector of multiplied series

$$(Y_1, Y_1[Y_2/Y_1], \ldots, Y_1[Y_2/Y_1] \ldots [Y_i/Y_{i-1}], \ldots, Y_1[Y_2/Y_1] \ldots [Y_N/Y_{N-1}]). \qquad (5.3)$$

This can be simplified to

$$(Y_1, \ldots, Y_N), \qquad (5.4)$$

which is the original Y vector, our goal. Formula 5.1 can be implemented quite compactly with the following R expression:

```
c(Y[1],Y[1]*exp(cumsum(Ylogrets)))
```

We can see from this output sequence that prices which match the original Y can be generated from the log returns of Y using this R expression:

```
> Y = c(30,29,28,28,30,32,31)
> Ylogrets = diff(log(Y))
> round(Ylogrets,4)
[1] -0.0339 -0.0351  0.0000  0.0690  0.0645 -0.0317
> Yprices = c(Y[1],Y[1]*exp(cumsum(Ylogrets)))
> Yprices
[1] 30 29 28 28 30 32 31
```

This scheme of generating prices from log returns will be used in an upcoming section. Now we can write a utility to convert log returns to prices, *toPrices()*:

```
Y=c(1.3,1.2,1.3,1.4,1.5,1.4,1.3,1.4,1.5)

toPrices <- function(Y1,Ylogrets){
  Yprices = c(Y1,Y1*exp(cumsum(Ylogrets)))
  Yprices
}
Y
toPrices(Y[1],diff(log(Y)))
#assert
sum(Y-toPrices(Y[1],diff(log(Y)))<.00000001) == length(Y)
```

The output from running the last few lines of code after the function is below. We can see there that the assertion comparing Y to the recreated Y from its log returns via the function *toPrices()* is TRUE.

```
> Y
[1] 1.3 1.2 1.3 1.4 1.5 1.4 1.3 1.4 1.5
> toPrices(diff(log(Y)))
[1] 1.3 1.2 1.3 1.4 1.5 1.4 1.3 1.4 1.5
> #assert
> sum(Y-toPrices(diff(log(Y)))<.001) == length(Y)
[1] TRUE
```

Consider the process of going from log returns to prices one step further. Our log returns are named in Formula 5.4 and they are the incremental week-to-week, day-to-day, or second-to-second changes. Thinking in terms of day-to-day, for example, each of the rs is distributed $N(\mu_d, \sigma_d^2)$, where d denotes *daily*:

$$r_2, \ldots, r_N. \tag{5.5}$$

Our desire is to examine what happens to the distribution as we reconstruct prices from these log returns. If we look at how to construct Y_is where $2 \leq i \leq N$ for period of length N, we know from our reconstruction Formula 5.1 that

$$Y_i = Y_1 \exp(r_2 + \cdots + r_i). \tag{5.6}$$

Formula 5.6 is another form of reconstruction formula. We can choose any time period, but we will focus on one year for now. If the original prices are stocks quoted daily, we set $N = 252$. If the prices are for foreign exchange rates, we set $N = 365$ for data sources with no breaks: every day has a closing price at the end of the day. We will choose $N = 365$, the FX convention. If $r_2, \ldots, r_N$ is our path from day 2 to day N, we use Formula 5.1 to see that

$$Y_{365} = Y_1 \exp(\sum_{j=2}^{365} r_j) = Y_1 \exp(r_2 + \cdots + r_{365}). \tag{5.7}$$

The summation has 364 terms where each term is distributed $N(\mu_d, \sigma_d^2)$. The summation of normal variates is normal with mean equal to the sum of the means and variance equal to the sum of variances. If the summation portion of Formula 5.7

$$U_i = \sum_{j=2}^{i} r_j, \tag{5.8}$$

then $U_i \sim N(\mu_U, \sigma_{U_i}^2)$ where $\mu_{U_i} = (i - 1)\mu_d$ and $\sigma_{U_i}^2 = (i - 1)\sigma_d^2$. Since $U_i = U$ is distributed normally, $N(\mu, \sigma^2)$, we know that $V = \exp(U)$ is distributed log-normally, $LN(\mu, \sigma^2)$. Since we have $(i - 1)$ terms r_i in this case, summarizing:

$$U_i \sim N((i-1)\mu_d, (i-1)\sigma_d^2) \text{ and } V_i = \exp(r_2 + \ldots + r_i) \sim LN((i-1)\mu_d, (i-1)\sigma_d^2). \tag{5.9}$$

By Formula 5.6, Y_i/Y_1 is distributed $LN((i - 1)\mu_d, (i - 1)\sigma_d^2)$ as well.

5.2   Normal Mixture Models of Price Movements

The Gaussian or normal distribution always has kurtosis 3, which means that the size of the tails are consistently the same value, regardless of the variance. A *Gaussian mixture model or normal mixture model* can be used to obtain the required heavier tails, meeting a criterion that the kurtosis be greater than 3 as we would expect. In order to simulate the market distribution for a normal mixture random variable X, a mixture can be used which is a combination of two normal distributions: the first distribution with random variable Y has a smaller variance than the second with random variable Z (Hogg and Craig, 1978; Ruppert, 2011). Both $Y \sim N(0, \sigma_1^2)$ and $Z \sim N(0, \sigma_2^2)$, where $\sigma_1 < \sigma_2$. One can use a uniform distribution for a random variable U with a threshold set at the decimal level where the first or the second is used:

$$X = \begin{cases} Y, & \text{if } U < .9 \\ Z, & \text{otherwise.} \end{cases} \tag{5.10}$$

This simple scheme can be implemented in R using the *runif()* function for the uniform distribution and two instances of the *rnorm()* function with one of two expected variates with each of the two variances. The function *rmixture()* implements the normal mixture with $\mu = 0$ and σ_1 and σ_2 provided. The single line of code after the function is a unit test of it. The unit test histogram plot is shown in Figure 5.1.

```
rmixture <- function(N,sigma1,sigma2=0,thresh=.9) {
  variates = vector(length=N)
  U = runif(N)
```

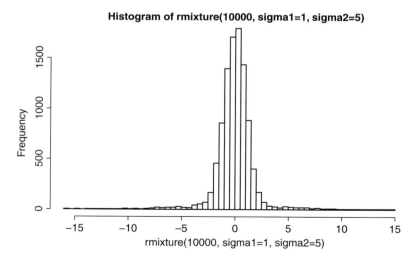

Histogram of rmixture(10000, sigma1=1, sigma2=5)

Figure 5.1   Extreme events in the market can be modeled with a normal mixture model: above is a histogram with $\mu = 0$ and $\sigma_1 = 1$ and $\sigma_2 = 5$. The tails have occurrences of variates that are five times greater than the standard normal distribution.

```
   for(i in 1:N)
     variates[i] = rnorm(1,0,sd=sigma1)
   if(sigma2 != 0) { #only mixture if sigma2 != 0
     for(i in 1:N)
       if(U[i] >= thresh)
         #replace original variate with mixture variate
         variates[i] = rnorm(1,0,sd=sigma2)
   }
   variates
}
hist(rmixture(10000,sigma1=1,sigma2=5),breaks=50)
```

In order to use the mixture model in a price simulation, we need a way to convert returns into prices. If log returns are normally distributed, that matches the conventional financial markets assumptions. However, with our new mixture model in hand, *rmixture()*, we want to modify our assumption such that the log returns are distributed according to the normal mixture model. This is in order to obtain the extreme events in the tails as needed.

The R function *simPricePath()* below will generate a price path from a normal or a normal mixture model. If *sigma2* is supplied it will choose a normal mixture using $\mu = 0$ and *sigma1* and *sigma2*. Y is our normal variable and Z is our normal mixture random variable. Once the log returns are generated, *toPrice()* is used to map log returns into prices. Figures 5.2 and 5.3 provide a way to compare *Yprices* to *Zprices*. We can see that the mixture model, as expected, produces a jumpier prices series, Figure 5.3.

```
simPricePath <- function(initPrice,N,seed,sigma1=.05,
                         sigma2=0,thresh=.9) {
  #Non mixture model
  set.seed(seed)
  Xlogrets = rmixture(N,sigma1,sigma2,thresh=thresh)
  Xprices = toPrices(initPrice,Xlogrets)
  list(Xprices,c(Xlogrets))
}
#unit test
seed=26
sigma1=0.007157
N=365
par(mfrow=c(2,2)); maxy=10*.007
Y <- simPricePath(1.3,N=365,seed=seed,sigma1)
Yprices  <- Y[[1]]
Ylogrets <- Y[[2]]
plot(Yprices,type='l')
plot(Ylogrets,type='l',ylim=c(-maxy,maxy))
points(Ylogrets)
Z <- simPricePath(1.3,N=365,seed=seed,sigma1,sigma2=4*sigma1)
Zprices  <- Z[[1]]
Zlogrets <- Z[[2]]
```

```
plot(Zprices,type='l')
plot(Zlogrets,type='l',ylim=c(-maxy,maxy))
points(Zlogrets)
sd(Ylogrets)
sd(Zlogrets)
par(mfrow=c(1,1))
plot(density(Ylogrets))
lines(density(Zlogrets),col=4)
```

Figure 5.4 provides a density plot for *Ylogrets* and *Zlogrets* generated from the above final three lines of code. The right tail being thicker for *Zlogrets* corresponds to the large movement after the 50th time step in Figure 5.3. Comparing the fourth moments of the non-mixture and the mixture model, we can see from the output below that the kurtosis of the mixture model is quite a bit larger than the kurtosis of the non-mixture model.

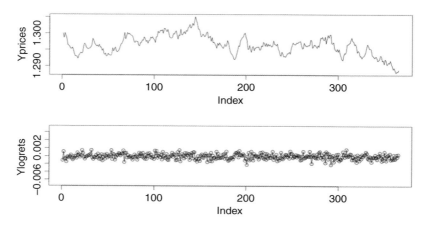

Figure 5.2   Daily normal model-generated prices for a time series *Y* 365 days long. The kurtosis of these log returns in the bottom chart is in the normal range, 2.9, versus 14.6 for Figure 5.3.

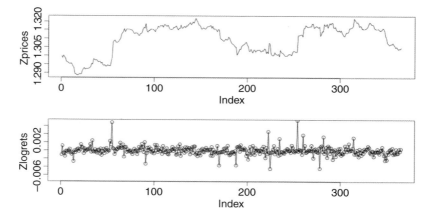

Figure 5.3   Normal mixture model-generated prices for a time series *Z*. There is similarity with Figure 5.2 except that jumps occur in the log returns which cause corresponding jumps in the prices.

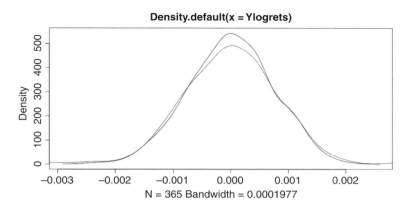

Figure 5.4   Kernel density estimate of normal model and normal mixture model-generated log returns

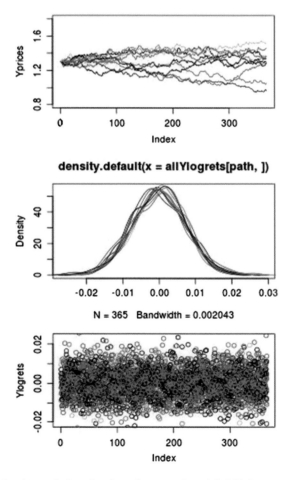

Figure 5.5   Simulated prices, density, and plot of variates for normal model, 365 days.

```
> library(moments)
> KurtYlogrets = length(Ylogrets)^(-1)*sd(Ylogrets)^
+   (-4)*sum((Ylogrets - mean(Ylogrets))^4)
> KurtYlogrets
[1] 3.393385
> kurtosis(Ylogrets)
[1] 3.412056
> #measure Kurtosis of mixture
> KurtZlogrets = length(Zlogrets)^(-1)*sd(Zlogrets)^
+   (-4)*sum((Zlogrets - mean(Zlogrets))^4)
> KurtZlogrets
[1] 12.09176
> kurtosis(Zlogrets)
[1] 12.15829
```

We can see in the output sequence above that, whether measured by our coded kurtosis formula using Equation 3.34 or by the R *kurtosis()* routine, the kurtosis of the mixture distribution is quite a bit larger. It is a little more than three times four, the kurtosis of the normal distribution.

Simulating multiple paths with for 365 days starting at the EUR per USD price of 1.3000 is possible by calling *simPricePath()* in a loop. We can do this with the underlying normal and normal mixture models to compare the behavior. Below is the normal code first, with plots shown in Figure 5.5:

```
#Multiple paths
library(moments)
par(mfrow=c(3,1))
mapToCol <- function(d)
  if(d==7) 1 else if(d==8)
    2 else if(d==15) 3 else if(d==23) 4 else d
allYlogrets = matrix(nrow=10,ncol=N)
for(path in 1:10) {
  Y <- simPricePath(1.3,N,seed=path,sigma1=.007157)
  Yprices <- Y[[1]]; Ylogrets <- Y[[2]]
  if(path == 1) plot(Yprices,type='l',ylim=c(.8,1.8))
  else lines(Yprices,col=mapToCol(path))
  allYlogrets[path,] = Ylogrets
}
for(path in 1:10) {
  if(path==1) plot(density(allYlogrets[path,]),main="")
  else lines(density(allYlogrets[path,]),
            col=mapToCol(path))
}
mean(Ylogrets)
sd(Ylogrets)
for(path in 1:10) {
  if(path==1) plot(allYlogrets[path,],ylab='Ylogrets')
  else points(allYlogrets[path,],col=mapToCol(path))
}
```

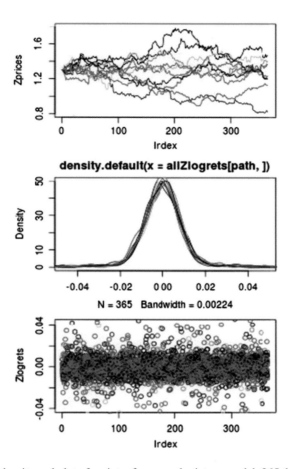

Figure 5.6   Simulated prices, density and plot of variates for normal mixture model, 365 days.

Now comes the normal mixture code, with plots shown in Figure 5.6. Our *sigma*1 = 0.007157 as this corresponds to annualized 13.7 percent volatility, a typical value. In the mixture code below we quadruple that to 4 ∗ *sigma* 10 percent of the time.

```
#mixture
allZlogrets = matrix(nrow=10,ncol=N)
for(path in 1:10) {
  Z <- simPricePath(1.3,N,seed=path,sigma1=.007157,
                   sigma2=4*.007157)
  Zprices <- Z[[1]]; Zlogrets <- Z[[2]]
  if(path == 1) plot(Zprices,type='l',ylim=c(.8,1.8))
  else lines(Zprices,col=mapToCol(path))
  allZlogrets[path,] = Zlogrets
}

for(path in 1:10) {
  if(path==1) plot(density(allZlogrets[path,]),main="")
```

```
   else lines(density(allZlogrets[path,]),
              col=mapToCol(path))
}
mean(Zlogrets)
sd(Zlogrets)
for(path in 1:10) {
  if(path==1) plot(allZlogrets[path,],ylab='Zlogrets')
  else points(allZlogrets[path,],col=mapToCol(path))
}
```

As we can see below, this causes our volatility to go from 0.007157 to 0.010179 on a daily basis, an increase of 34.6 percent, seemingly not that great, compared to the impact it has on the paths.

```
> sd(Ylogrets)
[1] 0.007559591
> sd(Zlogrets)
[1] 0.01017884
> sd(Zlogrets)/sd(Ylogrets)
[1] 1.34648
```

5.3   Sudden Currency Price Movement in 2015

On Thursday, January 15, 2015, the Swiss Central Bank switched policies regarding their currency, the Swiss Franc, abbreviated CHF, and that sent other related currencies weaker and the CHF stronger. The price for CHFEUR went from 0.8323 CHF per EUR to 0.8884 then to 0.9983 in only three days, according to daily data downloaded via the *get.hist.quote()* utility call below. This is unheard of in currency markets because that represents 557 and 1099 ticks respectively. A tick is the minimum upward or downward movement in the price of a security. For the CHFEUR security, the amount per tick (0.0001) is roughly 10.09 dollars per contract held. 557 ticks represent $5621 and $11,091 moves per contract held which is quite a bit for the investor who is long Euros and short the Swiss Franc when their investment has lost value so quickly.

```
library(tseries)

tmixture <- function(N,sigma1,sigma2=0,sigma3=0)
#three level mixture with state changes
{
  variates = vector(length=N)
  mode = 1
  B = rbinom(365,1,1/365)
  for(i in 1:N)
    variates[i] = rnorm(1,0,sd=sigma1)
  if(sigma2 != 0) { #only mixture if sigma2 != 0
    for(i in 1:N)
      if(B[i] == 1) {
```

```
      mode = 2
      #replace original variate with mixture variate
      variates[i] = rnorm(1,0,sd=sigma2)
      print(sigma2)
      print(variates[i])
    } else if (mode == 2) {
      variates[i] = rnorm(1,0,sd=sigma3)
    }
  }
  variates
}
#S<-get.hist.quote("CHF/EUR",provider="oanda",
#               start="2014-01-30",end="2015-01-29")
setwd(paste(homeuser,"/FinAnalytics/ChapV",sep=""))
S<-rev(read.csv("CHFperEUR.csv",header=TRUE)[,2])
```

Market data provided by Oanda Corporation through *get.hist.quote()* for CHF/EUF was pre-downloaded via two commented out commands and placed into the file called CHFperEUR.csv. Another way to obtain market data is to go to the elegant and powerful Quandl.com web site API, then download and invert the ECB/EURCHF prices, which are also provided in reverse order, as shown below:

```
library(Quandl)
S2<-1/rev(Quandl('ECB/EURCHF',
          start_date="2014-01-30",end_date="2015-01-29")[,2])
```

We resume our code sequence by setting up a 2×2 plotting grid and finding log returns of the actual prices for plotting below.

```
par(mfrow=c(2,2))
diffLogS <- diff(log(S))
plot(diffLogS,type='p',ylim=c(-.08,.08))
plot(S,type='l',col='blue',ylim=c(.60,1.05),
    xlab="One Year: ealry 2014 - early 2015",
    ylab="actual CHF per EUR")
S[351:359]

diffLogS351 <- diff(log(S[1:351]))
diffLogS351mean <- mean(diffLogS351)
diffLogS351mean
diffLogS351dailyVol <- sd(diffLogS351)
diffLogS351dailyVol
diffLogSjumpMean = mean(diff(log(S[351:353])))
sd(diff(log(S[351:353])))/diffLogS351dailyVol
diffLogSlast <- diff(log(S[355:365]))
sd(diffLogSlast)/diffLogS351dailyVol
```

We use a binomial random variable, $B \sim Bn(n,p)$, where $n = 365$, the number of days for the simulation, and $p = \frac{1}{365}$, the probability of the jump event occurring each day. We also need to know the magnitude of the mixture of standard deviation, *sigma*1. In terms of historical volatility, the daily volatility is calculated from the first 351 days below and the figure after that is the number of "sigmas" movement that the jump represents.

```
> diffLogS351 <- diff(log(S[1:351]))
> diffLogS351mean <- mean(diffLogS351)
> diffLogS351mean
[1] 6.068558e-05
> diffLogS351dailyVol <- sd(diffLogS351)
> diffLogS351dailyVol
[1] 0.0006194764
> diffLogSjumpMean = mean(diff(log(S[351:353])))
> sd(diff(log(S[351:353])))/diffLogS351dailyVol
[1] 73.00818
> sd(diff(log(S[351:353])))/diffLogS351dailyVol
[1] 57.15945
> diffLogSlast <- diff(log(S[355:365]))
> sd(diffLogSlast)/diffLogS351dailyVol
[1] 17.8339
```

If we apply the R code sequence to CHF prices, we can get a handle on how drastic this move was historically. We know that three standard deviations for a normally distributed random variable is fairly rare. The two largest days of movement represent a 73-times sigma move! It caused turmoil, especially outside the Euro-zone countries. It caused investors to continue to flock toward safe havens like the United States and Switzerland, which are outside the Euro zone (Swiss Move Roils Global Markets, 2015).

The following code block makes use of a three-level mixture called *tmixture()*. Here are the three phases of the mixture:

- In the beginning, until the binomial random variable $B = 1$, the mixture is purely normal with a small variance. This phase represents the Swiss Government enacting its policy of keeping the CHF currency weak and approximately tied to four-fifths of the EUR.
- Once the binomial random variable $B = 1$, a normal variate is selected with a standard deviation 73.00 times the original *sigma*1.
- Once the event has occurred, the currency moves with normal to higher volatility. The simulated prices appearing after the jump event use a *sigma3* which is 17.84 times *sigma1*.

In summary,

$$Y = \begin{cases} Z \sim N(0, \sigma_1), & \text{while } B = 0 \text{ then} \\ U \sim N(0, \sigma_2), & \text{while } B = 1 \text{ then} \\ V \sim N(0, \sigma_3), & \text{afterward where } \sigma_2 = 73.00\sigma_1 \text{ and } \sigma_3 = 17.84\sigma_1. \end{cases} \quad (5.11)$$

Once the model is built it can generate scenarios which are inspired by this currency crisis but not identical to it. The scenario with seed 196 is particularly similar to the January

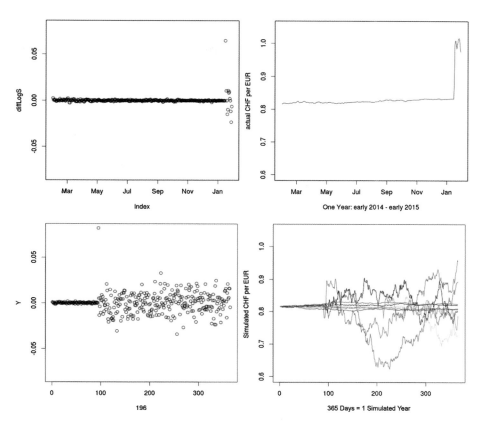

Figure 5.7 Daily prices for CHFEUR from 2014-01-24 to 2015-01-13. The top two depict actual price and the bottom two are simulated prices. The huge rise in prices occurs on the 352nd and 353rd days in this series after the Swiss Central Bank switched policies regarding its currency. The left plots are the log returns while right plots are prices. The top-right chart is scaled for the first 351 days before the jump. The bottom-left chart is a plot of the normal variates of the three-way mixture model with the singularity occurring randomly at the 95th day in the first simulated path. The mixture model of log returns is then mapped into 10 price paths as seen on the bottom-right. The path going lower in price than any other is a path where two jump events occur.

2015 event with exactly one large singularity. The binomial portion of the mixture model can generate from zero to two such events typically in a one-year window.

```
b = 196
for(path in b:205) {
  N=365;
  set.seed(path)

  Y <- tmixture(N,diffLogS351dailyVol,
                73.00818*diffLogS351dailyVol,
                17.84*diffLogS351dailyVol)
```

```
if(path == b)
  plot(Y,ylim=c(-.08,.08),xlab=path)
Yprices = c(S[[1]],S[[1]]*exp(cumsum(Y)))
if(path == b)
  plot(Yprices,col=14,type="l",ylim=c(.60,1.05),
      xlab="1825 Days = 5 Simulated Years",
      ylab="simulated CHF per EUR")
else
  lines(Yprices,col=mapToCol(path%%24))
print(path)
Sys.sleep(2)
}
```

Figure 5.7 at the top shows a chart of the sample variable, S, which contains daily CHFEUR prices plotted with and without the extreme movement. The left plots are the log returns while right plots are prices. The top-right are the actual prices. The bottom-right is of a simulation similar event with Y displayed over a five-year daily series.

When considering the risk of trading and investing in foreign exchange markets, extreme movements like this are always possible. If one did not think such a large move was possible in the FX markets, seeing this event occur will change one's mind. It is important to study these events from an analytics perspective in order to build risk models which take these extreme event possibilities into account.

5.4   Exercises

5.1. Understanding the inverse of the difference of the logs mapping.

Without using the R *cumsum()* function, write *mycumsum()*, a function that takes in a length N vector of values and performs the mapping of Formula 5.1. What values do you get for *c(15,15*exp(mycumsum(c(-0.0339, -0.0351, 0.0000, 0.0690, 0.0645 -0.0317))))*?

5.2. Tailoring a Gaussian Mixture Model to the Market.

Use the code in the chapter as necessary and modify it to formulate a Gaussian mixture model which will produce 30,000 prices from 29,999 log returns. This would correspond to approximately one month of one-minute prices for the EURUSD security. Use an initial price of 1.3400 EUR per USD. Use $\sigma_Y = 0.0002$ and $\sigma_Z = 0.0006$ for the normal random variables Y and Z.

(a) Use variates from the uniform distribution to form a two-part mixture so that the kurtosis of the 29,999 log returns is approximately 10 where 3 is the kurtosis of the Gaussian distribution. Your uniform random variable,

$$X = \begin{cases} Y, & \text{if } U < h \\ Z, & \text{otherwise} \end{cases} \tag{5.12}$$

U comes from the uniform distribution. You may use trial and error to find the proper threshold, h, to tailor the distribution to this kurtosis.

(b) Plot both the generated prices and the log returns. Plot the density of the log returns.

(c) Is this the density of the normal distribution?

6 Time Series Analysis

You work for an airline in the operations department. They ask you to reach into the historical company and industry datasets and figure out the expected loading for every flight in their book for this coming year. This ties directly into projected revenue. In the back of your mind, you know that expenses for the company need to be offset by revenue. It doesn't help to be overly optimistic because the risk of not meeting the projections carries with it the risk of future disappointment.

What should you do? Passenger boardings are cyclical. There are risks of a downturn. But a downturn could impact profitability of the entire company. The price of oil and jet fuel is important. Mergers happen every year which change the competitive landscape and make some routes more efficient.

Time series analysis can certainly help. Just like confidence intervals in statistics (please see also the Appendix), there is a band of uncertainty around any of the projections. The expected airline passenger loadings is a random variable. Passenger boarding is one of several arenas we will explore with the help of tools in R.

6.1 Examining Time Series

We begin with a quick survey of the types of times series we will model. We can use the quantmod and PerformanceAnalytics packages, firstly. We will define the vector of symbols to be downloaded. The symbols GSPC, VIX, TNX, refer to the S&P 500 index, the CME volatility index, and the ten-year treasury yield, respectively. Use the getSymbols() function to download the time series for the symbols in sym.vec between the dates of January 3, 2003 and September 10, 2015. If the quantmod and PerformanceAnalytics packages are not yet installed, they can be installed with the commands install.packages("quantmod", dependencies=TRUE) and install.packages("PerformanceAnalytics", dependencies=TRUE).

```
> library(quantmod)
> library(PerformanceAnalytics)
> sym.vec <-c("^GSPC","^VIX")
> getSymbols(sym.vec, from = "2005-01-03", to = "2015-09-16")
```

```
[1] "GSPC" "VIX"
```

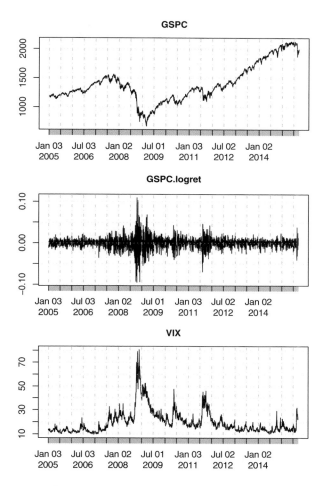

Figure 6.1 Prices, log returns and the volatility index of the S&P 500 index from January 3, 2003 to September 10, 2015.

The first plot is of the S&P 500, shown in Figure 6.1. We see the peak of the market in early 2007 and then the steep decline as the housing crisis hit. We see the market bottom out in mid 2009 and begin a large rally that lasts through mid 2015. We see minor corrections in 2011 and 2012 due to uncertainty surrounding the government debt in the Euro zone, and a significant sell-off in mid 2015 due to uncertainty surrounding China's economy. An interesting aspect of this time series is the fact that negative returns tend to clump together (bear market) and positive returns tend to clump together (bull market).

Now we extract the adjusted price of the S&P 500.

```
> GSPC <- GSPC[, "GSPC.Adjusted", drop=F]
```

We then use the `CalculateReturns()` function to calculate the log returns of the price vector. We are interested in log returns because if the overall price distribution

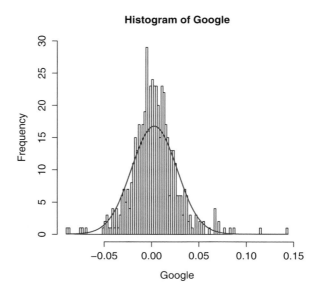

Histogram of Google

Figure 6.2   Histogram of Google log returns from August 20, 2004–September 13, 2006 with overlay of density of a normal random variable with the same mean and standard deviation as Google log returns. We observe the excess kurtosis commonly seen in stock returns: clustering of small returns around the mean, as well as large deviations out in the tail of the distribution.

is log-normally distributed then the log returns are normally distributed and their joint distribution follows a multivariate normal distribution.

```
> GSPC.logret = CalculateReturns(GSPC, method="log")
```

The CalculateReturns() function first takes the log() of the price time series and then takes the difference. Since the difference is the current value minus the previous value, the first component of the log return vector is not defined. To illustrate this we take the difference of a sequence of numbers one through ten.

```
> GSPC.logret[1]

             GSPC.Adjusted
2005-01-03            NA

> GSPC.logret[1] = 0.0
```

We plot the returns in Figure 6.1 and observe one of the main features of financial return: volatility that changes with time. We see there are "quiet" or "calm" times when the market is not very active, and then there are "loud" or "stormy" times when the market is extremely active. The statistical term for this time-varying volatility is *heteroskedasticity*, and is one of the main reasons financial data is so difficult to model.

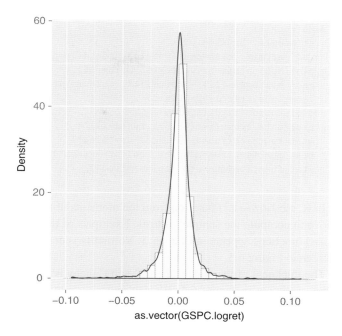

Figure 6.3   Histogram and estimated density of log returns of the S&P 500 index from January 3, 2003 to
September 10, 2015.

```
> par(mfrow=c(3,1))
> plot(GSPC)
> plot(GSPC.logret)
> plot(VIX)
```

Closely related to the burstiness of market returns is behavior of what is known as
priced volatility, represented here by the VIX and shown in Figure 6.1. Loosely speaking, the VIX is an average over implied volatilities of a basket of options. Implied
volatilities are figures which are between 0.0 and just over 1.0 and represent the standard deviation of the movement of the underlying security. For the VIX, the underlying
security is the S&P 500 Index.

The VIX is known as the market's "fear factor" because it represents how much
investors are demanding to assume market risk at a given time. If the market is quiet
then investors will likely not demand much to bear market risk. If, on the other hand,
market behavior is violent then investors will likely demand much more to bear market
risk. This is indeed what we observe in Figure 6.1. During the market crash associated with the 2008 housing crisis we see the VIX spike to levels as high as 80 percent,
whereas during the long boom after the housing crisis we see the VIX fall to levels as
low as 11 percent or 12 percent.

```
> library(TSA)
> library(ggplot2)
```

```
> data(google)
> hist(google, breaks=100)
> curve(dnorm(x, mean=mean(google), sd=sd(google)), add=TRUE, col="blue")
> ggplot(NULL,aes(x=as.vector(GSPC.logret),y=..density..)) +
+    geom_histogram(fill="cornsilk", colour="grey60", size = 0.2) +
+    geom_density(colour="blue")
> dt4<-function(x) dt(x,df=4)
> ggplot(data.frame(x=c(-5,5)),aes(x=x)) +
+    stat_function(fun=dnorm, colour="blue") +
+    stat_function(fun=dcauchy, colour="green") +
+    stat_function(fun=dt4, colour="red")
```

In R, the *kurtosis(x)* function from the moments library will use the moment method above to compute the sample kurtosis. Examples of the use of the *skewness()* and *kurtosis()* functions appears in Chapter 5. Normality is depicted in Figure 6.2. Kurtosis can be seen in Figure 6.3.

The thickness of the tails of the $t(4)$ and Cauchy is evident from the plot of the densities as shown in Figure 6.4. We can underscore this by randomly sampling 10,000 random variable samples from each of the three distributions, computing the kurtosis of each sample, and comparing to the kurtosis of the S&P 500 log returns. We see what has been previously documented, namely that observed market returns follow a $t(4)$ reasonably well. Returns have higher kurtosis than that of a standard normal, and comparable to that of a $t(4)$ distribution as seen in the output below. The extreme, fat tails of the Cauchy are illustrated by a kurtosis over two orders of magnitude greater than

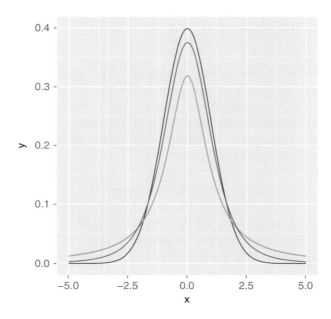

Figure 6.4   Densities of a standard normal (blue), a Cauchy (green), and t distribution with four degrees of freedom (red).

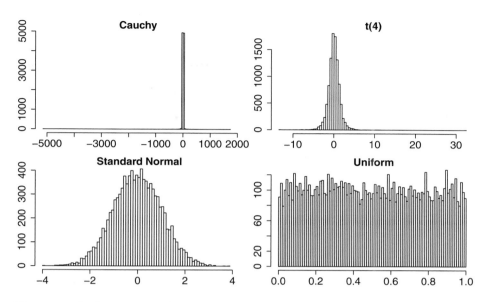

Figure 6.5   Histograms of a Cauchy, a *t* distribution with four degrees of freedom, a standard normal distribution, and a uniform distribution.

the kurtosis of the *t*(4) or market returns as seen in Figure 6.5. As expected, the normal random variable has an excess kurtosis of close to zero.

```
par(mfrow=c(2,2))
hist(rcauchy(n=10000), main="Cauchy",breaks=100)
hist(rt(n=10000,df=4), main="t(4)",breaks=100)
hist(rnorm(n=10000), main="Standard Normal",breaks=100)
hist(runif(n=10000), main="Uniform",breaks=100)
set.seed(255270)
kurtosis(rcauchy(n=10000))
kurtosis(rt(n=10000,df=4))
kurtosis(rnorm(n=10000))
kurtosis(GSPC.logret[c(-1)]) #remove 1st elem
kurtosis(runif(n=10000))
```

6.2   Stationary Time Series

In *time series analysis* we are generally concerned with isolating different types of structure in the time series under study. Typical types of structure include trend and cyclicality. In finance we often encounter exponential trend growth, and seasonal cyclicality. We will examine several different examples of time series to illustrate different types of trend and cyclicality (Cryer and Chan, 2010). Other sources are Shumway and Stoffer (2006) and Hamilton (1994). Our analysis uses the R package TSA by Kung-Sik Chan and Brian Ripley. We are interested in two classes of time series: stationary and non-stationary. Stationarity has two levels: weak and strong. Weak stationarity implies that both the mean and covariance structure of the time series are constant in time:

$$E(Y_t) = \mu$$
$$\gamma_j = E(Y_t - \mu)(Y_{t-j} - \mu) \, for \, all \, t.$$

Strong stationarity goes beyond the first and second moments and says that the underlying probability distribution function itself does not change in time, i.e.:

$$F_Y(y_{t+j_1}, \cdots, y_{t+j_n}) = F_Y(y_{j_1}, \cdots, y_{j_n}) \, for \, all \, t \, and \, j_1, \cdots, j_n.$$

The distinction is in the behavior of the higher moments. We can imagine a distribution whose third moment changes with time but whose first and second moments do not change with time. Such a time series would be weak-sense stationary but not strong-sense stationary.

6.3   Auto-Regressive Moving Average Processes

The main tool for examining stationary time series is the Auto-Regressive Moving Average (ARMA) process. An *ARMA(p, q)* process is defined as

$$Y_t = \mu + \phi_1 Y_{t-1} + \phi_2 Y_{t-1} + \cdots + \phi_p Y_{t-p}$$
$$+ e_t - \theta_1 e_{t-1} - \theta_2 e_{t-2} - \cdots - \theta_q e_{t-q},$$

where $\phi_1 y_{t-1} + \phi_2 y_{t-1} + \cdots + \phi_p y_{t-p}$ is the auto-regressive component, $\theta_1 e_{t-1} + \theta_2 e_{t-2} + \cdots + \theta_q e_{t-q}$ is the moving average component, μ is the process mean, and e_t is the error process. The error process (also called the innovation process) is the difference between the observed value of a variable at time t and the model forecast of that value based on information available up to time t.

6.4   Power Transformations

Analysis of non-stationary time series requires us to expand our tool set. Essentially, the goal is to take a time series that is non-stationary and carry out a series of operations on it so that the resulting time series is stationary. The main operations we use are transformation and differencing. In transformation we apply a function to the time series in an attempt to reduce heteroskedasticity, i.e. make the variance more stable in time. Typical transform functions are the natural log function: $\log(x)$ and the square root function: $\sqrt{x}$. Both these functions can be generalized into a family of transformations called the *power transformation*. Power transformations were introduced by Box and Cox (1964). Given a parameter λ, the power transformation is defined by

$$f(x) = \begin{cases} \frac{x^\lambda - 1}{\lambda} & \text{for } \lambda \neq 0 \\ \log x & \text{for } \lambda = 0. \end{cases} \tag{6.1}$$

To show that the power transform $f(x) = \log(x)$ when $\lambda = 0$ we use l'Hospital's rule from calculus and show that as $\lambda \to 0$, $\frac{x^\lambda - 1}{\lambda} \to \log(x)$. We first recall $e^{\log(x)} = x$, $\log(x^\lambda) = \lambda \log(x)$ and $\frac{d}{dx}e^x = e^x$ so that we can rewrite $x^\lambda = e^{\lambda \log(x)}$ and then taking the derivative, giving us

$$\frac{dx^\lambda}{d\lambda} = \frac{de^{\lambda \log(x)}}{d\lambda} \tag{6.2}$$

$$= \log(x)e^{\lambda \log(x)} \tag{6.3}$$

$$= \log(x)\left(e^{\log(x)}\right)^\lambda \tag{6.4}$$

$$= \log(x)x^\lambda. \tag{6.5}$$

Applying l'Hospital's rule gives us

$$\lim_{\lambda \to 0} \frac{x^\lambda - 1}{\lambda} = \lim_{\lambda \to 0} \left(\frac{\frac{d}{d\lambda}(x^\lambda - 1)}{\frac{d}{d\lambda}\lambda}\right) \tag{6.6}$$

$$= \lim_{\lambda \to 0} \left(\frac{\log(x)x^\lambda}{1}\right) \tag{6.7}$$

$$= \log(x). \tag{6.8}$$

With the general transformation defined, the question now is how to find the appropriate value for λ. This appropriate value is the one that produces a transformed series most similar to a normal random variable. This depends on the time series and is estimated via the R function BoxCox.ar().

6.5   The TSA Package

The TSA package is a time series analysis package written by Kung-Sik Chan and Brian Ripley. The package contains functionality to estimate, forecast, and plot time series models. It also includes functionality to estimate spectra of time series which involve the decomposing of functions into combinations of sinusoids. We will not cover spectral analysis in this book, however. If you have not already installed the TSA package, it can be installed with the R command install.packages("TSA").

We begin by loading the TSA package.

```
> library(TSA)
```

The first time series we examine is *tempdub*, which is the average monthly temperature recorded in Dubuque, Iowa from January 1964 to December 1975. This is a good example of a well-behaved time series. We can see in Figure 6.6 that the mean is reasonably constant, and the cyclicality is seasonal and highly stable. We see that summers and winters vary in their severity and months in which extremes are reached, but these are minor deviations.

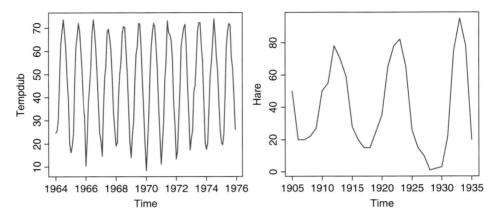

Figure 6.6   Two cyclical time series. Left: Average monthly temperature in Dubuque, Iowa. Right: Hare abundance in the Hudson Bay, Canada. We observe stable cyclicality over decades with a period of around ten years. We also observe variation in the slopes of the rise and fall of hare population, probably due to variation in environmental factors.

```
> data(tempdub)
> plot(tempdub,col='blue')
```

Given the highly structured nature of the *tempdub*, we expect it to be stationary. We can test stationarity formally using the Augmented Dickey–Fuller test. The null hypothesis of the Augmented Dickey–Fuller test is non-stationarity, so to reject the null hypothesis we need to see a small p-value. We carry out the Augmented Dickey–Fuller test below and note a p-value small enough to reject non-stationarity at the $\alpha = 0.05$ level. We therefore conclude that *tempdub* is stationary.

```
> adf.test(tempdub)

Augmented Dickey-Fuller Test

data:  tempdub
Dickey-Fuller = -11.077, Lag order = 5, p-value = 0.01
alternative hypothesis: stationary
```

A natural way to model a highly stationary times series such as *tempdub* is the *seasonal means* model. In the seasonal means model we assume a number of parameters for the model, one for each segment of time – months in this case. We assume the observed time series can be described as

$$Y_t = \mu_t + X_t, \tag{6.9}$$

where μ_t is the cyclical component and X_t is the random component such that $E(X_t) = 0$. In our case here, we want to estimate the expected average for each of 12 months. We assume a constant average for each month: $\beta_1, \beta_2, \cdots, \beta_{12}$ so that the expected average temperature for each of the 12 months is given as

$$\mu_t = \begin{cases} \beta_1 & \text{for } t = 1, 13, 15, \cdots \\ \beta_2 & \text{for } t = 2, 14, 26, \cdots \\ \vdots & \\ \beta_{12} & \text{for } t = 12, 24, 36, \cdots. \end{cases} \tag{6.10}$$

To fit the seasonal means model to the *tempdub* dataset we define indicator variables that indicate the month to which each of the data points corresponds. The TSA package has functionality by which we can extract the month of the dataset. We then regress the temperature on the extracted month, and view the summary of the linear regression. We see the average temperature for each of the months. Note that the -1 in the regression suppresses the intercept.

```
> month <- season(tempdub)
> model1 <- lm(tempdub ~ month - 1)
> summary(model1)

Call:
lm(formula = tempdub ~ month - 1)

Residuals:
    Min      1Q  Median      3Q     Max
-8.2750 -2.2479  0.1125  1.8896  9.8250

Coefficients:
                Estimate Std. Error t value Pr(>|t|)
monthJanuary      16.608      0.987   16.83   <2e-16 ***
monthFebruary     20.650      0.987   20.92   <2e-16 ***
monthMarch        32.475      0.987   32.90   <2e-16 ***
monthApril        46.525      0.987   47.14   <2e-16 ***
monthMay          58.092      0.987   58.86   <2e-16 ***
monthJune         67.500      0.987   68.39   <2e-16 ***
monthJuly         71.717      0.987   72.66   <2e-16 ***
monthAugust       69.333      0.987   70.25   <2e-16 ***
monthSeptember    61.025      0.987   61.83   <2e-16 ***
monthOctober      50.975      0.987   51.65   <2e-16 ***
monthNovember     36.650      0.987   37.13   <2e-16 ***
monthDecember     23.642      0.987   23.95   <2e-16 ***
---
Signif. codes:  0 '***' 0.001 '**' 0.01 '*' 0.05 '.' 0.1 ' ' 1

Residual standard error: 3.419 on 132 degrees of freedom
Multiple R-squared:  0.9957, Adjusted R-squared:  0.9953
F-statistic:  2569 on 12 and 132 DF,  p-value: < 2.2e-16
```

Since we are modeling a highly stationary process we expect the model to fit very well. This is what we see. The estimates for each month are highly significant, the standard error is less than 1 degree for any given month, and the R^2 is a whopping 0.9957, which means the model is accounting for 99.57 percent of all variation we see in the data.

While seasonal patterns such as *tempdub*, above, records quite stable, other types of cyclicality are less stable. The dataset `hare` records yearly hare abundances for the main drainage of the Hudson Bay in Ontario, Canada and was based on trapper questionnaires. We see in Figure 6.6 behavior that is obviously cyclical, but it is less stable than the temperature measurements. Instead of a yearly period, we see a period that is variable with an average of about ten years. We can reason that, at peak, hare population, it is too high and the environment cannot support it, so hares die off or are eliminated by predators. When enough hares have died off and the environment has recovered, then the population begins to move to a new peak. We could also hypothesize some type of multi-year pattern in the weather or behavior of the sun that leads to cyclicality in the hare population. In any case, the problem is that the periodicity is not stable. During some cycles the increases and decreases are steeper, while in other cycles the increases and decreases are more gradual. This, no doubt, is connected to the season timing, predator density, weather, and other factors which cumulatively result in a situation that is more difficult to model than the temperature example above.

```
> data(hare)
> plot(hare,col='blue')
```

For *hare*, we test for stationarity by applying the Augmented Dickey–Fuller unit root test, and since the reported p-value is greater than 0.05 we accept at the $\alpha = 0.05$ level the null-hypothesis of non-stationarity. There is enough instability in the series to reject stationarity with a p-value > .05.

```
> adf.test(hare)

Augmented Dickey-Fuller Test

data:  hare
Dickey-Fuller = -3.5051, Lag order = 3, p-value = 0.06064
alternative hypothesis: stationary
```

It could be that heteroskedasticity, or variation in the magnitude of the cycles, is a problem. If so, then applying a power transform could stabilize the variance. The Box–Cox procedure solves for the value of λ that produces a transform closest to a normal random variable with constant variance, as well as produces confidence interval for that optimal λ value. We carry out the Box–Cox procedure to estimate the optimal power transform parameter λ. The resulting confidence interval is seen in Figure 6.7. We observe that $\lambda = 0.5$ is well within the confidence interval and decide on a square root transform.

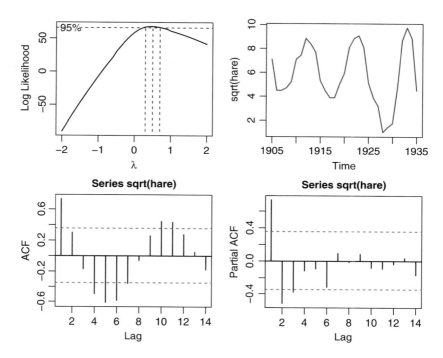

Figure 6.7   From upper left: Box–Cox confidence interval for Hare series, square-root transform, autocorrelation function, and partial autocorrelation function.

```
> par(mfrow=c(2,2))
> BoxCox.ar(hare)
> plot(sqrt(hare),col='blue')
> acf(sqrt(hare))
> pacf(sqrt(hare))
```

We examine a plot of the square-root of the *hare* dataset in Figure 6.7 and notice that the degree of heteroskedasticity, or non-constant variance, has been reduced significantly. While the trough heteroskedasticity is still apparent, the peak heteroskedasticity has been largely eliminated. We can now again test for stationarity, this time of the square root transformed process. Testing for stationarity of the square-root transformed time series yields a p-value of 0.01, which is too small to accept the null hypothesis of non-stationarity at the 5 percent level. We therefore reject the null hypothesis of non-stationarity and conclude that the square root of the *hare* time series is stationary.

```
> adf.test(sqrt(hare))

Augmented Dickey-Fuller Test

data:  sqrt(hare)
Dickey-Fuller = -4.479, Lag order = 3, p-value = 0.01
alternative hypothesis: stationary
```

With stationarity reasonably established we can turn toward the structure of the $ARMA(p, q)$ process. That is, we must identify p: the order of the auto-regressive component, as well as q: the moving average component. We need three tools for this:

1. a plot of the ARMA subsets;
2. the autocorrelation function; and
3. the partial autocorrelation function.

The plot of ARMA subsets gives the lags of the AR and MA components that minimize the Bayesian Information Criterion (BIC) and can be seen in the upper panel of Figure 6.8. (The BIC is defined in the Appendix.) The ARMA subset plot serves as a first indication of what lags might be of interest in modeling the series. This occurs at several AR and MA lags, and we choose the lags that are corroborated by the autocorrelation function and partial autocorrelation functions.

```
layout(matrix(c(1,1,2,3), 2, 2, byrow = TRUE))
plot(armasubsets(y=hare,nar=7,nma=7))
acf(sqrt(hare))
pacf(sqrt(hare))
```

The above block of code produces the subsets and correlation graphs of Figure 6.8.

The autocorrelation function (ACF) indicates which lags of the MA component are of interest, and the partial autocorrelation function (PACF) indicates which lags of the AR component are of interest. They allow us to winnow the model down to the essentials. In

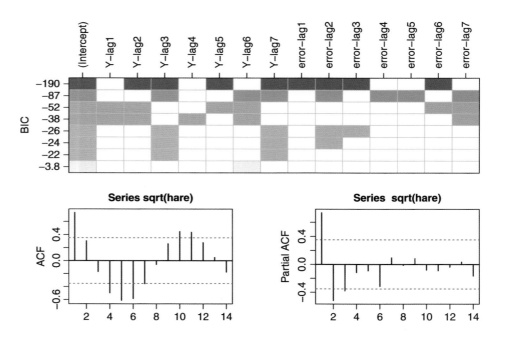

Figure 6.8   ARMA subsets, autocorrelation, and partial autocorrelation of transformed hare series.

Figure 6.8, the ARMA subset plot on top indicates that AR lags of 2, 3, 5, and 7 are of interest while MA lags of 1, 2, 3, and 6 are of interest. The three significant lags of the partial autocorrelation function indicate that the AR component of the model will be of order three. The oscillating but exponentially decaying behavior of the autocorrelation function indicates the MA component will be of order zero.

The ACF indicates no MA component, and the PACF indicates lags of 1, 2, and 3. We examine the partial autocorrelation function and conclude that lags 1 and 2 are significant. Lag 3 is borderline, but since both lags 1 and 2 are strongly significant we will include lag 3 in the model as well. We prefer models to be as simple as possible so that estimation of parameters can be as precise as possible, so we conclude that an $AR(3)$ model is appropriate. This leads us to choose an $ARMA(3, 0)$.

We fit the $AR(3)$ model as an $ARIMA(3, 0, 0)$ model using the `arima()` function so that $p = 3, d = 0$ and $q = 0$ in $ARIMA(p, d, q)$ in the *TSA* package. ARIMA will be defined further in the next section.

```
> m1.hare <- arima(x=sqrt(hare),order=c(3,0,0))
```

We now examine the autocorrelation function of the residuals with the goal of finding structure to be modeled. The goal of modeling the time series is to incorporate all of the structure into the model. If we succeed at this then the residual errors left over should exhibit no discernible structure. In time series, this phrase "no discernible structure" typically means the error terms are independent of each other, exhibit no autocorrelation, and (ideally) are normally distributed. Given the lack of significance in the autocorrelation of the residuals as seen in Figure 6.9 we are led to believe we have modeled most of the structure in the time series. To be sure, we carry out the Ljung–Box test, seen in the lower panel of Figure 6.9, which tests for autocorrelation of the residual errors with the null hypothesis of the test being no autocorrelation. As expected, the Ljung–Box test produces a p-value high enough that we accept the null hypothesis of no autocorrelation (independence) of error terms and we conclude we have incorporated all structure in the time series into the model errors of the model.

To corroborate the results of the Ljung–Box test and further bolster our claim of residual error independence, perform a *runs* test on the residuals. The runs test examines the prevalence of "runs" in the series, i.e. streaks where the series is above or below the median, with the null hypothesis being independence. If we have too many *or* too few runs in the series then it is evidence that the series is not random. We carry out the runs test below and observe a p-value high enough that we accept the null hypothesis of independence of the error terms.

```
> runs(rstandard(m1.hare))

$pvalue
[1] 0.602

$observed.runs
[1] 18
```

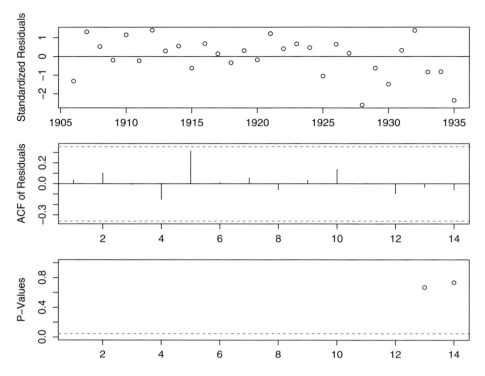

Figure 6.9   Standardized residuals, autocorrelation of residuals, and Ljung–Box test for independence of residuals of *hare*.

```
$expected.runs
[1] 16.09677

$n1
[1] 13

$n2
[1] 18

$k
[1] 0
```

With the independence of error terms established, we wish to determine if they are normally distributed or not. We first examine the histogram of the residuals in Figure 6.10 and notice a couple of outliers on the left and a conspicuous lack of a tail on the right of the distribution. This negative skew and prominent left tail might lead us to question the normality of the residuals.

```
> tsdiag(m1.hare)
> par(mfrow=c(1,2))
```

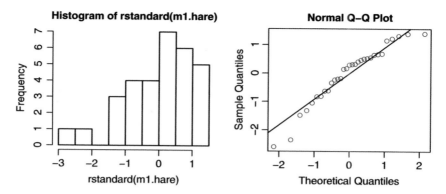

Figure 6.10   Histogram of the residuals of the *AR*(3) model fit to *hare*.

```
> hist(rstandard(m1.hare))
> qqnorm(rstandard(m1.hare),col='blue')
> qqline(rstandard(m1.hare))
```

The next tool we use to determine normality is the Q–Q plot. Since our goal is to produce a model with residual errors that are independent and normally distributed, we compare the standardized residuals to a standard normal random variable using the qqnorm() function. If the residuals were perfectly normal, then the dots would all be plotted very close to the line. We examine the quantile–quantile normal plot of the residuals in Figure 6.10 and observe that, while most are quite close to the line, there are a couple that show significant deviation. This again highlights the prominent left tail (negative residuals) and indicates that further analysis of the residuals is needed.

With both the histogram and Q–Q plot ambiguous, we proceed to perform the Shapiro–Wilk test of normality on the residuals. The Shapiro–Wilk test takes normality as its null hypothesis and so, observing a p-value of over 0.05, we accept the null hypothesis of normality of residuals. However, the p-value of the Shapiro–Wilk test is just barely over 0.05, which we expect given the ambiguity of the histogram and Q–Q plot. So we conclude that the residuals are normal, but just barely.

```
> shapiro.test(residuals(m1.hare))

        Shapiro-Wilk normality test

data:  residuals(m1.hare)
W = 0.93509, p-value = 0.06043
```

Lastly, in Figure 6.11 we plot the predicted forecast as well as the 95 percent confidence intervals around the hare predicted forecast. We define the function to square the vector and we plot the squared predicted forecasts as well as 95 percent forecast

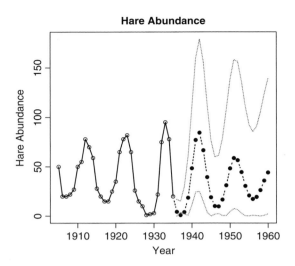

Hare Abundance

Figure 6.11   Predicted hare abundance in the Hudson Valley.

confidence intervals of the model for 25 time steps ahead. We observe that the prediction confidence interval increases with the overall level of prediction and widens as prediction time is further in the future.

```
> square<-function(x) {y=x^2}
> plot(m1.hare,n.ahead=25,xlab='Year',ylab='Hare Abundance',
+       pch=19,transform=square,
+       col='blue')
```

Let us now summarize the model diagnostic process. Once we have used the Box–Cox procedure to arrive at an optimal transform and looked at the ACF/PACF to arrive at model order, we fit the model. After we have fit the model we have a couple of tools at our disposal to ascertain the quality of the model. The goal in modeling a time series is to incorporate any discernible structure into the model. If we have done this to a sufficient degree, then we should be able to observe no structure in the model residuals, i.e. the part of the data that is left over after taking away what is predicted by the model. If the residuals are truly random, we expect them to exhibit some specific properties:

1. They should be either normally distributed or very close to normally distributed. If this is the case, then we can make the argument that whatever is generating the residuals is essentially unrelated to the structure of the time series.
2. The residuals should be uncorrelated in the sense that knowing the current and/or past time value of the residuals tells us nothing or close to nothing about future values of residuals.

We have a couple of tools in our toolbox to help us.

1. The Shapiro–Wilk test is a test for normality in that if we pass the *shapiro.test()* function the residuals of the model and observe a p-value of at least 0.05 then we can feel confident that the residuals are normally distributed. A p-value of between

0.01 and 0.05 is a "grey area" and a p-value below 0.01 means our claim of normal residuals is probably false.

2. The *tsdiag()* function takes as its argument a fitted model and returns three plots, each a diagnostic tool in itself.

   (a) The top plot is a simple plot of the standardized residuals, i.e. the residuals minus their mean and divided by their standard deviation. If we are claiming normality, then we should see few points outside +/−2, and very few outside +/−3. If we observe any points at +/−4 or beyond, then our claim of normality is probably false.

   (b) The second panel of the *tsdiag()* output shows the autocorrelation function of the model residuals. We should see no more than 1 in 20 residuals outside the dashed red line. If we see more than this, or if we see residuals far outside the red dashed line, then it is an indication that there is significant structure in the residuals, i.e. structure that should have been incorporated into the model.

   (c) The third panel shows the results of the Ljung–Box test for independence. If we observe points significantly above the red dashed line then we can assume that the model residuals are sufficiently independent of one another.

6.6 Auto-Regressive Integrated Moving Average Processes

Many times in the analysis of time series we see non-stationarity due to a growth trend in the series or instability in the variance of the process. We can see both in the Johnson & Johnson earning time series in Figure 6.12. We see an exponential growth trend due to earnings growing with the overall economy, and we see a periodic component since earnings tend to be weakest in the fourth quarter and strongest in the first and third quarters. As the economy grows we see a mean that is increasing exponentially and we see a periodic component that is stable but also increasing exponentially in severity with time. We approach such a series by first transforming to homogenize the variance (see Figure 6.12) and then differencing to remove the trend left after transformation.

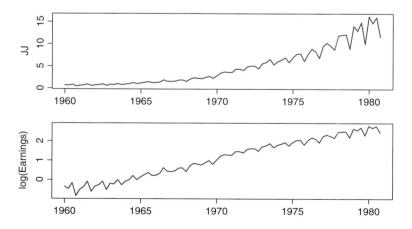

Figure 6.12   Quarterly earnings per share of Johnson & Johnson, Inc. (above) and log of earnings (below).

This process of differencing to produce a stable ARMA process leads us to the topic of Auto-Regressive Integrated Moving Average (ARIMA) models.

```
> data(JJ)
> plot(JJ,col='blue')
> par(mfrow=c(2,1))
> plot(JJ,col='blue')
> plot(log(JJ),ylab='log(Earnings)',type='l',col='blue')
```

A time series $\{Y_t\}$ follows an *Auto-Regressive Integrated Moving Average process* if the dth difference $W_t = \nabla^d Y_t$ is a stationary ARMA process. If W_t in turn follows an $ARMA(p, q)$ process then we say that Y_t is an $ARIMA(p, d, q)$ process.

To begin, let us consider an $ARIMA(p, 1, q)$ with $W_t = Y_t - Y_{t-1}$ so that in terms of the differenced series W_t we have

$$W_t = \mu + \phi_1 W_{t-1} + \phi_2 W_{t-1} + \cdots + \phi_p W_{t-p} \tag{6.11}$$

$$+ e_t - \theta_1 e_{t-1} - \theta_2 e_{t-2} - \cdots - \theta_q e_{t-q}, \tag{6.12}$$

and in terms of the original observed series we have

$$Y_t - Y_{t-1} = \mu + \phi_1(Y_{t-1} - Y_{t-2}) + \phi_2(Y_{t-2} - Y_{t-3}) + \cdots + \phi_p(Y_{t-p} - Y_{t-p-1})$$

$$+ e_t - \theta_1 e_{t-1} - \theta_2 e_{t-2} - \cdots - \theta_q e_{t-q},$$

which is an $ARIMA(p, 1, q)$ process. Note that if the first differenced process were still not stationary (as indicated by an Augmented Dickey–Fuller test p-value of less than 0.05) then we would difference again, resulting in an $ARIMA(p, 2, q)$ process, but most processes need only be differenced one time. After we have transformed the process to stabilize the variance, we must often difference once to remove any trend that is left after the transform. The next section will document such an example.

As we will see in the next section, if the series shows a strong quarterly or yearly cyclicality, we can expand the ARIMA process to accommodate a seasonal component. This is called a multiplicative seasonal ARIMA model and is specified as

$$ARIMA(p, d, q) \times (P, D, Q)_s,$$

with non-seasonal orders p, d, and q as well as seasonal orders P, D, and Q with seasonal period s.

6.7   Case Study: Earnings of Johnson & Johnson

Let us now return to our example with exponential growth as well as a quarterly seasonal component. The dataset *JJ* is the quarterly earnings per share from Q1 of 1960 to Q4 of 1980 of the US company, Johnson & Johnson, Inc. While this series is non-stationary due to its exponential growth, we can model it effectively due to the stable rate of exponential growth and seasonal cyclicality. We also observe heteroskedasticity in that earning volatility at lower levels is lower than earning volatility at higher levels.

The first step in our analysis of the earnings time series is to take the logarithm of it. This converts the exponential trend to a linear trend and can be seen in Figure 6.12. The next step is to remove the linear trend by differencing the logged series. The resulting series will be the basis for further analysis and can be seen in Figure 6.13.

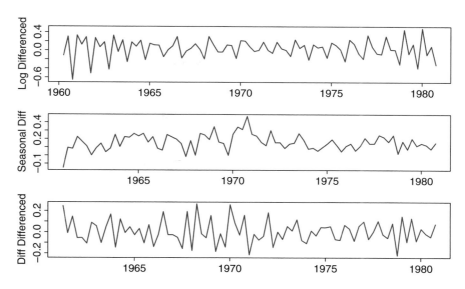

Figure 6.13   Lagged quarterly earnings per share of Johnson & Johnson, Inc.

```
> par(mfrow=c(3,1))
> plot(diff(log(JJ)),ylab='log differenced',type='l',col='blue')
> plot(diff(log(JJ),lag=4),ylab='seasonal diff',type='l',col='blue')
> plot(diff(diff(log(JJ),lag=4)),ylab='diff differenced',type='l',
+      col='blue')
```

The cyclicality of the log-diff series is obvious and we will further document it with a couple of diagnostic tools. The first is to examine the autocorrelation, seen in Figure 6.14. We calculate and graph the sample ACF of the first differences and observe that the cyclical (lag 4) component has been removed. We observe further that the first lag is significant, and this will lead us to set the MA component of the ARIMA process to p = 1. We proceed to obtain the seasonal differenced series by differencing at $lag = 4$ and test this seasonal differenced series for stationarity. We observe a p-value of 0.01 so can conclude stationarity at the $\alpha = 1$ percent level but not at the $\alpha = 5$ percent level.

```
> series<-diff(diff(log(JJ),lag=4))
> adf.test(series)

Augmented Dickey-Fuller Test

data:  series
Dickey-Fuller = -6.8701, Lag order = 4, p-value = 0.01
alternative hypothesis: stationary
```

```
> par(mfrow=c(1,2))
> acf(as.vector(series),ci.type='ma')
> pacf(as.vector(series),ci.type='ma')
```

We set $d = 1$ because we differenced the series once and set $q = 1$ because the ACF shows a significant correlation at lag 1. We now turn to examination of the seasonal

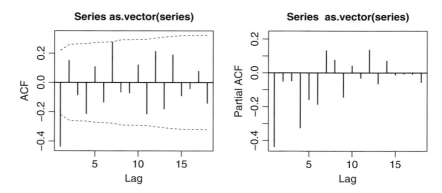

Figure 6.14   Autocorrelation and partial autocorrelation of seasonally differenced quarterly earnings per share of Johnson & Johnson, Inc.

differenced series. We observe the ACF in Figure 6.14 and see significant MA lags at 1. We observe the PACF and see significant AR lags at 1 and 4. However, if we fit an $ARIMA(1, 1, 1) \times (0, 1, 1)_4$ or $ARIMA(4, 1, 1) \times (0, 1, 1)_4$ we observe AR component estimates that have large standard errors. Based on this we fit an $ARIMA(0, 1, 1) \times (0, 1, 1)_4$ model to the log of the series. Using the seasonal ARIMA notation developed earlier, in $ARIMA(p, d, q) \times (P, D, Q)_s$ we set $s = 4$ because we have quarterly cyclicality (4 cycles per year), $Q = 1$ because we differenced at period 4 once, and $D = 1$ because we difference once after seasonal difference to obtain stationarity.

```
> model<-arima(x=log(JJ),order=c(0,1,1),seasonal=
+                       list(order=c(0,1,1),period=4))
> model
Call:
arima(x = log(JJ), order = c(0, 1, 1), seasonal = list(order = c(0, 1, 1),
                       period = 4))

Coefficients:
          ma1      sma1
       -0.6809   -0.3146
s.e.    0.0982    0.1070

sigma^2 estimated as 0.007931:  log likelihood = 78.38,  aic = -152.75

> shapiro.test(residuals(model))

    Shapiro-Wilk normality test

data:  residuals(model)
W = 0.98583, p-value = 0.489

> tsdiag(model)
> plot(model,n1=c(1975,1), n.ahead=8, pch=19, ylab='Earnings',
                       transform=exp,col='blue')
```

As described in section 6.5, the R tsdiag() function plots time series diagnostics, we use it in the above code with the results in the Figure 6.15. In the upper panel we see nearly all standardized residuals falling within $+/- 2$ and exhibiting no discernible trend. In the middle panel we see no significant auto correlation lays in the residuals. In the lower panel we observe easily accepted null hypotheses of independence at all lags. These three panels let us comfortably conclude that the residuals are independent and normally distributed, and that the ARIMA model has incorporated all discernible structure.

With normality established, we now turn to prediction of the series, predicting eight quarters ahead starting in 1975, exponentiating the output of the ARIMA model, and plotting 95 percent confidence intervals, shown in Figure 6.16.

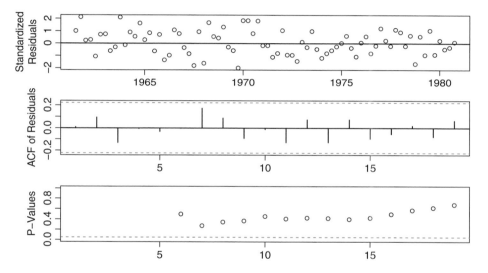

Figure 6.15   Standardized residuals, autocorrelation of residuals, and Ljung–Box test for independence of residuals for Johnson & Johnson for eight quarters from 1980 to 1982.

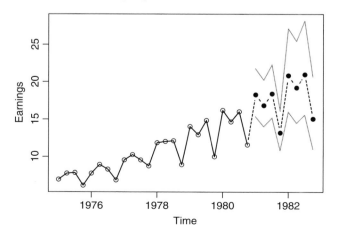

Figure 6.16   Predicted earnings of Johnson & Johnson for eight quarters from 1980 to 1982.

6.8   Case Study: Monthly Airline Passengers

From 1960 to 1972 airline travel increased by a factor of five or more. The cyclicality is depicted in Figure 6.17. The ACF of the difference of key airline passenger transforms is depicted in Figure 6.18.

```
> data(airpass)
> par(mfrow=c(3,1))
> plot(airpass,ylab="Air Passengers",col="blue")
> plot(log(airpass),ylab=" Log of Air Passengers",col="blue")
> plot(diff(log(airpass)), ylab="Diff of Log Air Passengers",col="blue")
> points(diff(log(airpass)),
+          x=time(diff(log(airpass))),
+          pch=as.vector(season(diff(log(airpass)))))
> layout(matrix(c(1,2,3,4), 2, 2, byrow = TRUE))
> acf(as.vector(diff(log(airpass))),main="differenced")
> acf(as.vector(diff(diff(log(airpass)),lag=12)),
>                    main="seasonal differenced")
> plot(diff(diff(log(airpass)),lag=12),col="blue",
>                    ylab="seasonal differenced")
> hist(diff(diff(log(airpass)),lag=12),main="histogram",
>                    xlab="difference")
```

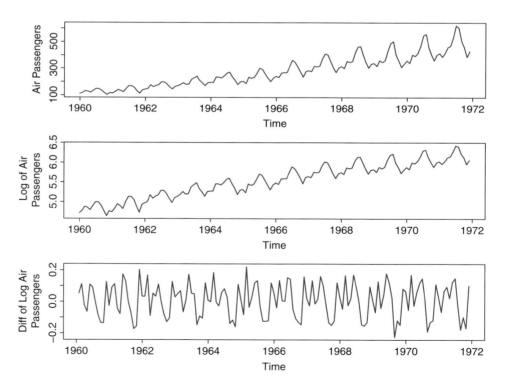

Figure 6.17   Plot of airline passengers, log of airline passengers, and difference of log airline passengers.

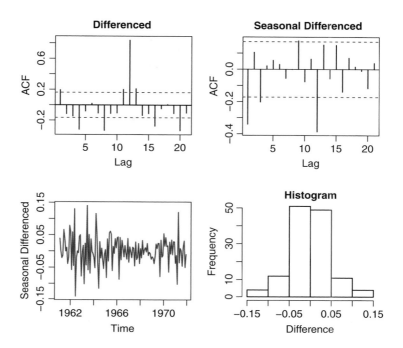

Figure 6.18 From top left: ACF of difference of log air passengers, ACF of seasonal difference of difference of log air passenger miles, and histogram of seasonal difference of difference of log air passenger miles.

Carrying out the ARIMA model estimation on the monthly airline passenger series, we observe standard error (marked s.e. below) of model estimates about one-fifth of the absolute value of the estimates themselves, indicating that the estimates are precise and reliable.

```
> mod <- arima(log(airpass), order = c(0,1,1),seasonal=
                         list(order=c(0,1,1),period=12))
> mod
Call:
arima(x = log(airpass), order = c(0, 1, 1), seasonal =
                  list(order = c(0, 1, 1), period = 12))

Coefficients:
          ma1      sma1
       -0.4018   -0.5569
s.e.    0.0896    0.0731

sigma^2 estimated as 0.001348:  log likelihood = 244.7,  aic = -485.4
```

Turning to analysis of the model residuals, we wish to examine the standardized residuals, the autocorrelation function of the residuals, and the Ljung–Box test for independence of residuals. We see in the upper panel of Figure 6.19 that the standardized

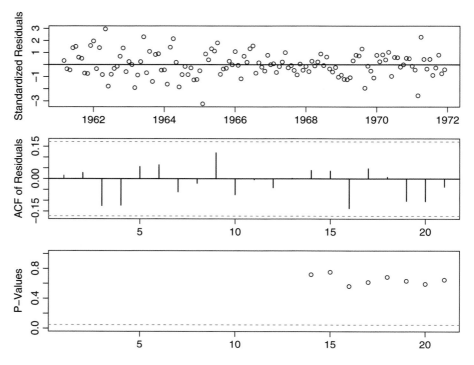

Figure 6.19   Standardized residuals, autocorrelation of residuals, and Ljung–Box test for independence of residuals for monthly airline passenger miles.

residuals are reasonably well behaved, with only a couple outside +/− 3. We see in the middle panel no autocorrelation of residuals, and in the lower panel we see that the Ljung–Box test easily accepts the null hypothesis of independence of residuals.

```
> tsdiag(mod)
```

To confirm, we carry out the Shapiro–Wilk test for normality of the residuals, and observe a p-value of over 0.15, leading us to accept the null hypothesis of normally distributed residuals.

```
> shapiro.test(residuals(mod))

Shapiro-Wilk normality test

data:  residuals(mod)
W = 0.98637, p-value = 0.1674
```

With the model estimated and the residuals analyzed, we can turn to prediction. In Figure 6.20 we predict monthly airline passenger numbers three years out into the future, and observe that the 95 percent confidence intervals increase with the overall level of the prediction and widen as the prediction moves further into the future.

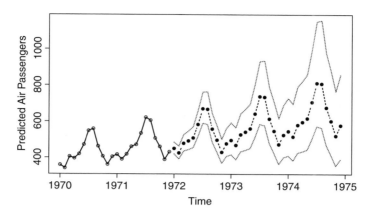

Figure 6.20   36 months' predicted air passengers.

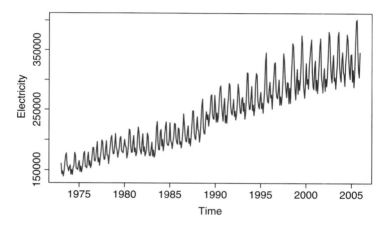

Figure 6.21   Monthly US electricity generation for three decades, 1973 to 2005.

```
> plot(mod,n1=c(1970,1),n.ahead=36,pch=19,
+      ylab="Predicted Air Passengers",transform=exp,col="blue")
```

6.9   Case Study: Electricity Production

We next consider in Figure 6.21 a more difficult series, namely *electricity*, which is monthly US electricity generation (in millions of kilowatt hours) of all types: coal, natural gas, nuclear, petroleum, and wind, from January 1973 to December 2005. In this series we see structure that is more difficult to deal with. We begin by loading the dataset and plotting it.

```
> data(electricity)
> plot(electricity,col='blue')
```

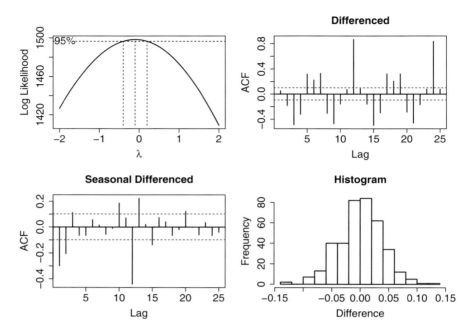

Figure 6.22   From upper left: Box–Cox estimate of the transform parameter λ, autocorrelation function of differenced series, autocorrelation of seasonal differenced series, histogram of seasonal differenced series.

We see in Figure 6.21 that stable cyclicality is still present, since electricity generation is greatest during the hottest days of summer and coldest days of winter. However, we also see a growth trend in electricity usage. As the economy and population of the country grows, so will electricity usage. This growth trend is easy enough to model. What is more difficult to model is the changing variance. We can see that variability at lower levels of usage is lower and that variability at higher levels of usage is higher. This phenomenon is known as heteroskedasticity and to deal with it we will need to carry out a power transformation. Given the stable exponential growth of the *electricity* time series, we might guess that a log transform is appropriate. We carry out the Box–Cox procedure to estimate the optimal λ and confidence interval. We see in Figure 6.22 that λ = 0 is well within the confidence interval, and is very close to being the optimal value of λ, so we conclude that a log transform is appropriate.

```
> layout(matrix(c(1,2,3,4), 2, 2, byrow = TRUE))
> BoxCox.ar(electricity)
> acf(diff(log(as.vector(electricity))),main="differenced")
> acf(diff(diff(log(as.vector(electricity)))),lag=12),
+      main="seasonal differenced")
> hist(diff(diff(log(as.vector(electricity)))),lag=12),
+      main="histogram",xlab="difference")
> mod2 <- arima(log(electricity), order = c(0,1,1),
+                      seasonal=list(order=c(0,1,1),period=12))
```

```
> mod2
Call:
arima(x = log(electricity), order = c(0, 1, 1), seasonal =
                  list(order = c(0, 1, 1), period = 12))

Coefficients:
          ma1      sma1
      -0.5049   -0.8299
s.e.   0.0753    0.0319

sigma^2 estimated as 0.0007344:  log likelihood = 831.35,  aic = -1658.7

> tsdiag(mod2)
> shapiro.test(residuals(mod2))

Shapiro-Wilk normality test

data:  residuals(mod2)
W = 0.99232, p-value = 0.03925

> plot(mod2,n1=c(2004,1),n.ahead=24,pch=19,
+       ylab="Predicted Electricity Production",transform=exp,col="blue")
```

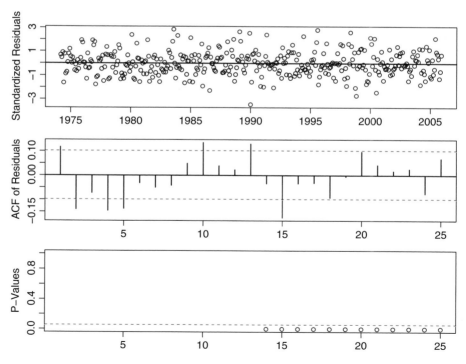

Figure 6.23   Standardized residuals, autocorrelation of residuals, and Ljung–Box test for independence of residuals for monthly electricity production.

In Figure 6.23 we see that the residuals are not as well behaved. The residual plot in the upper panel of the figure shows values larger than $+/-3$, indicating more extreme values than we like to see. In the middle panel we see more significant correlations than the 1 in 20 we expect at the 5% significance level. In the lower panel we see that the Ljung-Box test rejects independence at all lags. These results are consistent with a Shapiro-Wilks test that rejects normality. The conclusion is that while we have modeled most of the structure in the series, there is still some structure left in the residuals, most likely of a non-linear nature.

6.10   Generalized Auto-Regressive Conditional Heteroskedasticity

As we have discussed previously, many financial time series have a variance that changes with time. Generalized Auto-Regressive Conditional Heteroskedasticity (GARCH) models give us a framework to model this phenomenon. While $ARMA(p, q)$ processes have both auto-regressive $AR(p)$ and moving-average $MA(q)$ components, GARCH processes have a similar structure:

$$\sigma_{t|t-1}^2 = \omega + \beta_1 \sigma_{t-1|t-2}^2 + \cdots + \beta_p \sigma_{t-p|t-p-1}^2$$
$$+ \alpha_1 r_{t-1}^2 + \cdots + \alpha_q r_{t-q}^2.$$

In the GARCH framework the series we are trying to model: σ_t^2 is analogous to y_t in the ARMA framework, and squared returns r_t^2 in GARCH are analogous to the innovations e_t in ARMA. The β coefficients determine how past values of volatility σ_t^2 affect the present value of σ_t^2, and the α coefficients determine how past values of squared returns r_t^2 affect the present value of σ_t^2. We can see the forcasted electricity production in Figure 6.24.

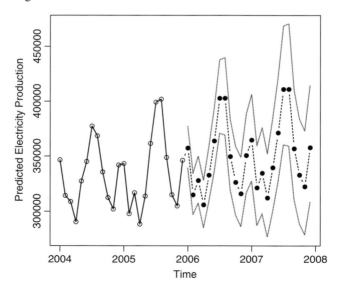

Figure 6.24   Predicted electricity production with 95 percent confidence intervals for 24 months.

6.11   Case Study: Volatility of Google Stock Returns

We turn now to an analysis of the daily returns of Google stock from August 20, 2004 to September 13, 2006. We load the dataset *google* and plot it as shown in Figure 6.25. We notice heteroskedasticity in the returns, with variability higher at some times and lower at other times.

Note that Google time series comprises returns, not raw prices. If we want to recon-struct the original price series we can recall that returns are created by first differencing the series then taking the log of it: *return <- diff(log(price))*. To create the price vector from the return vector, we must invert this process. We sum the process cumulatively and then take the exponential of each value in the vector. In R this is accomplished with the *cumsum()* and exp() functions, respectively, and as outlined in Chapter 5. Note that this price series is scaled to a starting value of 1. To reconstruct the actual price series we would multiply by the price of Google at the start of the series: $50.12, which is the closing price on August 19, 2004. The price series reconstructed from returns is shown in Figure 6.26.

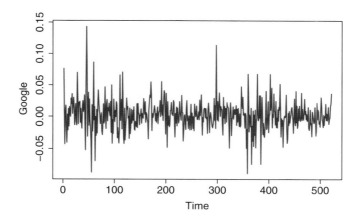

Figure 6.25   Daily returns of Google stock from August 20, 2004 to September 13, 2006.

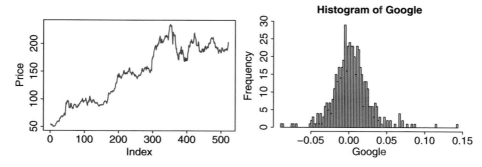

Figure 6.26   Left: daily price of Google stock. Right: histogram of daily returns of Google stock. The period is from August 20, 2004 to September 13, 2006.

```
> data(google)
> plot(google,col='blue')
> price <- exp(cumsum(google)) * 50.12
> plot(price,type='l',col='blue')
```

We next consider the histogram of Google returns over the time series. We observe the heavy tails that are common in financial time series. While the histogram of Google's returns do resemble a normal distribution, we must carry out a Shapiro–Wilk test for normality.

```
> hist(google,breaks=100)
> shapiro.test(google)

Shapiro-Wilk normality test

data:  google
W = 0.94779, p-value = 1.365e-12
```

We notice two things from the Shapiro–Wilk test for normality. First, from the p-value close to zero, that the null hypothesis of normality is easily rejected. Second, we note the dependence of the presence of extreme values on the reported p-value. If we run the Shapiro–Wilk test for normality on the Google returns with all returns greater than 6 percent removed, we observe a p-value of over 0.44 in which case the null hypothesis of normal distribution is easily accepted. So while the returns are reasonably well behaved, the presence of extreme values leads to the rejection of normality. We also see below that if we count the number of days on which we have an absolute value of return greater than 6 percent, they amount to only 17 days.

```
> sum(abs(google)>0.06)
[1] 17
> shapiro.test(google[abs(google)<=0.06])

Shapiro-Wilk normality test

data:  google[abs(google) <= 0.06]
W = 0.99686, p-value = 0.4403
```

We now turn toward characterization and modeling of the daily return process. The first step is to examine the autocorrelation function and partial autocorrelation function of the series to look for cyclicality. We observe in Figure 6.27 significant lags, we conclude that the returns are essentially uncorrelated over time.

```
> par(mfrow=c(2,2))
> acf(google)
> pacf(google)
> acf(google^2)
> pacf(google^2)
```

To model the return process we need the mean to be zero. We calculate the mean of the daily return series

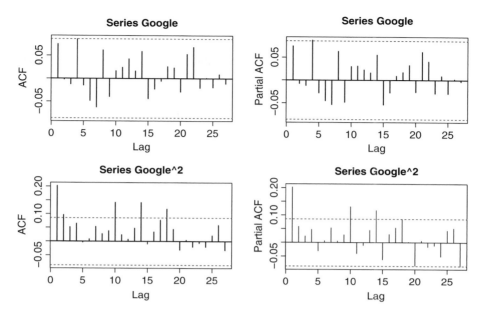

Figure 6.27   Autocorrelation function of daily returns of Google stock from August 20, 2004 to September 13, 2006.

```
> mean(google)
[1] 0.002685589
```

and see that the mean return ≈ 0.27 percent per day. This sounds small but amounts to 0.6804 or 68 percent annualized. We carry out a one-sided t-test and conclude that with a p-value of much smaller than 0.05, we reject the null hypothesis that the mean return is zero and conclude the alternative that the mean return is greater than zero. We will need to subtract the mean when we model the return series in a GARCH framework.

```
> t.test(google, alternative='greater')

One Sample t-test

data:  google
t = 2.5689, df = 520, p-value = 0.00524
alternative hypothesis: true mean is greater than 0
95 percent confidence interval:
 0.000962967            Inf
sample estimates:
  mean of x
0.002685589
```

The next step is to test for Auto-Regressive Conditional Heteroskedasticity (ARCH). The McLeod–Li test carries out this hypothesis test with a null hypothesis of constant variance, or homoskedasticity. We observe in Figure 6.28 that the null hypothesis of constant variance is easily rejected.

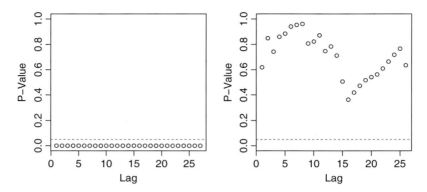

Figure 6.28   On the left we see the McLeod–Li test for ARCH of daily returns of Google stock from August 20, 2004 to September 13, 2006 with consistently low values leading us to reject the null hypothesis on constant variance. On the right we see the McLeod–Li test for a sequence of 500 independent normal random variables with mean 0 and standard deviation 1 with high values indicating acceptance of the null hypothesis of constant variance.

```
> par(mfrow=c(2,1))
> McLeod.Li.test(y=google)
> McLeod.Li.test(y=rnorm(500))
```

To put this in perspective, let's carry out the McLeod–Li test under conditions of known constant variance, i.e. a vector of 500 standard normal random variables. We observe that all p-values are above the critical level and most are substantially over the critical value.

Now that heteroskedasticity is established; we need to determine the correct order of the GARCH(p,q) process. We calculate the extended autocorrelation function for both the absolute value of the return vector and the square of the return vector, both of which indicate that a GARCH(1,1) process is appropriate. We also carry out the extended autocorrelation function eacf() and see at the (1,1) position the "northwestern"-most vertex of a triangle of o'S with x's both above and to the left. This corresponds to auto regressive and moving average components each having lag 1. This corroborates our findings in the autocorrelation function and partial autocorrelation functions.

```
> eacf(google^2)

AR/MA
  0 1 2 3 4 5 6 7 8 9 10 11 12 13
0 x x o o o o o o o o x  o  o  o  x
1 x o o o o o o o o x  o  o  o  x
2 x o o o o o o o o x  o  o  o  x
3 x x x o o o o o o x  o  o  o  x
4 x x x o o o o o o o  o  o  o  o
5 x x x o o o o o o o  o  o  o  o
6 x x x x o o o o o o  o  o  o  o
7 o x x o o x o o o o  o  o  o  o
```

Having decided upon a GARCH(1,1) process to model the return series, we have a model equation of

$$\sigma^2_{t|t-1} = \omega + \beta_1 \sigma^2_{t-1|t-2} + \alpha_1 r^2_{t-1} \tag{6.13}$$

and we wish to estimate ω, α_1, and β_1 from the return series. We fit the model to the data and examine the output. We see that the estimates of ω, α_1, and β_1 are all highly significant. We see from the result of the Jarque–Bera test that the null hypothesis of joint zero skew and zero kurtosis is easily rejected. We also observe from the Box–Ljung test that the null hypothesis of independence of residuals is easily accepted.

```
> m1 <- garch(x=google-mean(google),order=c(1,1),reltol=1e-6)
> summary(m1)
Call:
garch(x = google - mean(google), order = c(1, 1), reltol = 1e-06)

Model:
GARCH(1,1)

Residuals:
    Min       1Q    Median       3Q       Max
-3.60772 -0.59914 -0.04721  0.54559   5.56378

Coefficient(s):
    Estimate  Std. Error  t value Pr(>|t|)
a0 5.246e-05   1.276e-05    4.111 3.94e-05 ***
a1 1.397e-01   2.335e-02    5.984 2.17e-09 ***
b1 7.698e-01   3.722e-02   20.682  < 2e-16 ***
---
Signif. codes:  0 '***' 0.001 '**' 0.01 '*' 0.05 '.' 0.1 ' ' 1

Diagnostic Tests:
Jarque Bera Test

data:  Residuals
X-squared = 201.25, df = 2, p-value < 2.2e-16


    Box-Ljung test

data:  Squared.Residuals
X-squared = 0.010978, df = 1, p-value = 0.9166
```

With the volatility modeled we can now plot it. We observe in Figure 6.29 that the conditional variance of returns can vary greatly over time, with periods of relatively low volatility very quickly giving way to large spikes of volatility. We see in Figure 6.30 a joint plot of Google's return series, price series, and conditional variance of returns series. We observe spikes in variance coinciding with periods of greater uncertainty and movement in both the return series and the price series.

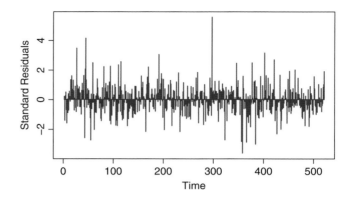

Figure 6.29   Standard residuals for Google.

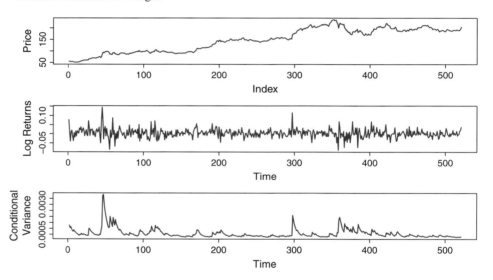

Figure 6.30   Joint plot of returns, price, and volatility of Google stock from August 20, 2004 to September 13, 2006.

```
> plot(residuals(m1),type='h',ylab='standard residuals',col='blue')
```

```
> par(mfrow=c(3,1))
> plot(price,type='l',col='blue',ylab='price')
> plot(google,type='l',col='blue',ylab='log returns')
> plot((fitted(m1)[,1])^2,type='l',
+        ylab='conditional variance',xlab='time',col='blue')
```

We can see the Q–Q plot of the residuals from GARCH(1,1) in Figure 6.31.

```
> par(mfrow=c(2,2))
> plot(residuals(m1),col="blue",main="Residuals")
> hist(residuals(m1))
> McLeod.Li.test(y=residuals(m1),main="McLeod-Li")
```

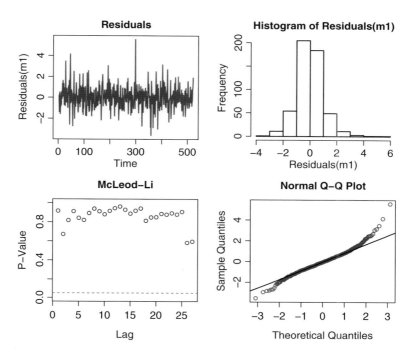

Figure 6.31 Q–Q plot of residuals from GARCH(1,1) model of Google returns.

```
> qqnorm(residuals(m1),col='blue')
> qqline(residuals(m1))
> shapiro.test(residuals(m1))

Shapiro-Wilk normality test

data: residuals(m1)
W = 0.96922, p-value = 5.534e-09
```

Under a $GARCH(1, 1)$ model we can calculate a process variance. Assuming stationarity and noting that $\sigma_t^2 = E(r_t^2) - E^2(r_t) \approx E(r_t^2)$ since $E(r_t)$ is close to zero, we can take expectations of both sides of the equation $\sigma_{t|t-1}^2 = \omega + \beta_1 \sigma_{t-1|t-2}^2 + \alpha_1 r_{t-1}^2$ above, yielding:

$$\sigma^2 = \omega + \beta_1 \sigma^2 + \alpha_1 \sigma^2$$

which, when we solve for σ^2, using our $\alpha_1 = a1$ and $\beta_1 = b1$ estimates from the *garch()* summary above, gives us

$$\sigma^2 = \frac{\omega}{1 - \alpha_1 - \beta_1} = \frac{0.00005}{1 - 0.1397 - 0.7698} = 0.00052, \tag{6.14}$$

which is very close to the calculated variance of the return process:

```
> var(google)
[1] 0.0005693958
```

In this chapter we have covered the main tools used to isolate and model structure in a time series. We have discussed how to detect stable periodic structure by way of autocorrelation and partial autocorrelation functions. We have discussed how to stabilize variability using the Box–Cox transformation, test for stationarity using the Augmented Dickey–Fuller test, and then model the time series in an ARMA framework. With the model defined and estimated we can turn to the tools in the TSA package for prediction estimates and confidence intervals. We have also discussed how to incorporate trend behavior into our characterization of time series via differencing. With the differenced series sufficiently stationary we discussed how to model series with trend in an ARIMA framework. Lastly, we discussed the phenomenon of heteroskedasticity, i.e. time-changing variance, and introduced the GARCH process for modeling heteroskedasticity.

6.12   Exercises

6.1. Public Transport Boardings

Install the TSA package with the command `install.packages("TSA")` if you have not already, and load it with the command `library(TSA)`.

In this exercise we use our time series analysis techniques to model and forecast the number of people who boarded light rail trains and city buses in Denver, Colorado.

(a) Load the boardings data with *data(boardings)* and examine its structure with *str(boardings)*.

(b) Extract the component we will analyze with *boardings <- boardings[,1]*.

(c) Plot the boardings data with *plot(boardings,col="blue")* and overlay the first letter of every month with *points(boardings, x=time(boardings), pch = as.vector(season(boardings)))*

(d) Calculate and view the ACF with *acf(as.vector(boardings))*. Is the yearly periodicity apparent? What about MA lags?

(e) Calculate and view the PACF with *acf(as.vector(boardings))*. Is the yearly periodicity apparent? What about AR lags?

(f) Model the boardings data as $ARIMA(4, 0, 3) \times (1, 0, 0)_{12}$. Note that the integrated part of the model is zero because we did not do any differencing for trend removal. Which estimates are the most precise? Which are the least precise?

m.boardings <- arima(boardings, order=c(4,0,3), seasonal = list(order = c(1,0,0), period=12)) m.boardings

(g) Examine the model residuals with *tsdiag(m.boardings)*. Are the residuals well-behaved? Are they reasonably normal? Are they reasonably independent?

(h) Test the residuals for normality with *shapiro.test(residuals(m.boardings))*. Does the Shapiro–Wilk test accept or reject normality?

(i) Predict 36 months ahead and plot the boardings data with predictions and 95 percent confidence interval with: *plot(m.boardings, n1=c(2004,1), n.ahead=36, col='blue')*

6.2. CO_2 Levels

In this exercise we use our time series analysis techniques to model and forecast the levels of CO_2 in the atmosphere.

(a) Load the dataset with *data(co2)* and plot it with *plot(co2, col="blue")*.

(b) Plot a partial window of the time series starting in 2001 with *plot(window(co2, start=c(2001,1)), col="blue")*.

(c) Define *months = c('J', 'F', 'M', 'A', 'J', 'J', 'A', 'S', 'O', 'N', 'D')* and lay the points over the line with *points(window(co2, start = c(2001, 1)), pch = months)*.

(d) Plot the ACF with *acf(as.vector(co2), lag.max=48)* and observe what appears to be a 12-month cycle.

(e) Plot the first difference with *plot(diff(co2))* and again observe the yearly cycle.

(f) Calculate the first and seasonal difference with, and plot it with, *series <- diff(diff(co2), lag=12) plot(series, ylab = 'First and Seasonal Difference')*.

(g) Plot the ACF and PACF of the first and seasonal differenced series with *acf(as.vector(series))* and *pacf(as.vector(series))*. What order of ARIMA model do you recommend?

(h) Fit and examine an $ARIMA(2, 1, 1) \times (0, 1, 1)_{12}$ model with *m.co2 <- arima(co2, order = c(2,1,1), seasonal = list(order = c(0,1,1), period = 12)) m.co2*.

(i) Examine model diagnostics with *tsdiag(m.co2)* test for normality with *shapiro.test(residuals(m.co2))*. Describe the residuals. Are they well-behaved? Are they normal?

(j) Plot predictions 48 months ahead starting in 2004 with 95 percent confidence intervals with the command `plot(m.co2, n1=c(2004,1), n.ahead=48, col = 'blue')`.

6.3. Exchange Rates

In this exercise we will analyze the volatility of the US dollar to Hong Kong dollar exchange rate.

(a) Load the US dollar/Hong Kong dollar data frame: *data(usd.hkd)*.

(b) Examine the structure of the data frame: *str(usd.hkd)*.

(c) Extract the *hkrate* component and make it a time series: *us.hk <- ts(usd.hkd$hkrate)*.

(d) Plot the time series: *plot(us.hk)*.

(e) Fit a GARCH(1,1) to the time series: *m2 <- garch(x = us.hk - mean(us.hk), order = c(1,1), reltol = 1e-6)*.

(f) Examine the model: *summary(m2)*.

(g) Plot the fitted model conditional variance: *plot((fitted(m2)[,1])$\hat{2}$, type='l', ylab = 'conditional variance', xlab = 'time', col='blue')*.

(h) Plot the model residuals with the command *plot(residuals(m2), col="blue", main = "Residuals")*. Do they look normal? Why or why not?

(i) Generate the histogram of the model residuals with the command *hist(residuals(m2))* Is it similar to a normal distribution? Why or why not?

(j) Test the model residuals for normality with the command *shapiro.test(residuals(m2))* Is normality accepted or rejected? Does this agree with your thoughts on the residual plot and histogram above?

7 The Sharpe Ratio

When comparing investments, an objective metric is necessary for measuring performance. We can use an analogy from sports. The American football quarterback efficiency ratio provides an analytical measurement of the success of the passer, an athlete at the quarterback position who is in the role of throwing the football to a receiver (rather than running the ball forward). Total yards are the number of yards gained from passing the ball successfully. Touchdowns for the passer are when a pass they throw results in a successful score through a 6-point touchdown. Completions are the number of successful plays involving a pass from the passer. Interceptions are when the pass throws a pass which is caught successfully by the opposing defense. For the US National Collegiate Athletic Association (NCAA), the formula is:

$$PssrRtg_{NCAA} = \frac{(8.4 \times Yds) + (330 \times TDs) + (100 \times Compl) - (200 \times Intcps)}{Atmps}.$$

(7.1)

The quarterback efficiency ratio allows college football coaches to measure a passing quarterback's performance against their peers on the same team or other teams. It has become an important metric for selecting the better quarterbacks in the league. While Aaron Rogers was a quarterback in college, playing for the University of California at Berkeley, also known as "Cal," he played two seasons with 5,469 total passing yards, 424 completions on 665 attempts with only 13 interceptions and a hefty 43 touchdown passes. This yielded, according to our formula above, a Cal career passer rating of 150.27. He was then drafted by the Green Bay Packers NFL team, thereby moving from playing at the college level to playing at the professional level. As predicted by his college passer rating, he became one of most prolific passers in the American National Football League, the NFL. After a great two-year career at Cal, he went on to hold the highest average passer rating in the NFL of his time, ranking first for all time as of the end of the 2014 season.

Just as the quarterback efficiency ratio formula provides an objective metric of the passer's performance for a season, when looking at the price behavior of common stocks, we need an analytical metric. Like athletic metrics, security returns are a reflection of the management team in place. Just as for the quarterback and the team, success is key and the management team needs to perform consistently, yielding good returns in order for investors to commit their capital. If the security price appreciates more than others, usually that is due to the talent and hard work of the management team and the employees of the company. Just as for the quarterback and the team, past successes can, in many cases, predict future success.

A drawdown of a security is when a sustained price depreciation occurs. Drawdowns can be pretty scary for the owner of a security. The investor observes as their investment loses value. If we see a stock chart with significant drawdowns, that is like having a quarterback on our team with a lot of interceptions. In either case, our confidence in the performance is severely impacted. We can no longer trust the athlete to succeed. Analogously, we can no longer trust the market, with our chosen securities, to generate gains.

Looking closely at the passer rating equation, Formula 7.1 above, it is clear that interceptions, which are mistakes, are penalized twice as much as pass completions, successes, are rewarded. This is because mistakes can be so costly to the team. Just like interceptions, the adverse market events are hard to overcome. Market drawdowns in value can ruin people's future retirement income or even their current income, so we need to be careful about how to analytically account for this.

7.1 Sharpe Ratio Formula

As a long-time standard for measuring investment efficiency, the Sharpe Ratio is important. Intuitively, the Sharp Ratio combines two important statistical moments of a random variable representing a security price time series (Sharpe, 1964). If the investment is a mixture of securities in a portfolio, P, the Sharpe Ratio is the mean return over and above the risk-free rate divided by the volatility:

$$\frac{E\{R_P\} - \mu_f}{\sigma_P}. \tag{7.2}$$

We can think of the volatility as a measure of risk. For every unit of risk, we have the excess return over and above the risk-free rate provided by taking that risk.

Figure 7.1 depicts high Sharpe Ratio stock prices in separate charts. These are actual daily price charts using historical data. The tickers symbols were omitted to create a sense of mystery. These might be deemed "good looking" to an investor in that they have drawdowns of short duration and continue to generally rise. We can think of these perhaps as the best quarterbacks in the NCAA, using our passer rating analogy.

7.2 Time Periods and Annualizing

Often, one can read books or journal articles quoting Sharpe Ratios, and they can seem too high or too low when remembering other instances. "Let's see, now, was that good Sharpe Ratio we talked about, 2.0 or 0.2?" It is important to recognize that it should be thought of as a unitless figure computed on a time series. The interval of the time series determines the implicit units.

For example, if there are log returns which were computed on a daily basis, those are unitless amounts, and they cannot be compared against log returns on a monthly basis. In order to compare the two, one of them must be converted.

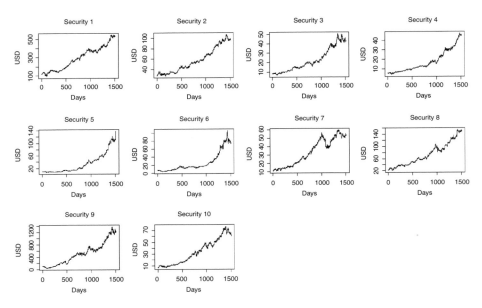

Figure 7.1   Ten stocks with the best Sharpe Ratios from a larger set of stocks. All of these exhibit a high rate of return relative to their volatility.

One of the most common conventions is to convert to an annualized basis. To convert a mean of daily returns or daily log returns, one can simply multiply by 252, the number of trading days per year. Similarly, when computing the variance of daily returns or daily log returns, one can simply multiply by 252 to obtain an annualized variance. However, since volatility is a standard deviation figure, one multiplies the volatility based upon daily prices by $\sqrt{252}$ to obtain an annualized volatility. Equations 3.31 and 3.32 describe converting from daily to annualized volatility.

All that being said, we will simply keep Sharpe Ratios in their simplest form without annualizing them due to the number of places they are being calculated.

7.3   Ranking Investment Candidates

The function *pruneBySharpe()* computes Sharpe Ratios independently and before they are needed for portfolio optimization. The pruning occurs after they are calculated. The candidate set of tickers is reduced according to the threshold *threshSR*. Figure 7.2 is the output of *pruneBySharpe()*, which shows the Sharpe Ratios both before and after the sorting and pruning.

```
pruneBySharpe <- function(prices,lab,meanv,sdevv,threshSR,mufree=0) {
  par(mar=c(4,4,1,1))
  par(mfrow=c(1,2))
  indepSharpes <- (meanv-mufree)/sdevv
  len = length(indepSharpes)
  plot(indepSharpes,ylab="SR",col=4)
```

```
   plot(sort(indepSharpes),ylab="SR",col=4)
   lines(1:len,rep(threshSR,len))
   indHighSharpes <- (indepSharpes > threshSR)
   #clean up NAs
   for(d in 1:length(indHighSharpes)) #clean up NAs
     if(is.na(indHighSharpes[d]))
       indHighSharpes[d] <- FALSE
   len = dim(prices)[1]
   wid = dim(prices)[2]
   smallerSz = sum(indHighSharpes)
   newPrices <- matrix(rep(0,len*smallerSz),
               nrow=len,ncol=smallerSz)
   newLab    <- vector(length=smallerSz)
   e <- 1
   for(d in 1:wid) {
     if(indHighSharpes[d]) {
       print(paste("e",e))
       newPrices[,e] <- prices[,d]
       newLab[e] <- lab[d]
       e <- e + 1
     }
   }
   print("completed Sharpe pruning")
   list(newPrices,newLab,indepSharpes)
}
#unit test:
library(huge)
data(stockdata)
D <- length(stockdata$data[1,])
p <- stockdata$data[,1:D]
l <- stockdata$info[1:D,1]
r <- findR(p)

res <- findCovMat(r)
meanv    <- res[[1]]
cov_mat  <- res[[2]]
diag_cov_mat <- res[[3]]
sdevv <- res[[4]]

res <- pruneBySharpe(p,l,meanv,sdevv,.035)
p    <- res[[1]]
l    <- res[[2]]
D    <- length(lab)
indepSharpes <- res[[3]]
print(paste('D =',D))
```

After running *pruneBySharpe()*, there is a big impact on our set of candidate securities, reflected in a new copy of the *prices* matrix. If we begin our process with an original covariance matrix, Σ computed via *findCovMat()* from **R**, the time series of log returns, then, after reducing the number of securities with *pruneBySharpe()*, Σ' needs

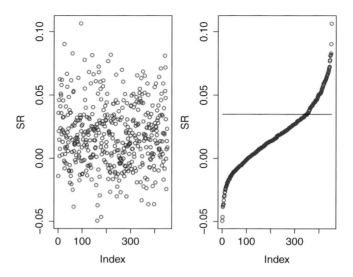

Figure 7.2   Output of the function *pruneBySharpe()*. On the left are the 452 unsorted candidates. On the right are the sorted candidates and the threshold as a horizontal line. 102 of them are above the threshold. We notice on the right that the majority of the candidates have positive Sharpe Ratios which is only possible with positive mean log returns. Since the candidates are 452 surviving stocks of the S&P 500 Index from 2003 to 2008 this is not surprising.

to be found. $\mathbf{\Sigma}'$ is a new covariance matrix coming from the new time series of log returns, $\mathbf{R}'$. This is done by the function *findCovMat()*, above. Also, as a guard against NAs creeping into the matrix from the log returns matrix, *isnaCheckCovMat* is utilized for detecting this.

In most cases, the Sharpe Ratio filter, implemented in *pruneBySharpe()*, will reduce our candidate securities quite a bit, depending upon the threshold we choose. Once the covariance matrix is recomputed, a check for any NA values prevents some unexplained errors.

```
isnaCheckCovMat <- function(R) {
  cor_mat = cor(R);
  print("Checking correlation data.")
  isNACor <- FALSE
  for(d in 1:D) { #check one row for bad data
    if(is.na(cor_mat[d,1])) {
      print(paste("NA for",d,lab[d]))
      cat(lab[d],file="badsyms.txt",append=TRUE,sep="\n")
      isNACor <- TRUE
    }
  }
  if(isNACor) stop("NA Cors recorded in badsyms.txt")
  diag_cov_mat <- diag(cov_mat)
  sdevv         <- sqrt(diag_cov_mat)
}
sdevv <- isnaCheckCovMat(r)
```

There are times when the process can wind up with duplicated prices for differently named securities, based upon the fact that two symbols can point to the same price series. It makes no sense to continue the process of selecting portfolio weight if we have a covariance matrix that cannot be utilized. One of the main criteria is that the price series for each candidate security being considered are unique. This is the first check performed in the *checkDeterminant()* function. Arbitrarily chosen time point day 20 is used and *price*[20, d] is compared to *price*[20, d + 1]. This test will fail if there are consecutive prices series in which day 20 prices are identical. From experience with our data source, this test is necessary.

In the second portion of *checkDeterminant()*, there is a progressive check of the determinant of either the correlation or covariance matrix. The algorithm proceeds like this. We begin with a core-sized correlation matrix of the price series, R_{small}, which is sized 5×5. We then add in a single vector of prices one by one, so that each iteration, R_{small} goes from size $d \times d$ to size $(d + 1) \times (d + 1)$.

```
checkDeterminant <- function(prices,R,lab,isSubDir=TRUE) {
  #incrementally build cov_mat to find singularities
  subdirStr = ifelse(isSubDir,"/NYSE","")
  D <- dim(R)[2]
  #First find out which pairs might be too cor
  scalar_cov = vector(length=D)
  for(d in 1:D){
    scalar_cov[d] = cor(R[,d],R[,8])
    print(paste(d,round(scalar_cov[d],6)))
  }
  #Look specifically for consecutive same prices[20,d],prices[20,d+1]
  for(d in 1:(D-1))
    if(prices[20,d] == prices[20,d+1]) { #arb pick 20th time point
      print("adding to badcors.txt")
      print(lab[d:(d+1)])
      system(paste("echo",lab[d],
        paste(">> ",homeuser,"/FinAnalytics/",dir,subdirStr,
            "/badcors.txt",sep="")))
    }
  for(d in 5:D){
    Rsmall = R[,1:d]
    small_cov_mat = cor(Rsmall)
    deter = det(small_cov_mat)
    print(paste(d,lab[d],deter,dim(Rsmall)[2]))
    if(deter <= 0.0) {
      system(paste("echo",lab[d],
        paste(">> ",homeuser,"/FinAnalytics/",dir,subdirStr,
            "/badcors.txt",sep="")))
      stop(paste(d,lab[d],"det =",deter))
    }
  }
}
checkDeterminant(p,r,1)
```

The determinant can become quite large or small in numeric terms, but must not go below zero. For example, for a set of 102 securities which survive the Sharpe Ratio threshold, the following results are reported by *checkDeterminant()*.

```
> checkDeterminant(p,r,1)
[1] "5 APD 0.737976891151175 5"
[1] "6 ARG 0.658016526839159 6"
[1] "7 AKS 0.608526624429268 7"
[1] "8 AKAM 0.587466012099102 8"
[1] "9 ATI 0.444410330824053 9"
[1] "10 AMZN 0.343231977428733 10"
[1] "11 AMT 0.230336200741275 11"
[1] "12 AON 0.162730053562088 12"
[1] "13 AAPL 0.134763127490828 13"
[1] "14 ADM 0.109717871386606 14"

. . .

[1] "92 UNP 3.69665092461679e-15 92"
[1] "93 X 2.71285159638293e-15 93"
[1] "94 VTR 2.1053706107129e-15 94"
[1] "95 VRSN 1.65020918169293e-15 95"
[1] "96 VNO 9.96678721117897e-16 96"
[1] "97 WAT 8.39710100408012e-16 97"
[1] "98 WDC 5.41680804131733e-16 98"
[1] "99 WMB 3.94165762115458e-16 99"
[1] "100 WEC 3.56197738805091e-16 100"
[1] "101 WYNN 2.51444920848486e-16 101"
[1] "102 XEL 1.78723110721909e-16 102"
```

We can see the numeric value becoming very close to zero. As it heads toward 1×10^{-16}, we finish all $D = 102$ of the prices successfully. *checkDeterminant()* is the kind of data engineering check which needs to succeed to prevent a long process from continuing forward with bad data.

7.4   The Quantmod Package

The Sharpe Ratio embodies such an important concept of finance that we should not limit it to only prices. Fundamental reported figures of companies, including income statements, are important metrics to track as harbingers of how the market will react in terms of price trends and volatility. The income statement is a summary of the profitability of the firm over a period of time. If a smooth, profitable income statement can be achieved by a company's managers, there is a better chance that price volatility will be low and the stock price trend will be desirable for investors. Let's think about how we might obtain these fundamental company metrics and, by forming a very short time series, measure their growth and volatility, much like we did for the price time series.

The R quantmod package makes important market-based datasets available from several major sources: yahoo, google, MySQL, FRED, csv, RData, and Oanda. Our examples use the google source (src='google'). From this source, several key reporting figures from company income statements can be read and trends can be calculated. We look at a small code segment for how to do this.

```
> library(quantmod)
> symbol='GOOG'
> getFinancials(symbol, src="google")
[1] "GOOG.f"
> GOOG.f$IS$A["Diluted Normalized EPS",]
2014-12-31 2013-12-31 2012-12-31 2011-12-31
     20.72      19.77      17.16      15.61
> 20.72/19.77
[1] 1.048053
```

We can query any of thousands of publicly traded companies. By setting the *symbol* to "GOOG" and invoking *getFinancials()* the developer can obtain a handle named "GOOG.f." Using this handle with the elements "IS" for income statement and "A" for annual and the attribute name "Diluted Normalized EPS" we obtain a series of four earnings per share figures in reverse chronological order, starting with the most recent. This comes in quite handy, as EPS growth, the ratio of any two of these EPS figures, can be calculated. The EPS growth is a unitless, normalized figure which can be compared with other EPS growth figures because the growth is not based upon the share price. The growth is a gross return figure. For example, the GOOG EPS growth rate from the end of 2013 to the end of 2014 is seen above as 1.048.

In order to prepare the MVO4 directory with cache files full of prices, we need the following initial logic. We set the size of the array of symbols, *lab*, and the *start* and *end* dates for populating the MVO4 directory with cache files.

```
library(tseries)
library(quantmod)
dir <- 'MVO4'
len <- 1006
isQtrly = FALSE
if(isQtrly) back = 5 else back = 4
if(isQtrly) stmt = 'Q' else stmt = 'A'
res <- readSubDirs(dir)
D1  <- res[[1]]
D2  <- res[[2]]
lab <- res[[3]]
D <- D1 + D2

start <- "2011-02-09"
end   <- "2015-02-09"
isPlotInAdjCloses <<- FALSE
isCacheEnabled    <<- TRUE
prices <- matrix(rep(NA,len*D),nrow=len,ncol=D)
#Must run acquirePrices if cache files do not yet exist:
library(tseries)
prices <- acquirePrices(prices,lab,len,D,D1,D2,dir,
             start=start,end=end,isSubDir=TRUE)
```

```
dir <- 'QMDM'
createDirs(dir,isSubDir=FALSE)
```

The following block of code will read the previously prepared quarterly or annual income statements into our data frame and call R function *na.omit()* to clear out records with spotty data. The Income Statement Data Frame named *cleanedISDF* will be returned. If this is the first time it has been run, it will not find the file and will send an NA back to the calling routine. If the file that is there does not contain income statement information for at least 50 percent of the tickers, the routine will send an NA back to the calling routine. In either NA case, the calling routine will need to obtain the income statement figures using the quantmod *getFinancials()* function.

```
readAndCleanISDF <- function(expectedLab,
                       dir='QMDM',stmt='A') {
  setwd(paste(homeuser,"/FinAnalytics/",dir,"/",sep=""))
  fn <- paste("IncomeStmts",stmt,".csv",sep="")
  #File must exist
  if(file.exists(fn)) {
    ISDF <- read.csv(fn,header = TRUE)
    relevantLab <- intersect(expectedLab,ISDF[,1])
    #count number of matching tickers: must have at least half
    if(length(relevantLab) > .50*expectedD) {
        #Remove entries with missing income stmt info
        cleanedISDF <- na.omit(ISDF)
        lab <- as.character(cleanedISDF[,1])
        D <- length(lab)
        cleanedISDF
    } else NA #missing income stmt recs
  } else NA #no file
}
```

By using *quantmod getFinancials()*, one can obtain three years of annual growth figures for a large set of stocks for comparison. The logic becomes a function with a singly-nested **for**-loop shown below. Inside the **for**-loop are four successive **tryCatch** statements to check for the presence of financial figures and *Net.Income, Total.Revenue, Gross.Profit,* and *Dil.Norm.EPS.*

```
obtainIncomeStmtFigures <- function(lab,dir='QMDM',isQtrly=TRUE) {
  #Read income stmt records via quantmod package
  #Only need to execute once for ETF
  D = length(lab)
  if(isQtrly) back = 5 else back = 4
  if(isQtrly) stmt = 'Q' else stmt = 'A'
  ncol = (2+4*back)
  #Try to read cached income stmts
  ISDF <- readAndCleanISDF(lab,
              dir=dir,stmt='A')
  if(!is.null(dim(ISDF))) return(ISDF)
  print("Income stmt file not found: using getFinancials()")
```

```
ISDF <- data.frame(matrix(nrow=D,ncol=ncol))
#colnams(ISDF) <- c("symbol","netinc",
#  "totrev3yr","gsprof3yr","dneps3yr")
for(d in 1:D) {
  symbol = lab[d]
  basedate = NA
  netinc = rep(NA,back); totrev = rep(NA,back)
  gsprof = rep(NA,back); dneps = rep(NA,back)
  print(symbol)
  isFound <- TRUE
  tryCatch( {
    getFinancials(symbol, src="google")
  }, error = function(e) {
    print(e); isFound <- FALSE
    netinc <- rep(NA,back); totrev <- rep(NA,back)
    gsprof <- rep(NA,back); dneps  <- rep(NA,back)
  } )
  if(isFound) {
    tryCatch( {
      Net.Income<-eval(parse(text=paste(
        symbol,'.f$IS$',stmt,'["Net Income",]',sep='')))
      if(is.numeric(Net.Income[1])) {
        netinc = round(Net.Income,2)
      } else {
        netinc = rep(NA,back)
      }
    }, error = function(e) {
      print(e); netinc <- rep(NA,back)
    } )
    tryCatch( {
      Total.Revenue<-eval(parse(text=paste(
        symbol,'.f$IS$',stmt,'["Revenue",]',sep='')))
      if(is.numeric(Total.Revenue[1])) {
        totrev = round(Total.Revenue,2)
      } else {
        totrev = rep(NA,back)
      }
    }, error = function(e) {
      print(e); totrev <- rep(NA,back)
    } )
    tryCatch( {
      Gross.Profit<-eval(parse(text=paste(
        symbol,'.f$IS$',stmt,'["Gross Profit",]',sep='')))
      if(is.numeric(Gross.Profit[1])) {
        gsprof = round(Gross.Profit,2)
      } else {
        gsprof = rep(NA,back)
      }
    }, error = function(e) {
      print(e); gsprof <- rep(NA,back)
    } )
```

```
    tryCatch( {
      Dil.Norm.EPS<-eval(parse(text=paste(
        symbol,'.f$IS$',stmt,'["Diluted Normalized EPS",]',sep='')))
      if(is.numeric(Dil.Norm.EPS[1])) {
        basedate = names(Dil.Norm.EPS)[1]
        dneps = round(Dil.Norm.EPS,2)
      } else {
        dneps = rep(NA,back)
      }
    }, error = function(e) {
      print(e); dneps <- rep(NA,back)
    } )
  }
  #print(basedate)
  items = c(symbol,basedate,netinc,totrev,gsprof,dneps)
  if(length(items) == ncol)
    ISDF[d,] = items
  }
  #ISDF #return income stmt net 3yr growth rates
  ISDF
}
```

getFinancials() is a tricky utility to use. The handle coming back is accessed via *eval()* because it does not seem to be able to go into a traditional R variable. (This returned handle, for example NASDAQ ticker PBIB, appears in the next section below.) Secondly, errors are common when the requested figures do not exist for a stock ticker. Hence, we make use of the R *tryCatch()* function to gracefully set empty values into variables. Once we have a source of gathering income statement figures, we rely upon it to write these to a CSV file for repeated consumption. Once the file is prepared by *obtainIncomeStmtGth()*, it can be written to a file and read back in later.

The next block of code finds all the possible candidate stock tickers in two files. After finding all the ticker symbols to query, the code block acts as an ETL (extract, translate, load) program which writes the resulting *ISDF* data frame out to a file.

```
writeISDF <- function(ISDF,dir='QMDM',stmt='A') {
  createDirs(dir)
  labNYSE <- as.character(
    read.csv("NYSE/NYSEclean.txt",
             header=TRUE,sep="\t")[,1])
  labNASQ <- as.character(
    read.csv("NASDAQ/NASDAQclean.txt",
             header=TRUE,sep="\t")[,1])
  lab <- c(labNYSE,labNASQ)

  ISDF <- obtainIncomeStmtFigures(lab,dir,isQtrly)
  savedISDF <- ISDF
  colnames(ISDF) <- c("symbol","basedate",
                      paste("netinc",0:(back-1),sep=""),
```

```
                      paste("totrev",0:(back-1),sep=""),
                      paste("gsprof",0:(back-1),sep=""),
                      paste("dneps",0:(back-1),sep="")))
  fileName = paste("IncomeStmts",stmt,".csv",sep="")
  write.csv(ISDF,fileName,row.names = FALSE)
}
#Check first to see if run is necessary
if(!file.exists(paste(homeuser,"/FinAnalytics/",dir,"/IncomeStmts",
                  stmt,".csv",sep=""))) {
  writeISDF(ISDF,stmt=stmt)
}
ISDF <- obtainIncomeStmtFigures(lab,dir='QMDM',isQtrly=FALSE)
dim(ISDF)
```

Our *tryCatch()*, and other exception handling above in *obtainIncomeStmtFigures()*, will produce NA results on our large income statement figure array for missing data elements. As a practical matter, graceful handling of erroneous results is an important issue in data science. R is particularly handy for data engineering by anticipating imperfect datasets, i.e., datasets with NAs, Infs, and NaNs.

The risk of using too short a range of daily prices for long-term investing is illustrated in Figure 7.3. When performing data mining using historical prices for a set of stocks, the stock STRM rises to the top of the heap on a chart from February 2013 to February 2014. It appears to be the best of the group when considering the 252 daily prices blended onto the same chart as gross returns. When downloading 1006 prices from February 2011 to February 2015, however, one can observe that the investor in STRM is not going to be thrilled at the performance in the last quarter of the chart, the most recent year, due to the significant drawdown. This case of STRM points out the risks of using a single year of historical prices. Consistency is hard to demonstrate in only one year.

7.5   Measuring Income Statement Growth

Gross return is simply the new figure divided by the initial figure. Positive gross returns, however, can result from both the initial and final figure being negative values. For example, Porter Bancorp, Inc. (NASDAQ:PBIB) has the following annual net income:

```
> symbol='PBIB'
> getFinancials(symbol, src="google")
[1] "PBIB.f"
> PBIB.f$IS$A["Net Income",]
2014-12-31 2013-12-31 2012-12-31 2011-12-31
    -11.15      -1.59     -32.93    -107.31
```

Computing one year's net income growth using the gross return method, we obtain the "rosy" 24.5 gross return figure below, which would make a program believe the

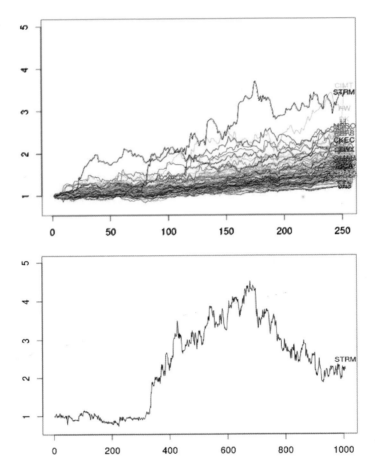

Figure 7.3   Two price time series: one year and four years. On the top is February 2013 to February 2014 which looks terrific to the investor of STRM. On the bottom is a longer series from February 2011 to February 2015. It shows the bigger picture that STRM was in a bullish regime which ended quite abruptly. Interestingly, the "head and shoulders" top seen around day 170 in the top chart also appears, but 252 days later in the bottom chart, around day 422.

stock candidate should be desired, when, in fact, it has a very pessimistic outlook as an investment candidate because all net income is negative!

$$netincgth = -11.15/-1.59 = 7.012579. \tag{7.3}$$

So we modify the gross return formula, which was meant for purely *nonnegative* values, to return NA. We eliminate the possibility of two negative figures making the gross return positive. We do this to be conservative, eliminating negative income statements and negative income statement growth.

```
#Compute gross returns or growth rates
#Use abs() and sign() to force NA when not positive
```

```
calcGth <- function(a,b) {
  if(is.na(a) || is.infinite(a) ||
      is.na(b) || is.infinite(b) || abs(a) < .001)
    return(NA)
  if(sign(a) == -1 && sign(b) == -1)
    return((-abs(b)/abs(a)))
  if(sign(a) == -1 && sign(b) == +1)
    return(NA)#((-a+b)/-a)
  if(sign(a) == +1 && sign(b) == -1)
    return(NA)#(-(a+abs(b))/a)
  return(round(abs(b)/abs(a),2)*sign(b))
}
#Unit tests:
calcGth(1.25,1.75)
calcGth(-1.25,1.75)
calcGth(1.25,-1.75)
calcGth(-1.25,-1.75)
calcGth(-1.25,NA)
calcGth(1/0,1.75)
calcGth(.0005,1.75)
```

Plotting the income statements helps us identify errant computations. The final code version which handles dividing by zero and NA figures and negative growth appears below. If we run the *plotIncomeStmts()* function on a slice of ten consecutive rows of *ISDF*, we can see the candidates':

- net income growth;
- total revenue growth;
- gross profit growth;
- diluted net earning per share growth.

plotIncomeStmtGth() is a test function to display any region of data in the income statement data frame, *ISDF*. The unit test statements at the bottom of the upcoming code block will display these four attributes in series.

```
plotIncomeStmtGth <- function(ISDF,back) {
#input: income stmt data frame: D x 17
  par(mar=c(4,4,2,1))
  par(mfrow=c(2,2))
  mapToCol <- function(d)
    if(d==7) 1 else if(d==8)
      2 else if(d==15) 3 else if(d==23) 4 else d
  mainVec = c("Net Income Growth","Total Revenue Growth",
              "Gross Profit Growth","Diluted Norm EPS Growth")
  D = dim(ISDF)[1]
  for(initFld in 2+c(1:4*back)) {
    isPlotted = FALSE
    for(d in 1:D) {
      symbol = as.character(ISDF[d,1])
      print(symbol)
```

```
finalFld = initFld - (back-1)
initAmt = as.double(ISDF[d,initFld])
finalAmts = as.double(ISDF[d,initFld:finalFld])
gthAmts = c()
for(i in 1:back)
  gthAmts = c(gthAmts,calcGth(initAmt,finalAmts[i]))
print(gthAmts)
if(initFld == 2+4*back) ylim=c(0.5,3.0) else ylim=c(0.5,3.0)
if(d == 1 || !isPlotted) { #initFld is gth baseline col
  if(!is.na(gthAmts[1])) {
      isPlotted = TRUE
      plot(gthAmts,xlab="Years",
        type='o',ylim=ylim,ylab="Gross Return",
        main=mainVec[(initFld-1)/back])
  }
} else {
  if(!is.na(gthAmts[1]))
    lines(gthAmts,type='o',
      col=mapToCol(d))
}
if(!is.na(gthAmts[1]))
  text(back-.05,gthAmts[back]-.01,symbol,cex=.75)
}
  cols <- sapply(c(1:D),mapToCol)
  print("------------")
}
}
#Unit test:
ISDFSlice=ISDF[(match('PCLN',ISDF[,1])-3):
              (match('PCLN',ISDF[,1])+6),]
ISDFSlice
plotIncomeStmtGth(ISDFSlice,back)
```

The resulting plots are depicted in Figure 7.4. It seems clear that PCLN has the most consistent growth positive rates of the ten neighbor candidates in the data frame in this small sample.

7.6   Sharpe Ratios for Income Statement Growth

The first figure we need for a Sharpe Ratio is the return. In this case, we will use gross returns. Without returns, our program will be trying to compare absolute revenue figures, which are much different in magnitude. For example, let's look at the stock Union Pacific, symbol UNP, and its two nearest neighbors in the *ISDF* data frame derived by calling the quantmod package.

```
> ISDFSlice=ISDF[(match('UNP',ISDF[,1])-1):
+ + (match('UNP',ISDF[,1])+1),]
> ISDFSlice
```

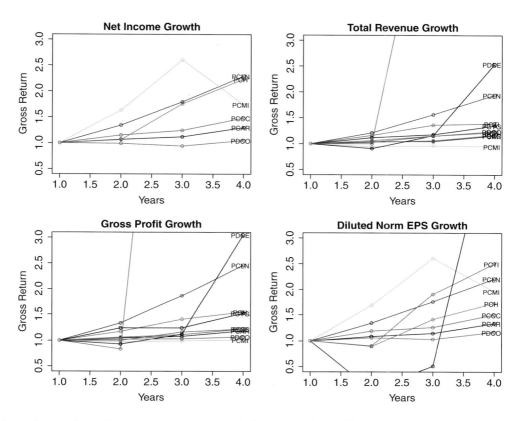

Figure 7.4 Computed growth rates as gross returns on the four years of annual income statements for common stocks, accessed via the *getFinancials()* utility. PCLN appears to have the highest consistent growth of the ten candidates. Those with negative growth rates are omitted via special cases in the algorithm. The year markers below mark the beginning of the respective year.

```
     symbol    basedate netinc0 netinc1 netinc2 netinc3
2087    UNP  2014-12-31 5180.00 4388.00 3943.00 3292.00
2088    UNS  2014-12-31   50.12   21.33   29.44   53.89
2089    UNT  2014-12-31  136.28  184.75   23.18  225.92
        totrev0   totrev1   totrev2   totrev3  gsprof0  gsprof1
2087 23988.00 21963.00 20926.00 19557.00 17891.00 16114.00
2088  1784.36  1788.09  1797.59  1780.57   533.38   538.19
2089  1572.94  1351.85  1315.12  1207.50   319.99   346.28
        gsprof2  gsprof3 dneps0 dneps1 dneps2 dneps3
2087 15175.00 13971.00   5.69   4.69   4.12   3.34
2088   563.46   543.95   2.28   2.06   1.92   2.54
2089   371.35   368.46   3.62   3.59   3.94   4.72
```

We can see above that UNP has total revenue figures that are ten to 20 times UNF and UNS. One thing we notice is that the income statement reporting is not all done on the same date. If it is early 2015, for example, we would like annual figures to be reported

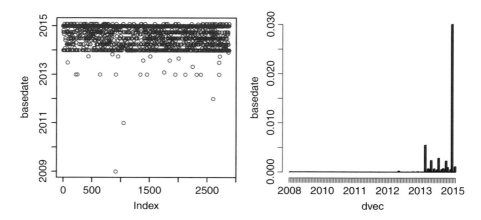

Figure 7.5   Scatter plot and histogram of the company income statement base dates. The most common date is 2014-12-31, seen on the right-hand histogram, where we are basing our analysis, and many base dates are within one or two months from that date.

on 2014-12-31. We can see from the following code run and Figure 7.5 that there, while 2014-12-31 is by far the most popular reporting base date, are others, depending upon the company's accounting and reporting cycle.

```
> #Take time out and look at the basedates.
> par(mfrow=c(1,2))
> dvec <- as.Date(ISDF[,2])
> plot(dvec,ylab="basedate",col=4)
> hist(dvec,breaks=100,col=4,ylab="basedate",main="")
> maxd = max(dvec)
> maxd
[1] "2015-02-01"
> #Below we can see the population of end periods:
> sum(dvec=="2014-12-31")/length(dvec)
[1] 0.5526681
> sum(dvec=="2014-09-30")/length(dvec)
[1] 0.04054054
> sum(dvec=="2014-06-30")/length(dvec)
[1] 0.04608455
> sum(dvec=="2014-03-31")/length(dvec)
[1] 0.03915454
> sum(dvec=="2013-12-31")/length(dvec)
[1] 0.1046431
```

We can see from the above results that only 55 percent of the base dates are exactly the ones we would expect, and also that the highest base date is 2015-02-01. That leaves 45 percent unaccounted for so far. The histogram gives us comfort, however, that the majority of the base dates are within range of what we need. 78 percent of the base dates are on the quarterly boundaries that we would expect. We can find this by adding up the five figures from 0.5526681 to 0.10464431 above.

Returning to the income statement figures themselves, we can scale these figures to a common base because company sizes are scaled in the stock market by the number of outstanding shares. If UNP has income statement figures which are ten times larger than a smaller company, then the chances are that the number of shares held by investors is roughly ten times the smaller company. When converting the figures to gross returns, they will behave like common share prices. All of the scaled figures will become gross returns and will be based upon the initial three-year back figures beginning at 1.0. This will be done in the function *findGth()*, below. In this function, the R *mapply()* function is used to apply our *calcGth()* function column-wise to the data frame. This very powerful R feature makes coding up the conversion to gross returns about as simple a task as we can expect.

```
findGth <- function(ISDF) {
  ISgthDF <- ISDF[,c(1:14)] #sets schema
  ISgthDF[,3] <- mapply(calcGth,ISDF[,6],ISDF[,5])
  ISgthDF[,4] <- mapply(calcGth,ISDF[,10],ISDF[,9])
  ISgthDF[,5] <- mapply(calcGth,ISDF[,14],ISDF[,13])
  ISgthDF[,6] <- mapply(calcGth,ISDF[,18],ISDF[,17])

  ISgthDF[,7] <- mapply(calcGth,ISDF[,5],ISDF[,4])
  ISgthDF[,8] <- mapply(calcGth,ISDF[,9],ISDF[,8])
  ISgthDF[,9] <- mapply(calcGth,ISDF[,13],ISDF[,12])
  ISgthDF[,10] <- mapply(calcGth,ISDF[,17],ISDF[,16])

  ISgthDF[,11] <- mapply(calcGth,ISDF[,4],ISDF[,3])
  ISgthDF[,12] <- mapply(calcGth,ISDF[,8],ISDF[,7])
  ISgthDF[,13] <- mapply(calcGth,ISDF[,12],ISDF[,11])
  ISgthDF[,14] <- mapply(calcGth,ISDF[,16],ISDF[,15])

  ISgthDF[,1] <- as.character(ISDF[,1])
  #dnepsgth2 means Dil.Net.EPS gth based upon two
  #figures: one 2 years back and one 3 years back
  colnames(ISgthDF) <- c("symbol","basedate",
      "netincgth2","totrevgth2","gsprofgth2","dnepsgth2",
      "netincgth1","totrevgth1","gsprofgth1","dnepsgth1",
      "netincgth0","totrevgth0","gsprofgth0","dnepsgth0")
  ISgthDF
}
```

Once the new ISgthDF data frame has the computed the gross returns in place, the R *colnames()* function relabels our columns with the income statement growth attribute name and how many years back the return represents.

Let us now revisit UNP and its neighbors, this time in the newly constructed data frame, *ISgthDF*. After scaling via the *findGth()* we can see that the gross returns are numbers near 1.0 as we expect for all three companies, UNF, UNP, and UNS, regardless of the initial figures.

```
> ISgthDF <- findGth(ISDF)
> cleanedISgthDF <- na.omit(ISgthDF)
> ISgthDF <- cleanedISgthDF
> ISgthDFSlice=ISgthDF[(match('UNP',ISgthDF[,1])-1):
+ (match('UNP',ISgthDF[,1])+1),]
> ISgthDFSlice
        symbol   basedate netincgth2 totrevgth2 gsprofgth2
1297       UNF 2014-08-30       1.24       1.11       1.09
1298       UNP 2014-12-31       1.20       1.07       1.09
1299       UNS 2014-12-31       0.55       1.01       1.04
        dnepsgth2 netincgth1 totrevgth1 gsprofgth1 dnepsgth1
1297         1.24       1.23       1.08       1.13       1.22
1298         1.23       1.11       1.05       1.06       1.14
1299         0.76       0.72       0.99       0.96       1.07
        netincgth0 totrevgth0 gsprofgth0 dnepsgth0
1297          1.03       1.03       1.03       1.02
1298          1.18       1.09       1.11       1.21
1299          2.35       1.00       0.99       1.11
```

We can also compare UNP to its transportation industry section peers by using *match()* and placing those subscripts into a four-element vector with which to index *ISgthDF*.

```
> ISgthDF[c(match('CNI',ISgthDF[,1]),
+ match('KSU',ISgthDF[,1]),
+ match('NSC',ISgthDF[,1]),
+ match('UNP',ISgthDF[,1])),]
        symbol   basedate netincgth2 totrevgth2 gsprofgth2
275        CNI 2014-12-31       1.09       1.10       1.11
737        KSU 2014-12-31       1.14       1.07       1.09
915        NSC 2014-12-31       0.91       0.99       0.99
1298       UNP 2014-12-31       1.20       1.07       1.09
        dnepsgth2 netincgth1 totrevgth1 gsprofgth1 dnepsgth1
275          1.15       0.97       1.07       1.04       1.09
737          1.07       0.93       1.06       1.07       1.17
915          1.00       1.09       1.02       1.03       1.09
1298         1.23       1.11       1.05       1.06       1.14
        netincgth0 totrevgth0 gsprofgth0 dnepsgth0
275           1.21       1.15       1.17       1.24
737           1.43       1.09       1.12       1.25
915           1.05       1.03       1.08       1.09
1298          1.18       1.09       1.11       1.21
> lab <- as.character(ISgthDF[,1])
> D   <- length(lab)
```

We find that going back two years from 2014-12-31, UNP beat its peers in many categories except for CNI for the most recent Gross Profit Growth (*gsprofgth0* = 1.11 for UNP vs. *gsprofgth0* = 1.17 for CNI). Going back one year or last year, KSU was the one peer to best compete with UNP. In the most recent year, KSU had Net Income Growth of 43 percent (*netincgth0* = 1.43).

Now that the gross returns are in place in the *ISgthDF* data frame, we again use another form of the R apply function, called *apply()* this time, to apply the *mean()* and *sd()* statistical functions across specific columns, selected by the *cols* vector to find our two key elements of the Sharpe Ratio. By calling *findIncomeStmtSR()*, which operates by dividing the means by the standard deviations, we indeed have the Sharpe Ratios of our favorite four income statement metrics as well as obtaining the four scatter plots of Figure 7.6.

```
findIncomeStmtSR <- function(ISgthDF,cols,
                  main="") {
  #Find Income Stmt Sharpe Ratio
  SRvec <- apply(ISgthDF[,cols],1,mean)/
    apply(ISgthDF[,cols],1,sd)
  plot(SRvec,cex=0,main=main)
  text(SRvec,ISgthDF[,1],cex=.75)
  SRvec
}
```

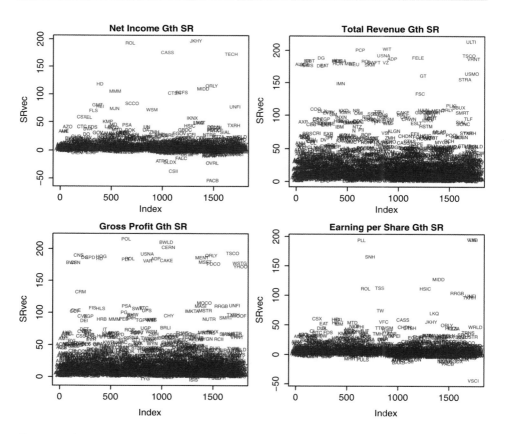

Figure 7.6   Four growth rate mean returns over volatility. These are Sharpe Ratios of income statement metrics by stock ticker.

We have four income statement growth metrics and we could consider those candidates as either the best in *any* category or the best in *all* categories. For the case that we need to use the strictest criteria, "all," our function *findBestAllIncomeStmtSR()* will take in the Sharpe Ratio vectors for the four income statement figures, find out which candidate stocks, identified by their index in the data frames, will meet a given minimum threshold, *thresh*. Only those stocks which meet the threshold in *all four* will be marked TRUE in the *indAllSR* Boolean vector which is returned by the function.

```
findBestAllIncomeStmtSR <- function(
  vecSR1, vecSR2, vecSR3, vecSR4, thresh=50) {
  #From 4 SR vectors, find those that meet thresh
  indVec1SR = vecSR1 > thresh
  indVec2SR = vecSR2 > thresh
  indVec3SR = vecSR3 > thresh
  indVec4SR = vecSR4 > thresh
  indAllSR = indVec1SR & indVec2SR &
   indVec3SR & indVec4SR
  indAllSR
}
```

Stitching the pieces together, our Sharpe Ratio function above, *findIncomeStmtSR()* is called once for each income statement attribute.

```
par(mfrow=c(2,2))
cols  <- c(3,7,11) #netincgth2, netincgth1, netincgth0
ignSR <- findIncomeStmtSR(ISgthDF,cols,
        main="Net Income Gth SR")

cols  <- c(4,8,12) #totrevgth2, totrevgth1, totrevgth0
trgSR <- findIncomeStmtSR(ISgthDF,cols,
        main="Total Revenue Gth SR")

cols  <- c(5,9,13) #gsprofgth2, gsprofgth1, gsprofgth0
gpgSR <- findIncomeStmtSR(ISgthDF,cols,
        main="Gross Profit Gth SR")

cols  <- c(6,10,14) #dnepsgth2, dnepsgth1, dnepsgth0
esgSR <- findIncomeStmtSR(ISgthDF,cols,
        main="Earning per Share Gth SR")
```

Figure 7.6 has our four income statement metric Sharpe Ratios from running the code above. The highest tickers bubble to the top of the chart. If we hand-pick the top two of each and plot their historical prices for five years, from 2010 to 2015, we see drawdowns in the price plot of Figure 7.7, produced by the code below. Note that the *getHistPrices()* quote utility code appears in Section 8.6.

```
#Let us look at price charts for top two of each
#PLL no longer exists as a ticker, May, 2015
topSRlab <- c('ROL','JKHY','WIT','ULTI',
```

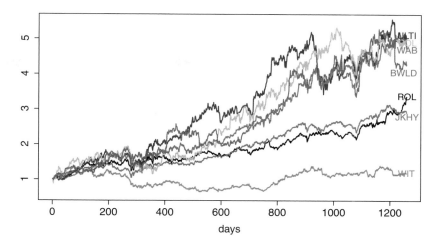

Figure 7.7   Price history scaled via gross return for eight stocks: the top two from each of the four income statement attributes. This is weaker than other possible criteria. Significant drawdowns occur in our historical sample.

```
                'POL','BWLD','PLL','WAB')
prices <- getHistPrices(topSRlab,rep(1/8,8),252*5-1,
        start="2010-07-01",end="2015-06-30",
        startBck1="2010-06-30",startFwd1="2010-07-02")
plotMultSeries(prices,topSRlab,rep(1/8,8),8,
            cc="days",ret="",ylim=c(.6,5.5))
```

We can see vividly in the figure that it is not enough to have a good Sharpe Ratio in *any* of the attributes. If this were our portfolio, we see large drawdowns for ULTI and POL, leading us to rethink our criteria.

Intending to revise our criteria to be the stricter, requiring *all* four criteria to be equally weighted, we now create a new data frame in the code below, called *ISgthSRDF*.

```
ISgthSRDF <- data.frame(as.character(ISgthDF[,1]),
                        ignSR,trgSR,gpgSR,esgSR)
colnames(ISgthSRDF) <- c("symbol","ignSR",
                    "trgSR","gpgSR","esgSR")
cleanedISgthSRDF <- na.omit(ISgthSRDF)
ISgthSRDF <- cleanedISgthSRDF
ISgthSRDF[match('UNP',ISgthSRDF[,1]),] #sample
ISgthSRDF[match('INTC',ISgthSRDF[,1]),] #sample
ISgthDF[match('UNP',ISgthDF[,1]),] #sample
ISgthDF[match('INTC',ISgthDF[,1]),] #sample
```

When we put this data frame together, we try a small test to see how an industrial, UNP, compares to a technology stock, INTC, for the past three years for income statement growth.

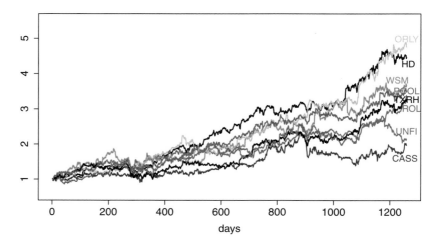

Figure 7.8   Stricter criteria yield a more positive gross return history: eight stocks which were the top in the combined income statement Sharpe Ratio competition.

```
> ISgthSRDF[match('UNP',ISgthSRDF[,1]),] #sample
      symbol    ignSR trgSR    gpgSR     esgSR
1298     UNP 24.61656  53.5 43.17975 25.25137
> ISgthSRDF[match('INTC',ISgthSRDF[,1]),] #sample
      symbol    ignSR   trgSR    gpgSR    esgSR
2073    INTC 4.709579 25.0735 10.57691 5.084924
```

We know that, for this time window, technology stocks such as INTC are outshone by those which take advantage of very high oil prices to outcompete their peers in the transportation sector, such as UNP. To be sure of the figures, we consult Google Finance and find that these Sharpe Ratios appear to be correct. We can calculate that the INTC Diluted Normalized EPS growth is 1.43 versus 1.70 for UNP. Spotting a lower Diluted Normalized for INTC in 2013 than in 2011, we now know that this figure will penalize it due to negative growth. Knowing from Figures 7.7 and 7.8 that using the stricter criteria of *findBestAllIncomeStmtSR()*, we can now use it in the large on our thousands of candidates.

The following code block finished with our best candidates from an income statement growth view so far. In Figure 7.8, rather than hand-picking the best eight from each chart, we set a proper threshold into the strict function *findBestAllIncomeStmtSR()* which will skim off the "cream of the crop" with the following code:

```
ind8SR <- findBestAllIncomeStmtSR(
  ignSR,trgSR,gpgSR,esgSR,thresh=40)
sum(ind8SR)
top8SRlab <- as.character(ISgthSRDF[,1])[ind8SR]
top8SRlab
prices <- getHistPrices(top8SRlab,rep(1/8,8),252*5-1,
                    start="2010-07-01",end="2015-06-30",
```

```
                          startBck1="2010-06-30",startFwd1="2010-07-02")
plotMultSeries(prices,top8SRlab,rep(1/8,8),8,
               cc="days",ret="",ylim=c(.6,5.5))
```

The results of the *thresh* = 40 run of *findBestAllIncomeStmtSR()* is *ind8SRlab*, a vector of tickers or labels.

```
> top8SRlab
[1] "HD"   "ROL"   "WSM"   "CASS"  "ORLY"  "POOL"  "TXRH"  "UNFI"
```

Figure 7.8 is produced by running the remainder of the code on the eight tickers to obtain daily price quotes.

Following this same process, we expand the candidate selection to *thresh* = 25 in order to give the optimizing engine coming up in Chapter 8 a chance to combine ISSR selection with price history in its weighting scheme.

```
> indAllSR <- findBestAllIncomeStmtSR(
+                ignSR,trgSR,gpgSR,esgSR,thresh=25)
> sum(indAllSR)
[1] 33
> topSRlab <- as.character(ISgthSRDF[,1])[indAllSR]
> D = length(topSRlab)
> len = dim(ISgthSRDF)[1]
> topSRlab
 [1] "AME"  "AZO"  "CSX"  "CTC"  "EL"   "FDS"  "HD"
 [8] "KAMN" "KMP"  "MD"   "MMM"  "MTD"  "NKE"  "NRT"
[15] "PCP"  "PX"   "ROK"  "ROL"  "SNA"  "UA"   "WSM"
[22] "CASS" "HSIC" "IKNX" "JKHY" "NTRS" "ORLY" "PAYX"
[29] "PCLN" "POOL" "SIAL" "TXRH" "UNFI"
```

Figure 7.9 shows us that there are some candidates of the 33 which achieve a 300 percent to 400 percent gross return when collecting their price history with the following code block. The suspiciously flat line at 1.0 are quotes for CTC. KMP and CTC are no longer quoted in Yahoo! or Google Finance, so must be eliminated; thus D becomes 31 before portfolio optimization.

The function *plotIncomeStmtSRTops()* takes one of the four income statement Sharpe Ratio (ISSR) vectors and an indicator Boolean vector which indicates the highest Sharpe Ratios as TRUE for the ISSR vector and plots, with the stock ticker name, the ratios. The *rnorm()* R normal variate function dithers the tickers, names horizontally to attempt to randomly separate them for better readability. This works to a degree, but when the density is higher, one needs to investigate the R data structure to find specific results.

```
plotIncomeStmtSRTops <- function(isSRvec,indAllSR,
                        lab,minSR,maxSR,type=1) {
  set.seed(200)
  par(mar=c(4,4,2,1))
  par(mfrow=c(1,1))
  numPoints = length(isSRvec[indAllSR])
```

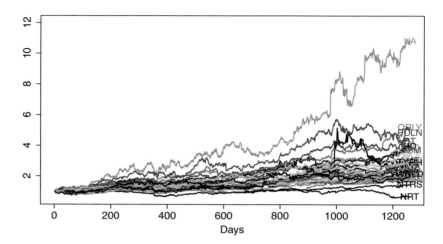

Figure 7.9   D = 33 candidate stock tickers and their in-sample performance. Clearly for this time window, UA has the best in-sample price behavior for this set of high income statement Sharpe Ratio (ISSR) stocks. ORLY, PCLN, and HD also have high gross returns.

```
if(type == 1) {
  plot(rep(type,numPoints),isSRvec[indAllSR],cex=0,
    xlim=c(0,5),main="All Income Stmt Gth SR",
    ylim=c(minSR,maxSR),xlab="Income Stmt Gth Type",ylab="SR")
} else {
  points(rep(type,numPoints),isSRvec[indAllSR],cex=0)
}
text(rep(type,numPoints)+.20*rnorm(numPoints),
     isSRvec[indAllSR],ylim=c(minSR,maxSR),
     as.character(lab[indAllSR]),cex=.75,col=type)
}
maxSR <- max(ignSR[indAllSR],trgSR[indAllSR],
             gpgSR[indAllSR],esgSR[indAllSR])
minSR <- min(ignSR[indAllSR],trgSR[indAllSR],
             gpgSR[indAllSR],esgSR[indAllSR])
plotIncomeStmtSRTops(ignSR,indAllSR,ISgthSRDF[,1],minSR,maxSR,1)
plotIncomeStmtSRTops(trgSR,indAllSR,ISgthSRDF[,1],minSR,maxSR,2)
plotIncomeStmtSRTops(gpgSR,indAllSR,ISgthSRDF[,1],minSR,maxSR,3)
plotIncomeStmtSRTops(esgSR,indAllSR,ISgthSRDF[,1],minSR,maxSR,4)
```

The plot, shown in Figure 7.10, becomes cluttered quickly. ORLY automotive parts can be seen in all four series. Many cannot be seen, but it is possible to inquire about any given ticker with a code sequence such as that in the output below for UA athletic wear.

```
> #track UA's IS SR for all 4 categories
> UAidx = match('UA',ISgthSRDF[,1])
> ignSR[UAidx]; trgSR[UAidx]; gpgSR[UAidx]; esgSR[UAidx]
    1283
35.77816
```

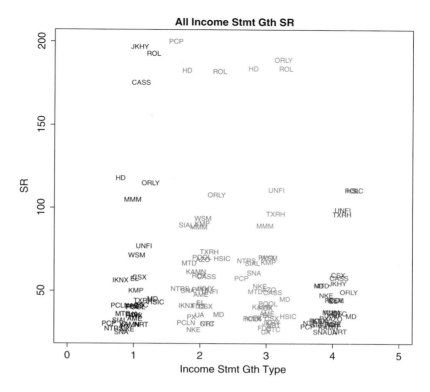

Figure 7.10   33 candidate stock tickers and their income statement Sharpe Ratios (ISSR) for 1 = Income Growth, Net; 2 = Total Revenue Growth; 3 = Gross Profit Growth; 4 = Diluted Normalized Earning per Share Growth.

```
      1283
35.50081
      1283
25.49725
      1283
25.36479
```

Even though the UA ticker is obscured by others, we can see from the *match()* and array-indexing operations that the ISSRs are 35.78, 35.50, 25.50, and 25.36.

Now that we have developed Sharpe Ratio logic for the price and income statement datasets by stock ticker, these can be used in subsequent optimization and learning algorithms in upcoming sections.

7.7   Exercises

7.1. Finding Best Sharpe Ratios

Write another version of *pruneBySharpe()* called *myPruneBySharpe()* in R, which uses the negative subscript feature introduced in Chapter 2 to eliminate prices in the *prices* matrix and ticker symbols in the *lab* vector and adjust the value of the *D* scalar. Use the *list()* operator to return the three variables for prices, ticker symbols, and *indepSharpes*. Use any of the code from *pruneBySharpe()* you need. Use the unit test from the *pruneBySharpe()* function of Chapter 7 for testing *myPruneBySharpe()*. Show the output of testing *myPruneBySharpe()*.

7.2. Data Visualization for Income Statement Growth

Produce the plot in Figure 7.10 by locating and running the code which invokes *findBestAllIncomeStmtSR()*. Experiment and find a better way to separate the ticker symbols horizontally by storing them in a list or dictionary as necessary, rather than the purely random method of Section 7.6. Imagine a radius around them of an appropriate length which you will determine in order to prevent most conflicts in the plot.

7.3. Error Handling with Datasets

Use the *elimSyms()* code from Section 4.10 on Securities Data Cleansing to perform a unit test function called ESUT() of this utility. The function performs a cleaning of the *prices* matrix and *lab* vector based upon what transpired in the *acquirePrices()* process as recorded in the files of the form *bad*.txt*. Write a unit test using at least 20 tickers you choose and disqualify 30 percent of those tickers using one of the *bad*.txt* files. Hint: You may use the first three lines of code from APUT() to assign dir, l1, l2 in a similar way. Best to choose ESUT as the dir name. Create a *badsyms.txt* file in each of the two sub-directories NYSE and NASDAQ to form two lists of symbols to eliminate from prices and lab.

8 Markowitz Mean-Variance Optimization

This chapter focuses on an applied statistical approach to the data mining of equities, price trends in order to gain insight into selecting the most desirable portfolios on the basis of return, volatility, and inter-security time series correlation. Historical prices can very well tell the story of the times of the data collection: volatile, trending bullish or bearish, oscillating or crashing, based upon what market events have occurred. Figure 3.3 shows the price behavior of several stocks with the Great Recession in the early portion of the charts. Generally, some securities are very sensitive to the events of the times while others manifest a higher degree of independence. In any case, the simulations ensure that each security is treated analytically according to its historical nature.

Classically, when analyzing desirable equities portfolios, one can focus on two very different approaches. They are

- fundamental analysis of company balance sheets, which can involve factors for book equity to market equity ratios, etc. (Fama and French, 1995, 1996); or
- the price behavior of their common stock in the global market (Markowitz, 1952, 1959; Ruppert, 2011).

In later chapters we will consider the former analysis, but in our financial analytics experiment in this chapter, we choose the latter, which is consistent with the approach of many market practitioners. The raw price behavior of the common stock is recorded and can be observed and obtained by participants worldwide. The publicly available price data is the driver. The theory surrounding the analysis of the prices in portfolios began in the 1950s.

Depending upon the return and volatility of the historical prices, as well as the covariance of an individual security to the remaining securities, preference is given to those with higher return and lower volatility and lower covariance.

8.1 Optimal Portfolio of Two Risky Assets

The basic idea of a portfolio is to place a set of securities into a basket with weights representing the amount of investment in each. Each investment return is a random variable. In the case of two investment returns, X and Y, if a and b are the investment weights, we are interested in how the variance of the portfolio turns out. We know from the derivation in Section 3.6 that:

$$Var(aX + bY) = E(aX + bY)^2 - E^2(aX + bY)$$
$$= a^2 Var(X) + b^2 Var(Y) + 2abCov(X, Y).$$

The special case of two risky assets in a portfolio, where $Var(X) > 0$ and $Var(Y) > 0$, is an especially good example to see optimization at work. As an investor, we are always interested in minimizing risk, which corresponds to minimizing the variance.

If we assume that our first weight $a = w_d$ represents the debt portion of a portfolio which would hold fixed income securities such as a bond and that our second weight $b = w_e$ represents the equity portion of a portfolio which would hold stocks, then the two weights must make up the whole portfolio so:

$$w_d + w_e = 1.$$

Actually, it is not necessary for either a or b to represent any particular type of investment, we simply chose debt and equity as an example. Substituting in $a = w_d$ and $b = w_e = 1 - w_d$ and using some differential calculus for finding the minimum, we can determine a formula for the minimum variance debt proportion. Our new formula for the portfolio variance appears below:

$$\sigma_P^2 = w_d^2 \sigma_d^2 + (1 - w_d)^2 \sigma_e^2 + 2w_d(1 - w_d)\sigma_{de}$$
$$= w_d^2 \sigma_d^2 + \sigma_e^2 - 2w_d \sigma_e^2 + w_d^2 \sigma_e^2 + 2w_d \sigma_{de} - 2w_d^2 \sigma_{de}.$$

Now we take the derivative with respect to w_d since we are interested in the best weight for the debt portion. We will also obtain the best weight for the equity portion since there are only two portions in this case.

$$\frac{\partial \sigma_P^2}{\partial w_d} = 2w_d \sigma_d^2 - 2\sigma_e^2 + 2w_d \sigma_e^2 + 2\sigma_{de} - 4w_d \sigma_{de} = 0$$
$$w_d(2\sigma_d^2 + 2\sigma_e^2 - 4\sigma_{de}) = 2\sigma_e^2 - 2\sigma_{de}$$
$$w_d = \frac{2\sigma_e^2 - 2\sigma_{de}}{2\sigma_d^2 + 2\sigma_e^2 - 4\sigma_{de}}.$$

The minimum variance portfolio debt proportion is

$$w_d = \frac{\sigma_e^2 - \sigma_{de}}{\sigma_d^2 + \sigma_e^2 - 2\sigma_{de}}$$
$$= \frac{\sigma_e^2 - \sigma_d \sigma_e \rho}{\sigma_d^2 + \sigma_{e2} - 2\sigma_{de}}$$

since $Cov(X, Y)\sigma_{XY} = \sigma_X \sigma_Y \rho$ for any two random variables X and Y. And so the minimum variance portfolio equity proportion is

$$w_e = 1 - w_d.$$

To visualize this relation, below is an R program which will plot it.

```
mu_d = .05
mu_e = .12
sigma_e = .30
sigma_d = .20
```

```
sigma_de = .003
w_d = seq(0,1,.01)
mu_P    = vector(length=length(w_d))
sigma_P = vector(length=length(w_d))
sr_P    = vector(length=length(w_d))
```

Initialization code is above and sets up the five parameters and vectors to record 100 values for μ_P, σ_P, and μ_P/σ_P, the Sharpe ratio. Below is the main loop which iterates and constructs the curves in those vectors.

```
for(u in 1:length(w_d)) {
  mu_P[u]    = mu_d*w_d[u] + mu_e*(1-w_d[u])
  sigma_P[u] = sqrt(w_d[u]^2*sigma_d^2 +
       (1 - w_d[u])^2*sigma_e^2 +
       2*w_d*[u](1 - w_d[u])*sigma_de)
  sr_P[u] = mu_P[u] / sigma_P[u]
}
par(mfrow=c(1,2))
plot(sigma_P,w_d,type="l",ylab="w_d",col=6)
ind_min_var_P = sigma_P == min(sigma_P)
w_d[ind_min_var_P]
points(sigma_P[ind_min_var_P],w_d[ind_min_var_P])
text(sigma_P[ind_min_var_P]+.04,w_d[ind_min_var_P],
  paste("<-(",round(sigma_P[ind_min_var_P],4),",",
  w_d[ind_min_var_P],")"),cex=.75)
```

Figure 8.1 depicts the curve and optimal w_d. By inspecting the Boolean array *ind_min_var_P*, we find that the minimum value of $\sigma_P = 0.1702$ or 17.02 percent when $w_d = 0.70$. The code above is for the leftmost plot of Figure 8.1. The code below is for the rightmost plot.

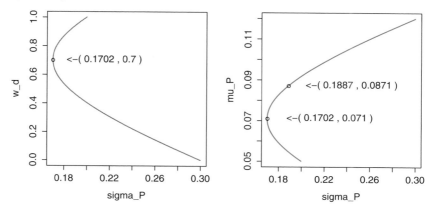

Figure 8.1   Two weights, w_d and w_e share a portfolio. The value for w_d which yields the minimum variance portfolio is depicted on the left plot. The value for μ_P which yields the minimum variance portfolio appears below the value for μ_P which yields the tangency or best Sharpe ratio portfolio on the right plot. The plots assume $\mu_d = 0.05, \mu_e = 0.12, \sigma_e = 0.30, \sigma_d = 0.20, \sigma_{de} = 0.003,$ $0 \leq w_d \leq 1.$

```
#Now plot sigma_P as a function of mu_P
plot(sigma_P,mu_P,type="l",ylab="mu_P",col=2)
mu_P[ind_min_var_P]
points(sigma_P[ind_min_var_P],mu_P[ind_min_var_P])
text(sigma_P[ind_min_var_P]+.045,mu_P[ind_min_var_P],
  paste("<-(",round(sigma_P[ind_min_var_P],4),",",
  mu_P[ind_min_var_P],")"),cex=.75)
```

By inspecting the Boolean array *ind_opt_p*, we find that the value of $\sigma_P = 0.1887$ or 18.87 percent when $w_d = 0.47$.

```
ind_opt_P = sr_P == max(sr_P)
mu_P[ind_opt_P]
points(sigma_P[ind_opt_P],mu_P[ind_opt_P])
text(sigma_P[ind_opt_P]+.045,mu_P[ind_opt_P],
     paste("<-(",round(sigma_P[ind_opt_P],4),
     ",",mu_P[ind_opt_P],")"),cex=.75)
```

Figure 8.1 depicts three important concepts in Portfolio Theory.

- The *efficient frontier* is the entire curve of the rightmost plot of Figure 8.1. All along the curve, we can see what the optimal variance is for a given level of return.
- The *minimum variance portfolio* has a return and variance is the lower of the two selected points in the rightmost plot of Figure 8.1.
- The *tangency portfolio* which has the best Sharpe ratio is the upper of the two selected points in the rightmost plot of Figure 8.1.

8.2   Quadratic Programming

The formula for portfolio optimization can be recognized and cast into a Quadratic Programming (QP) problem. When using R, fortunately, there is a quadprog package for solving these problems using a well-known fast algorithm published in 1982 and 1983 (Goldfarb and Idnani, 1982, 1983). The R package is quite useful for solving mean-variance problems in finance. Quadratic Programming has been around for decades; however, having it available in a language for statistical computing is new. *solve.QP()* is the name of the solver function within the package. Its specification appears below:

```
Usage

solve.QP(Dmat, dvec, Amat, bvec, meq=0, factorized=FALSE)

Arguments

Dmat
matrix appearing in the quadratic function to be minimized.

dvec
vector appearing in the quadratic function to be minimized.
```

```
Amat
matrix defining the constraints under which we want to
minimize the quadratic function.

bvec
vector holding the values of b_0 (defaults to zero).

meq
the first meq constraints are treated as equality
constraints all further as inequality constraints
(defaults to 0).

factorized
logical flag: if TRUE, then we are passing R^(-1) (where
D = R^T R) instead of the matrix D in the argument Dmat.
```

Specifically, quadratic programming as implemented in the *quadprog* package minimizes the objective function as in

$$\operatorname*{argmin}_{b} \left(\frac{1}{2} \mathbf{b}^T \mathbf{D} \mathbf{b} - \mathbf{d}^T \mathbf{b} \right) \text{ under constraint } \mathbf{A}^T \mathbf{b} \geq \mathbf{b}_0, \tag{8.1}$$

where $\mathbf{D}$ is $p \times p$ and $\mathbf{A}$, a matrix of constants, is either $p \times p$ (this form states only inequality constraints) or $p \times (m + kp)$, for m equality and k sets of p inequality constraints, and $\mathbf{b}$, a vector of solution variables, is either $p \times 1$ or $(m + kp) \times 1$. We will discuss constraints shortly.

If we focus purely on QP for the time being, independent of the business problem of portfolio optimization, we can examine this key mechanism, that of implementing a solution to Formula 8.1. Let us say we want to solve a relatively simple mathematical minimization problem to find the optimal $\mathbf{b}$ (Laber and Zhou, 2013):

$$\operatorname*{argmin}_{\mathbf{b}} \left(x_1^2 + 2x_2^2 + 4x_3^2 - x_1 - x_2 + 5x_3 \right) \text{ u. c. } x_1 + x_3 \leq 1 \text{ and } x_1 \geq 5 \text{ and } x_2 \leq 0.$$

Translating this problem into the matrix notation of Formula 8.1, we now have

$$\mathbf{D} = 2 \begin{bmatrix} 1 & 0 & 0 \\ 0 & 2 & 0 \\ 0 & 0 & 4 \end{bmatrix} \text{ and } \mathbf{b} = [x_1 \ x_2 \ x_3]^T \text{ and } \mathbf{d} = [1 \ 1 \ -5]^T \tag{8.2}$$

and the (equality) constraint constants are

$$\mathbf{A}^T = \begin{bmatrix} -1 & 0 & -1 \\ 1 & 0 & 0 \\ 0 & -1 & 0 \end{bmatrix} \text{ and } \mathbf{b}_0 = [-1 \ 5 \ 0]^T. \tag{8.3}$$

Now, the R program which solves for $[x_1 \ x_2 \ x_3]^T$ is run with the following results:

```
> library(quadprog)
> library(tseries)
> P = 2*diag(c(1,2,4))
```

```
> d = c(1,1,-5)
> At = matrix(0,nrow=3,ncol=3)
> At[1,] = c(-1,0,-1)
> At[2,] = c(1,0,0)
> At[3,] = c(0,-1,0)
> b0 = c(-1,5,0)
> P
      [,1] [,2] [,3]
[1,]    2    0    0
[2,]    0    4    0
[3,]    0    0    8
> d
[1] 1  1  -5
> At
      [,1] [,2] [,3]
[1,]   -1    0   -1
[2,]    1    0    0
[3,]    0   -1    0
> b0
[1] -1  5  0
> xHat = solve.QP(P, d, t(At), b0)$solution
> xHat
[1]  5  0 -4
```

Note that $\mathbf{b} = [x_1\ x_2\ x_3]^T = [5\ 0\ -4]^T$ meets the constraints of $x_1 + x_3 \leq 1$ and $x_1 \geq 5$ and $x_2 \leq 0$ so our constraints are met.

The third argument to *solve.QP()* is confusing. Formula 6.1 states the constraints in terms of $\mathbf{A}^T$, but the third argument to the solver is specified as $\mathbf{A}$ itself. So the R code above populates a matrix variable which represents $\mathbf{A}^T$ called *At* and then that variable is transposed before supplying it to the solver. This is important and tricky!

8.3   Data Mining with Portfolio Optimization

With introductory experience with QP behind us, we can now apply it to financial data. In 1952 an analytic technique was invented by Harry Markowitz to optimize portfolios of equities. The emergence of this portfolio optimization approach began with his doctoral research (Markowitz, 1952, 1959). The very novel portion was the accounting that was made for risk in the portfolio. This work has been cited numerous times and used by investment advisors and fund managers throughout the world. Another researcher, Bill Sharpe extended the ideas while speaking of capital asset prices (Sharpe, 1964).

We call upon this Portfolio Theory to provide formal justification for comparing and blending equity securities on a long-term basis. Long-only is our strategy and we take advantage of publicly available data sources: daily closing prices. Portfolio Theory due to Markowitz and Sharpe (Sharpe, Alexander, and Bailey, 1999) can be used to classify investments in portfolio P:

- Begin with $\mathbf{R}$ an $N \times p$ dimensional log return time series matrix where $\mathbf{R} = (\mathbf{R}_1, \ldots, \mathbf{R}_p)$. Our goal is to find the optimal $\mathbf{w} = (w_1, \ldots, w_p)^T$. This $\mathbf{w}$ was known as **b** in Section 8.2. We define size N portfolio return vector $\mathbf{R}_P = \mathbf{Rw}$. When we have p time series of stock prices: S_{ij} at time i for equity security j, log returns are $R_{ij} = ln(S_{ij}/S_{i-1j})$. Note that if the $S_{1,j}$s are interest rates, then we simply set $R_{i,j} = S_{i,j}$ for all i and j since we expect the $S_{i,j}$s to be normally distributed. The full matrix of returns is

$$\mathbf{R} = \begin{bmatrix} R_{11} & R_{12} & \dots & R_{1p} \\ R_{21} & R_{22} & \dots & R_{2p} \\ \vdots & \vdots & \ddots & \vdots \\ R_{N1} & R_{N2} & \dots & R_{Np} \end{bmatrix}. \tag{8.4}$$

We can find

$$E\{\mathbf{R}\} = \boldsymbol{\mu} = \begin{bmatrix} \mu_1 \\ \vdots \\ \mu_p \end{bmatrix} \tag{8.5}$$

and $cov(\mathbf{R}) = \boldsymbol{\Sigma}$ which is of shape $p \times p$. Finding these matrices is a prelude to Markowitz-style mean-variance optimization.

- Now define $E\{\mathbf{R}_P\} = \mu_P = (\mu_1, \dots, \mu_p)^T \mathbf{w} = (E\{\mathbf{R}_1\}, \dots, E\{\mathbf{R}_p\})^T \mathbf{w}$ where $\mu_j = \frac{1}{N}\sum_{i=1}^{N} R_{i,j}$.
- Ranking investment choices and eliminating some altogether according to principles of higher return and less volatility and to the Sharpe Ratio:

$$\frac{E\{\mathbf{R}_P\} - \mu_f}{\sigma_P}$$

where $E\{\mathbf{R}_P\} = \mathbf{w}^T \boldsymbol{\mu}$ and

$$\sigma_P = \sqrt{\mathbf{w}^T \boldsymbol{\Sigma} \mathbf{w}}$$

A requirement for $solve.QP()$ is that $\boldsymbol{\Sigma}$ must be positive semidefinite (PSD). For this condition to hold, reducing its size by eliminating weak candidates and their returns will increase the chances of $\boldsymbol{\Sigma}$ being PSD.

Using QP for portfolio optimization entails finding the optimal variance portfolio given a mean using the objective function:

$$\mathbf{w}^T \boldsymbol{\Sigma} \mathbf{w}, \tag{8.6}$$

where $\boldsymbol{\Sigma}$ is $p \times p$ subject to both inequality and equality constraints (Karoui, 2009; Ruppert, 2011). Unlike in Section 8.2 above, we have *both* equality and inequality constraints, denoted eq and neq. Considering the vector, **b**, from Formula 8.1, we will state the equality constraints firstly as

$$\mathbf{A}_{eq}^T \mathbf{b} = \mathbf{b}_{eq}, \tag{8.7}$$

so that

$$\mathbf{A}_{eq}^T = \begin{bmatrix} \mathbf{e}^T \\ \boldsymbol{\mu}^T \end{bmatrix} \tag{8.8}$$

where $\mathbf{e}^T = (1, \dots, 1)$ a vector of p ones and $\boldsymbol{\mu}^T = (\mu_1, \dots, \mu_p)$

and

$$\mathbf{b}_{eq} = \begin{bmatrix} 1 \\ \mu_P \end{bmatrix}. \tag{8.9}$$

Applying Formula 8.1, in our case $\mathbf{D} = 2\Sigma$, $d = 0$, and $\mathbf{b} = \mathbf{w}$. So

$$\mu^T \mathbf{w} = \mu_P = \mu_P^T = (\mu^T \mathbf{w})^T = \mathbf{w}^T \mu, \tag{8.10}$$

and

$$\mathbf{e}^T \mathbf{w} = 1 = 1^T = (\mathbf{e}^T \mathbf{w})^T = \mathbf{w}^T \mathbf{e}. \tag{8.11}$$

We can restate Formula 8.7 as

$$A_{eq}^T \mathbf{b} = \begin{bmatrix} \mathbf{e}^T \\ \mu^T \end{bmatrix} \mathbf{w} = \begin{bmatrix} \mathbf{e}^T \mathbf{w} \\ \mu^T \mathbf{w} \end{bmatrix} = \begin{bmatrix} 1 \\ \mu_P \end{bmatrix} = \mathbf{b}_{eq}. \tag{8.12}$$

The inequality constraints can be stated as

$$\mathbf{A}_{neq}\mathbf{b} \geq \mathbf{b}_{neq}, \tag{8.13}$$

where $\mathbf{A}_{neq}$ is $p \times p$ (although it can in general be $p \times kp$) and $\mathbf{b}_{neq}$ is $p \times 1$.

Now, we consider the specific inequality constraints which amount to the "no short sales" constraint, a single equality constraint, stated simply as

$$\text{for all } i, 1 \leq i \leq p, w_i \geq 0, \tag{8.14}$$

but, more formally, as

$$\mathbf{A}_{neq}^T = \mathbf{diag}(p) \text{ and } \mathbf{b}_{neq} = \begin{bmatrix} 0 \\ . \\ . \\ . \\ 0 \end{bmatrix}, \tag{8.15}$$

where $\mathbf{diag}()$ is a diagonal matrix of size $p \times p$ with 1s on the diagonal and 0 everywhere else, and $\mathbf{b}_{neq}$ is equal to the vector of zeroes of size p so that Formula 8.13 is now stated in the form of Formula 8.12 using the specifics of Formula 8.14.

In order to form $\mathbf{A}$ and $\mathbf{b}$ we have the components for the equality and inequality or "no short sales" condition, so now

$$\mathbf{A}_{mat} = [\, \mathbf{A}_{eq} \mid \mathbf{A}_{neq} \,],$$

where $\mathbf{A}$ is $p \times (p + 2)$ and

$$\mathbf{b}_{vec} = [\, \mathbf{b}_{eq}^T \mid \mathbf{b}_{neq}^T \,]^T.$$

In Section 8.5 we will see a concrete example.

8.4   Constraints, Penalization, and the Lasso

Portfolio optimization is a very interesting application of non-linear optimization techniques. Since we have already discussed equality and inequality constraints in the portfolio optimization context, general optimization is worth diving into briefly in order to understand better what is going on with the optimization algorithm *solve.QP()*, the quadratic programming routine. Generally speaking, there is a domain in p-dimensions and the function to be optimized, f, is a surface in $(p + 1)$ dimensions. For example, if $p = 2$, as in our upcoming examples, then the function f is a surface in three dimensions. Optimizing consists of finding the domain point, $\mathbf{x} \in \mathbb{R}^p$, which gives us a minimal or maximal point in terms of the value of f. In the Markowitz and Sharpe tradition, we typically desire a mean return and then want the portfolio with the *lowest* covariance for that return. So we are finding a *minimum* point for the variance, or, equivalently, the standard deviation of the portfolio.

Constraints are conditions placed upon f which must be met for the optimization to be useful and valid. Our discussion of constraints here will be general, as we have already begun discussing portfolio optimization constraints. As we have seen in the prior section, constraints are specified as equalities and inequalities. Before the constraints become matrix form, we can think of the conditions in the form most commonly known as the Karush–Kuhn–Tucker (KKT) conditions stated as the main function followed by inequality and equality constraints:

$$minimize\ f(\mathbf{x})\ subject\ to\ g_i(\mathbf{x}) \le 0\ and\ h_j(\mathbf{x}) = 0$$
$$where\ i \in \{1, \ldots, l\}\ and\ j \in \{1, \ldots, m\}$$

where there are l inequalities and m equalities. The full equation for the KKT method is expressed

$$\mathbf{x}^* = \underset{\mathbf{x}}{\operatorname{argmin}} f(\mathbf{x})$$
$$= \underset{\mathbf{x}}{\operatorname{argmin}} \mathcal{L}(\mathbf{x}, \boldsymbol{\lambda}, \boldsymbol{\mu})$$
$$= \underset{\mathbf{x}}{\operatorname{argmin}} f(\mathbf{x}) + \sum_{i=1}^{l} g_i(\mathbf{x}) + \sum_{j=1}^{m} h_j(\mathbf{x}),$$

where $\mathcal{L}(\mathbf{x}, \boldsymbol{\lambda}, \boldsymbol{\mu})$ is known as the *Lagrangian* and depends also on $\boldsymbol{\lambda}$ and $\boldsymbol{\mu}$, which are vectors of *Lagrange multipliers*. For minimization, solving the above is accomplished by solving the system of equations in $p + l + m$ dimensions where x is p-dimensional:

$$\nabla f(\mathbf{x}) + \sum_{i=1}^{l} \nabla g_i(\mathbf{x}) + \sum_{j=1}^{m} \nabla h_j(\mathbf{x}) = 0, \tag{8.16}$$

where ∇f is the *gradient*, a p-dimensional vector of partial derivatives. We discuss an example of the KKT conditions for optimization below.

We can also apply a slightly less general but also highly useful technique of finding the Lagrangian equation for the optimization situation so long as we are purely focusing on equality constraints. Here is an illustration of the technique with a simple example. There is a need to minimize a formula as in:

$$minimize\ \mathbf{x}^T\mathbf{x}\ subject\ to\ \mathbf{A}\,\mathbf{x} = \mathbf{b}.$$

In this case, we will limit our example to $p = 2$ or two dimensions. We can think of $\mathbf{x} = (x, y)$ so, considering our third dimension as the function value, we have the three dimensional parabolic surface where $f(\mathbf{x}) = z = x^2 + y^2$. Now we know that, without the constraints, the minimum value of the function would be the domain point $(0, 0)$ when $z = 0$. However, we have an equality constraint, forcing us to consider the entire surface $x^2 + y^2$ intersected with the plane $\mathbf{Ax} = \mathbf{b}$. If we try a simple plane where $x + y = 2$, we can express that in our KKT form as $h(\mathbf{x}) = x + y - 2 = 0$ or in matrix form as

$$\mathbf{Ax} = \begin{bmatrix} 1 & 1 \\ 1 & 1 \end{bmatrix}\begin{bmatrix} x \\ y \end{bmatrix} = \begin{bmatrix} 2 \\ 2 \end{bmatrix} = \mathbf{b}.$$

Figure 8.2 depicts the contour of the $f(\mathbf{x}) = z$ with the equality constraint.

Another way to find the minimum of the same function is by using Lagrange multipliers. The Lagrangian method is not as general as the KKT method because of the limitation of pure equality constraints. For our example function and constraint here, we can apply it nonetheless. To obtain the Lagrangian form, we start with the expression for the function and add into the formula to be minimized the constraint equations:

$$minimize\ f(\mathbf{x})\ subject\ to\ g_i(\mathbf{x}) = 0\ where\ i \in \{1, \ldots, m\}.$$

With the Lagrangian, we use one λ multiplier for each equality constraint. We have one constraint in this example. If we rewrite the matrix equation $\mathbf{Ax} = \mathbf{b}$ as $x + y = 2$ then our Lagrangian is written as

$$\mathcal{L}(x, y, \lambda) = \underset{(\mathbf{x,y})}{argmin}\left\{x^2 + y^2 + \lambda(x + y - 2)\right\}.$$

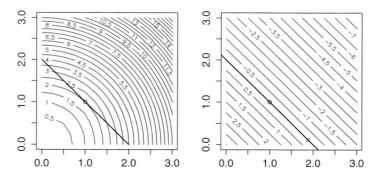

Figure 8.2   Contour plot of parabolic surface $f(x, y) = x^2 + y^2$ with constraint $x + y = 2$ and solution $(x, y) = (1, 1)$ on the left. On the right is the plane $z = -2x - 2y + 4$, our constraint when $\lambda = -2$.

We take the derivative of $\mathcal{L}$ with respect to each of x, y, and λ and set those to zero, then solve the equations:

$$\frac{\partial \mathcal{L}}{\partial x} = 2x + \lambda = 0 \tag{8.17}$$

$$\frac{\partial \mathcal{L}}{\partial y} = 2y + \lambda = 0 \tag{8.18}$$

$$\frac{\partial \mathcal{L}}{\partial \lambda} = x + y - 2 = 0. \tag{8.19}$$

By subtracting Equation 8.18 from 8.17 and dividing each side by 2, we get

$$x - y = 0.$$

From Equation 8.19 we also know that

$$x + y = 2.$$

Adding these two remaining equations, we determine that $x = 1$ and $y = 1$. The domain point for the minimum is at $\mathbf{x} = (x, y) = (1, 1)$ with a value of $z = x^2 + y^2 = 2$. We can see the solution point in Figure 8.2. We can also use Equation 8.18 to find that $\lambda = -2$ in our three-equation system. Our equality constraint $\mathbf{Ax} = \mathbf{b}$, which was written as Lagrange multiplier $\lambda(x + y - 2)$, is the plane $z = -2x - 2y + 4$ when $\lambda = -2$. This plane is depicted on the right side of Figure 8.2.

While we are discussing constraints, this is a good point at which to introduce a subject which has taken the machine learning community by storm. For many decades, in statistics, the important concept of a *shrinkage property* has been developed. It is now at the point where models are basically *expected* to have good shrinkage properties. Shrinkage is the idea that a given solution is more beneficial if it involves fewer and smaller parameter values. For example, in regression, it is our goal to not *overfit* a model to the specific dataset that we see. We want to use initial training dataset(s) to help us construct a model which can handle future test datasets which are not exactly like the training datasets. That way we have a model with, perhaps, more variance from the original test dataset.

Shrinkage can be achieved in many ways. One of the most popular ways is by adding a penalizing constraint with a limit on the size of the norm of the solution vector. The constraint, being an upper bound, has the effect of tightening or *lassoing* the results, hence the name LASSO. Inventively, the name LASSO stands for Least Absolute Selection and Shrinkage Operator. Mathematically it is relatively simple. We will use small letters, Lasso, for the name from now on.

In vector spaces, the ℓ_1 distance measure is the sum of the absolute value or magnitude of each component. If we are in p dimensions, then the vector x has the ℓ_1-norm of $\sum_{i=1}^{p} |x_i|$. This is known as the *Manhattan distance* because we can picture walking city blocks as pedestrians who need to keep to the streets due to the buildings blocking any side paths. The ℓ_2 distance measure is the square root of the sum of the components squared. If we are in p dimensions, then the vector x has the ℓ_2-norm of $\sqrt{\sum_{i=1}^{p} x_i^2}$ which has the effect of summing the magnitude of each component, then adjusting the size back via the square root. This is known as the *distance as the crow flies* for obvious reasons.

Of these two most common distance measures, for the Lasso, the ℓ_1 constraint is chosen due to its ability to provide better shrinkage properties. Geometrically, in $p = 2$ dimensions, the ℓ_1 distance measure forces one of the two components to dominate, forcing other components to zero. This can be seen in Figure 8.3 in the left plot. There is a function to be minimized shown as the contour plot. The diamond is the ℓ_1 constraint, $\sum_{i=1}^{2} |x_i| \leq 1$, appearing within the gradient of the function. Due to the diamond shape of the constraint, the optimization algorithm is forced to choose between one of the corner points of the constraint diamond, involving only the x or y component, because those are the points which are most likely to have the minimum value of the function to be minimized. So, we obtain shrinkage.

If, instead, the constraint were ℓ_2, the diamond shape would become a circle, and the point on that circle that would be minimal for $f(x, y)$ would involve a combination of x and y components, and we would lose our shrinkage property. In the case of Figure 8.3 the observer can see that, following the contour of $f(x, y)$ to the center or lowest z-valued point at $(0, 1)$, the Lasso diamond provides the sharp, distinct constraint with shrinkage.

More formally, to minimize the function

$$f(x, y) = (x - \frac{1}{2})^2 + (y - 2)^2 \text{ subject to } |x| + |y| \leq 1 \qquad (8.20)$$

we employ the KKT conditions. We will rewrite Formula 8.20 above as

$$f(x, y) = (x - \frac{1}{2})^2 + (y - 2)^2 \text{ subject to}$$
$$g_1(x, y) = x + y - 1 \leq 0$$
$$g_2(x, y) = x - y - 1 \leq 0$$
$$g_3(x, y) = -x + y - 1 \leq 0$$
$$g_4(x, y) = -x - y - 1 \leq 0.$$

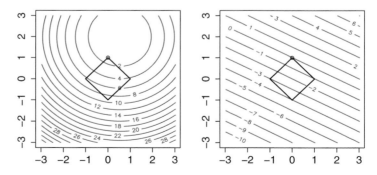

Figure 8.3   Contour plot of parabolic surface $f(x, y) = (x - \frac{1}{2})^2 + (y - 2)^2$ with Lasso-style constraint of $|x| + |y| = 1$ and solution $(x, y) = (0, 1)$ on the left. On the right is the contour plot of the constraint plane where $z = x + 2y - 2$ which is another form of the Lasso constraint. For comparison purposes both plots have the Lasso-style constraint diamond for $|x| + |y| = 1$.

Now, geometrically, we can see from Figure 8.3 that g_2 and g_4 are in a region of f which is higher in value so only g_1 and g_3 are important. We have two KKT multipliers, λ_1 and λ_3 corresponding to g_1 and g_3. Making use of the KKT formulation of Equation 8.16 the KKT gradients are

$$\nabla f(x, y) = (2x - 1, 2y - 4)$$
$$\nabla g_1(x, y) = (1, 1)$$
$$\nabla g_3(x, y) = (-1, 1),$$

so we can form our constraint solution equation with $l = 2$ inequality constraints as

$$\frac{\partial f}{\partial x} + \lambda_1 \frac{\partial g_1}{\partial x} + \lambda_3 \frac{\partial g_3}{\partial x} = 0$$

and

$$\frac{\partial f}{\partial y} + \lambda_1 \frac{\partial g_1}{\partial y} + \lambda_3 \frac{\partial g_3}{\partial y} = 0,$$

which can be calculated as

$$2x - 1 + \lambda_1 - \lambda_3 = 0$$
$$2y - 4 + \lambda_1 + \lambda_3 = 0.$$

So, combining all equations to obtain our $p + l = 4$ equation system, we now have

$$2x - 1 + \lambda_1 - \lambda_3 = 0$$
$$2y - 4 + \lambda_1 + \lambda_3 = 0$$
$$x + y = 1$$
$$-x + y = 1,$$

which can be written in matrix form as

$$\mathbf{Au} = \begin{bmatrix} 2 & 0 & 1 & -1 \\ 0 & 2 & 1 & 1 \\ 1 & 1 & 0 & 0 \\ -1 & 1 & 0 & 0 \end{bmatrix} \begin{bmatrix} x \\ y \\ \lambda_1 \\ \lambda_3 \end{bmatrix} = \begin{bmatrix} 1 \\ 4 \\ 1 \\ 1 \end{bmatrix} = \mathbf{b}$$

and solved as $\mathbf{u} = \mathbf{A}^{-1}\mathbf{b}$ via a small R program with output below to $(x, y, \lambda_1, \lambda_3) = (0, 1, \frac{3}{2}, \frac{1}{2})$:

```
> A = matrix(c(2,0,1,-1,
+               0,2,1,1,
+               1,1,0,0,
+               -1,1,0,0),nrow=4,ncol=4)
> b = c(1,4,1,1)
> u = solve(A) %*% b
> u
       [,1]
[1,]   0.0
[2,]   1.0
[3,]   1.5
[4,]   0.5
```

which tells us that the KKT-form equation

$$\mathbf{x}^* = \underset{\mathbf{x}}{\operatorname{argmin}} f(\mathbf{x}) = \underset{\mathbf{x}}{\operatorname{argmin}} \mathcal{L}(\mathbf{x}, \boldsymbol{\lambda}, \boldsymbol{\mu}) = \underset{\mathbf{x}}{\operatorname{argmin}} \mathcal{L}((x, y), (\lambda_1, \lambda_3))$$

$$= \underset{\mathbf{x}}{\operatorname{argmin}}\{(x - \frac{1}{2})^2 + (y - 2)^2 + \lambda_1(x + y - 1) + \lambda_3(-x + y - 1)\},$$

is solved with $\mathbf{x}^* = (0, 1)$ and $\boldsymbol{\lambda} = (\frac{3}{2}, \frac{1}{2})$. Our two λ terms are penalizing to the minimization problem because they increase the value of the overall formula to be minimized so long as the λs are positive. We find, using $\boldsymbol{\lambda} = (\frac{3}{2}, \frac{1}{2})$, that the two λ terms become $x + 2y - 2$, which form a plane in (x, y, z) space. Figure 8.3 shows the function $f(x, y)$ with the Lasso constraint on the left. On the right, the Lasso constraint is shown again against the contour of the plane where $x + 2y - 2$, which is our plane of interest when $\lambda_1 = \frac{3}{2}$ and $\lambda_3 = \frac{1}{2}$. We can see from the contour on the right that when the plane intersects the plane where $x + 2y - 2 = z = 0$ is where we have our solution point where $(x, y) = (0, 1)$.

Many of the Markowitz simulations shown in the literature involve a small handful of securities. These lower-dimensional simulations illustrate and instill confidence in the technique, and they spark curiosity on how the algorithm behaves when a large number of securities are being researched, hundreds here and in practice at investment firms. The goal for a portfolio manager or individual investor would be to supply the simulation a large number of candidate securities and see which of those candidates are marked as securities with a good return–risk ratio in the overall portfolio. It would be in scenarios like these that the true value of R language automation would be beneficial. While it is not very common, other work in high-dimensional Markowitz portfolios has been reported (Karoui, 2009).

In addition to return, measures of risk, including variance and covariance to the remaining securities, are important. Those securities with low to negative covariance to the others are favored even over those with higher Sharpe Ratios, due to their diversification contribution. As an example, one of the stocks, AmerisourceBergen (ABC), in the nine-dimensional case, is highly favored, as seen in Figure 3.3. The correlation is low to the others, as seen in the correlation matrix plot where the trough is apparent at the third row and column in Figure 3.4.

A natural progression of the Markowitz algorithm is scaling it up to many securities and, therefore, dimensions. This allows large sets of securities to be data-mined to find out if good values exist. Investors might not be aware of price characteristics until seeing these candidates emitted as results in the portfolio simulation.

Here is an outline of the steps used in this experiment to mine the data. The specific details which relate to code modules appear in Figure 8.5.

- Data collection
- Data pre-processing:
  Visualization of data
  Adjustment for splits
- Compute log returns
- Compute covariance matrix

- Simulation and optimization
- Visualization and storing of results

The data pre-processing steps prior to the automation steps are important to the knowledge discovery process when the results are revealed. Without them, inaccurate conclusions result from the inaccurate data. By using data visualization to examine and pay attention to the details of the data patterns, the automation steps can move ahead properly. And the process repeats as the automation code is developed. In cases like this, hundreds of charts are plotted to gain confidence of the validity of the data through inspection as introduced in Section 4.5.

8.5 Extending to High Dimensions

What are the practical implementation issues of using internet-based historical prices to measure key statistics in an R program? Without the data cleaning, incorrect returns, volatilities, and covariances will be computed (Bennett, 2014). When dealing with large datasets, the amount of data cleaning is commensurate to the dataset size.

We return to the *huge stockdata* dataset (Zhao, Liu, Roeder, Lafferty, and Wasserman, 2012). Our domain begins in the space of $\mathbb{R}^{452}$ because 452 of the S&P 500 Index stocks were kept in the index for the entire period of 2003 to 2008. We will be soon looking at a sample of size just over 1,200 from $\mathbb{R}^{452}$. The goal of *huge* is a somewhat different from our goal in this chapter, but considering this available dataset, originally used for graphical model structure learning experiments like those of Chapter 9, the large number of securities will give portfolio optimization a robust test in higher dimensions. So, as is commonly the case, an R package was used to leverage previous data collection work, after pre-processing of the data, for testing.

For this first-time use of the *solve.QP()* optimizer, we will track each of the steps. Data collection code and output is below. Leveraging the *huge stockdata* dataset can be done in six lines of code:

```
> library(huge)
> data(stockdata)
> len = length(stockdata$data[,1])
> D = dim(stockdata$data)[2]
> prices = stockdata$data[,1:D]
> lab = stockdata$info[1:D,1]
```

Data pre-processing, including visualization of data and adjustment for splits, code, and output, appears below. The *findR()* utility has the option to call the *splitAdjust()* utility. If *splitAdjusted* == FALSE already, it will call it. We do need to adjust *stockdata$prices* before we compute the log returns.

```
> isSplitAdjusted=FALSE
> daysPerYr=252; mufree = 0
> R <- findR(prices,
```

```
+ isSplitAdjusted=isSplitAdjusted) #side affects prices
[1] "split adjusting MMM 2 188 140.54 69.07"
...
[1] "split adjusting ABC 2 755 83.77 41.48"
...
[1] "split adjusting AAPL 2 543 88.99 44.86"
...
[1] "split adjusting EBAY 2 167 109.52 55.41"
[1] "split adjusting EBAY 2 537 172.18 85.44"
...
[1] "reverse split adjusting 125 ISRG 125 -2 7.49 14.64"
...
[1] "split adjusting QCOM 2 408 69.17 34.92"
[1] "split adjusting HSY 2 366 92.03 45.74"
...
[1] "reverse split adjusting 32 TIE 32 -10 1.9 18.77"
...
> displayCharts(prices,lab,nrow=6,ncol=4,sleepSecs=5)
...
[1] "451 ZMH"
[1] "452 ZION"
> dim(R)
[1] 1257  452
```

Next comes the code to find the covariance matrix. We look at the upper-left corner of the covariance matrix. Sharpe Ratios are computed as well for later.

```
> res    <- findCovMat(R)
> meanv <- res[[1]]
> cov_mat <- res[[2]]
> diag_cov_mat <- res[[3]]
> sdevv <- res[[4]]
> round(cov_mat[1:8,1:8],4)
        [,1]   [,2]   [,3]   [,4]   [,5]   [,6]   [,7]   [,8]
[1,] 1.3468 0.5412 0.3982 0.6838 0.7282 0.7022 0.5529 0.4677
[2,] 0.5412 2.4249 0.6008 0.9901 0.7854 0.8716 0.7769 0.8051
[3,] 0.3982 0.6008 1.5557 0.5182 0.4763 0.6424 0.5477 0.3988
[4,] 0.6838 0.9901 0.5182 5.0619 1.0390 1.4370 0.7675 0.8284
[5,] 0.7282 0.7854 0.4763 1.0390 4.1918 2.0683 0.9356 0.7662
[6,] 0.7022 0.8716 0.6424 1.4370 2.0683 9.0457 1.1346 0.6656
[7,] 0.5529 0.7769 0.5477 0.7675 0.9356 1.1346 5.7810 0.6727
[8,] 0.4677 0.8051 0.3988 0.8284 0.7662 0.6656 0.6727 3.6067
> Sharpe <- (meanv-mufree)/sdevv
> isSplitAdjusted <- TRUE
> isPlot <- TRUE
```

Simulation and optimization preparation code and output appears below. Our optimizer, *solve.QP()* expects to know *meq*, the number of columns of the *Amat* matrix which are dedicated to equality constraints, also known as *m*. As we examine the *Amat* constraint matrix for the *solve.QP()* optimizer, we note that it will be run essentially ℓ_1 or Lasso-constrained due to Formula 8.14 and the top half of Formula 8.12. Combining these conditions allows us to conclude that

$$\sum_{i=1}^{p} |w_i| = 1,$$

which is a stricter version of the classic Lasso $\sum_{i=1}^{p} |w_i| \leq s$ constraint where $s = 1$ (Bruder, Gaussel, Richard, and Roncalli, 2013). The ones down the first column of *Amat* below enforce the top half of Formula 8.12 and the ones down the diagonal of *Amat* and zeroes in the last p positions of *bvec* enforce Formula 8.13. The good news is that, by assuming no short sales, we are regularizing the covariance matrix and we can expect shrinkage in the recommended weights.

```
> isShorting <- FALSE
> Amat <- cbind(rep(1,D),meanv,diag(1,nrow=D)) #no short sales
> Amat[1:8,1:10]
                    meanv
[1,] 1 -0.03242621779461 1 0 0 0 0 0 0 0
[2,] 1  0.05612769998105 0 1 0 0 0 0 0 0
[3,] 1  0.02688130530390 0 0 1 0 0 0 0 0
[4,] 1  0.10358295996890 0 0 0 1 0 0 0 0
[5,] 1  0.04075647559033 0 0 0 0 1 0 0 0
[6,] 1  0.00537512486044 0 0 0 0 0 1 0 0
[7,] 1  0.15014719119253 0 0 0 0 0 0 1 0
[8,] 1  0.02523113946413 0 0 0 0 0 0 0 1
```

The simulation and optimization and visualization steps are incorporated into the function *findWeights()*. The code for this function appears below:

```
findWeights <- function(muP,cov_mat,Amat) {
  bvec = c(1,muP,rep(0,D)) #no short sales
  D <- dim(cov_mat)[1]
  result = solve.QP(Dmat=2*cov_mat,dvec=rep(0,D),
                    Amat=Amat,bvec=bvec,meq=2)
  result
}
```

Calling *findWeights()* in a loop with successively lower portfolio return goals allows us to see how *solve.QP()* brings more candidates into the set of nonzero-weighted stocks to diversify the portfolio. Figure 8.4 begins with finding the highest return possible, depicted in the *sort(meanv)* output, then 11 successive output plots go from high to low, 33.65 percent return down to 3 percent return on a log return basis. We can see in the first chart that the best individual stock return is 33.65 percent. We use that figure as our initial goal for the first run. We see how the $p = 452$ stocks get introduced, little by little, selected by having the best return for the risk they introduce into the portfolio.

```
par(mfrow=c(4,3))
maxMeanV <- max(meanv)
plot(sort(meanv),col=4)
```

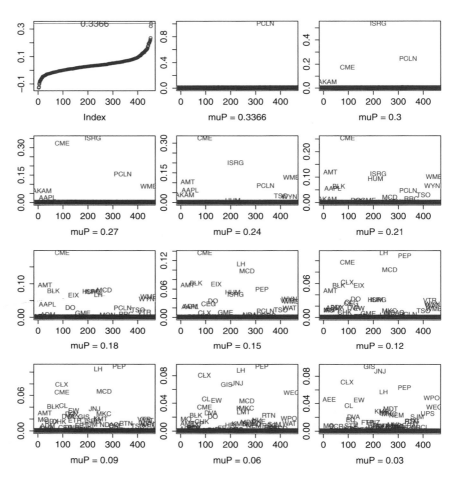

Figure 8.4   Results from initial runs of *solve.QP()* with *huge stockdata*, all of the 452 stocks of the S&P, to meet the highest return possible for the period 2003 to 2008. The first chart depicts the sorted individual stock returns so that we can determine the best possible pure return without regard for variance or covariance. The results from 11 runs appear after that with the weight, w_i for stock i on the vertical axis.

```
abline(h=maxMeanV,col=2)
text(D/2,maxMeanV,round(maxMeanV,4),col=4)
maxMeanV
for(muP in c(maxMeanV,.30,.27,.24,.21,
            .18,.15,.12,.09,.06,.03)) {
  result <- findWeights(muP,cov_mat,Amat)
  if(length(result[[1]])>0 && !is.na(result[[1]][1])) {
    summary(result)
    w = result$solution
    sum(w)
    round(w,4)
```

```
    plot(1:length(w),w,cex=.01,
         xlab=paste("muP =",round(muP,4)))
    text(1:length(w),w,lab,col=4,cex=.75)
  } else {
    stop("NA result")
  }
}


lab[w > 0.00001]
round(w[w > 0.00001],4)
t(w) %*% meanv
```

```
library(quadprog)
opt <- function(lab,meanv,cov_mat,isShorting,Nruns=100) {
  if(isShorting) {              #set the constraints matrix
    Amat = cbind(rep(1,D),meanv)
  } else {
    Amat = cbind(rep(1,D),meanv,diag(1,nrow=D)) #no short sales
  }
```

Let's note that, from the second case above, when *short_sales* = FALSE, when $D = 4$, for example,

$$\mathbf{A}_{mat} = \begin{bmatrix} 1 & \mu_1 & 1 & 0 & 0 & 0 \\ 1 & \mu_2 & 0 & 1 & 0 & 0 \\ 1 & \mu_3 & 0 & 0 & 1 & 0 \\ 1 & \mu_4 & 0 & 0 & 0 & 1 \end{bmatrix}$$

which is 4×6 in size where μ_i is the mean stock return for security *i*. Within the first two columns of this matrix, A_{mat}, is the right-hand side of constraint Equation 8.8.

```
  u = 1/2
  if(isShorting) {#set of Nruns possible target values
                  #for expect portfolio return
    muP = seq(.05,.60,length=Nruns)
  } else {
    muP = seq(min(meanv)+.0001,max(meanv)-.0001,
              length=Nruns) #no short sales
  }
  muP
  sdP = muP # set up storage for sdev of port rets
  weights = matrix(0,nrow=Nruns,ncol=D) #store port weights
  W <- 4
  u <- 1/2
  # find the optimal portfolios for each target expected return
  for (i in 1:length(muP))
  {
    if(isShorting) {
      bvec = c(1,muP[i])  # constraint vector
    } else {
      bvec = c(1,muP[i],rep(0,D)) #no short sales
```

```
}
#print(paste(2*cov_mat,rep(0,D),Amat,bvec))
```

Let's examine the constraints vector, *bvec*. The length is $p + 2$ or $D + meq$ where the first two positions correspond to the equality Equations 8.8 through 8.11. The remaining $p = D$ positions correspond to inequality Equations 8.13 and 8.14. When $D = 4$, *bvec* looks like below:

$$\mathbf{b}_{vec} = [\, 1 \; \mu_P \; 0 \; 0 \; 0 \; 0 \,].$$

Within the first two columns of this vector, $\mathbf{b}_{vec}$ is the right-hand side of Equation 8.9. Matrices $\mathbf{A}_{mat}$ and $\mathbf{b}_{vec}$ appear as parameters to *solve.QP()* below:

```
isPlot = TRUE

result = solve.QP(Dmat=2*cov_mat,dvec=rep(0,D),
         Amat=Amat,bvec=bvec,meq=2)
```

As stated in the usage summary in Section 8.2 above, the *meq* parameter to *solve.QP()* tells us the number of equality constraint columns in the *Amat* matrix. So $meq = 2$ in the calls to *solve.QP()* in the above code.

```
sdP[i] = sqrt(result$value)
#weights are contained in result solution
weights[i,] = result$solution

mufree = 1.3/daysPerYr # input value of risk-free int rate
sharpe =(muP-mufree)/sdP # compute Sharpe Ratios
ind = (sharpe == max(sharpe)) # Find maximum Sharpe Ratio

if(isPlot && (i%%10)==0) {
  print(i)
  par(mar=c(3.82,2.82,2.82,0.82))
  par(mfrow=c(ceiling((min(10,D+3))/W),W)) #3 extra plots
  for(d in 1:min(49,D)) {
    plot(round(weights[,d],3),xlab=lab[d])
  }
  plot(weights[i,],xlab=paste("weights,i =",i))
  plot(sharpe[1:i],xlab="sharpe",xlim=c(1,Nruns))
  plot(muP[1:i],xlab="mu",xlim=c(1,Nruns))
  Sys.sleep(5*u)
  }
 }
Sys.sleep(15*u)
round(weights[ind,],6)
```

The above section of code computes the Sharpe Ratio for all levels of *muP* and *sdP*, one for each *i*, the mean and standard deviation of the log returns for the portfolio *P*, and then displays the content of the current *weights* every 10th iteration of the

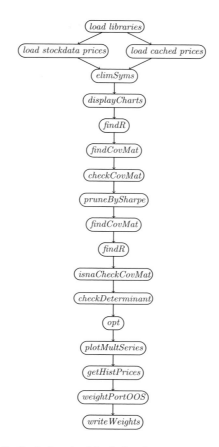

Figure 8.5   Sequencing for the Portfolio Optimizer (opt) including Pre-Processing Steps. Many of the functions have appeared in prior chapters.

```
for (i in 1:length(muP))
  w = vector(length=D)
```

loop as seen in Figure 8.6.

The remaining section of the *opt()* routine prints the weights greater than 0.001 after the main loop completes. Figure 8.5 helps us understand the internal steps. Figures 8.6 and 8.7 depict the individual weights over the time steps and how stocks cluster for volatility and mean return. Figure 8.8 depicts the final weights.

```
w[] = 0
for(d in (1:D)){
  weight = round(weights[ind,d],3)
  if(weight > .001)
    w[d] = weight
  print(paste(lab[d],weight*100,"%"))
}
for(i in 1:Nruns) if(ind[i]) print(i)
return(w)
}
```

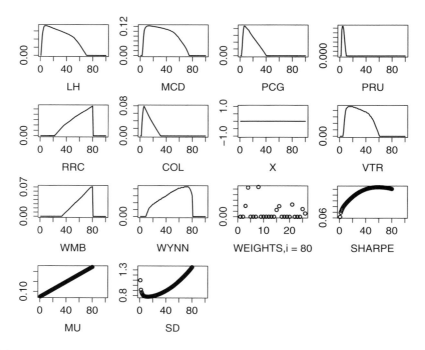

Figure 8.6   Weight values from optimizer when run is 80 percent completed ($i = 80$). All current weights are shown in the WEIGHTS plot. On the SHARPE chart one can see the peak is when $i= 60$.

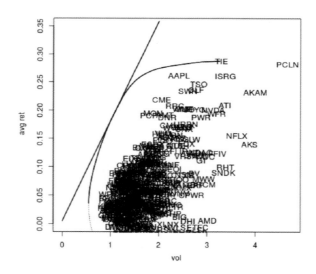

Figure 8.7   Volatility vs. mean return for entire *huge stockdata* set of ticker symbols. 24 of these rise above the Sharpe Ratio threshold.

8.6   Case Study: Surviving Stocks of the S&P 500 Index from 2003 to 2008

The nine-dimensional case was used to illustrate the charting and correlations as seen in Figure 3.3. However, using the *huge stockdata* dataset, the dimensions for our experiment can now be increased to $p = 452$ log-normal random variables in p dimensions of time series of 1,258 prices each.

The following code block will clean any bad prices, prune the candidates by Sharpe Ratio, recheck the matrices for NAs and a bad determinant, and run the optimizer for the *huge stockdata* dataset.

```
#huge case
res <- elimSyms(prices,lab,dir,isSubDir=FALSE)
prices <- res[[1]]
lab    <- res[[2]]
R <- findR(prices)
D <- dim(prices)[2]
res <- findCovMat(R)
meanv    <- res[[1]]
cov_mat  <- res[[2]]
diag_cov_mat <- res[[3]]
sdevv <- res[[4]]
checkCovMat(cov_mat)
mufree <- 0
res    <- pruneBySharpe(prices,lab,meanv,sdevv,.075)
prices <- res[[1]]
lab    <- res[[2]]
R   <- findR(prices)
res <- findCovMat(R)
meanv    <- res[[1]]
cov_mat  <- res[[2]]
diag_cov_mat <- res[[3]]
sdevv <- res[[4]]
sdevv <- isnaCheckCovMat(R)
checkDeterminant(prices,R,lab)
isShorting <- FALSE
daysPerYr <- 252
library(quadprog)
w <-opt(lab,meanv,cov_mat,isShorting)
t(cbind(lab[w > 0],w[w > 0]))
```

With these candidate stocks, the surviving candidates of the S&P 500 Index and their split-adjusted times series, the simulation was run without problems, producing a select handful of elite stocks which make a positive percentage contribution to the total portfolio. The time to complete the simulation is 22 minutes when running the R code in the RKWard environment on the Ubuntu Linux 11.10 (32-bit) operating system on an AMD V140 processor with 2GB RAM. A second configuration runs with the simulation code in the RStudio environment on Ubuntu Linux using Crouton under Google ChromeOS operating system using a Celeron 2995U processor with 2 GB RAM. The time to complete the simulation was less than one minute.

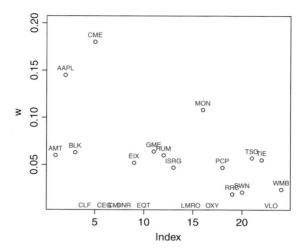

Figure 8.8   Zero and nonzero weight values for the 24 *huge stockdata* candidates. TIE and CVH may be eliminated due to mergers occurring after the dataset was sampled, as discussed in Section 4.7.

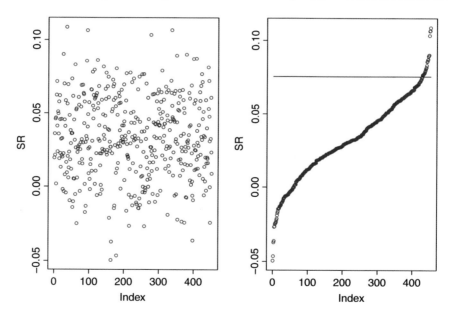

Figure 8.9   Sharpe Ratios of surviving stocks of the S&P 500 Index, January 2003 to January 2008.

The following code sequence sets up and runs the optimizer. Figure 8.9 depicts the Sharpe Ratio profile for this set of stocks.

```
#huge case
res <- elimSyms(prices,lab,dir,isSubDir=FALSE)
prices <- res[[1]]
lab    <- res[[2]]
```

```
R <- findR(prices)
D <- dim(prices)[2]
res <- findCovMat(R)
meanv      <- res[[1]]
cov_mat    <- res[[2]]
diag_cov_mat <- res[[3]]
sdevv <- res[[4]]
checkCovMat(cov_mat)
mufree <- 0
res      <- pruneBySharpe(prices,lab,meanv,sdevv,.075)
prices <- res[[1]]
lab      <- res[[2]]
R    <- findR(prices)
res <- findCovMat(R)
meanv      <- res[[1]]
cov_mat    <- res[[2]]
diag_cov_mat <- res[[3]]
sdevv <- res[[4]]
sdevv <- isnaCheckCovMat(R)
checkDeterminant(prices,R,lab)
isShorting <- FALSE
daysPerYr <- 252
library(quadprog)
w <-opt(lab,meanv,cov_mat,isShorting)
```

Here are the portfolio weights from *huge stockdata* candidate stocks:

```
> t(cbind(lab[w > 0],w[w > 0]))
       [,1]    [,2]     [,3]     [,4]     [,5]
[1,] "AMT"   "AAPL"   "BLK"    "CME"    "EIX"
[2,] "0.06"  "0.145"  "0.063"  "0.18"   "0.052"
       [,6]    [,7]    [,8]     [,9]     [,10]
[1,] "GME"    "HUM"   "ISRG"   "MON"    "PCP"
[2,] "0.064"  "0.06"  "0.047"  "0.108"  "0.047"
       [,11]   [,12]    [,13]    [,14]    [,15]
[1,] "RRC"    "SWN"    "TSO"    "TIE"    "WMB"
[2,] "0.019"  "0.021"  "0.057"  "0.055"  "0.024"
```

Via the optimizer, we go from having 26 candidates to 15 weighted stocks.

Our purpose is to report this experiment in financial analytics and present the process, experience and results for this first large group of several hundred candidate stocks. In the end, CME Group (CME) is the highest weighted stock in the simulated optimal portfolio, followed by Apple Inc. (AAPL). 94 percent of the stocks (428 of 452) are weighted at 0 and not used in the portfolio. The 24 stocks that are used are the most desirable stocks in the period of the dataset. The candidate tickers are all displayed and plotted in their standard deviation or volatility σ and average return, μ for the five year sample period in Figures 8.7 and weights are in Figure 8.8.

The optimizer, *opt()*, works with a fixed set of historical prices. Once it has completed, as time rolls forward, the analyst is, of course, very interested in how well the portfolio produces returns as new prices are revealed in the live market. After we have run the optimizer and found a recommended vector of weights, *w*, for a given set of symbols, *lab*, we can use the *get.hist.quote()* utility from the *tseries* package to call upon the Yahoo! database for price quotes. Since the number of days with quotes per year can vary a bit, there are three attempts to obtain the quotes. Any number of days can be requested as determined by the *start* and *end* parameters. Adjacent *start, startBck1* and *startFwd1* dates should be used as seen in the function *getHistPrices()*.

The utility function *weightPortOOS()* provides an out-of-sample portfolio vector *portv*, formatted as a gross return beginning at 1.0, using the *lab, len, D, w,* and *prices* provided. If the prices matrix is not provided, it will be found using *getHistPrices()*. While typically using the *w* vector of weights, it can also apply a naive $(1/D, \ldots, 1/D)$ equal vector of weights.

```
weightPortOOS <- function(lab,len,D,w,prices=NA,
                start="2013-11-29",end="2014-11-28",
                startBck1="2013-11-28",startFwd1="2013-11-27",
                isNaive=FALSE,cached=NA) {#len x D prices
  if(length(prices) == 1 && is.na(prices)) {
    obtainedPrices = getHistPrices(lab,w,len,start=start,end=end,
                startBck1=startBck1,startFwd1=startFwd1,cached=cached)
    existLen = dim(obtainedPrices)[1]
    prices = as.matrix(obtainedPrices[(existLen-len+1):existLen,])
  }
  numNonZeroWs = sum(ceiling(w))
  portv = as.vector(rep(0,len))
  D = length(w)
  for(i in 1:len) {
    for(d in 1:D) { #roll down a return line
      if(w[d] > 0)
        if(!isNaive)
          portv[i] = portv[i] +
              w[d]*prices[i,d]/prices[1,d]
        else
          portv[i] <- portv[i] +
              (1/numNonZeroWs)*prices[i,d]/prices[1,d]
    }
  }
  return(portv)
}
#unit test:
weightPortOOS(c('^GSPC'),252,1,c(1.0))
weightPortOOS(c('PCLN'),252,1,c(1.0))
weightPortOOS(c('^GSPC','PCLN'),252,2,c(.1,.9))
```

8.7   Case Study: Thousands of Candidate Stocks from 2008 to 2014

Using R's `tseries` package, the function *get.hist.quote()* can provide recent daily price quotes which are already split-adjusted. All that is needed is the ticker, the quote type

("Adj"), and the start and end dates of the requested series. The cache implemented in Section 4.9 works for our purposes with this time series. As explained in that section, there are two directories, NYSE and NASDAQ, where the tickers and their cached prices, named cached<ticker>.csv, are held.

Rather than burdening the portfolio optimizer with the mean return vector and covariance matrix for over four thousand stock time series, we choose to eliminate those which do not have desirable Sharpe Ratios. We discussed Sharpe Ratios extensively in Chapter 7. In Section 7.3, we covered how *pruneBySharpe()*, *findCovMat()*, *findR()*, *isnaCheckCovMat()*, and *checkDeterminant()* help us zero in on the final set of candidate stocks for the optimizer, *opt()*.

```
#Stocks: six years 2008 through 2014:
dir    <- "MVO6"
start <- "2008-02-14"
end    <- "2014-02-14"
isPlotInAdjCloses <- FALSE
isCacheEnabled <- TRUE
createDirs(dirs)
res <- readSubDirs(dir)
D1   <- res[[1]]
D2   <- res[[2]]
lab <- res[[3]]
len <- 1512
D <- D1 + D2
prices <- matrix(rep(NA,len*D),nrow=len,ncol=D)
library(tseries)
prices <- acquirePrices(prices,lab,len,D,D1,D2,dir,
                        start=start,end=end,isSubDir=TRUE)
```

Above we acquire the price vectors. Once available in *prices*, we can eliminate NA prices, and find the covariance matrix so that we can find the Sharpe Ratio of every security in the symbol list *lab*. After checking that matrix for anomalies, we can prune the symbol list down via the Sharpe Ratio filter, *pruneBySharpe()*. Successful checking for NAs and for bad determinants in sub-matrices allows us to proceed to the optimizer step, *opt()*.

```
res <- elimSyms(prices,lab,dir,isSubDir=TRUE)
prices <- res[[1]]
lab    <- res[[2]]
R <- findR(prices)
D <- dim(prices)[2]
res <- findCovMat(R)
meanv    <- res[[1]]
cov_mat  <- res[[2]]
diag_cov_mat <- res[[3]]
sdevv <- res[[4]]
checkCovMat(cov_mat)
mufree <- 0
res     <- pruneBySharpe(prices,lab,meanv,sdevv,.0456)
```

```
prices <- res[[1]]
lab    <- res[[2]]
R    <- findR(prices)
res <- findCovMat(R)
meanv <- res[[1]]
cov_mat <- res[[2]]
diag_cov_mat <- res[[3]]
sdevv <- res[[4]]

sdevv <- isnaCheckCovMat(R)
checkDeterminant(prices,R,lab)
isShorting <- FALSE
daysPerYr <- 252

library(quadprog)
w <- opt(lab,meanv,cov_mat,isShorting)
par(mfrow=c(1,1))
maxw = max(w+.02)
plot(w,ylim=c(0.01,maxw))
text(w,lab,cex=.55,pos=3,col=4)
t(cbind(lab[w > 0],w[w > 0]))
```

This next routine, *writeWeights()*, finds out the number of nonzero-weighted securities and writes them in descending weight order to a CSV file.

```
#Write out w and lab results to CSV file
writeWeights <- function() {
  numNonZeroWs = sum(ceiling(w))
  QPtype <- 1
  setwd(paste(homeuser,"/FinAnalytics/",dir,"/",sep=""))
  fileName = paste("resD",numNonZeroWs,"QP",toString(QPtype),
                   "Days",len,".csv",sep="")
  if(file.exists(fileName))
    stop(paste(getwd(),fileName,"already exists"))
  contents = cbind(lab,w)
  o <- order(-w)
  write.csv(contents[o,][1:numNonZeroWs,],file=fileName)
}
writeWeights()
```

The final weights are determined by the optimizer after a strict Sharpe Ratio filter was applied to a very large candidate set. Figure 8.10 depicts the situation after the call to *pruneBySharpe()*. After this step, 44 stocks remain as candidates. The final 13 nonzero-weighted stocks are shown in Figure 8.11. Figure 8.12 depicts performance in the market for a one-year period from March 6, 2014 to March 5, 2015. The optimizer was given a "cherry-picked" set of the highest Sharpe Ratio stocks to work with. Biotechnology stocks like TARO and growth stocks like DLTR are selected in the Sharpe Ratio filter based purely upon their six-year performance from February 14, 2008 to February 14, 2014. The optimizer chooses the weights with the set of constraints as discussed in Section 8.5.

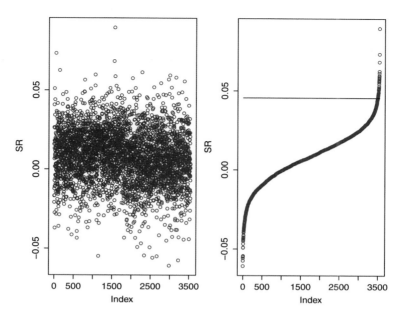

Figure 8.10   Sharpe Ratios of all four thousand-some candidates from February 2008 to February 2014. Some simple analysis tells us that it is TARO leading the pack for this time period at index 1718. The sorted Sharpe Ratios are on the right with the minimum threshold of 0.72 as the horizontal line.

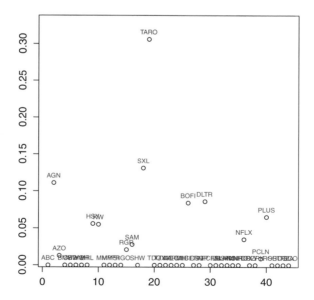

Figure 8.11   Zero and nonzero weight values for the four thousand-some candidates, using the cache files in directory MVO6. The 13 nonzero weights separate from the zero weights.

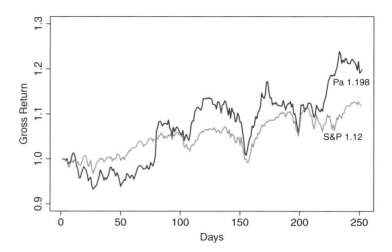

Figure 8.12   Gross return for the 13 stock portfolio weighted by the optimizer for one year from February 2014 to February 2015, marked to the actual market and out-of-sample. The biotechnology company TARO is the highest-weighted security and a surge in its price lifts the return of the portfolio to overcome the S&P 500 Index price in the first 100 days.

```
> t(cbind(lab[w > 0],w[w > 0]))
        [,1]      [,2]      [,3]      [,4]      [,5]      [,6]      [,7]
[1,]   "AGN"     "AZO"     "HSY"     "KW"      "RGR"     "SAM"     "SXL"
[2,]   "0.111"   "0.013"   "0.056"   "0.055"   "0.021"   "0.028"   "0.131"
        [,8]      [,9]      [,10]     [,11]     [,12]     [,13]
[1,]   "TARO"    "BOFI"    "DLTR"    "NFLX"    "PCLN"    "PLUS"
[2,]   "0.306"   "0.084"   "0.086"   "0.035"   "0.009"   "0.065"
```

8.8   Case Study: Exchange-Traded Funds

Like mutual funds, Exchange-Traded Funds, or ETFs, offer the investor exposure to various segments of the market. The investor can research the composition of each fund, which is a portfolio of stocks, all by itself. ETFs are gaining in popularity due to fees which are typically less than mutual funds for the same market segment. Like stocks, their price varies as the market demand changes during the day.

If we obtain a source of ETF tickers and use our R utility *get.hist.quote()* to obtain prices, then we can cache those prices for repeated runs of our Sharpe Ratio filter and the optimizer with the steps as laid out in Figure 8.5. It is interesting to compare the performance of ETFs to our earlier case studies of individual names from the NYSE and NASDAQ exchanges. Our ETF time period is three years back from the middle of 2015 due to the fact that many interesting ETFs just got their start and do not have a long history.

The controlling code for this case study is more abstract, now that all the utility functions have been defined previously. Our utility routine, *acquirePrices()* discovers whether prices for a ticker symbol have already been found on the internet and cached. If they have been found and cached, the routine will simply read the .csv cache file. The cached dataset obtained via *get.hist.quote()* is, again, a directory of files under in the *ETF* directory. The count is 1.25 million total rows in the 1,649 files for the ETF names coming over from ETFdb.com, but about 27 percent of those rows are NA because of the quote history for those names not being available or due to an error. The initial block of code will set the date range for the price history, which is of length *len*. It also sets the *dir* variable to find the caches prices and the *lab* vector of labels to the tickers found in the *ETFclean.txt* file.

```
#ETFs:
dir   <- "ETF"
start <- "2012-05-02"
end   <- "2015-05-01"
len <- 754
daysPerYr = 252
isPlotInAdjCloses <- FALSE
isCacheEnabled    <- TRUE
createDirs(dir,isSubDir=FALSE)
res <- readSubDirs(dir,isSubDir=FALSE)
D   <- res[[1]]
lab <- res[[2]]
prices <- matrix(rep(NA,len*D),nrow=len,ncol=D)
library(tseries)
prices <- acquirePrices(prices,lab,len,D,D1,D2,
                    start=start,end=end,dir,isSubDir=FALSE)
sum(is.na(prices[1,]))
price1v <- ifelse(is.na(prices[1,]),-1000,prices[1,])
plot(price1v,col=4)
```

Once executed, this block of code will obtain the three years of prices and report on missing prices. Between one-third and one-quarter of the ETF tickers do not have obtainable prices, as indicated by the following executed statements:

```
> sum(is.na(prices[1,]))
[1] 460
> price1v <- ifelse(is.na(prices[1,]),-1000,prices[1,])
> plot(price1v)
```

This is depicted in Figure 8.13 where, for display purposes, we have taken the liberty of assigning -1000 to those tickers where the first price in *prices*[1,] are NA. The *elimSyms()* utility function, called in the code sequence below, will remove those tickers with NA prices next, setting the stage for finding and checking the log return matrix, *R*, and the covariance matrix in *findCovMat()* and *checkCovMat()* and, ultimately, pruning the candidates by Sharpe Ratio. Figures 8.14 and 8.15 show the result of running *pruneBySharpe()*.

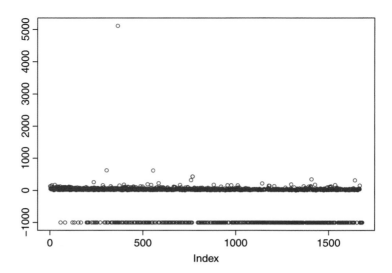

Figure 8.13   −1000 is assigned to ETF tickers with missing (NA) prices in order to depict the high density of the missing data.

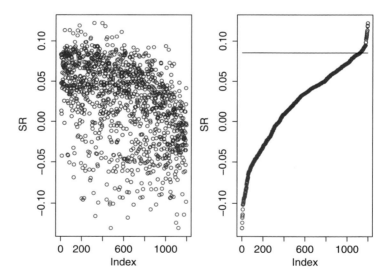

Figure 8.14   Sharpe Ratios of the 1,193 ETFs with valid price quotes on the left. The sorted Sharpe Ratios are on the right with the minimum threshold of 0.085 as the horizontal line.

```
res <- elimSyms(prices,lab,dir,isSubDir=FALSE)
prices <- res[[1]]
lab    <- res[[2]]
sum(is.na(prices[1,]))==0 #assert there are no NA prices in first row
isSplitAdjusted <- TRUE
R <- findR(prices)
```

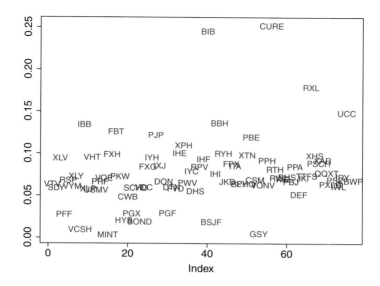

Figure 8.15   Mean log returns of the ETF candidates surviving the Sharpe Ratio filter. There are 76.

```
res <- findCovMat(R)
meanv    <- res[[1]]
cov_mat  <- res[[2]]
diag_cov_mat <- res[[3]]
sdevv <- res[[4]]
checkCovMat(cov_mat)
mufree <- 0
res      <- pruneBySharpe(prices,lab,meanv,sdevv,.085)
prices <- res[[1]]
lab      <- res[[2]]
sum(is.na(prices[1,]))
```

The remain steps leading to running the optimizer are as listed in the following code sequence. A new covariance matrix based upon the pruned candidate list is needed, as is a new *R* log return matrix.

```
R    <- findR(prices)
res <- findCovMat(R)
meanv     <- res[[1]]
cov_mat  <- res[[2]]
diag_cov_mat <- res[[3]]
sdevv <- res[[4]]
R <- findR(prices)
sdevv <- isnaCheckCovMat(R)
checkDeterminant(prices,R,lab,isSubDir=FALSE)
isShorting <- FALSE
library(quadprog)
w <- opt(lab,meanv,cov_mat,isShorting)
```

The covariance matrix needs to be checked for NA prices and for its determinant to detect the PSD problem introduced in Section 8.3. Finally, the *opt()* optimizer function is called and the plots in Figure 8.16 show that the optimal Sharpe Ratio is achieved when the iteration index ranging from 1 to 100, *i*, is equal to 21. The next code block plots the results of the optimizer run, depicted in Figure 8.17.

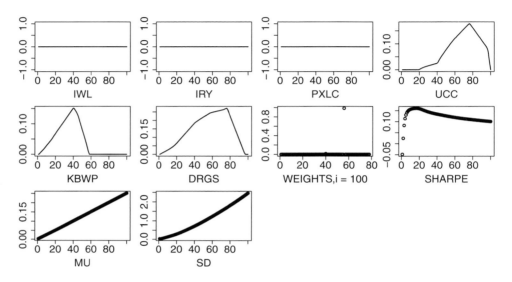

Figure 8.16   Weight values from optimizer when run is 100 percent completed (*i* = 100). All current weights are shown in the lower left-hand corner. On the SHARPE chart one can see the peak is when *i* = 21, as determined by the *ind* Boolean vector in the *opt()* routine.

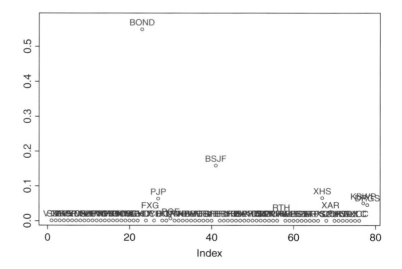

Figure 8.17   Weight values for the surviving 78 tickers of the 1,681 ETFdb.com candidates. The nonzero overlapping tickers in the lower-right corner are KBWP and DRGS.

```
portv <- weightPortOOS(lab,len,D,w,
                       start=start,end=end,cached=c("BSJF"))
sp <- weightPortOOS(c('^GSPC'),len=len,1,c(1.0),
                    prices=NA,start=start,end=end)
par(mfrow=c(1,1))
plot(meanv,col=4,cex=0)
text(meanv,lab,cex=1,col=4)

plot(portv,type="l",ylim=c(.5,1.9),
     main="",xlab="days")
lines(sp,type="l",col="green")
par(mfrow=c(1,1))
maxw = max(w+.025)
plot(w,ylim=c(0.01,maxw),col=4)
text(w,lab,cex=1,pos=3,col=4)
writeWeights()
```

To see the tickers and their weights which were favored by the optimizer, we can write a simple R expression:

```
> t(cbind(lab[w > 0],w[w > 0]))
      [,1]     [,2]     [,3]     [,4]     [,5]     [,6]
[1,] "BOND"   "FXG"    "PJP"    "PGF"    "BSJF"   "PPH"
[2,] "0.565"  "0.026"  "0.079"  "0.005"  "0.141"  "0.006"
      [,7]     [,8]     [,9]     [,10]    [,11]
[1,] "RTH"    "XHS"    "XAR"    "UCC"    "KBWP"
[2,] "0.018"  "0.069"  "0.029"  "0.003"  "0.058"
```

We see the BOND ticker being quite dominant at 56.5 percent and suspect that the optimizer may have been seduced into putting all it eggs into that basket by the data. A good way to see what is going on is to bring back our visualization function, *plotMultSeries()*, which was introduced in Figure 4.9 and listed in Section 4.8. Putting together a brief exploratory code block, we have

```
displayCharts(prices,lab,nrow=3,ncol=4,sleepSecs=2)
interestingIdxs <- c(1,2,11,23,27,41)
p <- length(interestingIdxs)
lab[interestingIdxs]
meanv[interestingIdxs]
sdevv[interestingIdxs]
justLab <- c(lab[interestingIdxs],'^GSPC')
sAndPprices <- getHistPrices(c('^GSPC'),c(1.0),len,
                             start=start,end=end)
justPrices <- cbind(prices[,interestingIdxs],sAndPprices)
p <- p + 1
plotMultSeries(justPrices,justLab,rep(1/p,p),p,ylim=c(.9,2.8))
```

the output of which is displayed in Figure 8.18 and in the output block below. In the figure, BOND and BSJF are shown at the bottom, and we can see in the R output below that separating the mean and standard deviation, the components of the Sharpe Ratio,

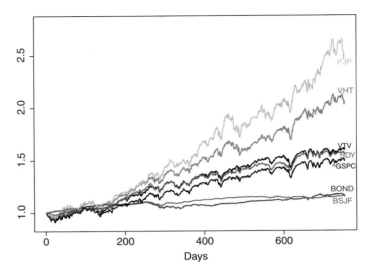

Figure 8.18   For return, we prefer the ETFs plotted in the top four price series which have more bullish and not as smooth charts as compared to our two optimizer-favored ETFs, BOND and BSJF, which appear as the bottom price series. The period is May 2012 to May 2015.

reveals that BOND and BSJF have a much lower mean return, less than 2 percent for three years, which disqualifies them from candidacy from a simply common-sense rule of thumb. Figure 8.18 makes us believe that they got into the recommended portfolio on their good "defense," low volatility, rather than their weak "offense."

```
> lab[interestingIdxs]
[1] "VTV"  "SDY"  "VHT"  "BOND" "PJP"  "BSJF"
> meanv[interestingIdxs]
[1] 0.06314663 0.05890903 0.09524277 0.01882325 0.12179788 0.01863257
> sdevv[interestingIdxs]
[1] 0.7362232 0.6921851 0.8373464 0.2192034 1.0193671 0.1786221
```

Figure 8.19 shows us that the "optimized" portfolio performance does not beat the benchmark in sample. With BOND at over 50 percent of the portfolio and a very low return, the portfolio will not beat the S&P 500 Index. This analysis shows us how much we must pay attention to the data. When moving to a new type of dataset, ETFs, we cannot simply turn the algorithmic crank and expect to get an optimized portfolio in the sense we are expecting! Exchange-Traded Funds present different historical time series than our stocks did.

We can prepend these names to the *badsyms.txt* file to exclude them from candidacy. Doing this reveals that VCSH is also in this camp of low return with low volatility where the optimizer favors that, so they are prepended to that file as well.

With stocks, the prices are subject to noisy and idocratic nature of the live equities market. An ETF, being a portfolio, can have a rather smooth price series. Our approach is based on the Sharpe Ratio for both the filtering threshold step and the optimization

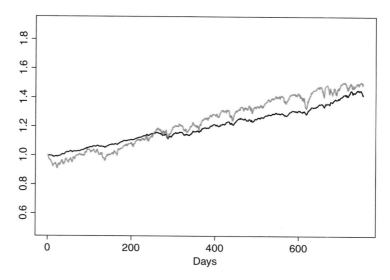

Figure 8.19   Portfolio gross return of ETF portfolio which (includes BOND and BSJF) plotted against the S&P 500 Index. The ETF portfolio has a lower gross return and appears in a darker color. The period is May 2012 to May 2015.

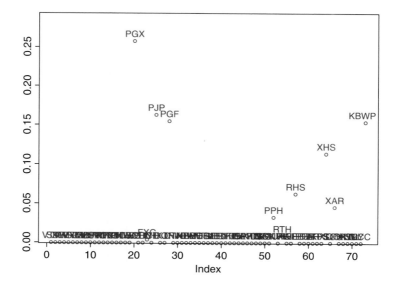

Figure 8.20   These are weight values after eliminating the four smoothest, low return and low volatility ETF tickers. This revised portfolio is more balanced.

step criterion. So ETFs with very low volatility can sneak by with correspondingly low mean return, which is not exactly desired in a bullish strategy. Using the *elimSyms()* function to exclude BOND, BSJF, and VCSH from being selected, we have the revised weights depicted in Figure 8.20, where ten of the now 73 candidates with high Sharpe Ratios are favored with a nonzero weight. This result is reasonably balanced. Figure 8.21

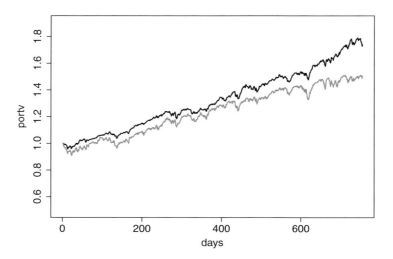

Figure 8.21   Revised ETF portfolio compared to the S&P 500 Index. The ETF portfolio is the upper line. The period is May 2012 to May 2015.

compares the performance of the ten ETF portfolio to the S&P 500 Index for the same time period. The numeric new portfolio weights per ticker appear below.

```
> t(cbind(lab[w > 0],w[w > 0]))
       [,1]     [,2]     [,3]     [,4]     [,5]
[1,]  "PGX"    "FXG"    "PJP"    "PGF"    "PPH"
[2,]  "0.258"  "0.004"  "0.163"  "0.155"  "0.033"
       [,6]     [,7]     [,8]     [,9]     [,10]
[1,]  "RTH"    "RHS"    "XHS"    "XAR"    "KBWP"
[2,]  "0.009"  "0.063"  "0.114"  "0.046"  "0.154"
```

From Figure 8.21 we can see that the revised portfolio beats the S&P 500 Index. Due to lack of historical prices for many ETFs, we only measure the performance in the sample.

```
> portv[len]
[1] 1.704891
> sp[len]
[1] 1.503441
> portv[len]-sp[len]
[1] 0.2014501
```

Measuring the difference in return over the three-year period reveals that the revised ETF portfolio return is 23.4 percent more than the benchmark.

We could regard the removal of poor-performing securities BOND, BSJF, and VCSH as over-fitting or tampering with rules. Any time we have undesirable results, however, we need to examine the rules to see if they still make sense. ETFs are a "different animal" from our individual names from before. Our Sharpe ratio filter, as implemented in *pruneBySharpe()*, apparently is not enough to work well with ETF candidates. We never screened the candidates for mean log return. So in the exercises, we propose trying this out with a new utility function, *pruneByMean()*.

So, in summary, when the price data is properly preprocessed, this iterative development process described here, including the QP algorithm, is an effective data mining approach. Consider that many data mining algorithms, including PageRank, created by Sergey Brin and Larry Page (Brin and Page, 1998), and supervised machine learning algorithms, including Classification and Regression Trees (CART) (Breiman, Friedman, Olshen, and Stone, 1984), are optimization algorithms. The goal of CART and related techniques is to minimize the difference between the values of the predicted response variables and the values of the actual response variables. Quadratic Programming is an optimization algorithm as well, so, due to similarity, can be considered a form of data mining. It can be applied to hundreds of candidate stocks with the dataset and, using the rules of Markowitz selection, the output is a select few best performers. With less advanced automation technology, it would be nearly impossible to review 452 stock charts and 568,616 adjusted closing prices and predict how to optimally weight the entries of the portfolio. But this high-dimensional optimization algorithm, as implemented with R packages and custom R code, makes the analysis feasible. In a related work to this chapter, an interesting set of results comes from a project with a variation to the initial Sharpe Ratio qualification step and individual limits on the optimizer weights (Benedict, Brewer, and Haddad, 2015).

8.9   Exercises

8.1. Examine the code of section 8.1. Write a one line R expression that evaluates to the value of w_d for the best shape ratio of the (w_d, w_e) portfolio.

For each case, below, the objective is to obtain a resulting weight file, prefixed by *res*, by piecing together the code sequence of Figure 8.5 and running it to completion. The optimizer, *opt()*, is the key step in the process.

8.2. Optimizing for Surviving Stocks of the S&P 500 Index
   Create a sub-directory called *huge* under the *FinAnaytics* directory on your computer if one does not already exist. This directory is used when the resulting weight file needs to be emitted. For the case that we use the R *huge* package, all the ticker symbols and prices are already loaded when the package is loaded using: library(huge). *stockdata* is the data frame for computing D and *len* and containing the necessary vectors: *prices* and *lab*. Locate in the book the code which loads these elements assuming *isHugeData* == TRUE. There is no need to create sub-directories or cache files. However, the prices are supplied unadjusted for stock splits. Use the code sequence to call *splitAdjust()* via the call to *findR()* (which computes log returns), making sure that *isSplitAdjusted* is set to FALSE beforehand, to adjust the prices.

8.3. Optimizing for Thousands of Candidate Stocks from 2008 to 2014

Create a sub-directory called *MVO6* under the *FinAnalytics* directory on your computer if one does not already exist. Under the *huge* directory, create *NYSE* and *NASDAQ* sub-directories. Locate the *NYSEclean.txt* and *NASDAQclean.txt* files on the book web site. Place those files into the *NYSE* and *NASDAQ* sub-directories, respectively. Use the code in Chapter 8 to download from the internet and create cache files or, if this was already done, read from cache files to acquire prices for the securities in the files *NYSEclean.txt* and *NASDAQclean.txt*. There should be approximately 2,200 symbols in each of these files. Use start <- "2008-02-14"; end <- "2014-02-14".

8.4. Optimizing for Exchange-Traded Funds

Create a sub-directory called *ETF* under the *FinAnalytics* directory if one does not already exist. In the case of ETFs there is no need for sub-directories under the *ETF* directory. Obtain the *ETFclean.txt* ticker symbol file from the book web site. There should be 1,681 symbols in the file. Place the *ETFclean.txt* file into the *ETF* directory. Use start <- "2012-05-02"; end <- "2015-05-01".

(a) Run the initialization code, which comprises everything after the #ETFs: comment, appearing in section 8.8 or from the book web site. Run the optimizer and display your weights of each ticker in the resulting weighted portfolio.

(b) As discussed in Section 8.8, before pruning by Sharpe ratio, write a function called *pruneByMean(prices,lab,meanv,threshMean)* which prunes the security candidate list based upon a mean log return threshold. Include *pruneByMean()* in the screening process prior to *pruneBySharpe()* choosing your own threshold to qualify a reasonable number of candidates. Perform another optimizer run in the *ETF* directory. Report the weights of each ticker in the resulting portfolio.

8.5. Optimizing for Best Income Statement Sharpe Ratio Stocks (Difficult)

Refer to Chapter 7's four categories (Income Growth, Net; Total Revenue Growth; Gross Profit Growth; Diluted Normalized Earning per Share Growth) and perform an optimizer run after setting up a two-level directory called *TopISSR* (with *NYSE* and *NASDAQ* sub-directories below it). This is an entirely new type of run for the optimizer, so original new code will be necessary. It should be based upon the same process, but use the Income Statement Sharpe Ratio (ISSR) rather than *pruneBySharpe()*. You can call your new selection function *pruneByISSR()*. What are the necessary arguments to *pruneByISSR()*? Report on what you expect your return to be for the portfolio, in-sample and out-of-sample. Chapter 8 has a useful function, *weightPortOOS()*, to help answer this question; use this function to obtain prices for out-of-sample runs. Use start <- "2011-02-09"; end <- "2015-02-09".

9   Cluster Analysis

Associations can be formed when like entities are grouped together into clusters. In high schools, during teenage learning years, clusters of the personalities are formed with students being classified into the "brains," the "jocks," and the "artists," for example. This personality model is simple in order to keep learning about the characteristics limited and tractable. As one grows past high school, one realizes just how simple the classification was.

Clustering is also useful for computer programs and is used extensively in the machine learning domain. Experiments have been reported that have attempted using Support Vector Machines (SVM) to analyze price and volume patterns in order to determine market direction as well as using undirected graphs to represent the dependence and clustering of hundreds of equity securities (as random variables) based upon co-movement (Ullrich, Seese, and Chalup, 2007; Fletcher, 2012; Fletcher, Hussain, and Shawe-Taylor, 2010).

Unlike the SVM studies, which intend to learn trading signals from the data, the undirected graph studies involve a less ambitious goal. Undirected graphs of mutually stochastically dependent market random variables are learned from time series training data from the market for each security, captured in the same trading time window. The graph contains an edge from a vertex, representing a security, to another edge, when sufficient co-movement exists.

When looking at the machine-learned structures as undirected graphs, the edges between vertices appear surprisingly close to our market intuition in that stocks in the same sector often move similarly.

9.1   K-Means Clustering

K-means aims to partition m observations $(x_1, \ldots, x_n)$, where each observation is a p-dimensional real vector, into $k \leq p$ cluster sets $\{\mathbf{C}_1, \ldots, \mathbf{C}_k\}$ with means $\{\bar{\mathbf{m}}_1, \ldots, \bar{\mathbf{m}}_k\}$, such that

$$\underset{\mathbf{C}}{\operatorname{argmin}} \sum_{i=1}^{k} \sum_{\mathbf{x} \in \mathbf{C}_i} ||\mathbf{x} - \bar{\mathbf{m}}_i||^2, \tag{9.1}$$

where $\bar{\mathbf{m}}_i$ is the mean of the points in $\mathbf{C}_i$ (MacQueen, 1967; Ledolter, 2013).

In the case of our portfolio of Section 8.5, we have p security price time series of length N observations, S of size $N \times p$, where $N = d \times y$ and $y = 6$ is the number of observed years and d is the number of trading days per year, typically 252. We will partition our y year time series into annual sample means $\bar{M}_{l,j}$ of log returns into a $6 \times p$ matrix $\bar{\mathbf{M}}$:

$$\bar{\mathbf{M}} = \begin{bmatrix} \bar{M}_{1,1} & \bar{M}_{1,2} & \dots & \bar{M}_{1,p} \\ \bar{M}_{2,1} & \bar{M}_{2,2} & \dots & \bar{M}_{2,p} \\ \bar{M}_{3,1} & \bar{M}_{3,2} & \dots & \bar{M}_{3,p} \\ \bar{M}_{4,1} & \bar{M}_{4,2} & \dots & \bar{M}_{4,p} \\ \bar{M}_{5,1} & \bar{M}_{5,2} & \dots & \bar{M}_{5,p} \\ \bar{M}_{6,1} & \bar{M}_{6,2} & \dots & \bar{M}_{6,p} \end{bmatrix}. \tag{9.2}$$

$\bar{\mathbf{M}}$ summarizes the matrix R where, once again, we assume that R contains log returns from price series $R_{i,j} = ln(S_{i,j}/S_{i-1,j})$. The $y \times p$ matrix $\bar{\mathbf{M}} = (\bar{M}_1, \dots, \bar{M}_p)$ and

$$\bar{M}_{l,j} = \frac{1}{d-1} \sum_{i=2+(l-1)\times d}^{l \times d} ln(S_{i,j}/S_{i-1,j}) = \frac{1}{d-1} \sum_{i=2+(l-1)\times d}^{l \times d} R_{i,j}. \tag{9.3}$$

26 stocks were selected by using historical prices from 2003 to 2008. Let's see how they perform out-of-sample moving time forward into the 2008 to 2014 markets. This upcoming function, *findRecentHugePrices()* will read in our portfolio ticker symbols and their respective weights from a file which was the output of an in-sample simulation using *opt()* from Chapter 8, and then look up more recent out-of-sample prices in the FinAnalytics/MVO6 directory in the user file system.

```
daysPerYr = 252
D <- NA

findRecentHugePrices <- function(dir,portFile) {
  #Take portfolio from portFile and find recent prices in cache.
  #Side effects Lab, W, D, len
  setwd(paste(homeuser,"/FinAnalytics/",dir,"/",sep=""))
  df   <- read.csv(portFile)
  lab <<- df[,2] #lab[2] is no longer expected to be FBMI
  w   <<- df[,3]
  indw <- (w > 0)
  lab  <- lab[indw]
  w    <- w[indw]
  D    <- length(lab)
  len <<- daysPerYr*6
  prices = matrix(rep(NA,len*D),nrow=len,ncol=D)
  #We have cache 2008 to 2014 prices in MVO6 dir
  dir = 'MVO6'
  d = 1
  for(l in lab) {
    fileName = paste('cached',l,'.csv',sep='')
    for(subdir in c('NYSE','NASDAQ')) {
      setwd(paste(homeuser,"/FinAnalytics/",dir,'/',
                  subdir,sep=''))
      if(file.exists(fileName))
        break
    }
```

```
    print(fileName)
    prices[,d] = read.csv(fileName,header=TRUE,
                              sep='')[,1]
    d = d + 1
  }
  #Validation of prices exist
  for(d in 1:D)
    if(is.na(prices[1,d]))
      stop(lab[d])

  plotMultSeries(prices,lab,w,D,ylim=c(.7,13))
  return(prices)
}
#This fails:
prices <- findRecentHugePrices('huge','resD26QP1Days1258.csv')
#This fails:
prices <- findRecentHugePrices('huge','resD25Days1258woTIE.csv')
#success:
prices <- findRecentHugePrices('huge','rebalresD24Days1258.csv')
R <- findR(prices)
```

This function reaches into the two sub-directories for the cached prices for 2008 to 2014 and attempts to find the prices for the portfolio securities. The last three executable lines are three attempts. Upon running them, we find that the first encounters problems:

```
...
[1] "cachedTSO.csv"
[1] "cachedGME.csv"
[1] "cachedTIE.csv"
 Error in file(file, "rt") :...
   cannot open file 'cachedTIE.csv':...
>
```

We discover after some searching on the internet that Titanium Metals Corp (NYSE: TIE) was purchased by Precision Castparts Corp (NYSE: PCP) in 2013. So we modify the file to remove TIE and rerun *findRecentHugePrices()* with the new file named *resD25Days1258woTIE.csv* to see if it will succeed. It does not succeed.

```
> prices <- findRecentHugePrices('resD25Days1258woTIE.csv')
...
[1] "cachedRAI.csv"
[1] "cachedWYNN.csv"
[1] "cachedCVH.csv"
 Error in file(file, "rt") :...
   cannot open file 'cachedCVH.csv':...
>
```

Even though CVH is in our portfolio, no cache file exists for it. Prices for our date range are not fully available for TIE and CVH. See Section 4.7 for more detail on these merger events. Since it is a small percentage of our portfolio, we decide to use the

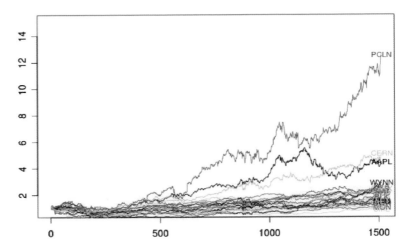

Figure 9.1   Plot of the six years of prices, 2008 to 2014, for the updated portfolio, out-of-sample, where $p = 24$ now. TIE and CVH have been eliminated.

utility function *adjustForMergers()*, provided in Chapter 4, to rebalance our portfolio, removing TIE and CVH, among $p = 24$ stocks now. Our third attempt, using *rebalresD24Days1258.csv*, is successful. Here are dimensions of the key market data matrix:

```
> dim(prices)
[1] 1512    24
```

Since *findRecentHugePrices()* calls *plotMultSeries()* let's take the opportunity to look at the output it produces, shown in Figure 9.1. Our first observation is that PCLN has an amazing chart over this time period. AAPL, CERN, and WYNN have good price appreciation as well.

For the first round of k-means clustering, we look exclusively at the annual mean of the log return. To fit the k-means approach we take the transpose of $\bar{\mathbf{M}}$, which is $\bar{\mathbf{M}}^T$, a 24×6 matrix. This provides the $m = 6$ vectors $(x_1, x_2, x_3, x_4, x_5, x_6)$ for the k-means algorithm. Cases $k = 2, 3, 4, 5$ are considered. The following two code segments assume that there are $m = 6$ years of $p = 24$ stocks prices, the *prices[]* matrix of size 1512×24. Firstly, we have the function *findMeanForYrs* which coalesces the log returns according to Formula 7.3.

```
library(stats)
#K-means clustering
findMeanForYrs <- function(prices) {
  D <- dim(prices)[2]
  R <- findR(prices)
  meanLogRet <- matrix(nrow=6,ncol=D)
  for(j in 1:D) { #security j
    R[,j] = 100*diff(log(prices[,j]))
    for(l in 1:6) { #year l
      meanLogRet[l,j] = 1/(daysPerYr-1)*
        sum(R[(2+(l-1)*daysPerYr-1):(l*daysPerYr-1),j])
    }
```

```
    }
    meanLogRet
}
meanLogRet <- findMeanForYrs(prices)
```

Now the straight line code sequence below will augment the *meanLogRet* matrix with proper columns and row names and run the R stats package *kmeans()* function four times.

```
meanLogRet <- findMeanForYrs(prices)
colnames(meanLogRet) <- lab
rownames(meanLogRet) <- c(2008,2009,2010,
                          2011,2012,2013)
round(meanLogRet[,1:4],4)    #sample first 4
meanLogRetT = t(meanLogRet)

round(meanLogRetT[1:4,],2)
```

In the output below, we can see the first five rows of $\bar{\mathbf{M}}^T$ matrix and the results of running the *kmeans()* R function.

```
> round(meanLogRetT[1:4,],2)
      2008  2009 2010  2011  2012 2013
CME  -0.39  0.18 0.02 -0.01  0.03 0.13
AAPL -0.10  0.28 0.22  0.13 -0.03 0.08
MON  -0.14 -0.01 0.00  0.02  0.12 0.03
MCD   0.02  0.06 0.08  0.12 -0.01 0.02
```

In the first column above we can certainly see the low log returns for the first three stocks. Our code sequence below goes from $k = 2$ to $k = 5$ with the output sorted by the cluster number:

```
> set.seed(1) #This kmeans call is based upon mean log ret by year
> grpMeanLogRet2 <- kmeans(meanLogRetT, centers=2, nstart=10)
> sort(grpMeanLogRet2$cluster)
CME AAPL  PCP  BLK ISRG  WMB WYNN CERN PCLN  MON  MCD  TSO  GME
  1    1    1    1    1    1    1    1    1    2    2    2    2
 LH  BCR  AMT  HUM  EIX  SWN ESRX  RRC  DVA  RAI  AET
  2    2    2    2    2    2    2    2    2    2    2
> grpMeanLogRet3 <- kmeans(meanLogRetT, centers=3, nstart=10)
> sort(grpMeanLogRet3$cluster)
CME ISRG  WMB WYNN  MON  MCD  TSO  GME   LH  BCR  HUM  EIX  SWN
  1    1    1    1    2    2    2    2    2    2    2    2    2
RRC  DVA  AET AAPL  PCP  AMT  BLK ESRX  RAI CERN PCLN
  2    2    2    3    3    3    3    3    3    3    3
> grpMeanLogRet4 <- kmeans(meanLogRetT, centers=4, nstart=10)
> sort(grpMeanLogRet4$cluster)
MON  MCD  GME   LH  BCR  AMT  HUM  EIX  SWN ESRX  RRC  DVA  RAI
  1    1    1    1    1    1    1    1    1    1    1    1    1
AET  CME  PCP  BLK ISRG  WMB WYNN  TSO AAPL CERN PCLN
  1    2    2    2    2    2    2    3    4    4    4
```

Below are the accumulated log returns for AAPL and PCLN. We can understand how PCLN and AAPL would appear in the same cluster above, number 4, when we see the cumulative log returns for the five years which are quite high by stock market standards, 59 percent and 99 percent!

```
> round(meanLogRetT[match('AAPL',lab),],2)
 2008  2009  2010  2011  2012  2013
-0.10  0.28  0.22  0.13 -0.03  0.08
> sum(meanLogRetT[match('AAPL',lab),])
[1] 0.5860594
> round(meanLogRetT[match('PCLN',lab),],2)
 2008  2009  2010  2011  2012  2013
-0.14  0.42  0.31  0.09  0.08  0.24
> sum(meanLogRetT[match('PCLN',lab),])
[1] 0.9943923
```

Below is the five-means resulting grouping.

```
> grpMeanLogRet5 <- kmeans(meanLogRetT, centers=5, nstart=10)
> sort(grpMeanLogRet5$cluster)
ISRG  CME  WMB WYNN  TSO AAPL  PCP  AMT  BLK ESRX  RAI CERN PCLN
   1    2    2    2    3    4    4    4    4    4    4    4    4
 MON  MCD  GME   LH  BCR  HUM  EIX  SWN  RRC  DVA  AET
   5    5    5    5    5    5    5    5    5    5    5
```

Now we consider the log returns of the entire time series in terms of the mean and standard deviation. The standard deviation can be found from the diagonal entries of the covariance matrix. Once the data frame is put together, *plot()* and *text()* display the five clusters as in Figure 9.2 where securities closer to the upper left-hand corner have a better Sharpe Ratio. All of these securities have a Sharpe Ratio for this sample of less than 1.

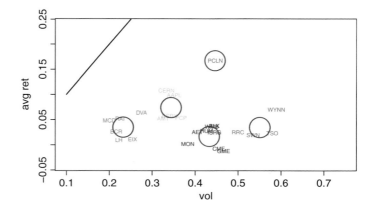

Figure 9.2   Five clusters based upon mean and standard deviation of six-year log returns.

```
#Now use entire time series mean and sd
R <- findR(prices)
cov_mat = cov(R/100)
mean_vect = apply(R,2,mean)
diag_cov_mat = diag(cov_mat)
sd_vect = sqrt(diag_cov_mat)*sqrt(daysPerYr)

meanLogRetVolByStockDF <-
    data.frame(ticker=colnames(meanLogRet),
    mean=mean_vect, sdev=sd_vect)

meanLogRetVolByStockDF[1:5,]
set.seed(1) #This kmeans call is based on mean log ret and vol
grpMeanLogRetVol <-
    kmeans(meanLogRetVolByStockDF[,c("mean","sdev")],
    centers=5, nstart=10)
o = order(grpMeanLogRetVol$cluster)
data.frame(meanLogRetVolByStockDF$ticker[o],
           grpMeanLogRetVol$cluster[o])
```

Three plot statements are required to spot the positions, place the text and mark the circle around the means.

```
par(mfrow=c(1,1))
plotMeans <- function(x,y,tickers,cluster,
                      centers) {
  par(mar=c(4,4,2.82,2.82))
  plot(x,y,type='n',
       xlim=c(0.1,.75),ylim=c(-.04,.24),
       ylab="avg ret",xlab="vol")
  text(x,y,labels=tickers,
       col=(cluster+1),cex=.55)
  points(centers[,2],centers[,1],cex=6.0,col=4)
  lines(x=c(.1,.25),y=c(.1,.25))
}
plotMeans(meanLogRetVolByStockDF$sdev,
          meanLogRetVolByStockDF$mean,
          meanLogRetVolByStockDF$ticker,
          grpMeanLogRetVol$cluster,
          grpMeanLogRetVol$centers)
```

Figure 9.1 is organized as if it came from a mean-variance analysis like those of Chapter 8. The desired location to reside in the plot is the upper-left corner where return is high and risk is low. Of course that is the ideal stock characteristic. None of the involved securities appears in that quadrant. The ticker, MCD, appears to be the closest to the 45-degree line.

Clustering via k-means groups similar securities based upon their return and volatility. It is sometimes the case that once a portfolio is suggested, particular securities should not be purchased due to already existing positions or for compliance reasons.

Alternative securities which approximate the originate candidate's price behavior can be found.

9.2   Dissecting the K-Means Algorithm

Clustering like items with the k-means algorithm is a form of optimization: finding the placement of the means such that the total distance between the clustered items and the means is minimal. The algorithm originally was published as a FORTRAN program in 1979 by Hartigan and Wong (1979). The mystery behind the k-means algorithm is revealed in the detailed treatment by Ledolter (2013).

We first discuss the distance measure. ℓ_2 distance is the direct route "as the crow flies" which involves computing the diagonal of a right triangle. In the problems of these sections, the items are two-dimensional: means are for one dimension and standard deviation for the other. From the Pythagorean Theorem, we know that

$$d(x_1, x_2) = \sqrt{x_1^2 + x_2^2}$$

and the code for this is below.

```
l2dist <- function(x,y) {
    sqrt((x[1]-y[1])^2 + (x[2]-y[2])^ 2)
}
#unit test
l2dist(c(3,4),c(0,0)) == 5
```

There is a simple unit test case of the 3, 4, 5 right triangle after the *l2dist()* function which should evaluate to TRUE.

There are three basic steps to the algorithm. The iteration time step is t.

- Initialization: Randomly choose k items as cluster means themselves, then proceed to the update step for the first iteration.
- Assignment: Iterate through each item $\mathbf{x}_i$ and assign it to a cluster $\mathbf{C}_j(t)$ with the closest mean $\bar{\mathbf{m}}_j$ so that the distance is minimized.

$$\mathbf{C}_j(t) = \left\{ \mathbf{x}_i : |\mathbf{x}_i - \bar{\mathbf{m}}_j(t)| \leq |\mathbf{x}_i - \bar{\mathbf{m}}_{j*}(t)| \ for \ all \ j* \in \{1, \ldots, k\} \right\}. \quad (9.4)$$

- Update: From the clusters that have been created in the assignment step, calculate k new means as the centroids of the items in each cluster. The summation and divisor is simply the arithmetic mean.

$$\bar{\mathbf{m}}_j(t+1) = \frac{\sum_{\mathbf{x}_j \in \mathbf{C}_j(t)} \mathbf{x}_i}{|\mathbf{C}_j(t)|}. \quad (9.5)$$

Now we see the R code for these three main steps as initial setup of p, the number of securities, and k, the number of clusters, the data frame which contains the means and standard deviation of the log returns for the stocks.

```
p = dim(meanLogRetVolByStockDF)[1]
k = 5
logRetVolWMeanDistDF <- data.frame(
  as.character(meanLogRetVolByStockDF[,1]),
  meanLogRetVolByStockDF[,2],
  meanLogRetVolByStockDF[,3],
  rep(0,p))
colnames(logRetVolWMeanDistDF) <-
  c("ticker","mean","sdev","jthMeanIdx")
logRetVolWMeanDistDF
```

The initialization occurs firstly, seen below. The initial cluster means are k randomly chosen items from the set of p items $x_1, \ldots, x_p$ using *sample()*.

```
#Initial: Randomly choose k units as cluster means first
set.seed(46510)
idxs <- sample(1:p, k)
clusterMeans <- matrix(
  c(meanLogRetVolByStockDF[idxs,2],
    meanLogRetVolByStockDF[idxs,3],
    idxs),nrow=5,ncol=3)
clusterMeans
newStepClusterMeans <- matrix(clusterMeans,
                    nrow=5,ncol=3) #clone initially
par(mfrow=c(4,1))
```

Then we introduce our function, *kmeansSteps()*, which contains our iterative steps. For our purposes with our current stock example, four iterations is enough, but, in general, it is best to loop until convergence is detected. We exclude (via **stop**) the case when initialization does not assign any items to one of the k clusters for simplicity in this introductory-level code block.

```
kmeansSteps <- function() {
  for(t in 1:4) {
    if(sum(is.na(clusterMeans)) > 1) stop
```

Below is the assignment step, described above in Formula 9.4. Loop through all p securities, consider the distance $d()$ to each of the k means and record the distance in *clusterMeans*. We do this on every step except for when $t = 1$.

```
  #Assignment step:
  if(t > 1)
    for(i in 1:p) {#find closest mean for i-th ticker
      min_l2dist <- 1e6 #start off w/infinity
      for(j in 1:k) {
        x1 <- logRetVolWMeanDistDF[i,2]
        x2 <- logRetVolWMeanDistDF[i,3]
        x  <- c(x1,x2)
        m  <- clusterMeans[j,1:2]
```

```
        l2dist_x_m <- l2dist(x,m)
        if(l2dist_x_m <= min_l2dist) {
          min_l2dist <- l2dist_x_m
          best_j      <- j
        }
      }
      logRetVolWMeanDistDF[i,4] <- best_j
    }
  else
    logRetVolWMeanDistDF[,4] <- sample(1:k, p, replace=TRUE)
  print(t(logRetVolWMeanDistDF[,c(1,4)]))
```

The update step appears below. The x_1 and x_2 coordinate cluster means are found for all $j \leq k$ clusters and then placed into the appropriate matrix.

```
#Update step:
for(j in 1:k) {
  print(paste("update step j =",j))
  x1ClusterMean <- mean(
    logRetVolWMeanDistDF[logRetVolWMeanDistDF$jthMeanIdx==j,2])
  x2ClusterMean <- mean(
    logRetVolWMeanDistDF[logRetVolWMeanDistDF$jthMeanIdx==j,3])
  newStepClusterMeans[j,1:2] <-
    c(x1ClusterMean,x2ClusterMean)
  newStepClusterMeans[j,3] <- TRUE #not needed now
}
```

The next block of instructions keep the user informed about the status of the iteration. The third and fourth statement display the former and new cluster means where the former is a faint gray color (col=8). Finally we have in the *clusterMeans* and *newClusterMeans* two matrices which could be compared with the small threshold to find out if convergence has occurred.

```
  print(newStepClusterMeans)
  plotMeans(logRetVolWMeanDistDF$sdev,
            logRetVolWMeanDistDF$mean,
            logRetVolWMeanDistDF$ticker,
            logRetVolWMeanDistDF$jthMeanIdx,
            newStepClusterMeans)
  points(clusterMeans[,1]~
          clusterMeans[,2],cex=9,col=8)
  points(newStepClusterMeans[,1]~
          newStepClusterMeans[,2],cex=9,col=9)
  clusterMeans <- newStepClusterMeans
  }
}
kmeansSteps()
```

Figure 9.3 depicts the time sequence of movements of the clusters as they are refined by the algorithm. In our Figure 9.2, we depicted the cluster as a circle. In Figure 9.3 we continue this, but the code appearing above will encircle those circles with larger circles

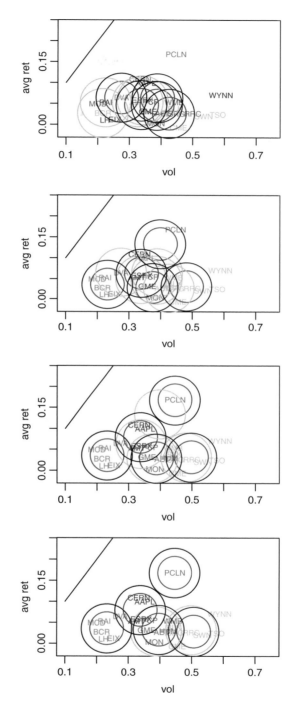

Figure 9.3   Movement of the cluster means for each step of our version of the k-means algorithm. The first plot shows initial random assignment and confusion. This is followed by three corrective steps. Light circles show former positions.

to highlight spreading out from their initial configuration to the final configuration. The number of required iterations before the k cluster means, $\bar{\mathbf{m}}_j(t)$, and k new cluster means, $\bar{\mathbf{m}}_j(t+1)$, are close enough to stop varies, depending on k and p.

Clustering securities in the volatility and average return dimensions groups securities with similar market behavior together. Investment preferences can be personal choices. If one likes the market behavior of the stock MON, then one may also be interested in similar behaving stocks in the same k-means cluster. K-means clustering provides recommendations of alternative securities like a recommender system would (Bystrom, 2013).

Having focused on the p dimensional case of clustering with respect to mean return and volatility where the x axis is volatility and the y axis is mean return, we now turn our attention to clustering with respect to covariance in p dimensions. We will be using a discrete structure called an undirected graph.

9.3   Sparsity and Connectedness of Undirected Graphs

Up to now, only the mean return and volatility has been considered for clustering. Now we begin to look at covariance. Gaussian Graphical Models (GGMs) are based upon the multivariate normal distribution, presented in the Appendix. The key parameter studied is Σ, the covariance matrix.

In order to examine a portfolio from a co-movement perspective, undirected graphs are quite useful. They are a way of organizing the relationships of random variables which correspond to the log returns of the individual stock price time series. If we have four hypothetical stocks, with ticker symbols W, X, Y, and Z, which may or may not move together, we can use a four-vertex graph to visualize the relationships. While this is a small graph, the clusters within small or large graphs of this type can be used for finding comovement among stocks which behave similarly in the same market conditions.

Undirected graphs can be represented by adjacency matrices. In a graph's adjacency matrix, A, we have a nonzero entry, $A_{i,j}$ if there is an edge between nodes i and j in the graph. Figure 9.4 shows a simple undirected graph where the rows and columns represent the nodes, W, X, Y, and Z. One possible adjacency matrix, where the nonzero entries are 1, is:

$$\mathbf{A} = \begin{pmatrix} 0 & 1 & 1 & 0 \\ 1 & 0 & 1 & 1 \\ 1 & 1 & 0 & 1 \\ 0 & 1 & 1 & 0 \end{pmatrix}. \tag{9.6}$$

Note that we do not consider a node i adjacent to itself as a convention so zeroes appear on the diagonal. The *density* of a graph, δ, can be found from the adjacency matrix by summing the total number of edges and dividing by the number of possible edges. The number of possible edges in a graph with p vertices is $p(p-1)/2$.

According to Portfolio Theory, investors are interested in portfolios with less comovement among the securities. Therefore, we desire graphs which are sparse, less

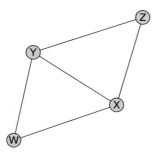

Figure 9.4 Simple undirected graph for four-dimensional adjacency matrix **A**.

connected, and less dense, in terms of the number of edges per vertex. These will be graphs with fewer clusters. This can be easily found from adjacency matrix A which has $p \times p$ dimensions:

$$\delta = \frac{\#actual\ edges}{\#possible\ edges} = \frac{\sum_{i=1}^{p} \sum_{j=1}^{j<i} A_{i,j}}{p(p-1)/2} \text{ and } \psi = 1 - \delta. \tag{9.7}$$

The ratio in the equation is the density. The *sparsity*, ψ, is defined to be one minus the density. For example, for our simple graph of Figure 9.4, $\psi = 1 - 5/6 = 1/6$. Our ideal independent movement market graph which the MVO algorithm is trying to find would have a density of 0 and a sparsity of 1. This is a graph with no edges and complete independence of the returns corresponding to the market random variables at each node. The worse possible graph would have a density of 1 and a sparsity of 0 from a variance optimization viewpoint. Under this measure, the adjacency matrix for W, X, Y, and Z with sparsity $\frac{1}{6}$ is just slightly more sparse than the worst case of 0.

Here is R code which will compute the sparsity using a graph's adjacency matrix.

```
computeSparsity <- function(A) {
  dimA = dim(A)
  if(dimA[1] == dimA[2]) {
    sumedges = 0
    p = dimA[1]
    for(i in 1:p)
      if(i > 1)
        for(j in 1:(i-1))
          sumedges = sumedges + A[i,j]
  } else return(NA)
  return(1-sumedges/((p*(p-1)/2)))
}
cells = c(0,0,1,1,
          0,0,1,1,
          1,1,0,1,
          1,1,1,0)
A = matrix(cells,nrow=4,ncol=4)
computeSparsity(A)
...
> computeSparsity(A)
```

```
[1] 0.1666667
> 1-computeSparsity(A) #density
[1] 0.8333333
```

A well-known metric, *local cluster coefficient*, is very common for measuring the degree of *connectedness* of a graph. If a graph like in Figure 9.4 were representing a social network, for example, and nodes X had friends Y and Z, then if Y and Z are also friends, which is fairly likely to be the case, then a triangle is formed in the graph. Essentially, the local cluster coefficient counts the number of completed triangles compared to the number of potential triangles that could exist (Fairchild and Fries, 2012). The formula for the local cluster coefficient, $c(v_i)$ for vertex v_i with $p \times p$ adjacency matrix A is

$$c(v_i) = \frac{\#connected\ triangles}{\#possible\ triangles} = \frac{\sum_{j=1}^{p} \sum_{k=1}^{p} A_{i,j} A_{j,k} A_{k,i}}{\binom{outdegree(v_i)}{2}} if\ outdegree(v_i) > 1\ else\ 1$$

(9.8)

and the entire graph's ($\mathbf{G} = (\mathbf{V}, \mathbf{E})$ where $\mathbf{E} \subseteq \mathbf{V} \times \mathbf{V}$) local cluster coefficient can be found by averaging the c of each vertex $v_i \in \mathbf{V}$:

$$C(\mathbf{G}) = \frac{1}{|\mathbf{V}|} \sum_{v_i \in \mathbf{V}} c(v_i),$$

(9.9)

which says to go through each vertex in the vertex set $\mathbf{V}$ and find each c.

As an example, consider again the graph in Figure 9.4. $c(W) = 1$ since $outdegree(W) = 2$ and the number of triangles is $\binom{2}{2} = 1$ and the number of possible triangles is 1, involving X and Y. This is also true for Z that $c(Z) = 1$. Now for vertices X and Y, $c(X) = \frac{2}{3} = c(Y)$ since $outdegree(X) = 3$ and so $\binom{outdegree(v_i)}{2} = 3$ and number of connected triangles is 2 of a possible 3. Averaging all four vertices gives us $C(\mathbf{G}) = (1 + 1 + \frac{2}{3} + \frac{2}{3})/4 = \frac{5}{6}$.

Here is R code which will compute the local clustering coefficient using a graph's adjacency matrix:

```
computeClusterCoeff <- function(A, isVerbose=FALSE) {
  N = dim(A)[1]
  degree = vector(length=dim(A)[1])
  avgdegree = vector(length=dim(A)[1])
  sumCC = 0
  for (i in 1:N) {
    sum = 0
    degree[i] = sum(A[i,])
    avgdegree[i] = degree[i]*(degree[i]-1)/2
    if(degree[i] < 2) {
      avgdegree[i] = 1; sum = 1
    } else {
      avgdegree[i] = dim(combn(degree[i],2))[2]
      for(j in 1:N) {
        for(k in j:N) {
          fact = A[i,j]*A[j,k]*A[k,i]
          if(fact > 0) {
            sum = sum + fact
            #print(paste(i,j,k,fact))
```

```
                }
              }
            }
          }
       if(isVerbose) print(paste(i,"===> cc num =",sum))
       if(avgdegree[i] != 0) {
          if(isVerbose) print(paste(i,
                        "===> clst coeff =",sum/avgdegree[i]))
          sumCC = sumCC + sum/avgdegree[i]
       }
    }
  sumCC/N
}
#Unit test
cells = c(0,0,1,1,
              0,0,1,1,
              1,1,0,1,
              1,1,1,0)
A = matrix(cells,nrow=4,ncol=4)
computeClusterCoeff(A,isVerbose=TRUE)
```

In this case, it so happens that the local clustering coefficient works out the same as the sparsity as seen in the output of *computeClusterCoeff()*.

```
> computeClusterCoeff(A,isVerbose=TRUE)
[1] "1 ===> cc num = 1"
[1] "1 ===> clst coeff = 1"
[1] "2 ===> cc num = 1"
[1] "2 ===> clst coeff = 1"
[1] "3 ===> cc num = 2"
[1] "3===> clst coeff = 0.666666666666667"
[1] "4 ===> cc num = 2" [1]
"4 ===> clst coeff = 0.666666666666667"
[1] 0.8333333
```

but this is generally not the case.

9.4   Covariance and Precision Matrices

While Chapter 5 demonstrated that the normal distribution is probably the exception rather than the rule for stock log returns, by approximating with it we can use recent developments in the theory of GGMs to model the portfolio interactions. The covariance matrix of the multi-dimensional normally distributed log returns for a portfolio is usually called Σ of size $p \times p$. There is an important result that states that the precision matrix

$$\Omega = \Sigma^{-1} \tag{9.10}$$

can be used to guide whether co-movement exists between pairs of multivariate normal random variables (Whittaker, 1990). Since our log returns are deemed to be of this distribution, we can apply it here.

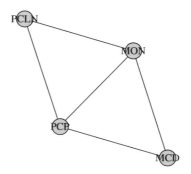

Figure 9.5   Undirected graph for four selected stocks from in-sample huge stockdata based upon prices from 2003 to 2008.

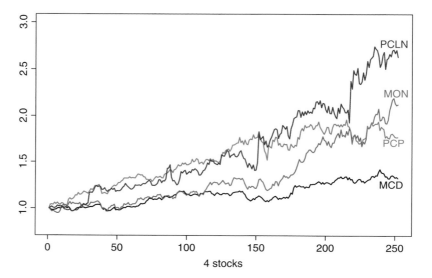

Figure 9.6   Price series for four stocks from in-sample huge stockdata for just 2007. PCLN and MCD are deemed to not move together by the precision matrix of Equation 9.10 and the graph of Figure 9.5. The horizontal axis is trading days for one year and the vertical axis is the prices scaled to 1.

Having a utility to build undirected graphs is essential. Below is the R code for taking the precision matrix, Ω above, from a covariance matrix, Σ above, and changing it to a graph adjacency matrix, then plotting the graph of Figure 9.5 and plotting the stock gross return chart of Figure 9.6. The *plotGraph()* utility can be called once we import prices and compute log returns for the stocks.

```
library(igraph)
library(tseries)
plotGraph <- function(lab,w,A) {
  D = dim(A)[1]
  indw = (w > .001)
  g <- graph.empty() + vertices(toupper(lab[indw]))
```

```
  threshold = .6
  for(i in 1:D) {
    if(w[i] > 0.0) {
      for(j in 1:max(1,(i-1))) {
        if(i != j && w[j] > .001 && A[i,j] != 0) {
          #print(toupper(lab[j]))
            g <- g + path(toupper(lab[i]),toupper(lab[j]))
        }
      }
    }
  }
  ug <- as.undirected(g)
  V(ug)$color <- "gold"
  V(ug)$label.cex = 1.1
  plot(ug,vertex.size=22.05)
}
plotGraph(c('W','X','Y','Z'),c(1/4,1/4,1/4,1/4),A)
```

Again we begin with the *huge stockdata* dataset. Our program so far has a *prices* matrix with 1,258 split-adjusted prices from 2003 to 2008. Let's look at four stocks of the 452. We can use the R function *match()* to locate our desired tickers in the *lab* vector in our dataset, giving us the vector *matchIdxs*. If we have these stocks in a proposed portfolio, MCD, MON, PCP, PCLN, we can find the covariance matrix of 100 times one year of the log returns using this upcoming sequence.

```
#Find covariance and precision Matrices
library(huge)
data(stockdata)
D = length(stockdata$data[1,])
len = length(stockdata$data[,1])
prices = stockdata$data[,1:D]
lab = stockdata$info[1:D,1]
isSplitAdjusted = FALSE
R <- findR(prices,isSplitAdjusted=FALSE) #Split-adjusts prices
dim(prices)
#Form small p  array of prices
ticker = c('MCD','MON','PCP','PCLN')
matchIdx = vector(length=4)
for(i in 1:4)
  matchIdx[i] = match(ticker[i],lab)
p = matrix(rep(0,252*4),nrow=252,ncol=4)
oneYr = (1258-251):1258
p[,1] = prices[oneYr,matchIdx[1]]
p[,2] = prices[oneYr,matchIdx[2]]
p[,3] = prices[oneYr,matchIdx[3]]
p[,4] = prices[oneYr,matchIdx[4]]
```

Below are the four vectors of computed log returns, r.

```
r = matrix(rep(0,251*4),nrow=251,ncol=4)
r[,1] = diff(log(p[,1]))
r[,2] = diff(log(p[,2]))
r[,3] = diff(log(p[,3]))
r[,4] = diff(log(p[,4]))
r100 = 100*r #100 x log rets
Sigma = cov(r100)
round(Sigma,2)
Omega = solve(Sigma)
round(Omega,2)
A = ifelse(round(Omega,2)!=0.00, 1, 0)
w = c(.25,.25,.25,.25)
plotGraph(ticker,w,A)
plotMultSeries(p,ticker,w,4,
              cc=paste(sum(w>0),"stocks"),
              ret="",ylim=c(.8,3))
```

which yields our covariance matrix:

$$\Sigma = \begin{pmatrix} 1.38 & 0.92 & 0.69 & 0.51 \\ 0.92 & 4.33 & 2.12 & 2.20 \\ 0.69 & 2.12 & 4.08 & 2.14 \\ 0.51 & 2.20 & 2.14 & 9.70 \end{pmatrix}. \tag{9.11}$$

Then, using the *solve()* and *round()* R functions, the precision matrix is found:

$$\Omega = \begin{pmatrix} 0.86 & -0.15 & -0.07 & 0.00 \\ -0.15 & 0.35 & -0.13 & -0.04 \\ -0.07 & -0.13 & 0.35 & -0.04 \\ 0.00 & -0.04 & -0.04 & 0.12 \end{pmatrix}. \tag{9.12}$$

The Ω precision matrix has the very nice property that, for any element of it, when $\omega_{i,j} = 0$, then we know that the log return series for security i is conditionally independent from the log return series for security j, given the remaining random variables for the other securities k where $k \neq i$ and $k \neq j$. This matrix works as an adjacency matrix when ignoring the diagonal elements, setting them to zero, and considering whether the other elements are equal to 0.00. Those elements that are not equal to 0.00 are considered to be equivalent to 1 in the corresponding adjacency matrix. We can conclude from this precision matrix, the first and fourth stocks, McDonald's and Priceline, MCD and PCLN, are not correlated because $\omega_{1,4} = \omega_{4,1} = 0$. Looking in Figure 9.5 we can see the undirected graph corresponding to Ω to show the co-movement of each weighted stock in the portfolio. The algorithm to construct the graph from an empty graph, $(\mathbf{V}, \{\})$, is

- first find the precision matrix from the covariance matrix;
- use the R *ifelse()* function to determine A, the adjacency matrix of the graph: inspect the precision matrix elements for whether they round to 0.00 and set $A[i,j]$ to 1 where the precision matrix value does not round to 0.00 at row i and column j;

- iterate through the lower triangle of adjacency matrix A and if row i, column j is 1 then add the edge (v_i, v_j) to edge set **E**.

The last step is what the above *plotGraph()* function does.

9.5 Visualizing Covariance

As one works with the GGMs, it becomes clear that whether an edge in the undirected graph should be present is subjective and needs to be adjustable. For example, if our p log return data series are such that the covariances are high among them, we could wind up with a strongly connected undirected graph with high density and low sparsity, a tight cluster that plots as a gnarled ball. A gnarled ball does not help an investor understand the inter-stock covariances. Our example matrices of the previous section for Σ and Ω serve as an example but are not typical of a large sample of stocks when $p > 4$. In fact, we find that it is somewhat rare for the Ω matrix to contain zeros! For the $p = 452$ *huge.stockdata* stocks, a small sample can tell us that at least half of the possible edges for a node such as EBAY will be claimed by the precision matrix, Ω, to be present. In other words, for row 139 corresponding to EBAY, stock index 139, approximately half of the columns in the adjacency matrix found from the precision matrix via the logic

```
A = ifelse(Omega!=0.00, 1, 0)
```

will be marked with a 1. Since a graph like that is not very useful, we need a mechanism to dial down the density or, equivalently, dial up the sparsity of the graph that is obtained in order for it to be a good visualization tool. Simply taking the inverse of the covariance matrix as our algorithm for the pseudo adjacency matrix, Ω, will have limitations. Depicting the relative dependence of node pairs is the purpose of the graph and this is a Boolean true or false situation. Either an edge is present or it is not. First, we would like to find the Sharpe Ratios of our 24 candidates and then, as a matter of convenience, enhance their labels with it.

```
findSixYrSR <- function(dir='huge',csvFile = 'rebalresD24Days1258.csv') {
  setwd(paste(homeuser,"/FinAnalytics/",dir,"/",sep=""))
  df <- read.csv(csvFile)
  lab <- df[,2]
  w <- df[,3]
  indw = (w > 0)
  lab <- lab[indw]
  isEnhanced <- FALSE
  w <- w[indw]
  D <- length(lab)
  daysPerYr = 252; mufree = 0
  recentPrices <- findRecentHugePrices('huge',
                            'rebalresD24Days1258.csv')
  R <- findR(recentPrices)
  cov_mat <- cov(R)
```

```
  meanv <- apply(R,2,mean)
  diag_cov_mat <- diag(cov_mat)
  sdevv <- sqrt(diag_cov_mat)
  Sharpe <- (meanv-mufree)/sdevv*sqrt(daysPerYr)
  Omega <- solve(cov_mat)
  prices <- recentPrices
  list(prices,R,cov_mat,meanv,sdevv,Sharpe,Omega,isEnhanced)
}
res <- findSixYrSR()
prices     <- res[[1]]
R          <- res[[2]]
cov_mat    <- res[[3]]
meanv      <- res[[4]]
sdevv      <- res[[5]]
Sharpe     <- res[[6]]
Omega      <- res[[7]]
isEnhanced <- res[[8]]
```

In order to depict the individual securities in a more meaningful way, there is a routine, *enhanceLab()*, to enhance the node labels to attach the Sharpe Ratio and the rounded weights for the six-year period. Small weights will round to 0 percent. The above routine finds the six-year Sharpe Ratio to compare securities: with the Sharpe vector computed then side effected by *findSixYrSR()*, the labels can be enhanced.

```
enhanceLab <- function(lab,Sharpe,w) {
  #Enhance lab with Sharpe and weight in percent
  D <- length(lab)
  shplab = vector(length=D)
  for(d in 1:D) {
    shplab[d] = paste(lab[d],
                paste(round(Sharpe[d],2),
                paste(round(100*w[d],0),'%',sep=''),sep='\n')
  }
  return(shplab)
}
shplab <- enhanceLab(lab,Sharpe,w)
```

The enhanced labels, called *shplab* as they are built, are listed below. We know from Chapter 8 that CME and AAPL were the highest weighted stocks of the 452 candidates at 16 percent and 12 percent, respectively. PCP and MON are next in line, listed below at 8 percent. Weighing in at 5 percent are MCD, TSO, LH, GME and BCR.

```
> shplab
 [1] "CME\n-0.04 16%"  "AAPL\n0.71 12%"  "MON\n0.01 8%"
 [4] "MCD\n0.61 5%"    "TSO\n0.1 5%"     "GME\n-0.07 5%"
 [7] "PCP\n0.37 8%"    "LH\n0.11 5%"     "BCR\n0.31 5%"
[10] "AMT\n0.41 5%"    "BLK\n0.21 5%"    "ISRG\n0.14 4%"
[13] "HUM\n0.17 3%"    "EIX\n0.11 3%"    "SWN\n0.09 2%"
[16] "ESRX\n0.42 2%"   "WMB\n0.21 2%"    "RRC\n0.13 1%"
[19] "DVA\n0.59 1%"    "RAI\n0.59 1%"    "WYNN\n0.3 1%"
[22] "CERN\n0.82 0%"   "PCLN\n0.95 0%"   "AET\n0.16 0%"
```

The code for *runGlassoAndDisplay()* appears below. We present it now and run it in a very introductory case of only four vertices to show how we can visualize covariance among the portfolio securities. A more in depth discussion of the Glasso algorithm fundamentals is forthcoming in the upcoming three sections.

```
runGlassoAndDisplay <- function(prices,lab,w,D,Sharpe,
                    isEnhanced=FALSE,lmratio = 0.33,trackIdx=9) {
  #Run the Glasso and record results in undir graph ug
  len = length(prices[,1]) # Does not impact R:
  Y = log(prices[2:len,1:D]/prices[1:(len-1),1:D])
  x.npn = huge.npn(Y, npn.func="truncation") # Nonparanormal
  out.npn = huge(x.npn,method = "glasso",
                cov.output = TRUE, nlambda=D,
                lambda.min.ratio = lmratio)
  out.npn
  #Find indicator array:
  indw = (w > .001)
  #Attach SR to lab
  if(!isEnhanced && D > 4) {
    shplab <- enhanceLab(lab,Sharpe,w)
    isEnhanced <- TRUE #shplab enhanced: e.g. "ISRG\n0.14 4%"
  }
  g <- graph.empty() + vertices(toupper(shplab[indw]))
  trackIdxEdges <- 0 #Track MCD
  for(d in D:D) { #focus on last version D
    for(i in 1:D) {
      if(w[i] > .001) {
        for(j in 1:i) {
          if(w[j] > .001 && out.npn$path[[d]][i,j] == 1) {
            #print(paste(i,j))
            #print(toupper(lab[i]))
```

Note that we augment the graph *g* by running this key line below which adds an edge from vertex *i* to *j* if there is a 1 in the final (*d*th version) of the adjacency matrix *out.npn* produced by the call to *huge()* for stocks with nonzero weights.

```
            g <- g + path(toupper(shplab[i]),toupper(shplab[j]))
            #Undir graph means need to count either case:
            if(j == trackIdx || i == trackIdx)
              trackIdxEdges <- trackIdxEdges + 1
          }
        }
      }
    }
  }
  ug <- as.undirected(g)
  V(ug)$color <- "gold"
  #V(ug)$offset <- 1.2
  V(ug)$label.cex = 0.8
  plot(ug,vertex.size=sqrt(500*w),ylab=
        paste("lmratio=",lmratio))
}
```

```
    print(paste("tracked outdegree:",trackIdxEdges))
    list(out.npn$path[[D]],shplab,isEnhanced)
}
```

Now that *runGlassoAndDisplay()* is defined, we can use it to display four simple graphs, depicting the difference in density or sparsity depending upon the setting of the *lmratio* parameter.

```
A = ifelse(Omega!=0.00, 1, 0)
lab4 <- c('MCD','MON','PCP','PCLN')
labIdxs <- sapply(lab4,function(x) match(x,lab))
prices4 <- prices[,labIdxs]
w = rep(1/4,4)
shplab <- lab[labIdxs]
par(mfrow=c(2,2))
res <- runGlassoAndDisplay(prices4,lab4,w,4,Sharpe,
                 lmratio=1.20,trackIdx=1)
A    <- res[[1]]
shplab <- res[[2]]
isEnhanced <- res[[3]]
res <-runGlassoAndDisplay(prices4,lab4,w,4,Sharpe,
                 lmratio=.95,trackIdx=1)
A    <- res[[1]]
shplab <- res[[2]]
isEnhanced <- res[[3]]
res <- runGlassoAndDisplay(prices4,lab4,w,4,Sharpe,
                 lmratio=.70,trackIdx=1)
A    <- res[[1]]
shplab <- res[[2]]
isEnhanced <- res[[3]]
res <- runGlassoAndDisplay(prices4,lab4,w,4,Sharpe,
                 lmratio=.45,trackIdx=1)
A    <- res[[1]]
shplab <- res[[2]]
isEnhanced <- res[[3]]
```

In Figure 9.7 we can see the result of running the code sequence above. We try four different levels for the parameter *lmratio* to the Glasso algorithm. The top-right graph has a sparsity of 1 and is totally unconnected. As we move to the right, we add an edge between MON and PCP and between PCLN and PCP. In the lower left, with *lmratio* = 0.7, we get a sparsity of $\frac{1}{6}$ and finally, the fully connected case appears when *lmratio* = 0.95 with a sparsity of 0. By setting *lmratio*, we can control the level of sparsity of the graph to make it appropriate for our use. It is not unlike the volume on a radio: we set it to the most useful setting.

Figure 9.8 shows the 452-stock graph in its entirety. We can see clustering occurring among subgroups. It is interesting to see that there are several outliers that move outside the large cluster to the fringes. These are relatively independently moving stocks. The code below will compute the required covariances for the *runGlassoAndDisplay()* function.

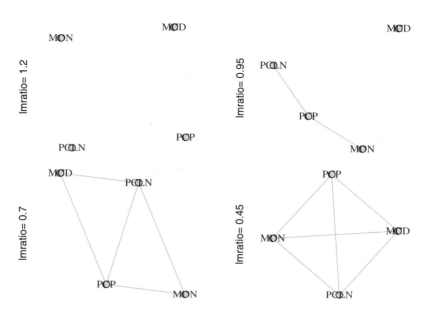

Figure 9.7   Penalization level determines whether edges are used to depict a covariance level. Sparsity varies
from 1 to 0 as *lmratio*=1.20 down to 0.45.

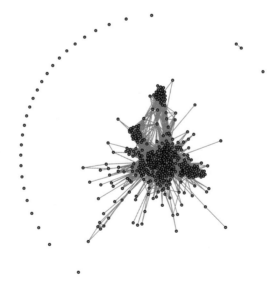

Figure 9.8   Unlabeled undirected graph node for 452 surviving stocks of the S&P 500 Index 2003 to 2008
using *huge.plot( )*.

```
w = rep(1/D,D)
Omega = round(solve(cov_mat),2)
Omega[1:8,1:8]
Aomega = ifelse(Omega!=0.00, 1, 0)
```

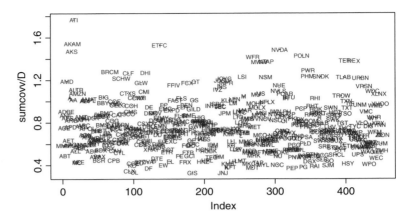

Figure 9.9   Comparison of the average covariances for the stocks of Figure 9.8. A lower average covariance for a stock implies more independence from other stocks in their log return behavior.

```
res <- runGlassoAndDisplay(prices,lab,w,D,Sharpe,
               lmratio=.45,trackIdx=4)
A    <- res[[1]]
shplab <- res[[2]]
isEnhanced <- res[[3]]
Aomega[1:8,1:8]
huge.plot(A)
```

Comparing the average covariance for stocks in the large set tells how clustered a stock is to others. Just like finding Sharpe Ratios on an individual stock basis was of interest in Chapter 7, determining the amount of covariance to other stocks is of interest here. Low covariance corresponds to low correlation and makes a stock a good candidate in a portfolio. We can see in Figure 9.9 that JNJ, PEP, HSY, and KFT, which are all consumer product stocks, have some of the lowest average covariances in the population. The code appearing below will perform the average covariance calculations, *sumcovv/D* and plot them by ticker symbol.

```
#Avg Cov
> saveList <- list(D,lab,prices) #save away
library(huge)
data(stockdata)
D = length(stockdata$data[1,])
len = length(stockdata$data[,1])
prices = stockdata$data[,1:D]
lab = stockdata$info[1:D,1]
isSplitAdjusted = FALSE
R <- findR(prices,isSplitAdjusted=FALSE) #Split-adjusts prices
dim(prices)
cov_mat <- cov(R)
sumcovv=vector(length=D)
for(i in 1:D)
  sumcovv[i]=sum(cov_mat[i,])-cov_mat[i,i]
```

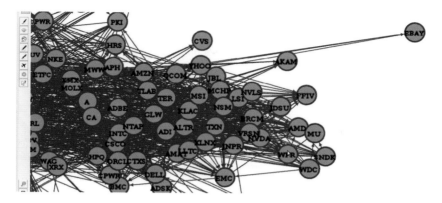

Figure 9.10   Zooming in with the Gephi tool on EBAY and EMC, two technology sector stocks. EBAY, upper right, has three associated stocks and EMC, lower center, has 23 associated stocks.

```
plot(sumcovv/D,type="p",cex=.1)
text(1:D,sumcovv/D,lab,col=4,cex=.55)
```

Exporting the edges from the graph of Figure 9.8 into a two-column CSV file for import into the open source graph drawing tool, *Gephi*, we can see the graph laid out using Gephi's Yifan Hu Proportional layout algorithm in Figure 9.10. The upcoming function *runGlassoAndDisplay()* emits the edge file records in the *write()* statement in the third nested **for**-loop. In Figure 9.10 we can see both EBAY with three connected nodes, AMZN, QCOM, and YHOO. EMC, on the other hand, has 23 connected nodes in the Gephi-displayed graph.

```
lab4    <- c('EBAY','EMC','PCLN','UPS')
labIdxs <- sapply(lab4,function(x) match(x,lab))
plot(sort(cov_mat[139,-139]),ylim=c(-.1,4),
     xlab="Sorted Index",ylab="Cov to other stocks")
points(sort(cov_mat[145,-145]),col=2)
points(sort(cov_mat[338,-338]),col=4)
points(sort(cov_mat[417,-417]),col=3)
text(rep(400,4),c(1.1,1.75,2.5,.5),lab4,cex=.75)
> D <- saveList[[1]]; lab <- saveList[[2]]; prices <-
> saveList[[3]]#restore
```

In Figure 9.11 we can see that, in general, EBAY has a lower covariance to the other stocks than EMC, especially at the tail end of the chart. The code for this chart appears above.

9.6   The Wishart Distribution

The sample covariance matrix Σ is derived from the sample from the MVN distribution. However, as pointed out in the literature of GGMs, the sample covariance matrix itself is

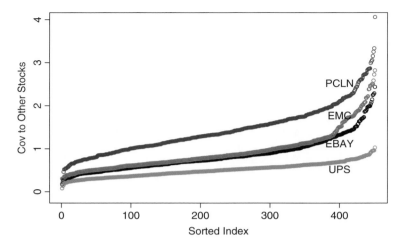

Figure 9.11 Comparison of four typical stock covariances, sorted across all other stocks in the candidate set. EBAY and EMC are seen in Figure 9.10 and PCLN, UPS are just typical stocks to compare as well. UPS has the least co-movement, followed by EBAY.

a parameter and has a Wishart distribution (Hastie, Tibshirani, and Friedman, 2009). The Wishart distribution represents the sums of squares and cross-products of n draws from an MVN distribution. The p.d.f. for the Wishart distribution is a very complex formula which is hard to visualize due to the dimensionality (see the Appendix for discussion of the various p.d.f.s, especially the MVN distribution for this discussion). If $\mathbf{X}$ is an $n \times p$ matrix where $x_i = (x_{i,1}, ..., x_{i,p})$ is drawn from the MVN$(0, \boldsymbol{\Sigma})$ distribution in p dimensions and $\mathbf{S}$ is the $p \times p$ sample covariance matrix defined as

$$\mathbf{S} = \frac{1}{n} \sum_{i=1}^{n} (x_i - \bar{x})(x_i - \bar{x})^T, \tag{9.13}$$

we say that $\mathbf{S} \sim W_p(\boldsymbol{\Sigma}, n)$, where $\mathbf{S}$ is positive definite. The density formula appears as Equation 9.14,

$$f(\mathbf{S}) = \frac{|\mathbf{X}|^{\frac{n-p-1}{2}}}{2^{\frac{np}{2}} \boldsymbol{\Sigma}^{\frac{n}{2}} \Gamma_p(\frac{n}{2})} \exp\left(\frac{-tr(\boldsymbol{\Sigma}^{-1}\mathbf{X})}{2}\right), \tag{9.14}$$

where $n > p-1$ is the degrees of freedom and the mean is $n\boldsymbol{\Sigma}$ and the function $\Gamma_p()$ is the multivariate gamma function in p dimensions. $\boldsymbol{\Sigma}$ denotes a positive definite scale matrix which can be thought of as a variance–covariance matrix from an MVN distribution.

There are multiple R packages containing a simulation of this distribution. We will focus on the R *sbgcop* package which has a Wishart random variate generator called *rwish()* taking the MVN covariance and the number of requested variates. Examining this distribution from R code is worthwhile to help understand the covariance and precision matrices used in GGMs.

Let us once again consider the $\boldsymbol{\Sigma}$ and $\boldsymbol{\Omega}$ matrices for our four stocks. The code sequence below will begin with $\boldsymbol{\Omega}$ and invert it to come up with another version of

Σ, called *Sig*, then use that to send to the *rwish()* function. We will ask for 100 "paths" or variates.

```
mapToCol <- function(d)
  if(d%%8==7) 1 else if(d==8)
    2 else if(d==15) 3 else if(d==23) 4 else d

library(sbgcop)
Omega = matrix(c(0.86, -0.15, -0.07,  0.00,
               -0.15,  0.35, -0.13, -0.04,
               -0.07, -0.13,  0.35, -0.04,
                0.00, -0.04, -0.04,  0.12),nrow=4,ncol=4)
A = ifelse(Omega!=0.00, 1, 0)
plotGraph(c('MCD','MON','PCP','PCLN'),rep(1/4,4),A)
Sig = solve(Omega)
p <- dim(Sig)[1]
df <- p+1

set.seed(138) # for replication
paths <- 100 # number of obs in our sampling dist
W.empir <- matrix( nrow = paths, ncol = length( c(Sig)) )
dim(W.empir)
for(i in 1:paths) {
  W.empir[i, ] <- c(rwish(Sig,nu=1))
  if(i == 1) {
    plot(as.vector(W.empir[i,]),type="l",
         ylim=c(-15,+90),ylab="rwish npaths=100")
  } else {
    lines(as.vector(W.empir[i,]),col=mapToCol(i))
  }
}
```

The code above computes the Wishart samples and stores them in the *W.empir* matrix. It then find plots the variates as 16-element paths for Figure 9.12. The code below produces the box plot of Figure 9.13 which depicts the distribution of each random variate in the Wishart matrix.

```
> boxplot(W.empir)
> meanW <- apply(W.empir,2,function(x) mean(as.vector(x)))
> matrix(round(meanW,2),4,4)
      [,1] [,2] [,3]  [,4]
[1,] 1.15 0.86 0.93  0.41
[2,] 0.86 4.08 1.95  2.62
[3,] 0.93 1.95 4.26  2.84
[4,] 0.41 2.62 2.84 11.19
> round(Sig,2)
      [,1] [,2] [,3] [,4]
[1,] 1.37 0.90 0.67 0.52
[2,] 0.90 4.21 1.98 2.06
[3,] 0.67 1.98 3.95 1.98
[4,] 0.52 2.06 1.98 9.68
```

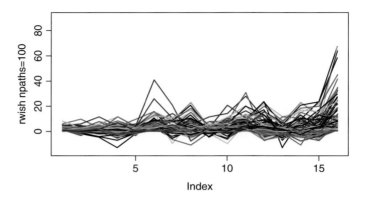

Figure 9.12   Variates of the *rwish()* function yielding 100 4 × 4 covariance matrices.

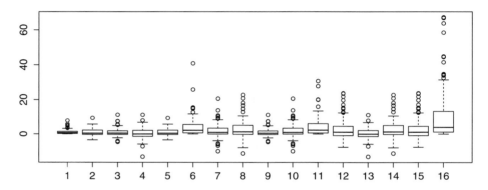

Figure 9.13   Box plots showing 16 covariance positions from the random variates of the Wishart distribution.

We can see that the starting point matrix, *Sig*, is similar in value to the *meanW* matrix, computed from the Wishart variates. We note that the final element in the fourth row and fourth column of the covariance matrix shows extra high covariance in the box plot (indexed at 16 on the horizontal axis), and this may very well be expected for the PCLN stock.

```
for(j in (1:16)) {
  if(j == 1) {
    plot(density(W.empir[j,]),
         xlim=c(min(W.empir),max(W.empir)),
         ylim=c(0,.8),main="")
  } else {
    lines(density(W.empir[j,]),col=mapToCol(j))
  }
}
```

Another view of the Wishart for this particular case of $p = 4$ and $\boldsymbol{\Sigma} = \boldsymbol{\Omega}^{-1}$ is depicted in Figure 9.14. The code to generate this graph appears above. Sixteen density plots are

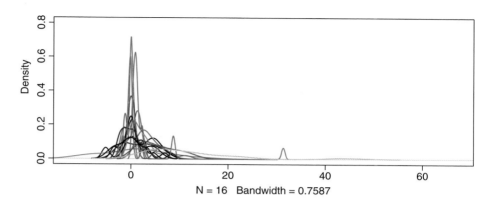

N = 16   Bandwidth = 0.7587

Figure 9.14   Superimposed density plots showing the Wishart distribution covariances. We can determine from the box plot of Figure 9.13 that the extra wide tail is from the element at position $p \times p = 16$.

superimposed in this view. Most of the distribution is centered between 0 and 1 but the outliers are driving the plot going out to the tails too.

9.7   Glasso: Penalization for Undirected Graphs

We mentioned the need for a mechanism to dial down the density or dial up the sparsity of the graphs. Having sparsity in the undirected graph is analogous to having shrinkage among parameters. The *Glasso* algorithm is an adaptation of the famous Lasso algorithm, discussed in Chapter 8, applied to undirected graphs. As with the Lasso, regularization parameters are used as a filter level. In this case we filter for the appropriate level of sparsity of the graph (Tibshirani, 1996). The log-likelihood function is

$$l(\mathbf{\Omega}) = \log(|\mathbf{\Omega}|) - tr(\mathbf{S\Omega}). \tag{9.15}$$

The constrained log-likelihood function can be found as

$$\mathbf{\Omega}^* = \operatorname*{argmin}_{\mathbf{\Omega}} l_C(\mathbf{\Omega}) = \operatorname*{argmin}_{\mathbf{\Omega}} \log(|\mathbf{\Omega}|) - tr(\mathbf{S\Omega}) - \sum_{(j,k)\notin\mathbf{E}} \gamma_{j,k}\omega_{j,k}. \tag{9.16}$$

In this second form of Equation 9.16, as we maximize the overall expression, the penalization sum works against the log-likelihood, reducing the overall value. So more edges mean more penalty from the summation term. This keeps the number of edges at a minimum. We stated earlier in Section 9.4 that the precision matrix, $\mathbf{\Omega}$, alone suggests way too many edges to be useful. This log-likelihood with the penalty is what we were looking for. Details of the Glasso algorithm can be found in the text (Hastie, Tibshirani, and Friedman, 2009) and the reference paper (Friedman, Hastie, and Tibshirani, 2008).

9.8   Running the Glasso Algorithm

The work on the *huge* package by Zhao, Liu, Roeder, Lafferty, and Wasserman provides an improvement before running the Glasso by running the non-paranormal step

(Zhao, Liu, Roeder, Lafferty, and Wasserman, 2012). The *huge* package uses the Glasso algorithm. We will use the Glasso algorithm to graphically visualize the co-movement of our stocks in the portfolio. Running the Glasso algorithm from *huge* with the non-paranormal step gives us back a much more useful graph, appearing in Figure 9.8, much sparser than the one that would come from the precision matrix.

The non-paranormal transform, *huge.npn()*, is used prior to calling the Glasso algorithm. The main routine to run the Glasso algorithm is called *runGlassoAndDisplay()* and the output can be used to produce graphs such as the top portion of Figures 9.15, 9.16, and 9.17. The code for the main routine, *runGlassoAndDisplay()*, was introduced earlier in Section 9.5. The loop after the *huge.npn()* and *huge()* calls builds the graph by using the *path()* function. The graph is then plotted using *plot()* on *ug*, the undirected graph. The most refined version of the graph, *out.npn$path*, is subscripted by *[[D]]*.

9.9   Tracking a Value Stock through the Years

A stock that tends to trade at a lower price than others relative to the fundamentals such as dividends, earnings, and revenue is called a *value stock*. Common characteristics of value stocks include a lower stock price-to-earnings ratio, higher dividend yield, and lower price-to-book ratio.

When simulating the MVO algorithm for the 452 *huge stockdata* securities using a Sharpe Ratio threshold, the 26 stocks are cleaned down to 24 stocks due to merger events occurring in our desired time window. The resulting 24 stock portfolio is determined as in Figure 8.8.

Simulating this portfolio out-of-sample forward in time for six years, from February 14, 2008 to February 14, 2014, we can think of a GGM and the annual portfolio return for each year, a total of six graphs. Each year begins and ends on February 14. For example, the year we are calling 2008 begins on February 14, 2008 and ends on February 14, 2009. We will examine the first three of the six graphs in this section, as they are the most interesting ones, given the market events in 2008 to 2011.

Let's trace the movement of a well-known value stock, a member of our portfolio. McDonald's Corporation, ticker MCD, became part the portfolio based upon its high performance over the *huge stockdata* period of 2003 to 2008, and it is given a strong 5 percent weight. Running a simulation forward from 2008 to 2014, MCD had a 0.061 Sharpe Ratio in the label of Figures through 9.17. We start tracking MCD by looking at Figure 9.15 and see that it appears in the middle of a dense cluster of correlation links in 2008. In the calculation statements below, we can see that MCD's annual return is 5.4 percent. As 2009 comes into play, MCD breaks out on its own. In 2009 it delivers 15.9 percent return as its restaurant chain proves to be a solid bet with frugal consumers during the days of the recovery from the Great Recession. Below are the returns for MCD for each of the six years:

```
> prices[252,4]/prices[1,4]-1
[1] 0.05411973
> prices[2*252,4]/prices[253,4]-1
```

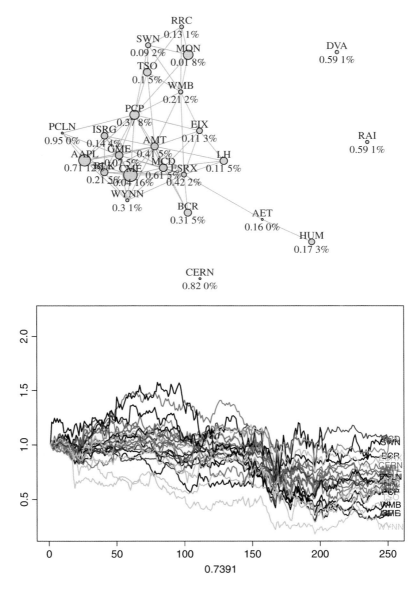

Figure 9.15   2008 return of 24 securities in co-movement graph and chart form. The first number attached to each vertex is the Sharpe Ratio for the current sample of prices: 2008 to 2014. The second is the portfolio weight of that ticker.

```
[1] 0.159067
> prices[3*252,4]/prices[252*2+1,4]-1
[1] 0.228165
> prices[4*252,4]/prices[252*3+1,4]-1
[1] 0.3467565
```

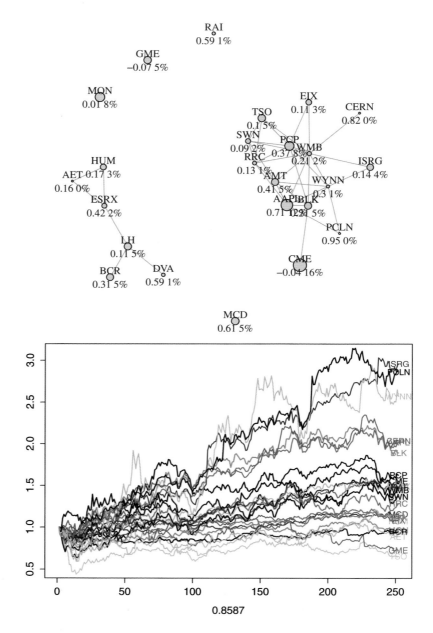

Figure 9.16   2009 return of 24 securities in co-movement graph and chart form.

```
> prices[5*252,4]/prices[252*4+1,4]-1
[1] -0.03004245
> prices[6*252,4]/prices[252*5+1,4]-1
[1] 0.05333184
```

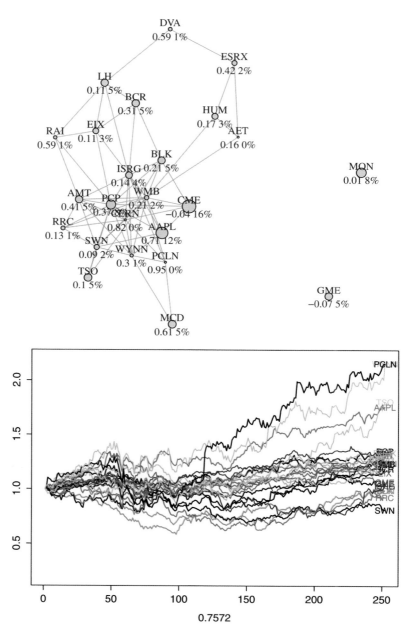

Figure 9.17 2010 return of 24 securities in co-movement graph and chart form.

- Figure 9.15 has an undirected graph and the 2008 actual prices plotted below, which have been scaled to an initial value of $1. In the figure, 2008 has a dense graph and bearish chart. MCD is connected to ten other stocks and has one of best returns of the group as we can see in the chart below the graph, in the MCD price path slightly above $1.

- Figure 9.16 shows 2009 with a bullish recovery in the chart and the graph above it shows independence of the stocks in the portfolio. MCD is deemed by the Glasso algorithm to be independent of the other 23 stocks in the portfolio, as its outdegree is 0.

- Figure 9.17, the 2010 chart, shows a compaction of the graph from 2009. The graph is fully connected so that no individual stock was breaking out and performing better than the remainder. Quantitative Easing went into Phase II late in the year and the market volatility was low. Return on stocks were moderately positive and quite positive for MCD at 22.8 percent. MCD itself exhibits a moderate level of dependence, not as great as in 2008, with an outdegree of 3. This time, interestingly enough, it "grabs on" to high flyer PCLN even though MCD itself enjoys a much higher weighting in the portfolio. Noting that one of its only three direct neighbors is Priceline, PCLN, and that is a very bullish association because over that time period PCLN has one of the highest rates of return of any stock in the NYSE or NASDAQ. While PCLN returns 115.6 percent in 2010, MCD, still a value stock, returns 22.8 percent.

From the returns calculated, 5.4 percent, 15.9 percent, 22.8 percent, 34.7 percent, – 3.0 percent, and 5.3 MCD can be viewed as a stock with good momentum. In 2010, it gets slightly absorbed into the fringe of the cluster and is comoving with high flyers. In 2011, the market starts to cool down, however, investors holding MCD are quite pleased with a 34.7 percent price appreciation.

The graphs of Figures 9.15 through 9.17 are produced by invoking the *huge* package. Not only it is of interest to view the graph plots, but we also want to consider our graph clustering measures: the sparsity and the clustering coefficient. Here is the R code which runs the Glasso procedure and computes the graph measures from Section 9.3.

```
runSixYrsGlasso <- function(daysPerPeriod,Sharpe,y=NA,sleepIntval=0,
                            isClusterCoeff=TRUE) {
 #Run Glasso alg from 2008 to 2014 by yr, qtr, mo
 totalPeriods= 6*daysPerYr/daysPerPeriod
 par(mfrow=c(1,1))
 sparsity = array(dim = c(totalPeriods))
 clustCoeff = array(dim = c(totalPeriods))
 portv = array(dim = c(totalPeriods))
 if(is.na(y)) yrange = c(1:totalPeriods) else yrange = c(y:y)
 for(y in yrange) { #2008:2009 to 2013:2014
   d1 = (y-1)*daysPerPeriod+1
   d2 = y*daysPerPeriod
   print(d1);print(d2)
   res <- runGlassoAndDisplay(prices[d1:d2,],lab,w,D,Sharpe,
                              lmratio=.6,trackIdx=4)
   A <- res[[1]]
   sparsity[y] <- round(computeSparsity(A),4)
   if(isClusterCoeff)
     clustCoeff[y] <- round(computeClusterCoeff(A),4)
   #compute portfolio return:
   portValue <- round( w %*% (prices[d2,]/prices[d1,]), 4)
   portv[y] <- portValue[1,1]
```

Using the system's *sleep()* utility, we can capture the plots for Figures 9.15 through 9.17.

```
Sys.sleep(sleepIntval)
if(daysPerPeriod == 252) { #yearly case
  if(y == 2) ylim = c(.5,3.1) else ylim = c(.2,2.2)
  plotMultSeries(prices[d1:d2,],lab,w,D,cc=sparsity[y],
                 ret=portV[1,1],ylim=ylim,isAlone=TRUE)
} else {
  portvDetail = array(rep(0,daysPerPeriod),
                      dim = c(daysPerPeriod))
  for(d in 1:D)
    portvDetail = portvDetail +
        w[d] * (prices[d1:d2,d]/prices[d1,d])
  plot(portvDetail,type='l',xlab="year",
     ylab="portfolio value")
}
Sys.sleep(sleepIntval)
}
return(list(sparsity,clustCoeff,portv))
} res <- runSixYrsGlasso(21,Sharpe,y=1)[[1]] #1 mo run
```

runSixYrsGlasso() plots the output as an undirected graph and stored results in three vectors of length 6 when our mode is yearly. In addition to each undirected graph is a scaled annual return plot for all the stocks in the portfolio. For the data gathering phase, the function splits the *prices[]* matrix by days with the R range *[d1:d2,]* into period covariance matrices. It is a function to observe, compute and transmit results for the period portfolio value, sparsity, and clustering coefficient. The **return** statement binds together the multiple results.

9.10   Regression on Yearly Sparsity

Let's consider looking at the six-year period with another perspective. Running the *runSixYrsGlasso()*, function yields our sparsity, clustering coefficient, and portfolio values.

```
glassoRes <- runSixYrsGlasso(252,Sharpe) #1 mo run
> yrlySparsity = glassoRes[[1]]
> yrlySparsity
[1] 0.7391 0.8587 0.7572 0.4819 0.8768 0.8043
> yrlyClustCoeff = glassoRes[[2]]
> yrlyClustCoeff
[1] 0.7513 0.7874 0.6299 0.7759 0.6500 0.7611
> yrlyPortV = glassoRes[[3]]
> yrlyPortV
[1] 0.6529 1.4432 1.2605 1.1493 1.1434 1.2274
```

A goal would be to predict the portfolio value direction, up or down, from knowing the other two independent variables about the comoment graph. In fact, we really want to predict the portfolio value direction, *lagged* one time period. This way, an investor can decide whether to invest short term in the portfolio during the expected bullish or bearish period coming up next.

The best linear regression equation is found by trying to use *sparsity*, *clustCoeff*, and *portv*, the portfolio value, to predict the lagged portfolio value, *shiftedPortV*. We can see that this is a poor regression plan from the fifth column p-values below:

```
Coefficients:
            Estimate Std. Error t value Pr(>|t|)
(Intercept)  6.83786    2.90470   2.354   0.143
sparsity    -1.83939    0.88964  -2.068   0.175
clustCoeff  -6.05451    3.44116  -1.759   0.221
portv        0.01173    0.39211   0.030   0.979
```

In fact, even taking away the *portv* and keeping the two graph measures still produces a poor regression result:

```
Coefficients:
            Estimate Std. Error t value Pr(>|t|)
(Intercept)    6.844     2.366   2.893   0.0629 .
sparsity      -1.835     0.718  -2.556   0.0835 .
clustCoeff    -6.049     2.806  -2.156   0.1201
```

What we can do with this very small set of data is seen below with a single dot(.) for the fifth column p-value:

```
Coefficients:
            Estimate Std. Error t value Pr(>|t|)
(Intercept)   1.6911    0.6480   2.610   0.0594 .
sparsity     -0.7741    0.8479  -0.913   0.4129
```

But this might not be surprising as the portfolio values move around quite a bit and we only have six points to work with. Note that the reader may end up with somewhat different results than these because of the number of data points involved in the 1,512 date time series and the number of securities involved.

Here is the final regression formula to predict the portfolio value. It only involves the *sparsity* independent random variable.

$$z_{yrly} = \beta_0^{yrly} + \beta_1^{yrly} \times yrlySparsity. \tag{9.17}$$

First, we set up a mapping of periods being years (mode 1) or quarters (mode 2) or months (mode 3) to fractional years in our period we are testing using a function *mapToYr()*. After finding the raw data in *runSixYrsGlasso()*, the regression procedure can be written, which goes as follows:

```
mapToYr <- function(per,mode=1) {
   if(mode==1) per+2007 else if(mode==2) per/4+2008
   else (per+2)/12+2008 }
```

```
fitLinReg <- function(sparsity,clustCoeff,portv,
                      daysPerPeriod,mode=1,LRTerms=3) {
  totalPeriods = 6*daysPerYr/daysPerPeriod
  periodsByYr = mapToYr(c(1:totalPeriods),mode=mode)
  shiftedPortV = c(1,portv[1:(totalPeriods-1)])
  if(LRTerms == 3) {
    lm <- lm(shiftedPortV ~ sparsity + clustCoeff + portv)
  } else if(LRTerms == 2) {
    lm <- lm(shiftedPortV ~ sparsity + clustCoeff)
  } else {
    lm <- lm(shiftedPortV ~ sparsity)
  }
  print(summary(lm))
  coef <- coef(lm)
  coef
  beta0 = coef[1]
  print(beta0)
  beta1 = coef[2]
  print(beta1)
  if(LRTerms >= 2) beta2 = coef[3]
  if(LRTerms == 3) beta3 = coef[4]
```

z can be found based upon the number of linear regression terms. *z*[1] is set to a filler value because the portfolio value series is shifted to the right.

```
if(LRTerms == 3)
   z = beta0 + beta1*sparsity +
   beta2*clustCoeff + beta3*portv
else if(LRTerms == 2)
   z = beta0 + beta1*sparsity +
   beta2*clustCoeff
else
   z = beta0 + beta1*sparsity
z[1] = 1.0
par(mar=c(4,4,2.82,2.82))
par(mfrow=c(1,1))
plot(periodsByYr,sparsity,type='l',
     col=2,ylim=c(.2,1.5),xlab="year")
points(periodsByYr,sparsity,col=2)
if(LRTerms > 1) {
  lines(periodsByYr,clustCoeff,type='l',col=5)
  points(periodsByYr,clustCoeff,col=5)
}
lines(periodsByYr,shiftedPortV,type='l',col=4)
points(periodsByYr,shiftedPortV,col=4)
lines(periodsByYr,z,col=27)
lines(periodsByYr,rep(1,totalPeriods))
```

Below, we can compute our Boolean market direction variables, *indz* based upon the predictor and *indNonNegV*, the actual market random variable of whether that quarter has nonnegative portfolio value.

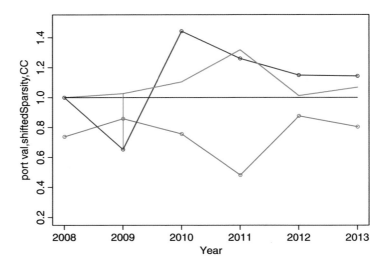

Figure 9.18   Plotting portfolio return against clustering. The top two series are the lagged portfolio value and predicted lagged portfolio value (without points). The bottom series is the co-movement graph sparsity. A vertical line segment is used to highlight the cases where the bull/bear prediction did not match the actual price level.

The final *sum()* in the *print()* function tells us how many successful Boolean predictions are made compared to the actual nonnegative portfolio value and is correct 80 percent of the time in predicting the next period's nonnegative or negative price. We use 1 for the first filler ($z = 1$) value due to the lag of one period.

```
indz = (z>=1)
indNonNegV = (shiftedPortV>=1)
print((sum(indNonNegV == indz)-1)/(length(indz)-1))
```

A series of vertical line segments is determined to highlight the cases where the bull/bear prediction did not match the actual price level with the R *lines()* below. Then the five newly computed vectors are returned after placing them into a list.

```
for(y in 2:totalPeriods)
  if(indz[y] != indNonNegV[y]) {
    lines(c(z[y],shiftedPortV[y])~
        c(mapToYr(y,mode=mode),mapToYr(y,mode=mode)),col="red")}
return(data.frame(z,sparsity,clustCoeff,portv,shiftedPortV))
}
```

For an annual basis, we can look at the chart of Figure 9.18 and see very few data points, but the predictor line, *z*, the line without marked points, is tracking somewhat to the sparsity. The case where it fails to predict is marked with a vertical line.

```
runGlassoAndLinReg <- function(daysPerPeriod,Sharpe,
                                mode=1,LRTerms=1) {
```

```
    totalPeriods = 6*daysPerYr/daysPerPeriod
    glassoRes = runSixYrsGlasso(daysPerPeriod,Sharpe)
    sparsity = glassoRes[[1]]
    clustCoeff = glassoRes[[2]]
    portv = glassoRes[[3]]
    lrres <- fitLinReg(sparsity,clustCoeff,portv,
                    daysPerPeriod,mode=mode,LRTerms=LRTerms)
    lrres
}
```

A period of one year may have too many bull and bear trends to subsume into one time slice. There is some movement in the sparsity which tracks somewhat to the lagged portfolio value. The dataset is very small when reduced down to one year of sparsity and value. In any case, we see some positive results, 80 percent prediction rate.

```
> yrlyDF  <- runGlassoAndLinReg(252,Sharpe,mode=1,LRTerms=1)
[1] 0.8
```

This is encouraging but only a modest success. We now turn to predict portfolio direction from the comovement graph quarterly and monthly.

9.11 Regression on Quarterly Sparsity

Let's consider retrying the type of chart of Figure 9.18 on a more granular, quarterly basis. After all, quarters can vary quite a bit in terms of the stock market's return. The six-year period contains 24 quarters. Again, we are looking for a trend between sparsity and clustering coefficient and the lagged portfolio value. Specifically, higher sparsity should yield higher portfolio returns, according to the hypotheses of the literature (Ang and Bekaert, 2003). Again we run R's *lm()* function and ask for the *summary()*. This time *daysPerPeriod* $= 63$ instead of 252. That means *totalPeriods* $= 24$.

```
Coefficients:
            Estimate Std. Error t value Pr(>|t|)
(Intercept)   0.9109     0.2001   4.552 0.000174 ***
sparsity      0.3042     0.1247   2.440 0.023655 *
clustCoeff   -0.1579     0.2178  -0.725 0.476579
```

The clustering coefficient, as seen in the above summary report, does not factor into the regression in a useful way. Rerunning the regression with only *sparsity* produces this summary:

```
Coefficients:
            Estimate Std. Error t value Pr(>|t|)
(Intercept)  0.77003    0.09355   8.231 3.67e-08 ***
sparsity     0.35562    0.12214   2.912  0.00809 **
```

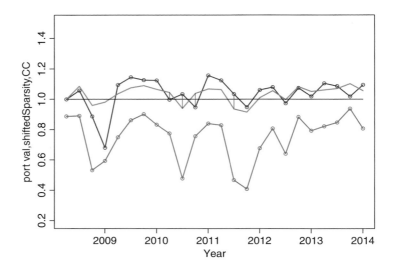

Figure 9.19   24 quarters of portfolio values. The top two series are the lagged portfolio value, marked without points, and the predictor, z. The lower series is the sparsity.

and with two and three asterisks for our βs, we become optimistic. The p-values reported are now well below 0.05.

Here is the regression equation which defines our predictor vector, z_{qtrly}, for which we need data for the independent random variables, $qtrlySparsity$ and $qtrlyClustCoeff$; however, once again, $qtrlyClustCoeff$ does not factor into the regression in a useful way. The β^{qtrly}s will be different values than for a yearly basis.

$$z_{qtrly} = \beta_0^{qtrly} + \beta_1^{qtrly} \times qtrlySparsity. \tag{9.18}$$

When we take out *clustCoeff* from the regression, we simply have the intercept and *sparsity* and Figure 9.19 shows the results from the quarterly regression from running the *runGlassoAndLinReg()* function with an 82.6 percent success rate.

```
> runGlassoAndLinReg(63,Sharpe,mode=2,LRTerms=1)
[1] 0.826087
```

Figure 9.20 shows a single slice of the quarterly run for the 23rd quarter. The graph is quite sparse. For the current period, it is also true that the market becomes quite bullish for these 63 days.

9.12   Regression on Monthly Sparsity

Many times in financial analytics we expect to find trends only to find out that logic and intuition is quite restricted in its application due to the highly random nature of the markets. However, in this case, we do see a relationship for the monthly period, as shown in Figure 9.21. Now, for the monthly period, we have $daysPerPeriod = 21$ and $totalPeriods = 72$.

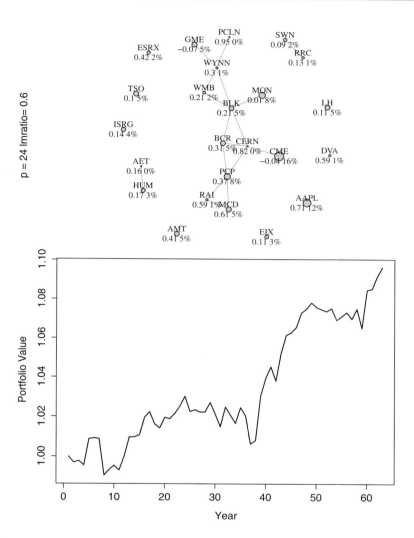

Figure 9.20 63 trading days of clustering graph and portfolio value chart for the 23rd quarter. A very bullish recovery is observed for the quarter.

For the monthly case, we have more points in the sample. We can see the regression summary below:

```
Coefficients:
            Estimate Std. Error t value Pr(>|t|)
(Intercept)  0.92992    0.03215  28.920   <2e-16 ***
sparsity     0.10862    0.04187   2.594   0.0115 *
```

Once again, our best linear regression formula has the single independent random variable.

$$z_{mnthly} = \beta_0^{mnthly} + \beta_1^{mnthly} \times mnthlySparsity \tag{9.19}$$

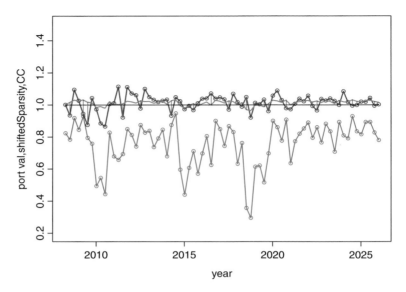

Figure 9.21   72 months of portfolio values. The top two series are the lagged portfolio value and the predictor, z, marked without points. The lower series is sparsity. The clustering coefficient is omitted.

```
> runGlassoAndLinReg(21,Sharpe,mode=2,LRTerms=1)
[1] 0.6478873
```

Our success rate is 64.7 percent. This begs the question, if we as investors focus on the sparsity as our primary predictor, can future potential returns be predicted in a bullish or bearish sense by using the sparsity and connectedness metrics on the Glasso-generated graphs? These modest successes suggest that perhaps they can on certain quarterly and monthly timescales; however, in the exercises we explore the out-of-sample case.

9.13   Architecture and Extension

The software architecture for clustering analytics involves the Glasso algorithm for finding the graph structures and linear regression to use the graphs as market signals for next period times of bullish or bearish regimes. Figure 9.22 is a structure chart showing the hierarchy of functions. Sharpe Ratios are needed to enhance the graph labels. Prices are needed to be able to find the log return, covariance, and inverse covariance matrices. Running the Glasso algorithm not only produces the plotted graphs and market charts, but keeps track of the graph metrics. Once the graph metrics are available, the linear regression can be attempted on the yearly, quarterly, and monthly periods.

We know that our predictions for yearly, quarterly, and monthly graphs are only offered in-sample at this point. There is an exercise for the ambitious reader to extend the regression by using the in-sample coefficients against out-of-sample data. 2014 and 2015 offer a full two years of available out-of-sample data for yearly, quarterly, and monthly cases. See the final exercise below for this.

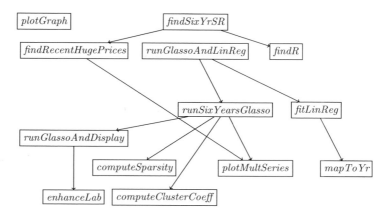

Figure 9.22   Structure chart showing the hierarchy of called functions.

9.14   Exercises

9.1. Draw the graph and find the sparsity and cluster coefficient for the adjacency matrix below:

$$\mathbf{A_1} = \begin{pmatrix} 0 & 1 & 1 & 0 & 0 \\ 1 & 0 & 1 & 0 & 1 \\ 1 & 1 & 0 & 1 & 1 \\ 0 & 0 & 1 & 0 & 0 \\ 0 & 1 & 1 & 0 & 0 \end{pmatrix}.$$

(a) Draw the undirected graph using node names U, V, W, X, and Y.

(b) Use Equations 9.7 and 9.9. Show all intermediate steps.

(c) Use the R utility functions *computeSparsity()* and *computeClusterCoeff()*.

9.2. Examining the variates of the Wishart distribution

The code for displaying Figure 9.12 appears in Section 9.6.

(a) Run the code with the seed set at 138. Display four histograms for *W.empir[,1]*, *W.empir[,6]*, *W.empir[,11]*, *W.empir[,16]* using 50 breaks.

(b) Explain why none of values appears to be negative.

9.3. Extending Clustering Prediction to Out-Of-Sample (OOS) Dataset (Difficult)

For the ambitious reader: extend the regression by using the in-sample coefficients against out-of-sample data. 2014 and 2015 offer a full two years of available out-of-sample data for yearly, quarterly, or monthly cases. Examine *runSixYrsGlasso()* and other prior routines in the chapter and book for loading prices and separate as necessary so that we can run a six-year in-sample and two-year out-of-sample simulation instead of the six-year in-sample simulation.

(a) Build and perform a yearly simulation.

(b) Build and perform a quarterly simulation.

(c) Build and perform a monthly simulation.

10 Gauging the Market Sentiment

The most common market regimes are the bull and bear regime. In Chapter 9 we discussed how to use the undirected Gaussian Graphical Model to gauge the market sentiment on a portfolio basis. Specifically the amount of sparsity – the number of absent edges in the graph – was an indication of the bullishness of the current market, to a degree.

Often it is hard to tell which regime the market is in. If this was easy to do, following a bullish or bearish trend would certainly be accomplished more frequently than it is currently. The time window of observation helps to determine the regime. Many market practitioners note that volatility is typically lower in a bull market than in a bear market. The panic that can set in during a crisis, which often are present in many bear markets, causes prices to fall faster than they typically rise. Sometimes this difference can be very pronounced, as those of us who experienced the 2000–1 and 2008–9 market drops know well.

Tools for determining market sentiment have a long history. This chapter begins with an application of a theory for market regime switching (Ang and Bekaert, 2004). The approach was introduced by Ang and Bekaert in the 2004 paper, "How regimes affect asset allocation." We proceed along the following lines. First, we load in raw prices and calculate the returns of our risky assets, in our case here the S&P 500 (SPY), the Swiss index (EWL), and the Japanese index (EWJ). These three assets roughly correspond to the geographic areas Ang and Bekaert found to be most important in international diversification. The economic rationale behind Ang and Bekaert's findings is that consumers are more able to delay purchases of durable goods (which tend to be produced in advanced manufacturing economies) and less able to delay purchases of service goods. For example, if I don't have a job, then I can delay the purchase of a new car, but I cannot delay paying my phone bill or my rent. Along this line of thinking, the ability to delay on the part of consumers leads manufacturing economies to show disproportionately poor returns during economic downturns. This in turn opens up an arbitrage opportunity. If we suspect that a given manufacturing economy will fare more poorly than a given service economy, then we can short (i.e. sell on credit with the broker) the manufacturing economy and long the service economy during the downturn. In this implementation we let Japan proxy as the manufacturing economy, Switzerland proxy as a small service economy, and use the S&P 500 as proxy for a large service economy.

10.1 Markov Regime Switching Model

We consider the sample time series $\{y_t\}_{t=1}^{T}$ where y_t are the log returns of the asset under consideration.

$$y_t = \mu_{S_t} + \sigma_{S_t}\epsilon_t \tag{10.1}$$

$$\epsilon_t \sim N(0, 1). \tag{10.2}$$

We assume there are two states: (1) bull and (2) bear. We further assume that the state variable $S_t \in \{1, 2\}$ is unobserved and must be inferred from the behavior of the log return process. The state process evolves according to a Markov chain with transition probabilities:

$$P(S_t = i | S_{t-1} = j) = p_{ij}.$$

A Markov chain is a random process that undergoes transitions from one state to another on a set of states as depicted in Figure 10.1.

Model parameter values $\theta = (\mu_1, \sigma_1, \mu_2, \sigma_2, p_{11}, p_{22})$ are estimated by maximum likelihood estimation, where μ_1 is the bull market mean, σ_1 is the bull market standard deviation, μ_2 is the bear market return, σ_2 is the bear market standard deviation, $p_{1,1}$ is the probability that we stay in a bull market given that we are in a bull market, and $p_{2,2}$ is the probability that we stay in a bear market given we are in a bear market.

We define the likelihood function to be maximized for the observed data as

$$L(\theta) = \prod_{t=1}^{T} f(y_t | \theta),$$

where

$$f(y_t | \theta) = \sum_i \sum_j f(y_t | S_t = i, S_{t-1} = j; \theta) P(S_t = i, S_{t-1} = j; \theta).$$

See the Appendix for a discussion of likelihood. Recall $\theta = (\mu_1, \sigma_1, \mu_2, \sigma_2, p_{11}, p_{22})$. We can write out $f(y_t | \theta)$, accounting for each of the four transition possibilities:

$$f(y_t | \theta) = \sum_i \sum_j f(y_t | S_t = i, S_{t-1} = j; \theta) P(S_t = i, S_{t-1} = j; \theta)$$

$$= \frac{1}{\sigma_1 \sqrt{2\pi}} e^{-\frac{1}{2}\left(\frac{y_t - \mu_1}{\sigma_1}\right)^2} P(S_t = 1, S_{t-1} = 1; \theta)$$

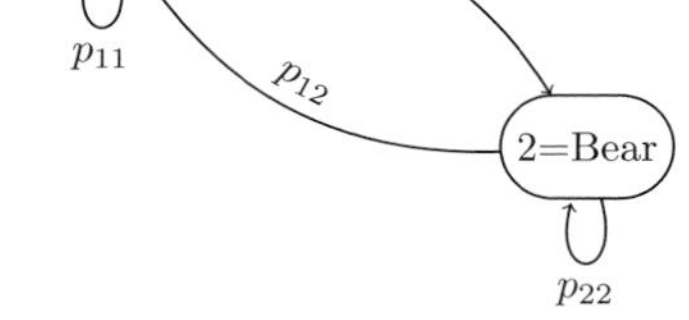

Figure 10.1 Regime switching state transition diagram.

$$+ \frac{1}{\sigma_1 \sqrt{2\pi}} e^{-\frac{1}{2}\left(\frac{y_t - \mu_1}{\sigma_1}\right)^2} P(S_t = 1, S_{t-1} = 2; \theta)$$

$$+ \frac{1}{\sigma_2 \sqrt{2\pi}} e^{-\frac{1}{2}\left(\frac{y_t - \mu_2}{\sigma_2}\right)^2} P(S_t = 2, S_{t-1} = 2; \theta)$$

$$+ \frac{1}{\sigma_2 \sqrt{2\pi}} e^{-\frac{1}{2}\left(\frac{y_t - \mu_2}{\sigma_2}\right)^2} P(S_t = 2, S_{t-1} = 1; \theta).$$

To simplify the above expression we use the $\phi(\cdot)$ notation probability density function:

$$\frac{1}{\sigma_i \sqrt{2\pi}} e^{-\frac{(y_t - \mu_i)^2}{2\sigma_i^2}} = \frac{1}{\sigma_i} \phi\left(\frac{y_t - \mu_i}{\sigma_i}\right)$$

where ϕ is the standard normal probability density function. Recall the definition of the standard normal distribution

$$\phi(x) = \frac{1}{\sqrt{2\pi}} e^{-\frac{1}{2}x^2}.$$

Note that we need the $\frac{1}{\sigma}$ multiplied by $\phi(\cdot)$ since the standard normal has standard deviation of $\sigma = 1$:

$$f(y_t) = \frac{1}{\sigma_i \sqrt{2\pi}} e^{-\frac{(y_t - \mu_i)^2}{2\sigma_i^2}}$$

$$= \left(\frac{1}{\sigma_i}\right) \frac{1}{\sqrt{2\pi}} e^{-\frac{1}{2}\left(\frac{y_t - \mu_i}{\sigma_i}\right)^2}$$

$$= \frac{1}{\sigma_i} \phi\left(\frac{y_t - \mu_i}{\sigma_i}\right).$$

Applying this notation and noting that constants will not affect the maximum likelihood estimation, we then have

$$f(y_t | \theta) = \frac{1}{\sigma_1} \phi\left(\frac{y_t - \mu_1}{\sigma_1}\right) P(S_t = 1, S_{t-1} = 1; \theta)$$

$$+ \frac{1}{\sigma_1} \phi\left(\frac{y_t - \mu_1}{\sigma_1}\right) P(S_t = 1, S_{t-1} = 2; \theta)$$

$$+ \frac{1}{\sigma_2} \phi\left(\frac{y_t - \mu_2}{\sigma_2}\right) P(S_t = 2, S_{t-1} = 2; \theta)$$

$$+ \frac{1}{\sigma_2} \phi\left(\frac{y_t - \mu_2}{\sigma_2}\right) P(S_t = 2, S_{t-1} = 1; \theta).$$

Applying Bayes' Rule to the joint state probabilities yields allows us to decompose the joint state probabilities $P(S_t = 1, S_{t-1} = 1; \theta)$ into the condition component $P(S_t = 1 | S_{t-1} = 1)$ and the marginal component $P(S_{t-1} = 1)$, for example.

$$f(y_t|\theta) = \frac{1}{\sigma_1}\phi\left(\frac{y_t - \mu_1}{\sigma_1}\right)P(S_t = 1|S_{t-1} = 1)P(S_{t-1} = 1)$$

$$+ \frac{1}{\sigma_1}\phi\left(\frac{y_t - \mu_1}{\sigma_1}\right)P(S_t = 1|S_{t-1} = 2)P(S_{t-1} = 2)$$

$$+ \frac{1}{\sigma_2}\phi\left(\frac{y_t - \mu_2}{\sigma_2}\right)P(S_t = 2|S_{t-1} = 2)P(S_{t-1} = 2)$$

$$+ \frac{1}{\sigma_2}\phi\left(\frac{y_t - \mu_2}{\sigma_2}\right)P(S_t = 2|S_{t-1} = 1)P(S_{t-1} = 1).$$

Once we have the conditional probabilities isolated, we can replace them with the components of our model. Recall that $p_{11} = P(S_t = 1|S_{t-1} = 1)$, $p_{12} = P(S_t = 1|S_{t-1} = 2)$, $p_{22} = P(S_t = 2|S_{t-1} = 2)$, and $p_{21} = P(S_t = 2|S_{t-1} = 1)$. Substitution yields

$$f(y_t|\theta) = \frac{1}{\sigma_1}\phi\left(\frac{y_t - \mu_1}{\sigma_1}\right)p_{11}P(S_{t-1} = 1)$$

$$+ \frac{1}{\sigma_1}\phi\left(\frac{y_t - \mu_1}{\sigma_1}\right)p_{12}P(S_{t-1} = 2)$$

$$+ \frac{1}{\sigma_2}\phi\left(\frac{y_t - \mu_2}{\sigma_2}\right)p_{22}P(S_{t-1} = 2)$$

$$+ \frac{1}{\sigma_2}\phi\left(\frac{y_t - \mu_2}{\sigma_2}\right)p_{21}P(S_{t-1} = 1).$$

For a Markov chain we have $p_{22} + p_{12} = 1$ and $p_{11} + p_{21} = 1$. Substitution yields the likelihood function in terms of $\theta = (\mu_1, \sigma_1, \mu_2, \sigma_2, p_{11}, p_{22})$, and the recursion, a formula for t defined in terms of the prior time period, $t - 1$, follows:

$$f(y_t|\theta) = \frac{1}{\sigma_1}\phi\left(\frac{y_t - \mu_1}{\sigma_1}\right)p_{11}P(S_{t-1} = 1)$$

$$+ \frac{1}{\sigma_1}\phi\left(\frac{y_t - \mu_1}{\sigma_1}\right)(1 - p_{22})P(S_{t-1} = 2)$$

$$+ \frac{1}{\sigma_2}\phi\left(\frac{y_t - \mu_2}{\sigma_2}\right)p_{22}P(S_{t-1} = 2)$$

$$+ \frac{1}{\sigma_2}\phi\left(\frac{y_t - \mu_2}{\sigma_2}\right)(1 - p_{11})P(S_{t-1} = 1).$$

Maximum likelihood estimation then yields the parameter estimates. Below we report the parameters of the Markov regime switching model as estimated by maximum likelihood via the R package fMarkovSwitching by Marcello Perlin (2006) and as described in Hamilton's Time Series Analysis (Hamilton, 1994) and Pennacchi's asset pricing work (Pennacchi, 2007). It is now difficult for the reader to reproduce these results because the *fMarkovSwitching* package has been made obsolete; however, we can discuss the results here. We expect the bull state to have a larger mean return and smaller

Table 10.1 Regime Standard Deviation.

	1	2
1	0.0235	0.0538

Table 10.2 State Means.

	1	2
1	0.0508	−0.0626

Table 10.3 State Standard Errors.

	1	2
1	0.0111	0.0031

Table 10.4 Transition Matrix.

	1	2
1	0.9668	0.0119
2	0.0332	0.9881

standard deviation, while the bear state is expected to have a smaller mean return and larger standard deviation, as seen in Table 10.1. This is what we observe below with state 1 standard deviation σ_1 being roughly half of state 2 standard deviation σ_2, as seen in Table 10.1. We also observe the contrast in means, with state 1 having a mean return μ_1 of roughly 5 percent and state 2 having a mean return μ_2 of roughly −6 percent.

We also observe the high persistence of each state, with each state having a probability of persisting to the next month of over 95 percent as seen in Table 10.4. This underscores the fact that both bull and bear markets tend to be persistent. In Ang and Bekaert we observe a bull–bear ratio of roughly 2 to 1, with the average bull market lasting 15 months and the average bear market lasting eight months.

10.2   Reading the Market Data

The first step in exploring the model of Ang and Bekaert is to read in the data files with security prices. Downloaded files for the S&P 500, the Japanese Index, and the Swiss Index for monthly closing prices are provided. We wish to contrast the bull vs. bear behavior of a balanced economy (S&P 500), a manufacturing economy (Japan), and service economy (Switzerland). We read the data into data frames and load the result of the regime switching maximum likelihood estimation. We then code 1.0 for a bull market state and zero otherwise.

```
setwd(paste(homeuser,"/FinAnalytics/ChapX",sep=""))

spy=read.csv("spy.csv",header=TRUE)
ewj=read.csv("ewj.csv",header=TRUE)
ewl=read.csv("ewl.csv",header=TRUE)
spy[1:3,]
smoothProbspy=read.csv("smoothProbspy.csv",header=TRUE)
smoothProbspy[1:3,]

#Plot series:
par(mfrow=c(5,1))
par(mar=c(1,2,1,1))
plot(spy[,5],type="l",col=4)
plot(ewj[,5],type="l",col=4)
plot(ewl[,5],type="l",col=4)
plot(smoothProbspy[,1],type="l",col=4)
#lines(smoothProbspy[,2],type="l",col=5)

stateProb=rep(0,length(ewl$Date))
for (i in 1:length(ewl$Date)){
  if (smoothProbspy$V1[i]>0.5){
    stateProb[i]=1.0
  }
} plot(stateProb,type="l",col=4)
```

We can now plot the three risky asset closing prices as well as state probabilities, verifying that bull states roughly correspond to segments of market positive trend. Figure 10.2 shows these time series plots.

Any type of covariance matrix and optimal portfolio calculation require returns, not raw prices. We will convert the raw prices to asset returns via the equation:

$$r_t = \frac{P_t - P_{t-1}}{P_{t-1}} = \frac{P_t}{P_{t-1}} - 1,$$

where R_t is current period return, P_t is current period price, and P_{t-1} is previous period price. These are net returns as defined in Chapter 3.

```
#sum(stateProb)
Rspy=rep(0,length(ewl$Date))
Rewl=rep(0,length(ewl$Date))
Rewj=rep(0,length(ewl$Date))
for (i in 2:length(ewl$Date)) {
  Rspy[i]=spy$Adj.Close[i]/spy$Adj.Close[i-1]-1
  Rewl[i]=ewl$Adj.Close[i]/ewl$Adj.Close[i-1]-1
  Rewj[i]=ewj$Adj.Close[i]/ewj$Adj.Close[i-1]-1
}
```

With our return vectors defined, we can construct the bull and bear return vectors. We do this by stepping through the state probability vector and assigning bull period returns to a bull return vector and bear period returns to a bear return vector.

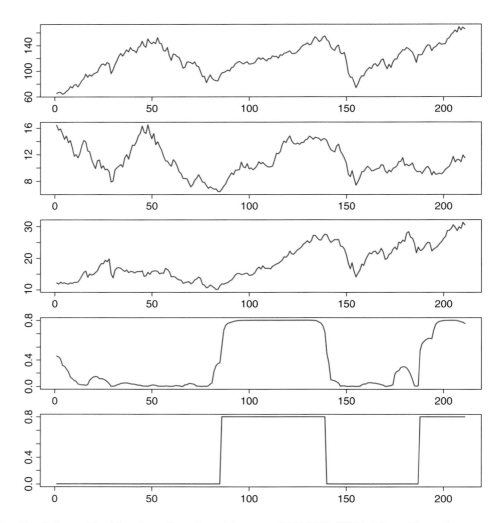

Figure 10.2 Top 3 charts: Monthly prices of our three risky assets (SPY, EWJ, EWL) followed by regime state probabilities for SPY followed by thresholded regime state for SPY.

```
a=1
b=1
#sum(stateProb)
bullRspy=rep(0,sum(stateProb))
bullRewl=rep(0,sum(stateProb))
bullRewj=rep(0,sum(stateProb))
bearRspy=rep(0,length(ewl$Date)-sum(stateProb))
bearRewl=rep(0,length(ewl$Date)-sum(stateProb))
bearRewj=rep(0,length(ewl$Date)-sum(stateProb))
for (i in 1:length(ewl$Date)) {
  if (smoothProbspy$V1[i]>0.5) {
    bullRspy[a]=Rspy[i]
    bullRewl[a]=Rewl[i]
```

```
    bullRewj[a]=Rewj[i]
    a=a+1
  } else {
    bearRspy[b]=Rspy[i]
    bearRewl[b]=Rewl[i]
    bearRewj[b]=Rewj[i]
    b=b+1
  }
}
#Plot series:
par(mfrow=c(3,1))
par(mar=c(2,2,1,1))
plot(bearRspy,type="l",col=4,main="S&P 500 Index")
plot(bearRewl,type="l",col=4,main="Swiss Index")
plot(bearRewj,type="l",col=4,main="Japanese Index")

hist(bearRspy,breaks=40,col=4,xlim=c(-.2,.2),main="S&P 500 Index")
hist(bearRewl,breaks=40,col=4,xlim=c(-.2,.2),main="Swiss Index")
hist(bearRewj,breaks=40,col=4,xlim=c(-.2,.2),main="Japanese Index")
```

We can now plot the return vectors in Figure 10.3 for the three assets and note coinciding periods of higher and lower volatility. We see the histograms which show the empirical distribution the individual asset returns in Figure 10.4.

```
> mean(bearRspy)
[1] 0.003797312
> mean(bearRewl)
[1] 0.00169756
> mean(bearRewj)
[1] -0.007118687
```

We can also see above the mean returns below and that the S&P has higher return than the Swiss and Japanese indices.

Using regime switching is one way to gauge market sentiment on the direction it is heading. Bayesian Reasoning is another way.

10.3   Bayesian Reasoning

In the previous chapters we used undirected graphs to collect groups of market random variables. In this chapter we use graphs once again; however, the edges will be directed showing expected causality and the nodes will represent Boolean predicates which can be true or false, with uncertainty represented by a probability. Bayesian Probability Networks have become important in the artificial intelligence (AI) and machine learning (ML) communities. Historically, computer science relegated any type of reasoning that involved uncertainty to AI, which embraced it (Pearl, 1998). The machine learning approaches, when compared to AI approaches, are more statistically thorough and rigorous. Bayesian Probability Networks, also known as Bayesian Networks (BN), span both AI and ML. They provide one of the more formal models for AI. Since these

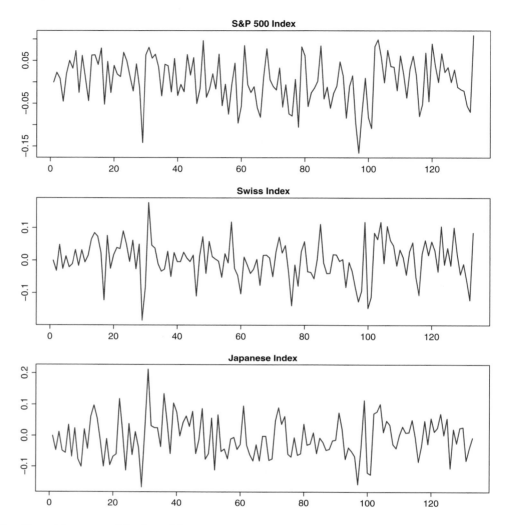

Figure 10.3   Bear state returns of the three risky assets.

networks have roots in logic, let us briefly discuss logic and graphs as they have been used in computer science.

The computer science literature is filled with approaches to automated reasoning. Propositional Logic provides the necessary mechanisms for reasoning about conditions for theorem proving, and there are programming languages such as Prolog (Colmerauer and Roussel, 1983) that evaluate predicates as a way of program execution. Propositional Logic assertions can be stated at points of control in software programs (Floyd, 1967; Hoare, 1969). Temporal Logic is a variation of Propositional Logic which incorporates reasoning about conditions at points in time for correctness proofs of software programs (Pnueli, 1977) and hardware circuits (Clarke and Emerson, 1981; Bennett, 1986). Both Propositional and Temporal Logic reason with certainty and are useful for verifying lower level computer engineering discrete Boolean logic.

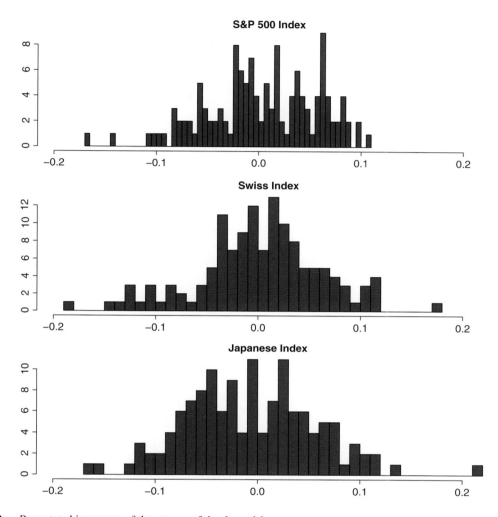

Figure 10.4   Bear state histograms of the returns of the three risky assets.

Bayesian reasoning attaches probabilities to predicates. If we have predicates *Grass-Soaked*, *Raining*, *SprinklerOn* in Propositional Logic, we have implications

$$(SprinklerOn => GrassSoaked) \text{ and } (Raining => GrassSoaked) \qquad (10.3)$$

where $v => w$ is defined as $\neg v \vee w$. In Temporal Logic, a gap in time can be described with the eventually operator ($\Diamond$) as in

$$(SprinklerOn => \Diamond GrassSoaked) \text{ and } (Raining => \Diamond GrassSoaked) \qquad (10.4)$$

With Bayesian Reasoning, the implications are embedded in the conditional probabilities:

$$P(GrassSoaked|SprinklerOn) \text{ and } P(GrassSoaked|Raining). \qquad (10.5)$$

Here we not only concern ourselves with whether the predicates are true but also the probability that they are true. We begin with the prior and posterior distributions as in (Ruppert, 2011) for computing the probabilities before and after we observe the events and then apply logic of the form of (Pnueli, 1977).

10.4   The Beta Distribution

The beta distribution is important in Bayesian Reasoning. Unlike the normal, which has a domain of all real numbers from $-\infty$ to ∞, its domain is the real numbers in the interval $[0, 1]$. When measuring the likelihood of a probability parameter, that, we know, must have a range $[0, 1]$, this distribution can be quite useful.

The beta probability density function is

$$P(X = x) = f(x) = \frac{\Gamma(\alpha + \beta)}{\Gamma(\alpha)\Gamma(\beta)} x^{\alpha-1}(1 - x)^{\beta-1} \ where \ \alpha, \beta \in 1, 2, 3, \ldots \qquad (10.6)$$

10.5   Prior and Posterior Distributions

Bayes Theorem allows us to reason about distributions before and after seeing the outcomes of a random variable. As stated in Chapter 3, Bayes Theorem can be stated as

$$P(Y_2|Y_1) = \frac{P(Y_1|Y_2)P(Y_2)}{P(Y_1)}. \qquad (10.7)$$

If we have a parameter or parameter set θ we can think about the *prior* distribution $\pi(\theta)$ before seeing observations Y and the *posterior* distribution $\pi(\theta|Y)$ after seeing those observations where we use the π when discussing densities of parameters as opposed to events. Applying Bayes Theorem to find $\pi(\theta|Y)$,

$$\pi(\theta|Y) = \frac{f(Y|\theta)\pi(\theta)}{f(Y)} = \frac{f(Y|\theta)\pi(\theta)}{\int f(Y|\theta)\pi(\theta)d\theta} = \frac{f(Y|\theta)\pi(\theta)}{C}, \qquad (10.8)$$

where the integral is no longer a function of θ and can be named a constant, C, which allows us to simplify the formula. C can be found such that the sum or integral of all probabilities for $\pi(\theta|Y)$ is 1.

If we want to develop a short-term trend following strategy based on market momentum, when we see a series of consecutive positive or negative returns, we update our beliefs about the upcoming return. Initially, before observation, we have an unbiased belief that a given market is bullish or bearish and so the $Beta(2, 2)$, with its symmetric continuous distribution, is a good fit for $\pi(\theta)$. For $Beta(2, 2)$ the p.d.f. is

$$\pi(\theta) = 6\theta(1 - \theta). \qquad (10.9)$$

Let Y be the number of times in five observations that we see a positive return. We are looking to overlay a logic structure on the simple log return Boolean values such as the following sequence. For example, for 21 consecutive adjusted closing prices, we have 20 log returns and 20 Boolean values of whether those log returns are positive.

```
> setwd(paste(homeuser,"/FinAnalytics/ChapX",sep=""))
> ec = read.csv("ECprices201305.csv")[,1]
> (diff(log(ec))>0)[1:20]
 [1] FALSE FALSE FALSE  TRUE  TRUE FALSE  TRUE FALSE FALSE  TRUE FALSE
[12]  TRUE FALSE  TRUE FALSE  TRUE  TRUE FALSE FALSE  TRUE
```

The sequence of TRUE/FALSE or 1/0 values for the sequence $Y_1, \ldots, Y_5$ is known to be, collectively, *Binomial*$(5, \theta)$, has a p.d.f. shown below and is depicted in the upper left side of Figure 10.5. (This distribution is covered in the Appendix.)

$$f(y|\theta) = \binom{5}{y} \theta^y (1 - \theta)^{5-y}. \tag{10.10}$$

So now, according to Formula 10.8, we can put together the two p.d.f.s from Formulas 10.9 and 10.10 into the posterior density of $Y_1, \ldots, Y_5$ being TRUE

$$\pi(\theta|5) = \frac{6\theta^6(1 - \theta)}{\int 6\theta^6(1 - \theta))d\theta} = \frac{6\theta^6(1 - \theta)}{C_5}. \tag{10.11}$$

Similarly, if all of the $Y_1, \ldots, Y_5$ are FALSE then the posterior density is

$$\pi(\theta|0) = \frac{6\theta(1 - \theta)^6}{\int 6\theta(1 - \theta)^6 d\theta} = \frac{6\theta(1 - \theta)^6}{C_0}. \tag{10.12}$$

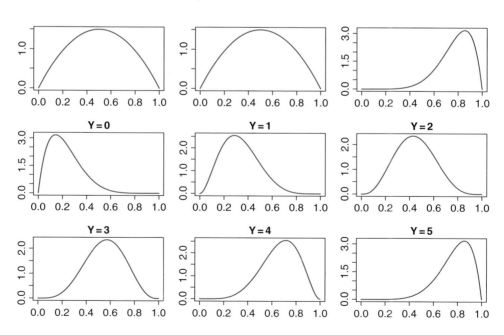

Figure 10.5   Two computations of the prior density. One computation of $\pi(\theta|5)$. Six computations of $\pi(\theta|y)$ where Y varies from 0 to 5, labeled above each plot.

Finding C_5 and C_0 can be done analytically or numerically. The R program below will simulate the various potential forms of the posterior distribution shown in Figure 10.5 with 10,000 trials and integrates numerically using the variables *postYis5DensTheta* and *postYis0DensTheta* in the **for**-loop from 1 to N, dividing the sum by N later.

```
N=10000
par(mar=c(2,2,2,2))
computePostDist <- function(n=5) {
  theta = vector(length=N)
  betaDensTheta  = vector(length=N)
  priorDensTheta = vector(length=N)
  postYisnDensTheta = vector(length=N)
  postYis0DensTheta = vector(length=N)
  postYisyDensTheta = matrix(rep(0,(n+1)*N),nrow=(n+1),ncol=N)
  for(i in 1:N) {
    theta[i] = i/N
    betaDensTheta[i] = dbeta(theta[i],2,2)
    #validate our expression for priorDensTheta
    priorDensTheta[i] = 6*theta[i]*(1-theta[i])
    postYisnDensTheta[i] = 6*theta[i]*(1-theta[i])*(theta[i])^n
    postYis0DensTheta[i] = 6*theta[i]*(1-theta[i])*(1-theta[i])^n
    for(y in 0:n)
      postYisyDensTheta[(y+1),i] = dbeta(theta[i],2,2)*
                                   dbinom(y,n,theta[i])
  }
  print(paste("Cn is",sum(postYisnDensTheta/N)))
  print(paste("C0 is",sum(postYis0DensTheta/N)))
  #
  postYisnDensTheta = N*postYisnDensTheta/sum(postYisnDensTheta)
  for(y in 0:n)
    postYisyDensTheta[(y+1),] = N*postYisyDensTheta[(y+1),]/
    sum(postYisyDensTheta[(y+1),])

  par(mfrow=c(ceiling((4+n)/3),3))
  plot(theta,betaDensTheta,type='l')
  plot(theta,priorDensTheta,type='l')
  plot(theta,postYisnDensTheta,type='l')

  #par(mfrow=c(2,3))
  for(y in 0:n)
    plot(theta,postYisyDensTheta[(y+1),],
         type='l',main=paste("Y =",y),ylab="prob")
} computePostDist()
```

In addition to computing and plotting the numerical version of the Beta p.d.f.s for each value $Y = y$, shown in Figure 10.5, the solution of $C_5 = C_0 = \frac{6}{56}$ is found.

```
> computePostDist()
[1] "Cn is 0.106983494617936"
[1] "C0 is 0.106983494617936"
```

Plugging these back into Formulas 10.6 and 10.8, we find that

$$\frac{\Gamma(\alpha + \beta)}{\Gamma(\alpha)\Gamma(\beta)} = \frac{\Gamma(9)}{\Gamma(7)\Gamma(2)} = 56$$

was easily calculated using R's *gamma()* function. So now we know that $\pi(\theta|5)$ is distributed *Beta(7,2)* and $\pi(\theta|0)$ is distributed *Beta(2,7)*.

10.6   Examining Log Returns for Correlation

Returns are believed to have nonzero correlations (Damodaran and New York University Stern School of Business). We can get an idea of how much this is true by examining a statistic that is designed for time series of prices or log returns: the autocorrelation function (ACF). The help page (accessed via ??acf) for the R *acf()* function references the book by Venables and Ripley from 2002 (Venables and Ripley, 2002). This book defines the *acf()* in terms of the mean of the whole series, and two portions of the series with the lag amount truncated off the front and rear to yield X_{s+t}, the lagged and truncated series, and X_s, the unlagged but truncated series, respectively.

$$c_t = \frac{1}{n}\sum_{s=1}^{n-t}(X_{s+t} - \bar{X})(X_s - \bar{X}) \ and \ r_t = \frac{c_t}{c_0}. \tag{10.13}$$

Implementing this algorithm by hand in R helps us understand the terms involved in this analytics metric. The R code which implements Equations 10.13 is presented below and, at the bottom, a comparison is made with native *acf()* values. In the code, we multiply the log returns by 100 to keep them away from 0. In the code R is *X*.

```
setwd(paste(homeuser,"/FinAnalytics/ChapX",sep=""))
ec = read.csv("ECprices201305.csv")[,1]
maxlag=30
n=59
acfval = vector(length=(maxlag+1))

R = 100*diff(log(ec[1:(n+1)]))
Rbar = mean(R)

for(lag in 0:maxlag) {
  R1=R[1:(n-lag)]
  R2=R[(1+lag):n]

  if(lag == 0)
    c0 = 1/n*sum((R-Rbar)*(R-Rbar))

  acfval[lag+1] = 1/n*sum((R1-Rbar)*(R2-Rbar))/c0
}
par(mfrow=c(1,2))
plot(R1,type='l',ylim=c(-.04,.04),col=5,
     main=paste("Lag =",maxlag))
lines(R2,type='l',col=3)
round(acfval,3)
```

```
acf <- acf(R, lag.max=maxlag)
acf
lines(0:maxlag,acfval,col=5)
```

Other than the indices being 0:30 instead of 1:31, the two methods of computing autocorrelation match, as seen below numerically and in Figure 10.6 graphically. The highest correlation occurs with the smallest lag, as expected. The case when the lag is 30 is shown in the left-hand plot where the lines display the two log return series *R1* and *R2*, which are the front and rear portions of *R[ ]* in the figure. *R1* and *R2* are taken from the May, 2013 EC price series.

```
> round(acfval,3)
 [1]  1.000 -0.223 -0.026 -0.010  0.003  0.150 -0.079  0.095
 [9] -0.082 -0.071  0.014 -0.080  0.063 -0.017  0.022 -0.111
[17] -0.041  0.047 -0.044  0.064 -0.012 -0.081 -0.122  0.144
[25] -0.028 -0.176  0.104  0.011 -0.076 -0.122  0.176
>
> acf <- acf(R, lag.max=maxlag)
> acf

Autocorrelations of series 'R', by lag

     0      1      2      3      4      5      6      7
 1.000 -0.223 -0.026 -0.010  0.003  0.150 -0.079  0.095
     8      9     10     11     12     13     14     15
-0.082 -0.071  0.014 -0.080  0.063 -0.017  0.022 -0.111
    16     17     18     19     20     21     22     23
-0.041  0.047 -0.044  0.064 -0.012 -0.081 -0.122  0.144
    24     25     26     27     28     29     30
-0.028 -0.176  0.104  0.011 -0.076 -0.122  0.176
```

This validates our implementation of Formula 10.13.

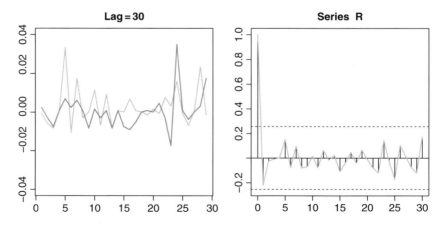

Figure 10.6   Times series of log returns and its lag of 30 periods with the autocorrelation computed two ways and compared graphically.

10.7   Momentum Graphs

If we have log returns R_1, R_2 for three consecutive quoted prices and S_1, S_2, S_3 for the two log returns, these can be summarized simply by two Boolean random variables Y_1 and Y_2, when considering the rise and fall of the prices.

$$Y_1 = \mathbf{1}_{R_1>0} \text{ and } Y_2 = \mathbf{1}_{R_2>0}, \qquad (10.14)$$

where $\mathbf{1}$ with a subexpression is the Boolean indicator function which has value 1 if true and value 0 if false. For example, when the prices were quoted in USD per EUR, these random variables can be used as momentum indicators whether prices are going up or down, like TRUE/FALSE values in Section 10.5, depending upon the prices or, equivalently, log returns so that

$$Y_1 = \mathbf{1}_{\log(S_2/S_1)>0} \text{ and } Y_2 = \mathbf{1}_{\log(S_3/S_2)>0}. \qquad (10.15)$$

Since consecutive prices are known to typically have some nonzero correlation, as demonstrated in Section 10.6, we can say that Y_1 and Y_2 have a dependency relationship as depicted in Figure 10.7 as

$$P(Y_1 = y_1) \text{ and } P(Y_2 = y_2 | Y_1 = y_1). \qquad (10.16)$$

This code sequence will help us look at a large set of prices and record our sample probabilities. In this case the robust set of prices are the 29,339 from the month of August, 2013 in the file named ECprices201308.csv.

```
setwd(paste(homeuser,"/FinAnalytics/ChapXI",sep=""))
ec = read.csv("ECprices201308.csv")[,1]
ind = diff(log(ec))>
len = length(ind)
sum = matrix(rep(0,4),nrow=2,ncol=2)
N = 0
for(t in 1:(len-1)) {
  Y1 = ind[t]
  Y2 = ind[t+1]
  if(!Y1 && !Y2) sum[1,1] = sum[1,1] + 1
  if(!Y1 && Y2)  sum[1,2] = sum[1,2] + 1
  if(Y1 && !Y2)  sum[2,1] = sum[2,1] + 1
  if(Y1 && Y2)   sum[2,2] = sum[2,2] + 1
  N = N + 1
}
prob = sum/N
ind
prob
prob/.25
sum(prob)
```

The following output shows the 2 by 2 matrix of computed probabilities. They may not look that far from $\frac{1}{4}$ until we divide them each by $\frac{1}{4}$ and see that, especially in the case of $P(Y_1)\&P(Y_2)$ in the lower right, we are quite surprised how far from $\frac{1}{4}$ they are.

Figure 10.7   One independent and one dependent random variable representing whether consecutive log returns are greater than 0.

```
> prob
           [,1]        [,2]
[1,] 0.2559566 0.2729659
[2,] 0.2730000 0.1980775
> prob/.25
           [,1]        [,2]
[1,] 1.023827 1.0918635
[2,] 1.092000 0.7923101
> sum(prob)
[1] 1
```

Even though we know that consecutive prices in historical markets have nonzero correlation, we have a desire to ask whether that correlation is positive or negative for our sample. Our one-month sample is large enough to get to within 1 percent of our expected 0.2500 probability. We can demonstrate this below where the final figure is in percent of 0.2500.

```
#Should we expect consec. logrets to be
#up then down with prob .2500?
set.seed(1001)
N <- 30000; vec<-rnorm(N); sum<-0
for(i in 1:(N-1)){
  if(vec[i]>0 && vec[i+1]<=0) sum<-sum+1
}
> sum/N
[1] 0.2506
> 100*sum/N/.2500
[1] 100.24
```

If Y_1 and Y_2 were positively correlated then $P(Y_1\&Y_2)$ would be greater than $\frac{1}{4}$ for a large enough sample. Instead $P(Y_1\&Y_2) = 0.1981$ and $P(\neg Y_1\&\neg Y_2) = 0.2560$. Summing across the bottom we also know that $P(Y_1) = 0.2730+0.1981 = 0.4711$ and down the right column we obtain $P(Y_2) = 0.2730 + 0.1981 = 0.4710$, properly rounded. We can use the latter of two forms of the probability multiplication formula

$$P(Y_1\&Y_2) = P(Y_1)P(Y_2|Y_1) \text{ if and only if } P(Y_2|Y_1) = \frac{P(Y_2\&Y_1)}{P(Y_1)} \qquad (10.17)$$

to compute $P(Y_2|Y_1)$ from $P(Y_1\&Y_2) = 0.1981$ and $P(Y_1) = 0.4711$ to be 0.4205. We know that Y_1 and Y_2 are dependent because $P(Y_1)$ is almost $\frac{1}{2}$ (actually 0.4711) and $P(Y_2)$ is almost $\frac{1}{2}$ (actually 0.4710) so $P(Y_1)P(Y_2) = 0.2219$ whereas $P(Y_1\&Y_2) = 0.1981$. If Y_1 and Y_2 were independent, then $P(Y_2|Y_1)$ would match $P(Y_2)$, but they do not: 0.4205 vs. 0.4710.

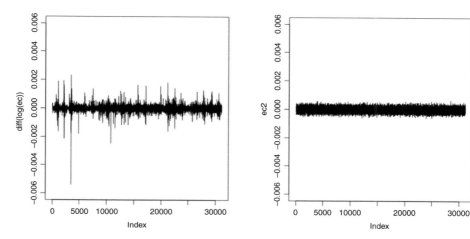

Figure 10.8   31,138 actual market price log returns and 31,138 simulated returns from the normal distribution on the same y scale. One can see that the standard deviation of the actual market log returns on the left is not constant.

We are working with Forex prices for EURUSD and these are typically modeled in computational finance literature as another Geometric Brownian Motion stochastic (GBM) process, much like in Chapter 14 and Figure 15.1. The interest rate differential provides the drift term μ of Equation 14.20. One very interesting analytics question is: How close to normal are the market log returns? We know that generating returns from the normal distribution allows for very few tail events as discussed in Chapter 5. What kind of tail events are in the market log returns? Another interesting question is: How do prices generated from a GBM process compare to the actual prices from market in terms of correlation?

Even our vector of 29,338 indicator variables from *ind* of the previous two R programs can tell us a little bit about how much correlation or independence exists. We know that if our sample values were independent from the normal distribution, then it would be true that $P(Y_1 \& Y_2) = P(Y_1)P(Y_2)$. So, if $P(Y_1) = 0.5$ and $P(Y_2) = 0.5$, then $P(Y_1)P(Y_2) = 0.25$. We know this from statistical independence, which is discussed in Chapter 3. However, in the case of the prices *ec* for August, 2013, $P(Y_1 \& Y_2) = 0.1981$ and $P(Y_1)P(Y_2) = 0.2219$ and these are pretty far off. Thus the independence assumption would have to be rejected. We can start to suspect some nonzero correlation in the prices. Let us look at the entire month of 31,138 prices and compare it to a generated sample from the normal distribution $N(\mu, \sigma^2)$ where μ and σ are set to the sample mean and standard deviation of the market price log returns. The program code allows us to compare the market log returns to simulated returns from the normal distribution. We can do that graphically first in Figure 10.8 which highlights the difference in consistency between actual log returns and log returns which are, in many cases, ideally simulated.

```
countInd <- function(R) {
  ind = R > 0
  len = length(ind)
```

```
    sumUp = 0; sumDn = 0
    N = 0
    for(t in 1:(len-4)) {
      if(is.na(ind[t])) {
        ind[t] = ind[t+1]
        print(ind[t])
      }
      Y1 = ind[t]
      Y2 = ind[t+1]
      Y3 = ind[t+2]
      Y4 = ind[t+3]
      Y5 = ind[t+4]
      if(Y1 && Y2 && Y3 && Y4 && Y5)
        sumUp = sumUp + 1
      if(!Y1 && !Y2 && !Y3 && !Y4 && !Y5)
        sumDn = sumDn + 1
      N = N + 1
      #print(paste(Y1,"->",Y2))
    }
    probUp = sumUp/N
    print(paste("Prob of seeing long ind",probUp))
    print(paste(round(probUp/(1/32)*100,2),"of 100 %"))
    probDn = sumDn/N
    print(paste("Prob of seeing shrt ind",probDn))
    print(paste(round(probDn/(1/32)*100,2),"of 100 %"))
    N
} #unit test:
pvec <- c(1.3,1.2,1.4,1.25,1.2,1.4,1.2,1.25,1.35,1.4,1.35,
          1.3,1.2,1.24,1.25,1.26,1.27,1.28,1.25,1.35,1.4,1.35,
          1.3,1.2,1.4,1.25,1.2,1.4,1.2,1.25,1.35,1.4,1.35,
          1.3,1.2,1.4,1.25,1.2,1.4,1.2,1.25,1.35,1.4,1.35)
countInd(diff(log(pvec)))

#Collecting 5 consecutive log ret directions
setwd(paste(homeuser,"/FinAnalytics/ChapX",sep=""))
par(mfrow=c(1,2))
ec = read.csv("ECprices201305.csv")[,1]
plot(diff(log(ec)),type='l',ylim=c(-.006,.006))
countInd(diff(log(ec)))

ec2 = rnorm(length(ec),0,sd(diff(log(ec))))
plot(ec2,type='l',ylim=c(-.006,.006))
countInd(ec2)
```

The *countInd()* function counts the number of times that the five Boolean indicator values, $Y_1, \ldots, Y_5$, like for our trade entry indicator functions, are all TRUE or all FALSE. In a symmetric and independent set of values, the indicator would be TRUE $P(Y_1, \ldots, Y_5) = \left(\frac{1}{2}\right)^5 = \frac{1}{32} = 0.03125$ of the time. When running *countInd()* on the log returns for EURUSD prices, we get a value less than that by quite a bit, as reported in the program output which is in percentage of $\frac{1}{32}$. With five consecutive positive log

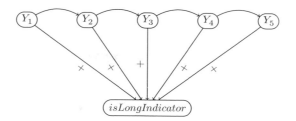

Figure 10.9 Six dependent random variables. *isLongIndicator* iff ($Y = 5$). The $+$ signs are to indicate a positive causal relationship.

returns being 44.4 percent less likely to occur in the up direction for the market sample than for the normal sample, this seems to say that the log returns have a reverting nature. They are less likely to sustain a run of either five up or five down returns than an ideal model of normal variates as seen in the segment below:

```
> countInd(diff(log(ec)))
[1] "Prob of seeing long ind 0.0173765015738421"
[1] "55.6 of 100 %"
[1] "Prob of seeing shrt ind 0.0261450504271857"
[1] "83.66 of 100 %"
[1] 31134
```

Stating it once again, we do not observe independence but rather a bit of anti-correlation in that $P(Y = 5) = \frac{0.5560}{32}$ and $P(Y = 0) = \frac{0.8360}{32}$, a bit smaller than $\frac{1}{32}$ which is what we would expect if they were independent events. Directed probabilistic graphs can be used to show causality. In this case, the analysis of the data is showing a bit of reverse causality in that in the market data it is less likely than in simulated data to see long and short indicators.

When entering a trade, we need to wait until a trend-following indicator is observed. If we think of a coin toss, the odds of seeing five consecutive heads is $(\frac{1}{2})^5 = \frac{1}{32}$. Due to the anti-correlation we can expect an indicator to occur more rarely than otherwise.

Bayesian probability networks allow one to formally reason about the market movements and justify a basic momentum indicator to be used in Chapter 11 for a trend-following trading strategy.

10.8   Exercises

10.1. Posterior Distribution with Another Indicator

Assume that your manager would like you to relax the trading indicator *isLongIndicator()* to only consider trades when the number of successive positive log returns or negative log returns is $Y_4 = 4$.

(a) Use the function *computePostDist()* to display the Beta distribution for this new case.

(b) Draw the directed probabilistic graph like Figure 10.9 for this set of random variables.

10.2. Independence of Market Random Variables

Assume that Y_1 and Y_2 are indicators of consecutive positive log returns for EURUSD price quotes as in Figure 10.7. When we collected approximately 30,000 log returns, we found the following sample occurrences which are our probabilities:

$$\begin{pmatrix} .24 & .27 \\ .23 & .26 \end{pmatrix}$$

(a) Determine $P(Y_1)$ and $P(Y_2)$ from the table as well as $P(Y_1 \& Y_2)$.

(b) If we round our computed probabilities to two digits, will we consider Y_1 and Y_2 independent for this sample?

11 Simulating Trading Strategies

Stories abound about people who say they bought a house 30 years ago, and it is now worth many times the purchase price. Staying invested in the housing market has historically been a safe bet. Just like a long-term investor in the housing market, a long-term individual stock market investor expects an upward-trending stock market when viewed decade by decade. The stock market investor remains in a long position, "long the stock market," until they decide to liquidate the position and realize any gains. In many cases this happens upon their retirement. This form of investing is one type of conservative strategy known as trend following: following the long-term upward trend until the desired profitability is achieved or until holding on to the investment is no longer feasible.

This chapter is all about trend following on a much more short-term basis: a matter of minutes or hours. It builds upon the market sentiment ideas of Chapter 10 and extends them.

11.1 Foreign Exchange Markets

If a United States corporation is expecting to make payments for purchased products in the Euro currency, they need to hedge their exposure to the Euro until the day the payment is required. Economically speaking, if the Euro increases in value before the payment date, and we wait to convert over our US currency into Euros, the payment effectively increases in value, against our will. The situation the company is in ends up being part of a trading strategy. A trend-following strategy to hedge exposure to the Euro involves buying the Euro and selling US Dollars at a point when the Euro is expected to increase or strengthen in value. If we own a forward or futures contract – the right to buy Euros at 1.1400 in the future – and the Euro currency then increases in value, as the Euros get more valuable we take comfort from the fact that we locked in at 1.1400, the lower rate. We tailor a contract to do this as long we think it is likely that an upward trend for Euro will exist. So, even though we just needed to make a payment, we are becoming a trader in the market.

Going beyond this simple payment example, for people speculating or hedging their long-term exposure to currency rates, another strategy is common. Since currency rates tend to grow much more slowly in return or percentage terms compared with stocks, a common strategy is *mean reversion*. If the Euro has been trading near

1.1400 US Dollars per Euro lately, it is not uncommon when it deviates from 1.1400 to come back to that amount. When it does, we say that it has "reverted" to the mean. A mean-reversion strategy involves buying the Euro currency when it has gone down as far as 1.1350 and expecting it to come back to 1.1400, at which time we plan to sell it. If things work out well, there are 0.0050 or 50 ticks of profit to be gained.

Keeping our attention on our shorter time frame, within a day, these two most basic types of investment strategies for a time series of prices are applicable: trend-following and mean reversion. On a short-term basis, with trend-following, a perceived trend is expected to sustain for a period of time so that the investor can profit. The investor believes a trend has begun by observing the market overall or a specific signal being triggered. As soon as possible, a position is established in the market. If the position is entered through a market order, the investor is subject to market price conditions at the time they enter the position. In order to fulfill the entry expectations, the goal is to complete the transaction as soon as possible. This is usually seconds or even milliseconds for a technically advanced firm, or hours or minutes for an individual manually entering the transaction on their own behalf or calling a broker to place the trade for them: essentially, "human speed."

With mean reversion in this short time span, the investor takes a long or short position with the expectation that prices will revert back toward a historical mean. If the investor is in a short position, they hold the opinion that prices are higher than the mean and are expected to fall back toward the mean. Two of the biggest challenges with mean reversion is to decide exactly what the value of the mean is, for prices to revert to, as well as the size of an excursion an investor is willing to tolerate before reversion occurs. If a bull market ensues after the short position is placed, it can be quite nerve-wracking to wait for prices to fall back to the mean. For example, in the bull markets for crude oil in the mid to late 2000s, reversion to some prices have still not yet occurred several years later in 2014. And in the currency world, many currencies such as the Canadian Dollar approached the value of the US Dollar in the five years from 2008 to 2013, whereas it had been only 65 percent of it as recently as 2003. Reversion to the 0.65 figure may never happen. In order to minimize this risk of non-reversion, stop loss limit orders can prevent a strategy from going awry when the trend is adverse to the investor's position. It limits the loss to be based upon the limit price. So long as the order can get filled in the market at or near the limit prices, the loss on the trade is capped. Sophisticated investors can overcome these obstacles and maintain a profitable mean reversion strategy by deploying limits orders.

Let us return to trend-following and look at a basic long and short strategy to earn a profit from trends in the foreign exchange market. Trend following can occur on a more short-term basis for those participating in futures markets with margin accounts. Day trading involves placing a position and liquidating it on the same day, staying "flat" or positionless overnight. There is enough price movement within the day to take advantage of strategies. The investor can speculate on either the long or short direction and must decide on the direction before placing the trade.

Futures are derivative securities which always have a time of expiry and are set in price roughly approximating the expected price at the expiry date. If one is participating in the currency futures markets on the EUR/USD currency pair, they typically speculate on a contract to either take EUR long and sell USD short simultaneously, or to take USD long and sell EUR short simultaneously. When interest rates are low, the price of the futures currency pair for expiry in one of four standard contract months each year, March, June, September, and December, is often close to the price of the "cash" or non-futures price which can be traded anytime. So trend-following a EUR/USD future is much like trend-following the EUR/USD cash security.

11.2   Chart Analytics

Strategies can be validated by performing chart analytics. Using historical prices and R as a simulation language for programming trend-following algorithms, one can back-test a strategy and get a feeling for its robustness and profitability. There are many commercial packages which simulate and display trades along with their status. But writing a simulator from scratch is a good exercise.

Figure 11.1 is a chart where each point represents the futures price of the Euro in US Dollars at a given minute. The futures market is open during trading hours for this chart for a full one-month period: June, 2013. EUR begins the month approximately 1.3000 and ends about there, but travels to as high as 1.3400 in between. For our purposes we will not be concerned with the exact open and closing time of the market. Typically the market is 24-hour except for an hour a day until Fridays, when there is a 48-hour break until the market reopens for Asia on Sunday. These time-of-day constraints can be built in after the basic strategy is up and running. For now, we will start with the basics of short-term trend-following as a long and short strategy.

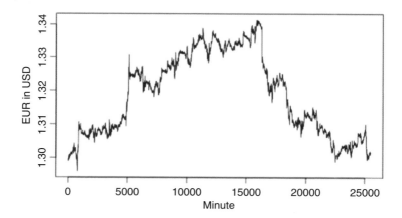

Figure 11.1   One month of minute-by-minute EUR/USD prices from June 2013.

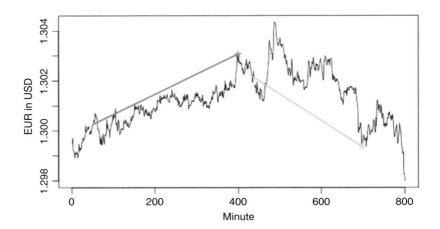

Figure 11.2   One long and one short trade in trend-following. In this example we have *stopAmt* = 0.0045 and *profAmt* = 0.0025. The prices are, again, from June 2013.

11.3   Initialization and Finalization

Administrative duties are required by most computer programs. Our market simulation needs to keep track of entry and exit prices for trades. It needs to ensure that no more than one trade is in effect at time, for our modest system here. One active trade at a time is our rule. It needs to separate long and short indicators and trade entries.

The following functions need to be executed before and after each simulation run. It makes heavy use of the super-assignment operator to perform the side-effects for the required resets. The constant *K* is the number of observed log returns and *KH* is double that amount, so that log returns prior to the trade entry decision can be observed and recorded to see how the market moves after trade entry.

```
reset <- function(S) {
  print("reset")
  K <<- 5; KH <<- 10
  LONG <<- 1; SHRT <<- 2; PROF <<- 1; LOSS <<- 2
  MaxTrades <<- round(length(S)/100)
  longProfTicks <<- 0
  longLossTicks <<- 0
  shrtProfTicks <<- 0
  shrtLossTicks <<- 0
  longProfLogDiffS <<- array(rep(0,MaxTrades,KH),c(MaxTrades,KH));
      longProfIdx <<- 1
  longLossLogDiffS <<- array(rep(0,MaxTrades,KH),c(MaxTrades,KH));
      longLossIdx <<- 1
  shrtProfLogDiffS <<- array(rep(0,MaxTrades,KH),c(MaxTrades,KH));
      shrtProfIdx <<- 1
  shrtLossLogDiffS <<- array(rep(0,MaxTrades,KH),c(MaxTrades,KH));
      shrtLossIdx <<- 1
  longProf <<- vector(length=MaxTrades)
```

```
  longLoss <<- vector(length=MaxTrades)
  shrtProf <<- vector(length=MaxTrades)
  shrtLoss <<- vector(length=MaxTrades)
  logProfIdx <<- 1
  longLossIdx <<- 1
  shrtProfIdx <<- 1
  shrtLossIdx <<- 1
}
```

winTicks and *totalTicks* below help implement the winning ratio calculation, which we will cover more in Section 11.8.

```
reportCounts <- function() {
  print(paste(longProfIdx-1,longLossIdx-1,
          shrtProfIdx-1,shrtLossIdx-1))
  print(paste("this sim longs =",counts[1],"shrts = ",counts[2]))
  winTicks = longProfTicks+shrtProfTicks
  totalTicks = longProfTicks+shrtProfTicks-
          longLossTicks-shrtLossTicks
  print(paste(round(winTicks),round(totalTicks),
          "winning ratio:", round(winTicks / totalTicks,4)))
  annHistVol
}
```

11.4   Momentum Indicators

A basic long and short trend-following strategy is to look for successive price changes showing momentum in the upward or downward direction as in Figure 11.3. A very simple indicator to determine if upward or downward momentum exists is a successive positive (negative) return for entering long (short) positions. Looking at the most recent log returns on the first 60 time points of the EURUSD chart, we have this output:

```
> ec = read.csv("ECprices201310.csv")[,1]
> diff(log(ec[40:100])) > 0
 [1]  TRUE FALSE FALSE FALSE  TRUE FALSE FALSE  TRUE FALSE FALSE
[11]  TRUE  TRUE FALSE FALSE FALSE  TRUE FALSE  TRUE FALSE FALSE
[21] FALSE  TRUE  TRUE FALSE FALSE FALSE FALSE FALSE  TRUE  TRUE
[31] FALSE FALSE FALSE FALSE FALSE  TRUE  TRUE  TRUE  TRUE  TRUE
[41]  TRUE FALSE FALSE FALSE FALSE FALSE FALSE  TRUE  TRUE FALSE
[51] FALSE  TRUE FALSE FALSE FALSE FALSE FALSE FALSE  TRUE  TRUE
```

There is one place where five or more consecutive upward returns appear: starting at the middle of the fourth row of Boolean values. This is fairly rare in the series and it is our long trade-entry indicator. Two time periods after the fifth Boolean (labeled 42) we will have entered our long trade: one period to look back and recognize the bullish signal and place an order and another period for the long order confirmation. Figure 11.3 shows seven consecutive trades on the first 5,000 minutes of prices with the first

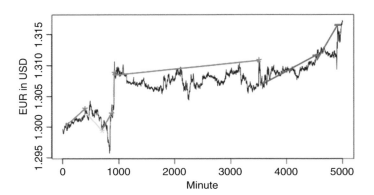

Figure 11.3   Seven trades in trend-following: long, short, long, long, long, short, and short. The four long trades are successful. Two of the short trades are unsuccessful and one is successful. In this example we have *stopAmt* = 0.0045 and *profAmt* = 0.0025. The prices are, again, from June 2013.

five successful in green (long) and yellow (short) and the last two unsuccessful in red (short). Brown is reserved for unsuccessful long trades.

11.5   Bayesian Reasoning within Positions

The argument for momentum with a given market, EURUSD in this case, can be made via the Bayesian ideas of prior and posterior distributions. For the prior case, since we know very little about what prices and log returns are coming in the future, we assume a very symmetric distribution. Then, as we start observing log returns and whether they are positive or not, our binomial random variable Y of Equation 9.5, we update our beliefs and form successive posterior distributions given Y. An argument can be made that if we see five successive positive log returns, $Y = 5$, then there is upward momentum in the bullish direction. Think of it as getting five consecutive heads in a row when flipping a coin, then changing any beliefs about the probability of heads being 50–50 to a Bayesian belief that heads are now more likely than tails for a while. Another argument can be made that this bullish price trend is very temporary and that prices will dissipate and revert back to where there were. It all comes down to the question: how long can the price trends sustain themselves? The position testing of this chapter is intended to find out more about this question.

Figure 10.5 tells us that prior and posterior reasoning has us believe that when $Y = 5$, the posterior distribution is $Beta(7, 2)$, whose p.d.f. appears in the lower right-hand corner. Two lines of R code can tell us the mean of this distribution which is at 0.7776, certainly biased toward another bullish success, expecting the upcoming log return to be positive.

```
> draws = rbeta(1000000,7,2)
> mean(draws)
[1] 0.777645
```

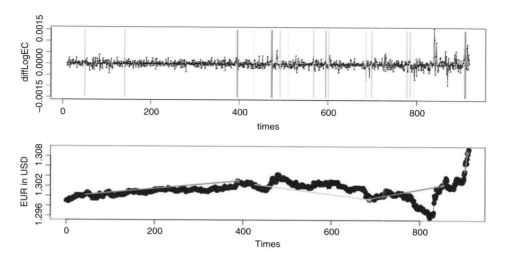

Figure 11.4   Log returns of EURUSD for 910 minutes of June, 2013 and position chart below.

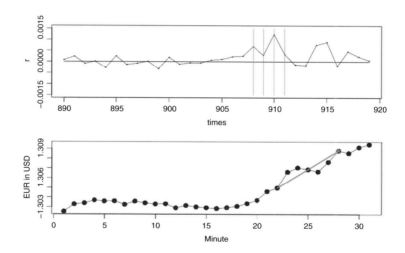

Figure 11.5   Fourth position from Figure 11.3 depicted above as log returns. The lower chart shows the trade lasting seven minutes for the expected 25-tick profit.

We can examine how often a five-stage indicator, depicted as a network in Figure 10.9, can occur in typical EURUSD log returns. If the five-stage indicator is observed, the position is entered and is held until resolved into a profitable or unprofitable position via a movement of 25 ticks or 45 ticks from entry in the direction of the position. Figure 11.4 imposes the log returns and prices next to each other for the first few minutes of June, 2013 with long and short indicators. Below that are EURUSD prices for the same period and short-term positions with long in green and short in yellow. The long indicators are in green and the short indicators are in yellow for the top chart with log returns.

The bottom chart shows the positions taken from the indicators in the top chart in the corresponding color. Figure 11.5 focuses on one position in this price series.

11.6   Entries

We have examined the conditions required to enter a trade. We simply proposed a heuristic rule which we felt might justify enough momentum in a market to begin to follow a trend. We know these trends do not last long in an intra-day market. The pair of functions *isLongIndicator()* and *isShrtIndicator()* are the indicators which use the posterior probability rationale of the previous chapter, where Y, the number of bullish or bearish successive prices in five consecutive minute time points, can be 0 through 5. We use this rule to justify a belief that a bull or bear market regime will begin and will sustain for long enough to earn a profit more often than not.

```
isLongIndicator <- function(logRetArr) {
  Y = sum(logRetArr[1:5] > 0)
  return(Y == 5)
}


isShrtIndicator <- function(logRetArr) {
  Y = sum(logRetArr[1:5] < 0)
  return(Y == 5)
}
```

The pair of functions are used throughout the market simulation as trade entry indicators. They are simple indicators which return whether five successive log returns of the price time series are all trending the same bullish (long) or bearish (short) direction. When either of these indicator functions returns TRUE the state goes from "no trade" to "preparing for trade entry" from one minute to the next.

The code to produce charts like the top chart of Figure 11.5 appears below. It uses five functions which are upcoming in this chapter: *isLongIndicator()*, *isShortIndicator()*, *reset()*, *reportCounts()*, and *sim()*. It is best to hold off from running the second portion of this code block until these functions are defined.

```
displayLogRetInds <- function(r,times) {
  plot(times,r,type='l',col=4,
       ylim=c(-.0015,.0015))
  points(times,r,cex=.2)
  len = length(r)
  lines(times,rep(0,len)) #plot x-axis

  longInd <- as.vector(rep(0,10)); j <<- 0
  shrtInd <- as.vector(rep(0,10)); k <<- 0
  for(i in 5:length(r)) {
    t = times[1]+i-1
    if(isLongIndicator(r[(i-4):i])) {
      j <<- j + 1
```

```
      longInd[j] <- i
      i = i + 5
      print(t)
   }
   if(isShrtIndicator(r[(i-4):i])) {
      k <<- k + 1
      shrtInd[k] <- i
      i = i + 5
      print(t)
   }
}
#Draw the potential entries:
if(j>0)
   for(i in 1:j)
      lines(c(longInd[i]+times[1]-1,
              longInd[i]+times[1]-1),
            c(-.0015,.0015),col="green")
if(k>0)
   for(i in 1:k)
      lines(c(shrtInd[i]+times[1]-1,
              shrtInd[i]+times[1]-1),
            c(-.0015,.0015),col="yellow")
longInd <<- longInd
shrtInd <<- shrtInd
}
```

The function *displayLogRetInds()* is merely to produce a figure. The code below that produced the top diagram of Figure 11.5.

11.7   Exits

Figure 11.3 depicts this strategy at work for seven trades, four profitable longs in green, one profitable short in yellow, and two unprofitable shorts in red over the first 5,000 minutes of the month of June, 2013 using *profAmt* = 0.0025 and *stopAmt* = 0.0045. A diagonal line terminated with an asterisk (*) depicts a profitable exit and a minus sign (−) depicts an unprofitable exit.

Backtesting is key for determining the exit strategy. Initially, it was believed that a good calibration was *profAmt* = 25 and *stopAmt* = 45; however, further testing found that *profAmt* 45 and *stopAmt* = 35 is a better choice for the sample dataset. So when sufficient momentum is observed at one time point, one minute later we enter a long trade and hold on until one of two events happens:

- The momentum continues and the price rises 0.0045 or 45 ticks above our entry price;
- The momentum dissipates and the price falls 0.0035 or 35 ticks below our entry price.

Symmetrically, the short trade has the profit target of 45 ticks below and stop of 35 ticks above the entry price. When either of these two exit signals occurs at a minute time point, we have exited the trade in the following minute time point. This strategy places a *profit target* and a *stop loss limit* to limit both directions of our trade. The profit target attempts to lock in a profit at a level proven to be reliable. The stop loss limit is to protect against the risk of a significant financial loss.

11.8   Profitability

Just like the stock market, the currency market has a convention for quoting prices. For the EUR/USD currency futures pair as traded on the Chicago Merchantile Exchange, 0.0001 represents a single *tick*, the smallest pricing unit, worth \$12.50 per contract bought or sold, for profit and loss settlements. For a ten contract investment, a movement of 45 ticks in the profitable direction is worth:

$$Profit \ = \ (10 \ contracts)(12.50 \ USD \ per \ contract \ per \ tick)(45 \ ticks) \ = \ 5625.00 \ USD.$$

For a ten contract investment, a movement of 35 ticks in the unprofitable direction is worth:

$$Loss \ = \ (10 \ contracts)(12.50 \ USD \ per \ contract \ per \ tick)(35 \ ticks) \ = \ 4375.00 \ USD.$$

11.9   Short-Term Volatility

Backtesting is a way to find the "beat" of the market that one is trading. By trial and error we found that approximately 45 ticks of profit and 35 ticks for a stop loss limit is about right consistently for our six-month by one-minute sample dataset. At 5625.00 USD per winning trade and 4325.00 USD per losing trade we would be allowed to have fewer winning trades per losing trade in order to maintain a profitable position.

With trending and mean reversion occurring and because of the volatility of prices, investors can speculate on the upcoming future prices, applying a strategy. As we simulate the market for one month, we also want to discover and keep in mind the volatility that was in effect for that month. Investor's intuition would tell us that an adequate level of volatility is necessary to have success in a trend-following strategy. If the trends we expect are occurring then those trends would be causing a higher standard deviation of log returns, and this should be reflected in the volatility.

Measuring volatility on the EUR charts, represented by price vector S, on a one-minute time basis, is as follows:

```
> S = ec
> logDiffS = diff(log(S))
> logDiffSmean = mean(logDiffS)
> N = length(logDiffS)
> minHistVol = sqrt(1/(N-1)*sum((logDiffS-logDiffSmean)^2))
> annHistVol = minHistVol*sqrt(60*24*252)
> annHistVol
[1] 0.1024109
```

See Section 3.4 for the general formula for historical volatility.

Simulating day trades on this one-minute Euro market on a price time series for one month begins with some R administrative code for setting constants, resetting counters, and reporting the results. The next section outlines this code.

11.10   The State Machine

At each time period where a single price for the security is present, we are in one of nine states, as depicted in Figure 11.6, where the positive or negative state value is kept in the *direction* variable in the R code. State (0) is the quiescent state with no active trade. The trade states are: (0) is no trade, (+1) is long, and (−1) is short. The fractional states are: (+.25) is transitioning from no trade to long, (−.25) is transitioning from no trade to short, (+.50) is transitioning from long to exiting because a loss limit is hit, (+.75) is transitioning from long to exiting because a profit target is hit, (−.50) is transitioning from short to exiting because a loss limit is hit, and finally (−.75) is transitioning from short to exiting because a profit target is hit.

Now we are ready for the main simulation loop which follows the finite state machine design of Figure 11.6.

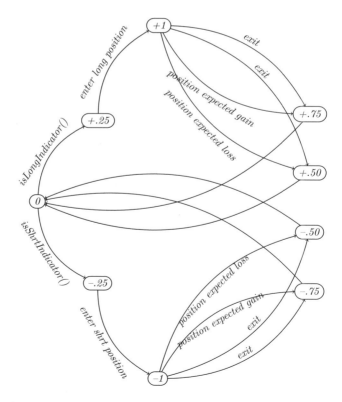

Figure 11.6   State machine for long and short positions.

```
sim <- function(S,mo,stopAmt=.0035,profAmt=.0045) {
  plot(S,type='l',col='blue4',xlab='minutes',
      ylab='EUR in USD')
  if(TRUE) #"blue"
    points(S,type='p',xlab="Minutes",ylab="EC",
          col='blue4',pch=16, cex=1.4)

  #simulate strategies on the incoming chart
  #We use 1e4 multiplier since logrets are only used for
  #pattern analysis
  logDiffS = 10000*diff(log(S))
  logDiffS = append(logDiffS, 0.0, after = 0); #log ret inds
  logDiffSmean = mean(logDiffS)
  N = length(logDiffS)
  minHistVol <<- sqrt(1/(N-1)*
                      sum((logDiffS/1e4-logDiffSmean/1e4)^2))
  annHistVol <<- minHistVol*sqrt(60*24*252)
  tradetrange = 0
  tradeSrange = 0
  direction = 0
  countT = 0; countF = 0
  logDiffSentry = array(rep(0,KH),c(KH))
```

We use five log returns as the trade entry indicators, and we analyze those five and the five prior to them. This results in skipping out to time period $KH + 1 = K + K + 1 = 5 + 5 + 1 = 11$ initially. The **while**-loop below is the main simulation loop, iterating over the length of the *logDiffS* log return price vector. There are four major code blocks below as we review it: long, long unwind, short, and short unwind, and these logic sections are marked in comments.

```
i = 11
while(i<=length(logDiffS)) {
  #long:
  if((direction == 0) && isLongIndicator(logDiffS[(i-4):i])
      ) {
    logDiffSentry = logDiffS[(i-(KH-1)):i]
    direction = +0.25 #buy upon next points
  }
```

The two element vector *tradetrange* (trade time range) and *tradeSrange* (trade stock price range) record the time, i, and price level, $S[i]$, of trade entry and exit. This simplifies the profit or loss calculation later.

```
  else if(direction == +0.25) {
      tradetrange = c(i)
      tradeSrange = c(S[i])
      print(paste("long: ",tradetrange,tradeSrange))
      countT <- countT + 1
      i <- i + 5 #fast fwd time for next indicator instance
      direction = +1
  }
```

On hitting the profit target of 45 ticks (below), we transition to the "exit position expected gain" state. Once in that state all trade exit tallies are completed.

```
#long unwind:
if((direction == +1) && ((S[i]-tradeSrange[1]) > profAmt)) {
  direction = +0.75
}
else if(direction == +0.75) {
  tradetrange = union(tradetrange, c(i))
  tradeSrange = union(tradeSrange, c(S[i]))

  print(paste("unwind long expected gain: ",tradetrange[2],
    tradeSrange[2],round(tradeSrange[2]-tradeSrange[1],5)))
  lines(tradetrange,tradeSrange,type="l",col="green",lwd=3)
  points(tradetrange[2],tradeSrange[2],
      cex=2,pch="*",col="green")

  longProf[longProfIdx] <<-
      tradeSrange[2]-tradeSrange[1] >= 0
  longProfLogDiffS[longProfIdx,] <<- logDiffSentry
  longProfIdx <<- longProfIdx + 1

  longProfTicks <<- longProfTicks + 10000*
      (tradeSrange[2] - tradeSrange[1])

  tradetrange = 0; tradeSrange = 0; direction = 0
}
```

On hitting the stop loss limit of 45 ticks (below), we transition to the "exit position expected loss" state. Once in that state all trade exit tallies are completed.

```
#long unwind:
if((direction == +1) && ((S[i]-tradeSrange[1]) <= -stopAmt)) {
  direction = +0.50
}
else if(direction == +0.5) {
  tradetrange = union(tradetrange, c(i))
  tradeSrange = union(tradeSrange, c(S[i]))

  print(paste("unwind long expected loss: ",tradetrange[2],
      tradeSrange[2],round(tradeSrange[2]-tradeSrange[1],5)))
  lines(tradetrange ,tradeSrange ,type="l",col="brown",lwd=3)
  points(tradetrange[2],tradeSrange[2],
      cex=3,pch="-",col="brown")

  longLoss[longLossIdx] <<-tradeSrange[2]-tradeSrange[1] < 0
  longLossLogDiffS[longLossIdx,] <<- logDiffSentry
  longLossIdx <<- longLossIdx + 1

  longLossTicks <<- longLossTicks + 10000*
      (tradeSrange[2] - tradeSrange[1])

  tradetrange = 0; tradeSrange = 0; direction = 0
}
```

Symmetrically, the logic applies to the short case.

```
#short:
if((direction == 0) && isShrtIndicator(logDiffS[(i-4):i])
    ) {
  logDiffSentry = logDiffS[(i-(KH-1)):i]
  direction = -0.25
}
else if(direction == -0.25) {
  tradetrange = c(i)
  tradeSrange = c(S[i])
  print(paste("shrt: ",tradetrange,tradeSrange))
  countF <- countF + 1
  i <- i + 5 #fast fwd time for next indicator instance
  direction = -1
}
```

Like for longs, on hitting the profit target (below), we transition to the "exit position expected gain" state.

```
#short unwind:
if((direction == -1) && ((tradeSrange[1]-S[i]) > profAmt)) {
  direction = -0.75
}
else if(direction == -0.75) {
  tradetrange = union(tradetrange, c(i))
  tradeSrange = union(tradeSrange, c(S[i]))
  print(paste("unwind shrt expected gain: ",tradetrange[2],
          tradeSrange[2],round(tradeSrange[1]-tradeSrange[2],5)))
  lines(tradetrange ,tradeSrange ,type="l",
        col="gold",lwd=3)
  points(tradetrange[2],tradeSrange[2],
        cex=2,pch="*",col="gold")

  shrtProf[shrtProfIdx] <<- tradeSrange[1]-tradeSrange[2] >= 0
  shrtProfLogDiffS[shrtProfIdx,] <<- logDiffSentry
  shrtProfIdx <<- shrtProfIdx + 1

  shrtProfTicks <<- shrtProfTicks + 10000*
    (tradeSrange[1] - tradeSrange[2])

  tradetrange = 0; tradeSrange = 0; direction = 0
}
if((direction == -1) && ((tradeSrange[1]-S[i]) <= -stopAmt)) {
  direction = -0.50
}
else if(direction == -0.50) {
  tradetrange = union(tradetrange, c(i))
  tradeSrange = union(tradeSrange, c(S[i]))
  print(paste("unwind shrt expected loss: ",tradetrange[2],
      tradeSrange[2],round(tradeSrange[1]-tradeSrange[2],5)))
```

```
      lines(tradetrange,tradeSrange,type="l",col="red",lwd=3)
      points(tradetrange[2],tradeSrange[2],
          cex=3,pch="-",col="red")

      shrtLoss[shrtLossIdx] <<-tradeSrange[1]-tradeSrange[2] < 0
      shrtLossLogDiffS[shrtLossIdx,] <<- logDiffSentry
      shrtLossIdx <<- shrtLossIdx + 1

      shrtLossTicks <<- shrtLossTicks+10000 *
          (tradeSrange[1] - tradeSrange[2])

      tradetrange = 0; tradeSrange = 0; direction = 0
    }
    i <- i + 1
  }
  return(c(countT,countF))
}
```

A portion of the *sim()* function output appears below. As it performs the trade entry and exit simulation, *sim()* logs individual position outcomes as a gain or loss and the entry and exit times and prices from the *tradetrange* and *tradeSrange* two-element vectors as well as the price difference. *reportCounts()* is a summary of each simulation run for a month of one minute data, showing the number of completed profitable longs, unprofitable longs, profitable shorts, and unprofitable shorts, as well as total long and total short positions. The winning ratio can be calculated from the following formula and appears near the bottom of this output segment:

$$WinRatio = (profitable\ ticks)/(profitable\ ticks - unprofitable\ ticks), \qquad (11.1)$$

where the *unprofitable ticks* are negatively signed.

First we set our current directory so that we pick up a file of prices from the upcoming Chapter. Then we can run a test of our built trading simulation functions.

```
setwd(paste(homeuser,"/FinAnalytics/ChapXI",sep=""))
par(mfrow=c(2,1))
start=890; end=920 #Limits chart to start:end
ec = read.csv("ECprices201306.csv")[,1]
ec = ec[start:end]
diffLogEC = diff(log(ec))
times=c(start:(end-1))
countInd(diffLogEC)
displayLogRetInds(diffLogEC,times)
ec = read.csv("ECprices201306.csv")[,1]
plot(start:end,ec[start:end],type="p",col=4)
reset(ec[1:800])
counts <- sim(ec[1:800],"01306",
              stopAmt=.0045,profAmt=.0025)
reportCounts()
ec = read.csv("ECprices201306.csv")[,1]
```

```
plot(ec[1:5000],type="l",col=4)
reset(ec[1:5000])
counts <- sim(ec[1:5000],"201306",
              stopAmt=.0045,profAmt=.0025)
reportCounts()
```

Here is a log of the seven simulated trades with the time as a minute number and simulated entry price, followed by the unwind or exit event with minute number and simulated exit price. The term "expected gain" means that a profit target was hit during minute t so that in minute $t + 1$ an exit will occur and there is an expected – but not a guaranteed – gain. The gain may not occur if the market moves significantly and out of the profit region, but this is highly unlikely. The term "expected loss" works similarly for the unprofitable case.

The last line is a trade entry whose exit does not occur within the first 5,000 minutes. There is no *unwind* event reported before we end the simulation.

```
> counts <- sim(ec[1:5000],"201306",stopAmt=.0045,profAmt=.0025)
[1] "long:    52 1.30027"
[1] "unwind long expected gain:   397 1.30306 0.00279"
[1] "shrt:    434 1.30216"
[1] "unwind shrt expected gain:   696 1.29936 0.0028"
[1] "long:    701 1.29964"
[1] "unwind long expected gain:   860 1.30224 0.0026"
[1] "long:    910 1.30498"
[1] "unwind long expected gain:   916 1.3088 0.00382"
[1] "long:    935 1.3085"
[1] "unwind long expected gain:   3500 1.31081 0.00231"
[1] "shrt:    3558 1.307"
[1] "unwind shrt expected loss:   4522 1.31164 -0.00464"
[1] "shrt:    4542 1.31091"
[1] "unwind shrt expected loss:   4909 1.31655 -0.00564"
[1] "long:    4978 1.31647"
```

The following code sequence dispatches six consecutive one-month-long simulations.

```
setwd(paste(homeuser,"/FinAnalytics/ChapXI",sep=""))
ec = read.csv("ECprices201305.csv",header = FALSE)[,1]
reset(ec)
counts <- sim(ec,"201305")
reportCounts()

ec = read.csv("ECprices201306.csv",header = FALSE)[,1]
reset(ec)
counts <- sim(ec,"201306")
reportCounts()

ec = read.csv("ECprices201307.csv",header = FALSE)[,1]
reset(ec)
counts <- sim(ec,"201307")
reportCounts()
```

```
ec = read.csv("ECprices201308.csv",header = FALSE)[,1]
reset(ec)
counts <- sim(ec,"201308")
reportCounts()

ec = read.csv("ECprices201309.csv",header = FALSE)[,1]
reset(ec)
counts <- sim(ec,"201309")
reportCounts()

ec = read.csv("ECprices201310.csv",header = FALSE)[,1]
reset(ec)
counts <- sim(ec,"201310")
reportCounts()
```

The output for one of the months might look like this:

```
...
[1] "long:   29242 1.29533"
[1] "unwind long expected gain:   29305 1.30128 0.00595"
[1] "shrt:   29319 1.3033"
[1] "unwind shrt expected gain:   30441 1.29858 0.00472"
[1] "shrt:   30490 1.29724"
[1] "unwind shrt expected loss:   30614 1.30068 -0.00344"
[1] "shrt:   30687 1.29849"
> reportCounts()
[1] "12 11 14 11"
[1] "this sim longs = 23 shrts =   26"
[1] "1221 2076 winning ratio: 0.5882"
[1] 0.09746766
```

A key success statistic is the reported winning ratio, *58.82* percent. At the very bottom is the reported annualized historical volatility of the price time series, *9.75* percent, which we can record and potentially study as a stimulus variable for the success of the strategy.

Figure 11.7 depicts the position activity for the 23 long and 26 short trades for the entire month of May 2013. The following color scheme is used to display the position activity:

- *green* is used for long profitable trades.
- *yellow* is used for short profitable trades.
- *brown* is used for long unprofitable trades.
- *red* is used for short unprofitable trades.

Once again, an asterisk marks the exit point of a position in both time and price level of profitable trades. A minus sign marks the exit point of a position of an unprofitable trade. Here the blue price charting lines are overpainted with large solid circles to help highlight the trade trajectories markers.

The output of the *plotMeanInds()* summary function displays the mean log returns so that time marches forward from left to right.

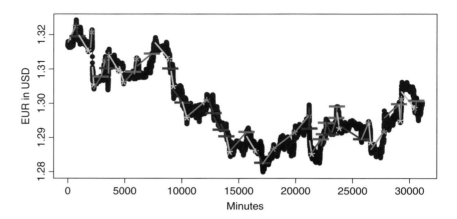

Figure 11.7   Entire month of long and short positions for May, 2013. Left to right, there is a mixture of all four outcomes: long, short, successful, unsuccessful, as time moves forward.

```
#post-simulation analysis of indicator distribution
plotMeanInds <- function() {
  par(mfrow=c(2,2))
  print(longProfLogDiffS[1:(longProfIdx-1),])
  plot(apply(longProfLogDiffS[1:(longProfIdx-1),],2,mean),
       xlab=paste("N =",longProfIdx-1),
       ylab="long prof: 1e5*logrets",ylim=c(-5,5),col=4)
  abline(h = 0,v = 5.5,col=8)
  print(longLossLogDiffS[1:(longLossIdx-1),])
  plot(apply(longLossLogDiffS[1:(longLossIdx-1),],2,mean),
       xlab=paste("N =",longLossIdx-1),
       ylab="long loss: 1e5*logrets",ylim=c(-5,5),col=4)
  abline(h = 0,v = 5.5,col=8)
  print(shrtProfLogDiffS[1:(shrtProfIdx-1),])
  plot(apply(shrtProfLogDiffS[1:(shrtProfIdx-1),],2,mean),
       xlab=paste("N =",shrtProfIdx-1),
       ylab="shrt prof: 1e5*logrets",ylim=c(-5,5),col=4)
  abline(h = 0,v = 5.5,col=8)
  print(shrtLossLogDiffS[1:(shrtLossIdx-1),])
  plot(apply(shrtLossLogDiffS[1:(shrtLossIdx-1),],2,mean),
       xlab=paste("N =",shrtLossIdx-1),
       ylab="shrt loss: 1e5*logrets",ylim=c(-5,5),col=4)
  abline(h = 0,v = 5.5,col=8)
}
plotMeanInds()
```

11.11   Simulation Summary

Examining the log returns just prior to trade entry, as seen in Figure 11.8, we see a certain smoothness to the log return levels just before a trade. As discussed in the previous chapter in the Bayesian Reasoning section, there is a low chance of five consecutive bullish or bearish log returns, rather like the chance of getting five heads in a row when

Table 11.1 Totals for six months for the strategy. The average winning percentage in the first column is 58.8 percent.

win pct	long	shrt	win ticks	tot ticks
58.8	23	26	1221	2076
45.5	20	24	823	1807
63.3	23	21	1204	1902
63.7	16	15	813	1276
62.3	14	17	677	1087
59.4	14	17	776	1305

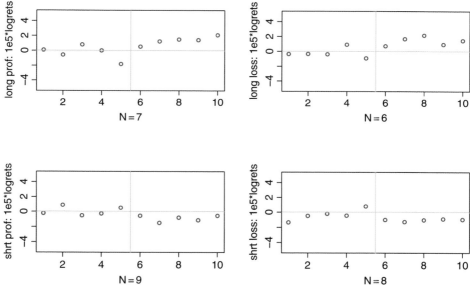

Figure 11.8 Mean of log returns as a function of the time steps before trade entry for trade sample size N. Long trades are in the upper portion. Profitable trades are on the left side. One can see with $KH = 10$ time points of log return history that the final $K = 5$ returns, to the right in each plot, are relatively smooth in terms of variability.

flipping a coin. We have been taking this rare event to mean that the market is changing to a bullish or bearish regime long enough for a profit to be made.

When factoring in slippage, which occurs between the back-test and the live trading, including the bid–ask spread, it can be quite difficult to use trend-following to gain an "edge."

Market data is filled with noise so that the signal-to-noise ratio is low. Data mining and machine learning techniques are of limited value in practice because of the high noise content (Kinlay, 2011). Investors use momentum rules that work when they spot them, but they often find that they only work "temporarily." Even with highly robust back-testing on large datasets, new indicators must be attempted to keep a profitable edge. At a modest 58.8 percent prediction rate for the strategy for a few hundred trades in Table 11.1, the need for strategies to be fully tested with a robust set of market data is clear. Strategies should be ready for modification or replacement by new strategies to stay profitable.

11.12   Exercises

11.1. Adding Conditions to the Trade Entry Criteria

Historical volatility may be an indicator of whether we are in a bullish or bearish trend following regime. Run the *sim()* simulator for the supplied six months of EC data (201305 through 201310) and record (1) the winning percentage and (2) the reported annualized volatility for each run which is displayed in the final lines of the output of *reportCounts()*.

(a) Plot (1) in the horizontal axis and (2) in the vertical axis.

(b) What is a simple condition on historical volatility that could be added to *isLongIndicator()* and *isShrtIndicator()* to attempt to improve the winning percentage?

(c) How does adding this additional criterion change the winning percentage?

11.2. Running the Simulator with Another Strategy

Assume that your manager would like you to modify the trading simulator to only consider long trades. Modify and run the simulator for this case. Run it for the six-monthly one-minute price files named ECprices20130xx, where xx is the month number. Keep track of the counts for each run and compare them to Table 11.1.

12 Data Exploration Using Fundamentals

As investigated in Chapter 7, income statements and balance sheets provide the investor with a view inside the company. As investors, we would like to know if gross revenue is growing year to year. We may also like to know the market value to book value ratio for a stock we own and compare it to the larger market. Knowing it will help us determine if the company could be overvalued in the stock market.

While "NoSQL," key–value, and graph databases are all the range of late, SQL databases still offer rapid querying and schemas that support years and decades of historical data. As we will see in this chapter, querying investment fundamentals can be accomplished in the R environment using the RSQLite package. The investor and data scientist can perform the required data mining with very little code, yielding beneficial results. We first begin with some definitions and formulas for investment fundamentals.

Since Chapter 7, and especially in Chapter 10, we focused on the price movement as the primary driver of our investment strategies. In Chapter 7, we had introduced four key income statement metrics and measured their Sharpe Ratio. In this chapter, like Chapter 7, the primary focus will be fundamental metrics of the company's balance sheet rather than price movements and their statistics. We are guided by our intuition and investment principles from classic industry references (Bodie, Kane, and Marcus, 2013; Greenblatt, 2006). In order to set the context regarding fundamentals, we define some basic investment terms and examples and then introduce our data mining package before examining our dataset.

12.1 The RSQLite Package

In order to apply some of these fundamental investment principles in a data mining setting, we need a package to perform the computations. *SQL* is a specialized language for declarative queries against relational databases (Chamberlin and Boyce, 1974). Query results are specified by the main query mechanism, the SELECT statement. *SQLite* is a widely deployed database engine which uses the SQL language. The source code for SQLite is in the public domain, accessible via http://www.sqlite.org/.

RSQLite is an R package to interface with the SQLite database engine, enabling R to work well with the large datasets we encounter in finance. To introduce the topic we will go over some basic examples, query balance sheet and income statements for commonly used financial ratios, and proceed to program a basic value formula. Assuming the RSQLite package is already installed, we load the DBI and RSQLite libraries, create a connection, and load the *mtcars* data frames into a SQLite table "mtcars" via the connection con, and list all fields in the *mtcars* table.

```
> library(DBI)
> library(RSQLite)
> con <- dbConnect(SQLite(),":memory:")
> dbWriteTable(con,"mtcars",mtcars)
[1] TRUE
> dbListFields(con,"mtcars")
 [1] "row_names" "mpg"      "cyl"      "disp"     "hp"    "drat"
 [7] "wt"        "qsec"     "vs"       "am"       "gear"  "carb"
```

With the table created we can select all entries from the *mtcars* table where the number of cylinders is four:

```
> result <- dbGetQuery(con,
+                       "SELECT * FROM mtcars WHERE cyl = 4")
> result
    row_names        mpg cyl  disp  hp drat    wt  qsec vs am gear
1      Datsun 710 22.8   4 108.0  93 3.85 2.320 18.61  1  1    4
2      Merc 240D 24.4    4 146.7  62 3.69 3.190 20.00  1  0    4
3       Merc 230 22.8    4 140.8  95 3.92 3.150 22.90  1  0    4
4       Fiat 128 32.4    4  78.7  66 4.08 2.200 19.47  1  1    4
5     Honda Civic 30.4   4  75.7  52 4.93 1.615 18.52  1  1    4
6  Toyota Corolla 33.9   4  71.1  65 4.22 1.835 19.90  1  1    4
7   Toyota Corona 21.5   4 120.1  97 3.70 2.465 20.01  1  0    3
8      Fiat X1-9 27.3    4  79.0  66 4.08 1.935 18.90  1  1    4
9   Porsche 914-2 26.0   4 120.3  91 4.43 2.140 16.70  0  1    5
10  Lotus Europa 30.4    4  95.1 113 3.77 1.513 16.90  1  1    5
11     Volvo 142E 21.4   4 121.0 109 4.11 2.780 18.60  1  1    4
```

Now let's query for all four-cylinder cars with miles per gallon greater than 30, and then disconnect from the SQLite database connection.

```
> result <- dbGetQuery(con,
+           "SELECT * FROM mtcars WHERE cyl = 4 AND mpg > 30")
> result
    row_names        mpg cyl disp  hp drat    wt  qsec vs am gear
1       Fiat 128 32.4    4 78.7  66 4.08 2.200 19.47  1  1    4
2     Honda Civic 30.4   4 75.7  52 4.93 1.615 18.52  1  1    4
3  Toyota Corolla 33.9   4 71.1  65 4.22 1.835 19.90  1  1    4
4   Lotus Europa 30.4    4 95.1 113 3.77 1.513 16.90  1  1    5
> dbDisconnect(con)
[1] TRUE
```

Now that we have looked at this simple automobile miles per gallon example, we will discuss investment metrics in the context of the RSQLite package.

12.2 Finding Market-to-Book Ratios

Turning to a finance application, we can introduce RSQLite by querying a database for financial ratios. Let's say we have an SQLite database on disk holding the balance sheet and income statement filings required by the SEC. We make use of the Compustat and the University of Chicago's Center for Research in Security Prices (CRSP) database tables.

After reading in the tables from the *.dta* files provided on the book's web site, we immediately write them using *dbWriteTable()* so that we can query them. Using Compustat's nomenclature, let's query the funda table for IBM's total assets, at, and total liabilities, lt.

```
> library(foreign)
> setwd(paste(homeuser,"/FinAnalytics/ChapXII",sep=""))
> funda <- read.dta("funda.dta")
> msf <- read.dta("msf.dta")
> con <- dbConnect(SQLite(),":memory:")
> dbWriteTable(con,"funda",funda,overwrite=TRUE)
[1] TRUE

> dbWriteTable(con,"msf",msf,overwrite=TRUE)
[1] TRUE

> dbListTables(con)
[1] "funda" "msf"

> query <- "SELECT tic, at, lt
+            FROM funda
+            WHERE fyear = 2010
+            AND tic ='IBM'"
> result <- dbGetQuery(con,query)
> result
  tic     at    lt
1 IBM 113452 90280
```

We can also calculate the market-to-book ratio M/B for IBM at the end of fiscal year 2010. We need price-per-share close annual calendar prcc_c, and common shares outstanding csho then multiply them together.

```
> query<-"SELECT tic, prcc_c, csho, at-lt AS bv
+          FROM funda
+          WHERE fyear = 2010
+          AND tic ='IBM'"
> result <- dbGetQuery(con,query)
> result
```

```
   tic prcc_c    csho    bv
1 IBM 146.76 1227.993 23172
> result$prcc_c * result$csho
[1] 180220.3
```

Note that common shares outstanding `csho` is in millions, which gives a total market cap of a little over \$180 billion. Dividing by shareholder equity, i.e. book value, gives a market to book value of

```
#market-to-book (M/B) ratio:
result$prcc_c * result$csho / result$bv
[1] 7.777501
```

Using SQLite we can also carry out the market-to-book ratio calculation in the database via the `AS` keyword. As our queries get longer we use the return character and indentation to give structure to the SQLite command.

```
> query<-"SELECT tic, at-lt AS bv, prcc_c*csho/(at-lt) AS mb
+           FROM funda
+           WHERE fyear = 2010
+           AND tic ='IBM'"
>           result <- dbGetQuery(con,query)
> result
   tic   bv      mb
1 IBM 23172 7.777501
```

We might be interested in the market-to-book ratio distribution over the whole market. So let's remove the restriction to only IBM and obtain the market-to-book ratio for every company listed in 2010.

```
> query <- "SELECT tic, prcc_c*csho/(at-lt) AS mb
+           FROM funda
+           WHERE fyear = 2010
+           AND tic IS NOT NULL
+           AND prcc_c IS NOT NULL
+           AND csho IS NOT NULL
+           AND seq IS NOT NULL"
> result <- dbGetQuery(con,query)
> result <- subset(result,mb > 0.0 & mb < 50)
```

We can no longer show the query result because it is far too large for a page, but we can calculate the summary statistics

```
> summary(result$mb)
   Min.  1st Qu.   Median    Mean  3rd Qu.    Max.
0.00004  0.98920  1.66400  2.99000  3.05300  49.79000
```

and plot a histogram of the market-to-book ratios as depicted in Figure 12.1.

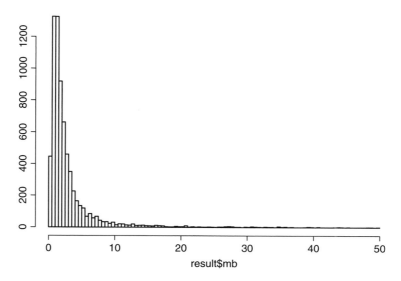

Figure 12.1 Histogram of the market-to-book ratios. The sample mean is approximately 3.0.

```
> hist(result$mb,breaks=100,main="")
```

12.3 The Reshape2 **Package**

When we query a database, the query is often returned in the form

```
> command <- "SELECT tsymbol,date,ret
+           FROM msf
+           WHERE date BETWEEN '2010-01-01' AND '2010-12-31'
+           AND tsymbol IN ('AAPL','GOOG')"
> result <- dbGetQuery(diskdb,command)
> result
   tsymbol      date          ret
1     AAPL 2010-01-29 -0.088591158
2     AAPL 2010-02-26  0.065379545
3     AAPL 2010-03-31  0.148470357
...
22    GOOG 2010-10-29  0.167196095
23    GOOG 2010-11-30 -0.094492406
24    GOOG 2010-12-31  0.068848766
```

where `tsymbol` takes on multiple values in the same column. This is awkward if we want to find the covariance matrix of a set of returns, which assumes that the returns are columns in a matrix. We could use *cbind( )* in the following fashion:

```
> c1 <- result[result$tsymbol=='AAPL',]$ret
> c2 <- result[result$tsymbol=='GOOG',]$ret
> cbind(c1,c2)
```

```
              c1          c2
 [1,] -0.08859116 -0.145224065
 [2,]  0.06537955 -0.005932669
 [3,]  0.14847036  0.076537602
 [4,]  0.11102126 -0.073044486
 [5,] -0.01612468 -0.076213397
 [6,] -0.02082687 -0.083767459
 [7,]  0.02274083  0.089672983
 [8,] -0.05500484 -0.071836688
 [9,]  0.16721511  0.168370277
[10,]  0.06072251  0.167196095
[11,]  0.03378956 -0.094492406
[12,]  0.03667043  0.068848766
```

but if the query is large and has missing values, this approach is unwieldy. The R package `reshape2` by Hadley Wickham provides a solution. We use the *melt()* function to reduce the data down to its most elemental, atomized components, and then re-cast this "molten" data in terms of the variables we want in the rows and columns. We return to our example with Apple and Google. We melt the query while naming *tsymbol* and *date* as *id* variables while *ret* is a measured variable.

```
> library(reshape2)
> result <- melt(result,id=c("tsymbol","date"))
> result
   tsymbol       date variable        value
1     AAPL 2010-01-29      ret -0.088591158
2     AAPL 2010-02-26      ret  0.065379545
3     AAPL 2010-03-31      ret  0.148470357
...
22    GOOG 2010-10-29      ret  0.167196095
23    GOOG 2010-11-30      ret -0.094492406
24    GOOG 2010-12-31      ret  0.068848766
```

We see that each individual measurement of *ret* has been named. The result is now molten. At this point we can recast with *date* as the only row variable, and both *tsymbol* and *ret* as column variables.

```
> dcast(result,date~tsymbol+variable)
         date    AAPL_ret      GOOG_ret
1  2010-01-29 -0.08859116 -0.145224065
2  2010-02-26  0.06537955 -0.005932669
3  2010-03-31  0.14847036  0.076537602
4  2010-04-30  0.11102126 -0.073044486
5  2010-05-28 -0.01612468 -0.076213397
6  2010-06-30 -0.02082687 -0.083767459
7  2010-07-30  0.02274083  0.089672983
8  2010-08-31 -0.05500484 -0.071836688
9  2010-09-30  0.16721511  0.168370277
10 2010-10-29  0.06072251  0.167196095
11 2010-11-30  0.03378956 -0.094492406
12 2010-12-31  0.03667043  0.068848766
```

We can also compute aggregation functions along variable values. For example, let's find the mean monthly return for each *tsymbol*.

```
> dcast(result,tsymbol~variable,mean)
  tsymbol           ret
1    AAPL 0.038788505
2    GOOG 0.001676213
```

And finally, let's check that these means agree with what we would have found using our initial approach of stripping the return columns out of the query result.

```
> mean(c1)
[1] 0.03878851
> mean(c2)
[1] 0.001676213
```

Using the *tseries* R package and our utility function *getHistPrices()*, we can collect daily prices using *get.hist.quote()* and plot them to compare the monthly analysis above to another view, using our *plotMultSeries()* function of Section 4.8.

```
library(tseries)
prices <- getHistPrices(c('AAPL','GOOGL'),c(.5,.5),252,
              start="2010-01-01",end="2010-12-31",
              startBck1="2009-12-31",startFwd1="2010-01-02")

plotMultSeries(prices,c('AAPL','GOOG'),c(.5,.5),2,
               cc="days",ret="",ylim=c(.6,1.5))
```

Figure 12.2 depicts the AAPL and GOOG daily quotes. For the year in question, AAPL does quite a bit better in the market than GOOG.

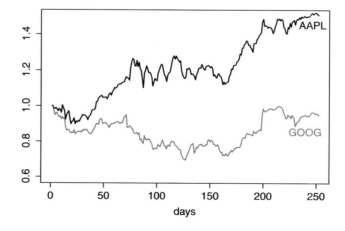

Figure 12.2   2010 adjusted daily closing prices for AAPL and GOOG scaled as gross returns.

12.4   Case Study: Google

Let's dig in a little deeper and look at the development of Google's market value to book value versus that of its industry. We first query the *funda* table to determine Google's market-to-book ratio

```
query <- "SELECT fyear, sich, (csho*prcc_f)/(at-lt) AS mb
        FROM funda
        WHERE fyear >= 2004
        AND tic IN ('GOOG')"
res1 <- dbGetQuery(con,query)
unique(res1$sich)
```

and proceed to query the market-to-book ratio for all firms that share Google's industry code: 7370.

```
query <- "SELECT tic, fyear, (csho*prcc_f)/(at-lt) AS mb
        FROM funda
        WHERE fyear >= 2004
        AND fyear <= 2013
        AND sich = 7370
    AND tic NOT IN ('GOOG')
        AND mb IS NOT NULL
        ORDER BY tic, fyear"
res2 <- dbGetQuery(con,query)
```

We can now melt the query and recast it, taking the median of all firm market-to-book by *fyear*.

```
library(reshape2)
res2 <- melt(res2,id=c("tic","fyear"),na.rm=TRUE)
res2 <- dcast(res2, fyear~variable, median)
```

We can now plot Google's M/B against the industry median M/B and that plot is in Figure 12.3. One way to interpret this graph is that Google "came back down to earth" with respect to its market value and book value. By 2012, the market value approaches the book value more closely.

```
par(mar=c(4,4,2,2))
plot(res1$fyear,res1$mb,type='l',ylim=c(0,1.1*max(res1$mb)),col='blue',
     xlab='year',ylab='Google M/B ratio versus industry median M/B ratio')
lines(res2$fyear,res2$mb,type='l',col='red')
legend(x=2008,y=15,legend=c("GOOG M/B","industry 7370 M/B"),
       col=c('blue','red'),lwd=c(1.5,1.5))
```

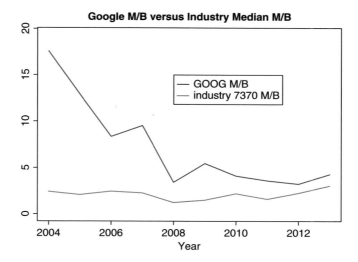

Figure 12.3   Google Market-to-Book vs. Industry Market-to-Book from 2004 to 2013.

12.5   Case Study: Walmart

We can combine information in the two databases and examine, say, the interaction between earnings per share growth and the price-to-earnings ratio for Walmart between 2002 and 2010. We first query the price table for Walmart's *tsymbol, price, split adjustment factor,* and *date* between the first day of 2002 and the last day of 2009.

```
query <- "SELECT tsymbol,prc,cfacshr,date
        FROM msf
        WHERE date BETWEEN '2002-01-01' AND '2009-12-31'
        AND tsymbol IN ('WMT')"
res1 <- dbGetQuery(con,query)
```

We now query the fundamentals table for Walmart's P/E defined as market cap divided by net income, and EPS defined as net income divided by common shares outstanding.

```
query <- "SELECT fyear, (csho*prcc_f)/ni AS pe, ni/csho AS eps
        FROM funda
        WHERE fyear >= 2002
        AND fyear <= 2010
        AND tic IN ('WMT')"
res2 <- dbGetQuery(con,query)
```

With both queries in hand we can plot the price activity of Walmart and contrast the rising EPS (tripling over the decade) with the falling P/E ratio (falling by roughly two-thirds). So while Walmart triples earnings per share over the decade, the market's expectation of future growth is falling rapidly. It falls enough that Walmart's price stays

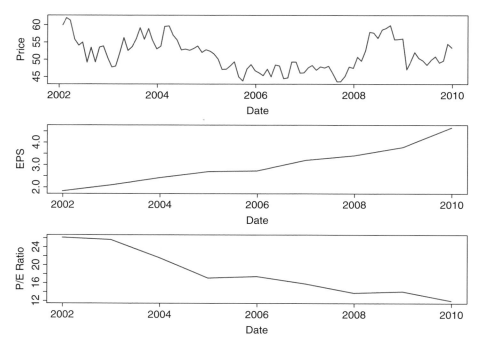

Figure 12.4   Stock Price, Earnings Per Share (EPS), and Price-to-Earnings (P/E) ratio for Walmart (WMT) from 2000 up until 2010.

in the same range over the entire decade. Figure 12.4 shows the price history along with the earnings per share and price–earnings ratio over the same decade.

```
par(mfrow=c(3,1))
plot(x=as.Date(res1$date),y=res1$prc,col="blue",type='l',
     xlab='date',ylab='price')
plot(x=res2$fyear,y=res2$eps,col='blue',type='l',
     xlab='date',ylab='EPS')
plot(x=res2$fyear,y=res2$pe,col='blue',type='l',
     xlab='date',ylab='P/E ratio')
```

12.6   Value Investing

Let's turn toward the implementation of a value-investing formula. In a value strategy we want to find quality companies that are underpriced. Let us use a nested sub-query to first query the funda table stocks in fiscal year 2010, that are not in the financials, that have a book value of over $1B, have an earnings yield of over 10 percent, have a cashflow-price yield of over 20 percent, and are based in the United States. With these tickers in hand we extract the return information for the next three years from the msf table, while adding 1 to the returns so they can be multiplied.

The query below is composed of two separate but related queries. The inner query is written as

```
SELECT tic
FROM funda
WHERE fyear = 2010
    AND (sich < 6000 OR sich &> 6999)
    AND seq > 1000
    AND ni/(prcc_f*csho) > .1
    AND ni/(prcc_f*csho) IS NOT NULL
    AND oancf/(csho*prcc_f) > 0.2
    AND oancf/(csho*prcc_f) IS NOT NULL
    AND fic = 'USA'
```

and carries out the value screen by selecting the stock symbols `tic` from the `funda` table which in fiscal year `fyear` = 2010 are not financial stocks (i.e. outside the 6000-7000 range), have a market cap of over 1 billion (`seq > 1000`), show an earnings yield `ni/(prcc_f*csho)` of greater than 10 percent, show a cashflow to market cap ratio `oancf/(csho*prcc_f)` of greater than 20 percent, and are domiciled in the United States (`fic = 'USA'`).

The outer query takes the stock symbols returned by the inner query and looks up in the `msf` (monthly stock file) table the stock ticker date, and the return for each month BETWEEN '2010-12-01' AND '2013-12-31', ordered by stock symbol `tsymbol` and return date `date`.

```
+ SELECT tsymbol,date, (1+ret) AS ret
+ FROM msf
+ WHERE date BETWEEN '2010-12-01' AND '2013-12-31'
+ AND tsymbol IN (
+    SELECT tic
+        FROM funda
+        WHERE fyear = 2010
+        AND (sich < 6000 OR sich > 6999)
+        AND seq > 1000
+        AND ni/(prcc_f*csho) > .1
+        AND ni/(prcc_f*csho) IS NOT NULL
+        AND oancf/(csho*prcc_f) > 0.2
+        AND oancf/(csho*prcc_f) IS NOT NULL
+        AND fic = 'USA')
+ ORDER BY tsymbol, date"
> result<-dbGetQuery(con,query)
```

We now load the R `reshape2` package, melt the data, and recast it in terms of ticker symbol `tsymbol`, taking the product prod of all returns for each `tsymbol`, and see the three-year accumulated return for each stock by ticker.

```
> result <- melt(result,id=c("tsymbol","date"),na.rm=TRUE)
> result <- dcast(result, tsymbol~variable, prod)
> result

    tsymbol        ret
1       ALK  2.6843125
2       CHK  1.3441437
```

```
3      EIX 1.3839577
4      ETR 1.0317614
5      GCI 2.4998424
6       MU 2.9921584
7      OSK 1.7608019
8     SKYW 0.9525674
9      STR 1.5271584
10       T 1.4854925
11     TER 1.4856662
12     TSN 2.1809760
13     UFS 1.3281121
14     VSH 0.9298738
15     WDC 2.5776105
```

Lastly, we average the cumulative returns and observe an equally weighted portfolio net return over three years of a little under 75 percent.

```
> mean(result$ret)
[1] 1.744296
```

Let's look more closely at this value formula and use it to further illustrate the reshape2 package. Our previous query yielded too many stocks to show all return info on a page, so let's make the criteria more stringent. Let's increase the required earnings yield to 15 percent and increase the required cashflow enterprise yield to 25 percent:

```
> query <- "SELECT tsymbol,date, (1+ret) AS ret
+             FROM msf
+             WHERE date BETWEEN '2010-12-01' AND '2013-12-31'
+                 AND tsymbol IN (SELECT tic
+             FROM funda
+                 WHERE fyear = 2010
+                     AND (sich < 6000 OR sich > 6999)
+                     AND seq > 1000
+                     AND ni/(prcc_f*csho) > .15
+                     AND oancf/(csho*prcc_f) > 0.25
+                     AND fic = 'USA')
+                 ORDER BY tsymbol, date"
> result <- dbGetQuery(con,query)
```

Now let's melt and recast with tsymbol and ret as column variables.

```
> result <- melt(result,id=c("tsymbol","date"),na.rm=TRUE)
> dcast(result, date ~ tsymbol + variable)

        date     MU_ret    UFS_ret    WDC_ret
1 2010-12-31 1.1033155 1.0032929 1.0119403
2 2011-01-31 1.3142144 1.1581929 1.0035398
3 2011-02-28 1.0559772 0.9939725 0.8988830
4 2011-03-31 1.0305481 1.0529748 1.2194245
5 2011-04-29 0.9869224 1.0135105 1.0673102
```

```
6   2011-05-31 0.9010601 1.1016986 0.9208543
7   2011-06-30 0.7333333 0.9276932 0.9926330
8   2011-07-29 0.9852941 0.8440667 0.9472237
9   2011-08-31 0.8018996 1.0046279 0.8557748
...
36  2013-11-29 1.1934389 1.0094440 1.0776965
37  2013-12-31 1.0308057 1.1096947 1.1220682
```

Finally, we find the cumulative return by taking the product, `prod`, of all entries for each `tsymbol` value:

```
> result <- dcast(result, tsymbol ~ variable, prod)
```

and observe a cumulative three-year equally-weighted portfolio return of

```
> mean(result$ret)

[1] 2.299294
```

or nearly 130 percent when we subtract 1 to convert it to a net return.

```
> query<-"SELECT tic FROM funda
+         WHERE fyear = 2010
+             AND (sich < 6000 OR sich > 6999)
+             AND seq > 1000
+             AND ni/(prcc_f*csho) > .15
+             AND ni/(prcc_f*csho) IS NOT NULL
+             AND oancf/(csho*prcc_f) > 0.25
+             AND oancf/(csho*prcc_f) IS NOT NULL
+             AND fic = 'USA'"
> result <- dbGetQuery(con,query)
> result

  tic
1  MU
2 WDC
3 UFS

> str(result)

'data.frame':   3 obs. of  1 variable:
 $ tic: chr  "MU" "WDC" "UFS"
```

We can download the price of the three top stocks picked by the value formula in 2010:

```
> library(quantmod)
> getSymbols(result$tic, from = "2010-12-01", to = "2013-12-31")

[1] "MU"  "WDC" "UFS"
```

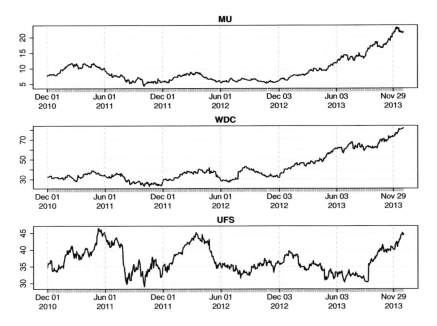

Figure 12.5   Prices of Micron Technology (MU), Western Digital Technologies (WDC), and Domtar Corp (UFS) from December 1st, 2010 to December 31st, 2013.

```
> MU <- MU[, "MU.Adjusted", drop=F]
> WDC <- WDC[, "WDC.Adjusted", drop=F]
> UFS <- UFS[, "UFS.Adjusted", drop=F]
```

Once the prices are in MU, WDC, and UFS series, we can plot them. Figure 12.5 depicts the price behavior of these three selected stocks. The market has not been as kind to UFS as the other two – MU and WDC – over the years 2010 to 2013.

```
> par(mfrow=c(3,1))
> plot(MU)
> plot(WDC)
> plot(UFS)
```

Now that our analysis and charting is complete, we can disconnect from the database.

```
> dbDisconnect(diskdb)
[1] TRUE
```

12.7   Lab: Trying to Beat the Market

We want to examine a value formula similar to that presented in *The Little Book that Beats the Market* by Joel Greenblatt (Greenblatt, 2006). Note that the PE and EP ratios are inverses of each other and contain the same information. We will keep the EP ratio as the measure of cheapness, but now use ROA as the measure of quality. Using the names of our database fields, we calculate the EP ratio as net income, `ni`, divided by market value of equity, `prcc_f*csho`, and we calculate the return on assets as net income, `ni`, divided by the sum of market value of equity, `prcc_f*csho`, and total liabilities, `lt`. As before, we screen for stocks with market cap greater than 1 billion with the condition `seq > 1000` and we screen for US-domiciled stocks with the condition `fic = 'USA'`. Define the query with the command

```
query<-"SELECT tic, ni/(prcc_f*csho) AS ep, ni/(csho*prcc_f + lt) AS roa
       FROM funda
       WHERE fyear = 2010
           AND (sich < 6000 OR sich > 6999)
           AND seq > 1000
           AND ep > .1
           AND ep IS NOT NULL
           AND roa > 0.1
           AND roa IS NOT NULL
           AND fic = 'USA'"
```

and execute then display the query with the command

```
res<-dbGetQuery(con,query)
res
```

12.8   Lab: Financial Strength

In this exercise we wish to screen for the companies in fiscal year 2010 that show financial strength. One proxy for financial strength is debt-to-equity ratio, which we screened for above. Another proxy for financial strength is the ability to pay down debt with earnings. Write a query to screen for stocks in fiscal year 2010 where total liabilities can be paid back with no more than two years' earnings. Net Income is given as `ni`, total liabilities (including total debt) is defined as `lt` in `funda`, and we define the ratio `ni/lt` as the quantity `pay`. Furthermore, we want market cap to be at least 1 billion, and we want only companies that are domiciled in the United States. We also screen for companies whose net income `ni` is positive.

```
query <- "SELECT tic, lt/ni AS pay
          FROM funda
          WHERE fyear = 2010
              AND seq > 1000
              AND fic = 'USA'
              AND pay < 2
              AND pay > 0"
```

Execute the query with the command

```
res <- dbGetQuery(con,query)
```

Show the stock tickers that meet this requirement with the following command:

```
res$tic
```

Plot the histogram of the pay variable with

```
hist(res$pay)
```

12.9   Exercises

12.2. Using RSQLite to Obtain Financial Statements

Write a SQL query inside an R program that finds the market capitalization of IBM, HPQ, ORCL, and SAP for comparison. Use the *funda* table.

12.2. Another View of Value Investing

Section 12.6 contains a query for finding underpriced companies. The four years, 2010 to 2013, calculation yielded a net return of about 75 percent when equally weighted in a portfolio. In this exercise we want to validate this net return result from another source. Use as many utility functions from the book as necessary to perform the following validation:

(a) Obtain daily quotes for the 15 tickers of Section 12.6 and place into a *prices* matrix of size N by 15. Hint: there is a utility function for this.

(b) Plot the prices, scaled to starting at 1.0 on the same chart. Hint: there is a utility function for this.

(c) Place the 15 stocks into a portfolio and find the portfolio value at the beginning and end of the time period. Use these two figures to calculate the net return.

(d) What is the name of the function in the book that will perform the quoting and portfolio weighting function? Hint: The name suggests this being done out-of-sample.

13 Prediction Using Fundamentals

The data mining and machine learning literature is now flush with scenarios about predicting baseball players' salaries from their prior year's number of hits and walks and about predicting the product sales from the prices, customer income, and level of advertising. These are amazing and noteworthy stories. They inspire data scientists to continue their cause. The classic examples feature a large two-dimensional array of cases as rows with the independent variables, also known as the stimulus variables, and the predictable variables, also known as the response variables, as columns. If we are predicting an athlete's salary, this figure is hand-tuned by the people who negotiate contracts. Better athletic production yields better salaries as athletes are constantly compared to one other. The salary is a figure updated usually one time per year at most. And only a handful of people are involved in setting the athlete's salary or the price of a consumer item. So these represent ideal cases in predictability.

Unfortunately, prediction in the case of financial analytics never turns out to be as accurate as in these sports and marketing areas. There is just more random noise in the financial markets with prices that are updated every second of every trading day. Thousands of participants are involved. Every security is affected by many other securities. For example, oil prices are affected not only by oil supply and demand and by the volume of trades at each incremental oil price level but by interest rates and various foreign exchange rates. Nevertheless, one can try these financial predictions using the same techniques in order to experiment and observe what can be predicted.

The process of attempting prediction yields at least two benefits. On the one hand, it may be possible to predict attributes from combinations of other attributes: in this case, response variables from stimulus variables. If this was the case, we can stand alongside those other successes in other areas of data science. On the other hand, prediction may not be possible or even all that useful, however; the collection exercise, getting all the data into rows and columns of the array, provides observations that can be made in an unsupervised learning sense. And discoveries can be made by applying thresholds or sorting and filtering the attributes to find maximally performing securities, as we are able to observe in Chapter 7.

13.1   Best Income Statement Portfolio

As we use our financial analytics techniques, we do not know in advance which technique will yield the best out-of-sample results. So we perform our analysis and experiments in the laboratory and then, as time marches on, we can observe the out-of-sample performance by collecting the new market prices. If we want to be bold, we also invest in the portfolio so that we have "skin in the game" and are living the unrealized profits and losses as the days pass by. If we decide not to be bold, we can simply observe the out-of-sample performance, but if it is satisfactory, as investors we may wish that we had invested in the portfolio. At that point, we cannot go back in time to reconsider our prior decision.

Chapter 7 provides two forms of Sharpe Ratios to qualify the best candidate stocks:

1. the Sharpe Ratio of daily prices;
2. the Sharpe Ratio of annual income statements, particularly:
   - Net Income Growth;
   - Total Revenue Growth;
   - Gross Profit Growth;
   - Diluted Net Earning per Share Growth.

By "growth" we specifically mean the gross return. We subjectively chose these four as key metrics which typically are important in annual reports and annual investor meetings. Up until now in this chapter, we concerned ourselves with stock candidates which were qualified using the first of these Sharpe Ratios. Since the portfolio optimization techniques here are general enough, one could look at another run of the optimizer where the candidate set is qualified using the second of these Sharpe Ratios. See the exercises of Chapter 8 for this proposal, called *Optimizing for Best Income Statement Sharpe Ratio Stocks*.

13.2   Reformatting Income Statement Growth Figures

To match our annual income statement figures over three years from Chapter 7, price vectors can be acquired from those three years and summarized into mean returns and volatility. Mean return is most of interest to the investor, although volatility is important to mitigate against taking too much risk. In terms of a hierarchy, we can think of the tree in Figure 13.1. In this section we will focus on the four lowest metrics which come from corporate income statements of publicly traded companies.

In Chapter 7, we built an income statement growth data frame with a row for each ticker symbol, called *ISgthDF*. We will begin with it and use it as a basis to form the *ISptrnDF* data frame. Now that we are concerned with prediction, we need to separate the dataset into the training rows and test rows as depicted in Figure 13.2. In-sample income statement figures from 2012 and 2013 are used, along with price growth, for training with each type of machine learning technique. For 2014, out-of-sample income

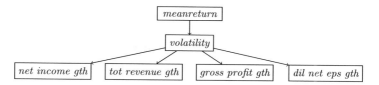

Figure 13.1   Tree showing the annual securities' statistics and their relative importance to investors from high to low. Having volatility below the mean return shows our bias toward having an adequate risk appetite.

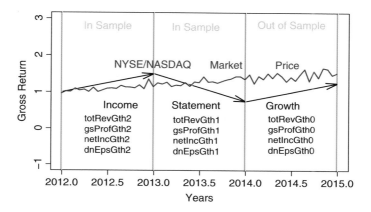

Figure 13.2   Timing of the historical data. The straight lines depict the fact that we use four snapshots (2012, 2013, 2014, 2015) which yields three gross returns for the four income statement figures and three log returns to compare to the S&P 500 Index.

statement figures are used to predict price growth for that year. The price growth is measured over and above the S&P 500 Index daily and annually using log returns.

In order to prepare the R environment for the upcoming routines and their execution, it is best to return to Section 7.4 and rerun that code to the end of Chapter 7. The following routine, *findPtrn()* transforms the *ISgthDF* into a longer and narrower data frame, called *ISptrnDF* for our training and test patterns. The code goes as follows. After setting the schema for the new data frame, the 2, 1, and 0 years back set of new *ISptrnDF* rows are created.

```
findPtrn <- function(ISgthDF) {
  N <- dim(ISgthDF)[1]
  ISptrnDF <- ISgthDF[c(1:(3*N)),c(1:9)] #sets schema
  #2 years back
  ISptrnDF[1:N,c(1,2)] <- ISgthDF[1:N,c(1,2)]
  ISptrnDF[1:N,c(3:7)] <- round(ISgthDF[1:N,c(3:7)],2)
  ISptrnDF[1:N,c(8:9)] <- rep(NA,2*N)
  ISptrnDF[1:N,7] <- rep(2,N)
  #1 year back
  ISptrnDF[(N+1):(2*N),c(1,2)] <- ISgthDF[1:N,c(1,2)]
  ISptrnDF[(N+1):(2*N),c(3:7)] <- round(ISgthDF[1:N,c(7:10)],2)
```

```
ISptrnDF[(N+1):(2*N),c(8:9)] <- rep(NA,2*N)
ISptrnDF[(N+1):(2*N),7] <- rep(1,N)
#0 year back
ISptrnDF[(2*N+1):(3*N),c(1,2)] <- ISgthDF[1:N,c(1,2)]
ISptrnDF[(2*N+1):(3*N),c(3:7)] <- round(ISgthDF[1:N,c(11:14)],2)
ISptrnDF[(2*N+1):(3*N),c(8:9)] <- rep(NA,2*N)
ISptrnDF[(2*N+1):(3*N),7] <- rep(0,N)

colnames(ISptrnDF) <- c("symbol","basedate","netincgth",
          "totrevgth","gsprofgth","dnepsgth","yrsback",
          "meanabvsp","sdev")
rownames(ISptrnDF) <- NULL
ISptrnDF
}
ISptrnDF <- findPtrn(ISgthDF)
D <- dim(ISptrnDF)[1]/3
lab <- ISptrnDF[1:D,1]
```

The last line finds D, the number of dimensions or securities involved: the data frame length is three times this figure, $2D$ for the in-sample data and D for the out-of-sample data where $D = p$ and p is another constant for the number of securities. A given security now has three row entries in *ISptrnDF* as seen in the example below, spaced D rows apart: two years back for 2012, one year back for 2013, and zero years back for 2014, indicated in the *yr* column.

```
> idx <- match('UNP',lab)
> ISptrnDF[c(idx,idx+D,idx+2*D),]
       sym    basedate netincgth totrevgth gsprofgth dnepsgth yr meanabv sdev
846    UNP  2014-12-31      1.20      1.07      1.09     1.23  2      NA   NA
2617   UNP  2014-12-31      1.11      1.05      1.06     1.14  1      NA   NA
4388   UNP  2014-12-31      1.18      1.09      1.11     1.21  0      NA   NA
```

The three records above have the row id, symbol, base date for the income statement figures, four income statement growth figures, years back, and unassigned mean of log returns above the S&P 500 Index and the standard deviation of log returns. In the next section we will cover assigning the last two equally important columns.

13.3   Obtaining Price Statistics

Let us consider the data frame that we work with for prediction. The data items in rows representing instances of random variables are tied to a point in time. Certainly when considering stock prices, the $N \times p$ two-dimensional array is ordered from low to high in occurrence time for the 1-through-N days and the ordering is required to be retained to keep the validity of the data. An $N \times p$ price dataset like this can be reduced to the main features: return and volatility which makes the output $p \times 2$ as it is used for subsequent prediction algorithms. When this is complete, other non-price-related statistics can be considered. Once again, a two-dimensional array can be constructed, but this time the non-price-related figures are adjacent columns to the price-related statistics. The new two-dimensional array is of size $p \times a$ where a is the number of attributes which can each serve as predictor or stimulus variables. In our case, we will return to the income statement figures to occupy these a places as column headers.

As early as Chapter 4, we discussed a reliable method for obtaining stock prices using the R *get.hist.quote()* function from the `tseries` package. We mention it here once again, although in this case the prices have been pre-fetched by the *getHist-Prices()* function of Chapter 8 and cached into files sitting in the MVO4 directory. This speeds up the loading of nearly 1 million prices for several thousand tickers.

Ultimately, an investor selecting stocks is interested in beating the market "bogie," the S&P 500 Index. Professional money managers have beating this bogie as a goal. Beating the bogie is not an easy task to accomplish consistently. Nonetheless, if this is our goal, we believe that it is best to scale our mean return to the performance of the bogie over the same time interval. If a stock has a gross profit growth which is, say, 10 percent higher in 2013 than in 2012, this is probably due to economic conditions being good and certain efficiencies of the company. When the mean return of the stock valued in the market increases so that it is 10 percent higher in 2013 than in 2012, however, there is a certain amount of systemic stock market optimism not due to efficiencies of the company. We propose subtracting out the mean return of the S&P Index from the mean return of the individual candidate stock. By this, we achieve two goals:

- We clearly focus on stocks whose mean return is higher than the S&P Index. Their adjusted mean return will be greater than 0.
- We scale the mean return of a given stock from year-to-year to the same baseline. This allows better year-to-year comparisons on price-based statistics.

We start with our large log return matrix R which is size $N \times p$. p is the number of stocks. In the code, we tend to use D instead of p. We also have one vector of length N for the S&P 500 Index log returns, called r. There are two very simple statistics we can compute: the sample means for a single stock and for the index from the log return series:

$$\bar{R}_j = \frac{1}{N} \sum_{i=1}^{N} R_{i,j} \text{ and } \mu_M = \frac{1}{N} \sum_{i=1}^{N} r_i. \tag{13.1}$$

In this case, N is the number of trading days, usually 252. After we have these means, we can begin adjusting the entire vector of stock means to be the mean *above*, positive or negative, the index mean:

$$\bar{A}_j = \bar{R}_j - \mu_M. \tag{13.2}$$

Firstly, we need the ability to read cached prices from the NYSE and NASDAQ directories. The function *findCachedPrices()* will do this for us. It contains a loop over the two directories.

```
dir <- 'MV04'
setwd(paste(homeuser,"/FinAnalytics/",dir,"/",sep=""))
len = 1006 #start with all four years

findCachedPrices <- function(dir,lab,prices,
                     start=NA,end=NA) {
  if(!is.na(start) && !is.na(end))
    prices <- prices[start:end,] #cut down size of prices
  d = 1
  for(l in lab) {
    attempts <- 0
    fileName = paste('cached',l,'.csv',sep=")
    for(subdir in c('NYSE','NASDAQ')) {
      setwd(paste(homeuser,"/FinAnalytics/",dir,'/',
               subdir,sep=""))
      attempts <- attempts + 1
      if(file.exists(fileName)) {
        break
      } else if(attempts == 2) {
        attempts <- -1 #unsuccessful
      }
    }
    if(attempts == -1) { #unsuccessful
      print(paste(fileName,"not in NYSE nor NASDAQ"))
      prices[,d] = rep(NA,len)[start:end]
    } else { #successful
      print(paste(fileName,"in",subdir))
      prices[,d] = read.csv(fileName,header=TRUE,
                        sep=")[start:end,1]
    }
    d = d + 1
  }
  #return vector may have NAs
  return(prices)
}
#unit test:
labtest <- c('AAN','MCD','PCLN') #2 NYSEs, 1 NASDAQ
dir    <- 'MV04'
len    <- 1006
D      <- length(labtest)
px <- matrix(rep(NA,len*D),nrow=len,ncol=D)
px <- findCachedPrices(dir,labtest,px,start=253,end=504)
```

The following code block will obtain three years of price history for the *D* stocks, but then trim that set down to three one-year vectors. It also obtains quotes for the S&P 500 Index for the matching time frame.

```
findCached3YrsBackPrices <- function(dir,lab,len) {
  #Go back 3 years in cached files for prices
  D <- length(lab)
```

```
  isSplitAdjusted <<- TRUE
  prices2 <- matrix(rep(NA,len*D),nrow=len,ncol=D)
  prices2 <- findCachedPrices(dir,lab,prices2,
                              start=253,end=504)

  prices1 <- matrix(rep(NA,len*D),nrow=len,ncol=D)
  prices1 <- findCachedPrices(dir,lab,prices1,
                              start=504,end=755)

  prices0 <- matrix(rep(NA,len*D),nrow=len,ncol=D)
  prices0 <- findCachedPrices(dir,lab,prices0,
                              start=755,end=1006)
  return(rbind(prices2,prices1,prices0))
}
D <- length(lab)
allPrices <- findCached3YrsBackPrices(dir,lab,len)
dim(allPrices)
prices2   <- allPrices[1:252,]
dim(prices2)
prices1   <- allPrices[253:504,]
dim(prices1)
prices0   <- allPrices[505:756,]
dim(prices0)
```

The next section of code retrieves the price vector for the S&P 500 Index so that we can find the log returns for μ_M.

```
library(tseries)
setwd(paste(homeuser,"/FinAnalytics/MV04",sep=""))

findSPprices <- function(fn="cachedGSPC.csv") {
  if(!file.exists(fn)) {
    pricesSP <- getHistPrices(c('^GSPC'),c(1),len,
                              start="2011-02-09",end="2015-02-09",
                              startBck1="2011-02-08",
                              startFwd1="2011-02-10")[,1]
    write.csv(pricesSP,file="cachedGSPC.csv",row.names=FALSE)
  } else {
    pricesSP <- read.csv("cachedGSPC.csv")[1]
    #error handling
    if(is.na(pricesSP[1,1])) {
      system('rm cachedGSPC.csv')
      findSPprices()
    }
  }
  pricesSP[,1]
}
pricesSP  <- findSPprices()
pricesSP2 <- pricesSP[253:504]
pricesSP1 <- pricesSP[504:755]
pricesSP0 <- pricesSP[755:1006]
```

Once we have the prices, we find the usual log returns; however, this time that is performed one year at a time. This time we also include the S&P 500 Index log returns in vectors *r2*, *r1*, and *r0*.

```
R2 <- findR(prices2)
R1 <- findR(prices1)
R0 <- findR(prices0)
r2 <- findR(as.matrix(pricesSP2,252,1))
r1 <- findR(as.matrix(pricesSP1,252,1))
r0 <- findR(as.matrix(pricesSP0,252,1))
```

The function *findOneYrPriceStats()* operates one year at a time. It finds the S&P 500 Index mean log return and subtracts that from the various securities mean log return. It also computes the standard deviation of the log returns or the volatilities.

```
findOneYrPriceStats <- function(R,r) {
  #Go back 3 years mean log ret and sdev
  meanSP       <- apply(r,2,mean)
  meanvAbvSP   <- apply(R,2,mean)-meanSP
  meanv        <- apply(R,2,mean)
  cov_mat      <- cov(R/100) #rescale back to logret wo 100 factor
  diag_cov_mat <- diag(cov_mat)
  sdevv        <- sqrt(diag_cov_mat)
  SR           <- meanvAbvSP/sdevv
  return(list(meanvAbvSP,sdevv))
}

res <- findOneYrPriceStats(R2,r2)
meanvAbvSP2 <- res[[1]]
sdevv2 <- res[[2]]
res <- findOneYrPriceStats(R1,r1)
meanvAbvSP1 <- res[[1]]
sdevv1       <- res[[2]]
res <- findOneYrPriceStats(R0,r0)
meanvAbvSP0 <- res[[1]]
sdevv0       <- res[[2]]
```

We have now collected raw data and computed price statistics for our candidates for one year back from February 9, 2015. February was chosen to allow one month of market reaction to the usual December 31st earnings report with nine extra days for the year-end holiday. *meanAbvSP2* stands for the mean log return above the S&P 500 Index mean log return two years back, *meanAbvSP1* for one year back, and *meanAbvSP0* for immediately back.

When we adjust the log return means by subtracting off the scalar value of the S&P 500 Index return, we can think of having a new array, A, with the same dimensions as our log return array, R. Each element is defined:

$$A_{i,j} = R_{i,j} - \mu_M \tag{13.3}$$

for row instances i and candidate stock columns j, as seen in the second line of code in the body of *findOneYrPriceStats()*, above. If we apply $\frac{1}{N}\sum_{i=1}^{N}$ to each side of 13.3 and use Formulas 13.1, we note that $\frac{1}{N}\sum_{i=1}^{N}\mu_M = \mu_M$ and obtain the following:

$$\bar{A}_j = \mu_j - \mu_M, \tag{13.4}$$

which says that the mean for our new series A_js are simply the mean of the R_j with μ_M subtracted from it for each j. μ_M is the S&P 500 Index mean log return for the same time period. If our goal is to perform better than the S&P 500 Index bogie, we should look at the distribution of individual stock mean return above the bogie, $\bar{A}_j = meanAbvSP$. Running an R *summary(meanAbvSP)*, where:

```
meanvAbvSP = c(meanvAbvSP0,meanvAbvSP1,meanvAbvSP2)
summary(meanvAbvSP)
```

we obtain the following results:

```
> summary(meanvAbvSP)
   Min. 1st Qu.  Median    Mean 3rd Qu.    Max.    NA's
-1.1380 -0.0635 -0.0033 -0.0111  0.0563  0.8118     435
```

which tells us that most of the $D = 1621$ candidate stocks perform slightly lower in mean return than the bogie (Mean -0.0111, Median -0.0033) over the three-year daily price sample.

Formula 13.4 is essentially p equations, which can be stated as one below:

$$[\bar{A}_1,\ldots,\bar{A}_p] = [\mu_1,\ldots,\mu_p] - \mu_M.$$

Performing more data analysis, we know that the standard deviation of our new random variables, $\bar{A}_j$ being simply the original $\bar{R}_j$ with a scalar mean subtracted, is the same as the original standard deviation. The term μ_M adjusts only the location of the distribution and not the scale of it. This can also be seen in the following formulas using their variances via 13.1 and 13.2, where we use $N - 1$ for N:

$$Var(A_j) = \frac{1}{N-1}\sum_{i=1}^{N}[A_{i,j} - \bar{A}_j]^2 \tag{13.5}$$

$$= \frac{1}{N-1}\sum_{i=1}^{N}[(R_{i,j} - \mu_M) - (\bar{R}_j - \mu_M)]^2 \tag{13.6}$$

$$= \frac{1}{N-1}\sum_{i=1}^{N}[R_{i,j} - \bar{R}_j]^2 \tag{13.7}$$

$$= Var(R_j), \tag{13.8}$$

where Formula 13.6 follows from Formulas 13.5 and the pair 13.3 and 13.4. The code in the upcoming section produces the three density plots of Figure 13.3 for each of the years 2012, 2013, and 2014.

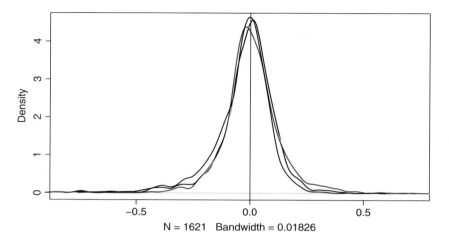

Figure 13.3   Plot of mean log return above the S&P 500 Index. Each curve contains $D = 1621$ tickers for a single year chosen from 2012, 2013, and 2014.

13.4   Combining the Income Statement with Price Statistics

Many investors believe that stocks move in a positive direction when they are able to grow key attributes of their income statement: net income, total revenue, gross profit, and (diluted net) earnings per share. Combining these historical income statement growth figures with historical mean return and volatility price statistics is of interest. So is the ability to predict future mean returns or, more realistically, classes of mean returns, based upon the prior year history.

The R data frame is the common mechanism to use the many data mining and machine learning packages. Forming a well-designed and clean data frame is the key to using Classification and Regression Trees. The following code block will form the data frame first. Then the data frame is inspected for NA via the *na.omit()* and the rows containing NAs will be removed.

```
augPtrn <- function(ISptrnDF) {
  #augment DF with price stats
  N <- dim(ISptrnDF)[1]/3
  ISptrnDF[1:N,c(8,9)] <-
    cbind(round(meanvAbvSP2,4),round(sdevv2,4))
  ISptrnDF[(N+1):(2*N),c(8,9)] <-
    cbind(round(meanvAbvSP1,4),round(sdevv1,4))
  ISptrnDF[(2*N+1):(3*N),c(8,9)] <-
    cbind(round(meanvAbvSP0,4),round(sdevv0,4))
  ISptrnDF
}
ISptrnDFcln <- na.omit(augPtrn(ISptrnDF))
D <- dim(ISptrnDFcln)[1]/3
lab <- ISptrnDFcln[1:D,1]
```

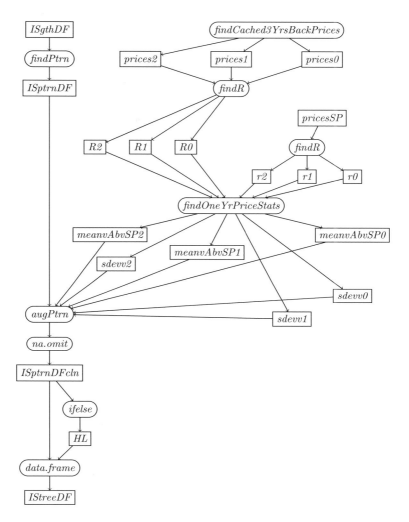

Figure 13.4 Tree showing the complex lineage of the *IStreeDF* data frame. Rounded rectangles are R functions. In practice, the prediction steps are not as complex as messaging the data into the proper form.

The *augPtrn()* function above updates the eighth and ninth columns of the data frame with *meanAbvSP* and *sdevv* vectors. *meanAbvSP* and *sdevv* are used as response variables to the four stimulus variables, *netincgth*, *totrevgth*, *gsprofgth*, and *dnepsgth*. We try a test case of stock NSC to view that the proper mean above the S&P 500 Index and the standard deviation was placed in the rows at positions 8 and 9.

```
> thisD <- dim(ISptrnDFcln)[1]/3
> idx = match('NSC',lab)
> ISptrnDFcln[c(idx,idx+thisD,idx+2*thisD),c(3:9)]
    netincgth totrevgth gsprofgth dnepsgth yr meanabv   sdev
```

587	0.91	0.99	0.99	1.00	2	-0.0445	0.0155
2358	1.09	1.02	1.03	1.09	1	0.0516	0.0136
4129	1.05	1.03	1.08	1.09	0	0.0174	0.0127

The data frame is now ready for prediction techniques to be applied. The entire process is depicted in Figure 13.4.

```
library(moments)
yb2logrets <- ISptrnDFcln[1:D,8]
yb1logrets <- ISptrnDFcln[(D+1):(2*D),8]
yb0logrets <- ISptrnDFcln[(2*D+1):(3*D),8]
alllogrets <- c(yb2logrets,yb1logrets,yb0logrets)
skewness(alllogrets)
kurtosis(alllogrets)
plot(density(yb2logrets),main="")
lines(density(yb1logrets),col=4)
lines(density(yb0logrets),col=9)
abline(v=0.0)
summary(alllogrets)
```

Running the *skewness()* and *kurtosis()* functions reveals that the skew is to the left as might be expected due to the fact that we are comparing to some of the best returns in the market: the S&P 500 equities.

```
> skewness(alllogrets)
[1] -1.008415
> kurtosis(alllogrets)
[1] 10.70697
```

The reported kurtosis above, being 10.71, much larger than 3, reveals that the distribution is far from normal, having heavy tails.

13.5   Prediction Using Classification Trees and Recursive Partitioning

Predictive techniques require a certain type of formal dataset design discipline. Classically, the supervised machine learning dataset is a two-dimensional table with rows being the instances and the columns being the attributes or random variables (Gareth, Witten, Hastie, and Tibshirani, 2013; Ledolter, 2013). Recursive-partitioning is no exception. In our case, the rows are the stock candidates and the columns are the predictive attributes which we believe are candidates for the algorithm is considered. In the row dimension, there is one more attribute. The rows are separated into three D-sized sections, one for each year. Due to the time series nature of financial data, the two oldest sections are used for training data and the remaining section is used for test data to try the prediction on.

With prediction, we make the assumption that there are stimulus variables which can be used to predict response variables. The input variables are known as stimulus or predictors for the response. These stimulus variables may have correlation among each other, but are generally considered to vary independently. Often we focus on a single response variable for simplicity. There is a class of techniques known as CART, which stands for *Classification and Regression Trees*. Depending upon the data type of the response variable, continuous or categorical, either a regression or classification tree is formed. Regression trees are used when the response variable is numeric or continuous. This may be the predicted response time for a request on a computer or a predicted rate of return, for example. Classification trees are used when the response variable is enumerated or categorical. This may be a predicted grade in the set $\{A, B, C, D, F\}$ or the predicted direction of a security in the next time period: up or down. There are many R packages for CART: *tree, rpart,* and *party* are some of the most popular. We will focus on *party* (Hothorn, Hornik, Strobl, and Zeileis, 2015). With most classifiers in R for CART, pruning the tree is an important step which often require rerunning, tuning the pruning parameter, and cross validating using subsets of the dataset. When using the *ctree* conditional inference tree within the *party* package, these parts are quite easy because the claim is that these steps are not necessary. As a benefit, this package also does a particularly good job of plotting the decision tree. In our case, the idea is to build a tree using the training set data by partitioning the training set into *subclasses* using Boolean decisions about one of the many predictor variables at each step. Just like any tree from the field of computer science, there is a single root node to begin at. Our data frame, *IStreeDF*, has our four income statement covariate stimulus variables which we would like to try out as predictors. Forming the tree involves, at each step in the build process, finding a covariate, among the four, which yields the best split.

We now describe the general algorithm between recursive partitioning for the case of a typical regression tree. Specific algorithms for both classification and regression trees vary as designed by the research team that implemented the algorithm. For details, it is best to consult the literature associated with the particular package.

If our predictors, X have v possible values, $X_1, \ldots, X_v$ in p dimensions, we find w distinct non-overlapping regions $R_1, \ldots, R_w$ such that for each X_i there is an R_j such that $X_i \in R_j$. Each region R_j has a single value $\hat{y}_{R_j}$ or the response variable. $\hat{y}_{R_j}$ is the mean of the response values for the $X_i's$ in R_j. We construct the regions so that the residual sum of squares,

$$RSS = \sum_{j=1}^{w} \sum_{i \in R_j} (y_i - \hat{y}_{R_j})^2, \tag{13.9}$$

is minimized with recursive partitioning. Going from region R_1 at the beginning to $R_1, \ldots, R_w$ at the end is a "greedy" algorithm in the sense that it only considers the current partitioning and the next best split without looking ahead into future states. This means that the *RSS* of Formula 13.9 is only minimized for each split move. For example, if there is a random variable vector X where

$$X = (X_1, X_2, X_3, X_4) = (dnepsgth, gsprofgth, totrevgth, netincgth),$$

then nodes 2 and 3 form regions where $\{X|X_1 \leq 1.03\}$ and $\{X|X_1 > 1.03\}$, respectively, where X_1 corresponds to *dnepsgth*. We find a cut point c when splitting on X_j that splits it into $R_1(j, c) = \{X|X_j \leq c\}$ and $R_2(j, c) = \{X|X_j > c\}$, regions with the greatest possible reduction in *RSS*.

The *RSS* is a good metric for minimizing the decision tree algorithm. Using $\hat{y}_{R_j}$, the mean response for the region, as the predicted y value for the regression tree case, when y is continuous, is fine. However, for a categorical y of K possible values in the classification tree case, we need a different metric. With categories, there is no $\hat{y}_{R_j}$ mean for each region so the *RSS* is undefined. We can think about the proportion $\hat{p}_{mk}$ of sample points of the training set that appear in the mth region that are from the kth class. For an ideally pure region corresponding to our single initial tree node, we would want all the y values to match identically, however, when we begin the recursive splitting process, and as a matter of practicality, impurity exists because of the diversity of y values in the single initial node. For example, if $K = 2$ and we begin at the lone starting region, and if we have 50 training set elements and 25 of the ys are in category 1 and 25 are of category 2, then the purity of the node is very low. We can think about the proportion of ys with the same value and we get $\hat{p}_{11} = \frac{1}{2} = \hat{p}_{12}$. Half of the population of ys do not match each other. So we start to recursively split the tree to try to obtain better node purity. As the tree becomes constructed, better node purity is achieved by adding nodes to the tree.

We can think about the error when classifying sample points as E_m for each region m. If $\hat{p}_{mk}$ are correctly classified together then $1 - max(\hat{p}_{mk})$ is a measure of the misclassified points. However, E_n turns out to be not of the proper sensitivity for constructing decision trees.

Two other common example metrics are the *Gini index*, G_m, and the *cross-entropy* or deviance, D_m for regions or, equivalently, tree nodes m. If we think of a simple decision tree with a set of regions corresponding to the tree nodes, in many cases, if $K = 2$ for binary classification, we are left with only two terms in the summation below:

$$E_m = 1 - max_k(\hat{p}_{mk}) \tag{13.10}$$

$$G_m = \sum_{k=1}^{K} \hat{p}_{mk}(1 - \hat{p}_{mk}) = \hat{p}_{m1}(1 - \hat{p}_{m1}) + \hat{p}_{m2}(1 - \hat{p}_{m2}) \tag{13.11}$$

$$D_m = -\sum_{k=1}^{K} \hat{p}_{mk} \log(\hat{p}_{mk}) = -\hat{p}_{m1} \log(\hat{p}_{m1}) - \hat{p}_{m2} \log(\hat{p}_{m2}). \tag{13.12}$$

We assume for this example that $K = 2$ and $\hat{p}_{m1} = .7$, meaning 7 of 10 points group together into a region and belong together.

$$E_m = 1 - max_k(\hat{p}_{mk}) = 1 - .7 = .3000$$
$$G_m = \hat{p}_{m1}(1 - \hat{p}_{m1}) + \hat{p}_{m2}(1 - \hat{p}_{m2}) = .7(.3) + .3(.7) = .4200$$
$$D_m = -\hat{p}_{m1} \log(\hat{p}_{m1}) - \hat{p}_{m2} \log(\hat{p}_{m2}) = -(.7) \log(.7) - (.3) \log(.3) = 0.6109.$$

We are showing formulas for the Gini index and cross-entropy side by side, above. We can see that they have similar values and can be spotted in Figure 13.5.

Our next goal is to visualize these three functions in R where we use p and $1 - p$ for $\hat{p}_{m1}$ and $\hat{p}_{m2}$. We can see the node impurity as the output of the following R code in Figure 13.5. We can see that two of the three are a smooth curved shape which lends well to optimization. For a more complete discussion of node-splitting criteria for CART, consult the literature (Hastie, Tibshirani, and Friedman, 2009; Gareth, Witten, Hastie, and Tibshirani, 2013; Ledolter, 2013).

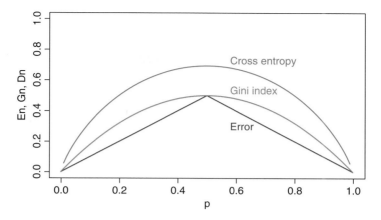

Figure 13.5 The three metrics for node impurity. The higher the impurity value, the more the region and node in the tree have values outside the class.

```
#Calc classification tree impurity
p = seq(0,1,.01)
En <- function(p) {1-max(p,1-p)}
Gn <- function(p) {p*(1-p)+(1-p)*p}
Dn <- function(p) {-p*log(p)-(1-p)*log(1-p)}
EnVec <- sapply(p,En) #error
GnVec <- sapply(p,Gn) #Gini
DnVec <- sapply(p,Dn) #cross-entropy

plot(p,EnVec,ylim=c(0,1),col=4,type="l",
     ylab="En,Gn,Dn")
text(c(.7),En(.7),"Error",col=4,cex=.95)
lines(p,GnVec,ylim=c(0,1),col=3)
text(c(.7),Gn(.7),"Gini index",col=3,cex=.95)
lines(p,DnVec,ylim=c(0,1),col=2)
text(c(.7),Dn(.7),"Cross-entropy",col=2,cex=.95)
```

If the dataset is robust in depth and density, for example, beginning in Chapter 7 the daily price series, which can be obtained for thousands of prior dates, goes back for hundreds of days, and that is a good situation. In the case of income statement figures, the series only goes back a handful of years. We are fortunate that these figures can be obtained by the `quantmod` package, but the limitation is that the depth is only four years for annual income statement figures.

In an ideal supervised learning world, we should have enough data to divide into training and test sets. In the case of income statements, only four deep, we are not sure whether this is feasible, due to the volatility of the income statement figures from year to year. Our STRM stock example from Chapter 7 illustrates the risk of using only one year of daily prices. We first need the *ISptrnDFcln* data frame to be augmented with a price growth level: Up and Down which are categories related to the mean above the S&P 500 Index, *meanabv*.

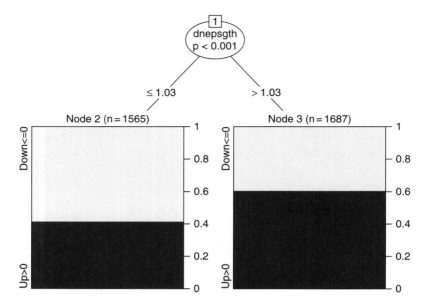

Figure 13.6   Recursively partitioned classification tree formed from $2D = 3242$ training rows from 2012 and 2013 income statement figures. In a nutshell, running the recursive partitioning tells us that stocks with Diluted Net Earnings per Share growth better than 3 percent (seen as *dnepsgth* gross return of over 1.03) will do better than the S&P 500 Index.

The following code forms response variable called *HL* for whether the mean return above the index is Up (> 0) or Down ($<= 0$). We make use of the R `party` package for recursive tree partitioning by, firstly, attaching a response attribute which tells us whether the result is *High* or *Low*. This is intended to be an indicator as to whether to buy the security or not. If the mean return is predicted to be up, we buy the security and plan to hold it for a while.

```
library(party)
attach(ISptrnDFcln)
train <- c(1:D,(D+1):(2*D))
length(train)==2*D

HL=ifelse(ISptrnDFcln$meanabv > 0,"Up>0","Down<=0")
IStreeDF = data.frame(ISptrnDFcln,HL)
```

Note the size of the training set defined by *train* in the code above is $\frac{2}{3}$ of the total dataset size. We next check once again that our new data frame *IStreeDF*, field *HL*, looks about right with a unit test case for the security *NSC* which appears to have the two types of years lately: *High* and *Low*.

```
> thisD <- dim(IStreeDF)[1]/3
> idx = match('NSC',lab)
> IStreeDF[c(idx,idx+thisD,idx+2*thisD),c(3:8,10)]
```

	netincgth	totrevgth	gsprofgth	dnepsgth	yr	meanabv	HL
575	0.91	0.99	0.99	1.00	2	-0.0445	Down<=0
2332	1.09	1.02	1.03	1.09	1	0.0516	Up>0
4089	1.05	1.03	1.08	1.09	0	0.0174	Up>0

Comparing the last column to the *meanabv* column, this test case looks fine. In fact, the column *netincgth* seems to be predicting the response *meanabv* for each year, with two years back being a poor year for income growth and a poor year for return above the S&P 500 Index; one year back being stronger year for income growth and for return above the S&P 500 Index; and the immediately prior year in between. Having inspected our data a bit, now we can proceed to find the training set subscripts, *train* and call the *ctree( )* recursive tree partitioning function.

```
attach(IStreeDF)
istree=ctree(HL ~ netincgth + totrevgth + gsprofgth + dnepsgth,
           data=IStreeDF, subset=train)
```

We now know our stimulus variable regions and our trained nodes that will be used in *istree* for prediction for any out-of-sample dataset. We left one third of the data out as out-of-sample in order to test prediction. Once the *istree* tree is built, we can pass it to the *predict()* function for predictions on the test set, *IStreeDF[−train,]*.

```
predRes <- predict(type="response",
                 istree, IStreeDF[-train,])
tbl <- round(table(predRes,IStreeDF[c(-train), "HL"])/D,3)
tbl
(tbl[1,1]+tbl[2,2])/sum(tbl)

par(mar=c(4,4,1,1))
par(mfrow=c(1,1))
plot(istree,cex=.25)
```

Notice that the only one mentioned of the four income statement figures in the tree is *dnepsgth*, Diluted Net Earnings per Share growth. This tells us that it is the most important predictor in the eyes of the `party` tree partitioning package as depicted in Figure 13.6. We can look again at the formula used to call the *ctree( )*:

```
meanabv ~ netincgth + totrevgth + gsprofgth + dnepsgth .
```

We can ask for a summary of the counts of the predicted response, up and down.

```
> sum(predRes == "Up>0")
[1] 819
> sum(predRes != "Up>0")
[1] 802
```

We can interpret these figures to be the number of securities which rise or fall in value above the S&P 500 Index over the time window, respectively.

We can request a description of the classification tree by having R display the contents of the variable *istree*. The output is below, with the four input, stimulus, or predictor variables listed and the response variable as well. Each line is a node of the tree. We can think of tree node 1 as the root and then the two lines for the branches which emanate out from root node 1 are listed in the next lines down.

```
> istree

Conditional inference tree with 2 terminal nodes

Response:  HL
Inputs:  netincgth, totrevgth, gsprofgth, dnepsgth
Number of observations:  3252

1) dnepsgth <= 1.03; criterion = 1, statistic = 25.908
   2)*  weights = 1565
1) dnepsgth > 1.03
   3)*  weights = 1687
> plot(istree)
```

We know that we are operating on a machine learning training set which is of size: > length(train) [1] 3242 and test set of one half that size. When running the code block below, which attempts to predict high mean return stocks from price statistics and income statement growth from two years back, we see the resulting confusion matrix, which is based upon two prediction classes for two labeled classes.

```
> predRes <- predict(type="response",
+                     istree, IStreeDF[-train,])
> tbl <- round(table(predRes,IStreeDF[c(-train), "HL"])/D,3)
> tbl

predRes   Down<=0  Up>0
  Down<=0   0.335 0.159
  Up>0      0.231 0.275
> (tbl[1,1]+tbl[2,2])/sum(tbl)
[1] 0.61
```

There are two basic categories of price movement which our response variables y_i can be assigned values from: *Down* $<= 0$ and *Up* > 0, where *Up* is the most bullish movement. We can look at the distribution of predicted low mean returns in the first three rows and see that the majority of the predicted lows are, in fact, *Down*. If we sum the upper left and lower right quadrants of the two-by-two matrix, we obtain 61.0 percent.

13.6   Comparing Prediction Rates among Classifiers

The majority of the coding effort was devoted to getting the price and income statement data organized to be useful for the `party` package utility. Being financial data, the market mean returns do not always reflect what is happening on the income statements due to the number of external factors that can affect market prices. Having stated that, however, the results here are encouraging. As delineated in the classic text, *Introduction to Statistical Learning* (Gareth, Witten, Hastie, and Tibshirani, 2013), where Logistic Regression, Linear Discriminant Analysis, and Quadratic Discriminant Analysis is used on the *Smarket* dataset, the prediction success rate can be improved from 52 percent to 60 percent by using more advanced techniques in the finance prediction domain. Any time we are sufficiently more successful than 50 percent in out-of-sample testing, we should call this a success.

We can try two more classifiers as a comparison to the `party` package recursive tree. The `randomForest` decision tree resamples the training set many times and averages the results. Often it can yield a more robust prediction result. Support vector machines (SVM) are one of the more classic statistical learning techniques which attempt to separate the dataset into clusters to match the response variable values. We combine the earlier code into the function *runClassifier()*, which has cases for the `party` package tree, `randomForest` package tree, and `e1071` package SVM.

```
library(party)
library(randomForest)
library(e1071)
attach(IStreeDF)
runClassifier <- function(IStreeDF,train,name="ctree") {
  if(name == "ctree") {
    classifier=ctree(HL ~ netincgth + totrevgth +
              gsprofgth + dnepsgth,
              data=IStreeDF, subset=train)
    predRes <- predict(type="response",
              classifier, IStreeDF[-train,])
  } else if(name == "randomForest"){
    set.seed(100)
    classifier=randomForest(HL ~ netincgth + totrevgth +
              gsprofgth + dnepsgth,
              data=IStreeDF, subset=train, mtry=4, importance=TRUE)
    predRes <- predict(type="response",
              classifier, IStreeDF[-train,])
  } else if(name == "svm") {
    classifier <- svm(formula=HL ~ netincgth + totrevgth +
              gsprofgth + dnepsgth,data=IStreeDF, subset=train,
              kernel="sigmoid",na.action=na.omit, scale = TRUE)
    predRes <- predict(type="response",
              classifier, IStreeDF[-train,])
  }
  par(mar=c(4,4,1,1))
  par(mfrow=c(1,1))
  if(name == "ctree" || name == "randomForest")
    plot(classifier,cex=.25)
  tbl <- round(table(predRes,IStreeDF[c(-train), "HL"])/D,3)
  print(tbl)
  print(tbl[1,1]+tbl[2,2]/sum(tbl))
}
```

```
runClassifier(IStreeDF,train,"ctree")
runClassifier(IStreeDF,train,"randomForest")
runClassifier(IStreeDF,train,"svm")
```

While we strive for perfection in prediction, 100 percent success rates, in finance, we are challenged by the thousands of market participants who randomly help determine a security's price. More than for biological and marketing analytics problems, financial markets problems have patterns which are constantly interrupted by random and occasionally extreme events.

Let's think about it. If it were easy to get an 80 percent success rate predicting and then investing in securities, everyone would be jumping on board. In practice, it is very tricky because the success rates are not guaranteed and are up against the threat of losing large sums of money or losing gains by not getting the required price entries. Transaction costs also factor into the final results in a significant way.

Classifier	Winning percentage
party tree	61.0
random forest	55.2
support vector machine	44.9

In spite of this, so long as our prediction rates are well enough above 50 percent that we can cover our transaction and employee costs, in the long run profits can be obtained using predictive recursive partitioning. 61.0 percent for this case involving three years of prices for the decision tree is reasonably good. At this point, further investigations to these are exercises and challenges for the reader to extend the foundation of this chapter.

13.7   Exercises

13.1. Setting Up Directory Structure and Acquiring Market Prices

Set up a directory under *FinAnalytics* called *MVO4* with sub-directories *NYSE* and *NASDAQ*. Locate the ticker symbol files *NYSEclean.txt* and *NASDAQclean.txt* and place them in their respective sub-directories. Examine the logic used for unit testing the *acquirePrices()* function to invoke it properly to obtain cache files in *NYSE* and *NASDAQ* sub-directories. There should be one cache file for each symbol in the *NYSEclean.txt* and *NASDAQclean.txt* files as outlined in Table 4.1; however, not all symbols will succeed when downloading. Be sure to use *readSubDirs()* to set the symbol vector, *lab* and the dimension variables $D = D1 + D2$. Note that $D1$ should be approximately 2233 and $D2$ should be approximately 2248.

Create a two-dimensional matrix called *prices* full of NAs and then invoke *acquirePrices()* to obtain D price vectors of length *len* covering the period: start = "2011-02-09" end = "2015-02-09" As *acquiringPrices()* is running, look into the *NYSE* directory to see that proper cache files are being created with non-NA prices. If NAs are being produced consistently it is good chance that the *start* and *end* dates do not match the *len* variable.

13.2. Expanding the Unit Test

Locate the logic for the function *findCachedPrices()* of Chapter 13. Expand the unit test of Section 13.3 to contain 12 *NYSE* and 12 *NASDAQ* symbols. Among these 24 symbols, it is fine if there are up to six symbols with unobtainable prices. What happens to the returned matrix in the case that there are no cache files for these symbols?

13.3. Obtaining S&P 500 Index Prices

Use the following invocation of *getHistPrices()* to obtain the index prices for comparison to the individual stock prices:

```
pricesSP <- getHistPrices( c('^GSPC'), c(1), len, start = "2011
-02-09", end = "2015-02-09", startBck1 = "2011-02-08", start
Fwd1 = "2011-02-10") write.csv( pricesSP, file = "cachedGSPC.
csv", row.names=FALSE)
```
creating the file *cachedGSPC.csv* in the *MVO4* directory.

13.4. Executing the Prediction Using Fundamentals

Obtain and execute the remaining code of Chapter 13 on the newly created directory structure. Examine whether the text results and plots are as expected.

13.5. Expanding the Dataset for Cross Validation

Once there are several elements in the dataset, cross-validation involves training on a subset of training data, followed by testing. In Chapter 13 we had only imported three years of prices, where two years were used for training. Expand the program logic to import five years of data for training and testing. Leave one year out of the four possible years of training data and run the `party` prediction training and test logic. By leaving one year out, there are four possible training sets. Report on the prediction rate for each training set. In your report, plot the resulting tree that is built by each called instance of *ctree()* in order to see the thresholds for each random variable used. Report the four prediction success rates for each case of leaving one year out of the sample.

14 Binomial Model for Options

Derivative securities provide a flexible and more sophisticated exposure to the market than simply owning the stock. In this section, we will concern ourselves with a particular type of derivative security known as an *option*. Options give the purchaser the right, but not the obligation, to purchase or sell the underlying security at a given price. This right will expire at the maturity date.

That is correct: the user of the option can determine the price that they want to pay for the underlying security. However, there is no guarantee that the price of the underlying will be reached, and so the proposal can become worthless when it reaches its expiration. Additionally, there is a fee for having this right. It is known as the *option premium*.

With American options, the right to exercise can occur at any time of any date after the purchase of the option. With European options, the right to exercise can only occur at maturity (Hull, 2006).

When one owns a stock, they are subjected to all the highs and the lows that can occur while holding the position. With an option, however, one is only subject to exposure in either the long (call) or short (put) direction. Valuing options is a non-trivial exercise due to the stochastic nature of the underlying security. A relatively simple option model which is used quite often in the options trading world is called the *binomial tree*. Our purpose here is to help explain how options operate so we can build an analytics framework later.

14.1 Applying Computational Finance

In computational finance, one uses probability and statistics to reason about financial instruments in algorithms. In order to makes sense of the binomial tree and another related model called the binomial asset pricing model, we assume *investors* in securities:

- Keep bank accounts;
- Invest in underlying securities like stocks.

In our case here, the best way to illustrate the options market is using an option trading game. Hypothetical stock investor, Smitty, believes in increased demand for GOOG stock, buys 1 share on Monday ($t = 0$), sells on Friday ($t = T$); GOOG has 50–50 probability of going up (p) or down (q) by \$1 per day. GOOG stock is trading at \$800 per share on Monday. Here is the situation over time:

$$n = 0, 1, 2, 3, 4 \text{ or } t = 0, \left\{\frac{1}{N}\right\}, \left\{\frac{2}{N}\right\}, \left\{\frac{3}{N}\right\}, \left\{\frac{4}{N}\right\}.$$

From these times and potential stock prices we can form a lattice (N is the number of trading days in a year). Use a coin toss to determine the daily direction: up (H) or down (T).

Let's look at one single day of GOOG stock price, $S(t)$, as seen in Figure 14.1. The time-based random variable representing the stock value, $S(t)$, is a stochastic process. The buyer of the stock on Monday ($t = 0$) is long and concerned with expected value of stock on Friday ($t = T$). From Figure 14.2, there are 16 paths in the full lattice of possible outcomes. In this version, the basic form of a binomial tree is shown with the original stock price, S, and its evolution to future prices in the up, u, or down, d, direction. Each time step, the current price is multiplied by either u or d. Figure 14.3 shows approximate stocks prices when $S = 800$. Freezing time at T, there is an expected value at the end of our experiment:

$$\mathbb{E}\left[S(T)\right] = 804p^4 + 802 \cdot 4p^3q + 800 \cdot 6p^2q^2 + 798 \cdot 4q^3p + 796q^4$$

$$= \left\{804\frac{1}{16} + 802\frac{4}{16} + 800\frac{6}{16} + 798\frac{4}{16} + 796\frac{1}{16}\right\} = 800$$

$$P(S(T) > S(0)) = \left\{\frac{1}{16} + \frac{4}{16}\right\} = \frac{5}{16} = .3125 = P(S(T) < S(0)). \tag{14.1}$$

Options investor Billie believes that GOOG is overvalued and buys a put option GOOG on Monday and sells on Friday. A put option is a type of derivative security derived from the right to sell GOOG stock short at a "strike" price $K = 801$ and has the ability to either:

- exercise it for profit it if GOOG price goes down to 800, 798, or 796 on Friday where the profit is the *strike minus price at expiration*;
- let it expire worthless if GOOG price goes up to 802 or 804.

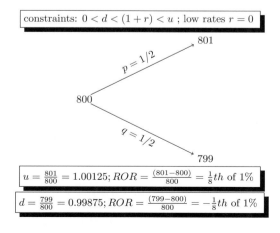

Figure 14.1   Transitioning from one day to the next where the stock price can go up or down at market close.

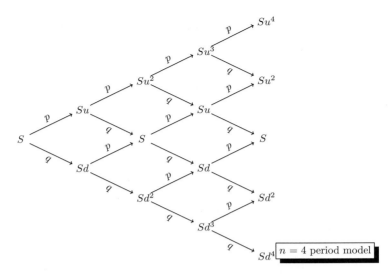

Figure 14.2   All possible outcomes beginning with stock price S. There are 16 possible paths from the root node to period $n = 4$.

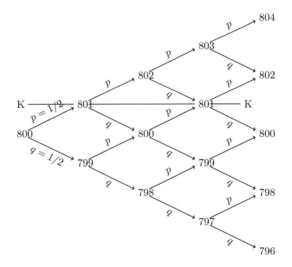

Figure 14.3   Lattice drawn this time with the strike price $K = 801$.

The owner of a put option has bearish viewpoint. They profit from the quantity $K - S(T)$ when it is greater than zero. The option payoff is the expected value at T:

$$\mathbb{E}\left[max(K - S(T), 0)\right] = \sum_{s} max(K - s, 0) \cdot P(S(T) = s)$$

$$= (max(801 - 804, 0)P(HHHH) +$$

$$max(801 - 802, 0)(P(HHHT) + P(HHTH)) +$$

$$max(801 - 802, 0)(P(HTHH) + P(THHH))+$$
$$max(801 - 800, 0)(P(HHTT) + P(HTHT))+$$
$$max(801 - 800, 0)(P(THTH) + P(TTHH))+$$
$$max(801 - 800, 0)(P(HTTH) + P(THHT))+$$
$$max(801 - 798, 0)(P(TTTH) + P(TTHT))+$$
$$max(801 - 798, 0)(P(THTT) + P(HTTT))+$$
$$max(801 - 796, 0)P(TTTT))$$
$$= 0p^4 + 0 \cdot 4p^3q + 1 \cdot 6p^2q^2 + 3 \cdot 4q^3p + 5q^4$$

$$\mathbb{E}\left[max(K - S(T), 0)\right] = 1\frac{6}{16} + 3\frac{4}{16} + 5\frac{1}{16} = 1.4375. \tag{14.2}$$

So $1.4375 is what the option is priced at, commonly known as the *premium* value.

Our third investor, Mayer, is not sure that GOOG is going to go down in value but does not think it's going way up either, so wants to sell a put option with strike price at 801 and profit from collecting the premium, hopefully not having to pay the option holder any payout. Mayer is taking the other side of the put option. We know that the value today of this option, as it is expected to possibly payout in the future, is $1.4375. Mayer's sold put profit worse case is $1.4375 − $5 = $ −3.5625 in the case when the put option has reached maximum value to the owner.

This three-player game is best played using a single coin tossed four times to represent the heads or tails value at the end of Monday through Friday. Before tossing the first coin, on Monday, Figure 14.4 shows the payouts, where Smitty buys the stock for $800, Billie buys the put option for $1.44 and that premium goes directly to Mayer. By Friday, as seen in Figure 14.5, depending upon the outcomes of four tosses, Smitty gets back the current price of GOOG, Billie gets zero or the difference between the strike price and the GOOG stock price if that price is below the strike price, and Mayer must pay

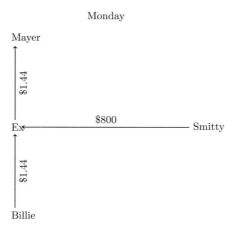

Figure 14.4 Initial payouts on the first day. Ex represents the stock options exchange.

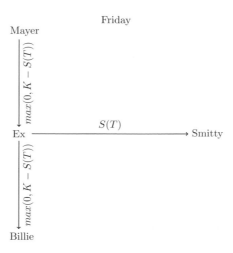

Figure 14.5   Payout to each investor at expiry.

zero or the difference between the strike price and the GOOG stock price if that price is below the strike price. These three investors represent typical investors in an options market.

14.2   Risk-Neutral Pricing and No Arbitrage

In computational finance there is an important elementary principle called *risk-neutral pricing*. While the risk-averse investor minimizes their risk, and the risk-seeking investor is attracted to risk, in this theoretical situation, the *risk-neutral* investor is neither risk-seeking nor risk-averse. While it is hard to believe, knowing what we do about personalities, that such an actual type of person exists, it is the most reasonable assumption to be made in order for the general case of option valuation to work out. By assuming the investors are risk-neutral, there is *no preference* between single guaranteed outcome and multiple outcomes so long as their expect value is the same. Any more complex assumptions cause additional complications, and they do not necessarily add to the accuracy of the analysis.

Another elementary principle is known as the *no arbitrage condition*. *Arbitrage* is a theoretical condition where investors can profit from a transaction that involves no negative cash flow at any probabilistic or temporal state, such that there is positive cash flow in at least one state. It is the possibility of a risk-free profit at zero cost. "No arbitrage" means that arbitrage, when it exists, disappears quickly. As market participants quickly take any profits from arbitrage very quickly, and since it is hard to introduce random variables for arbitrage, this common assumption seems reasonable.

14.3   High Risk-Free Rate Environment

We performed our basic binomial tree option calculations assuming that the interest rates were zero. While the risk-free rate, μ_f, the rate paid by a treasury bond from a stable issuer such as the United States Government, has been close to zero through the early part of the 2010 decade, this was certainly not always the case. In the late 1970s and early 1980s, some of the highest recorded risk-free rates prevailed.

To illustrate how high these rates can go, and how they affect the binomial tree, consider a story from that period. An Illinois family purchased a home in 1972 for $80,000. In 1984 that same family sold the same home for $380,000. Let us find the annualized rate of return, r_A and use it as a proxy for prevailing risk-free interest rates like μ_f.

$$380000 = 80000 \cdot (1 + r_A)^{12} \tag{14.3}$$

$$r_A = 14\%. \tag{14.4}$$

Now r_A is an annualized real estate appreciation rate, and it can be used as a proxy for interest rates. In order to obtain a daily interest rate, such as we have been using in our binomial tree, we need to solve for r in this formula:

$$(1 + r_A) = (1 + r)^N|_{N=250}. \tag{14.5}$$

Solving for r, we determine that

$$r = 0.00052425. \tag{14.6}$$

The Binomial Asset Pricing Model says that risk-neutral probability of the stock price going up, p, is related to the factor by which it goes up, u, and down, d, and the rate, r (Shreve, 2004a):

$$p = \frac{1 + r - d}{u - d}. \tag{14.7}$$

Similarly, the probability of the stock price going down, $q = 1 - p$, is related to the factor by which it goes down, d, and up, u, and the risk-free interest rate, r:

$$q = \frac{u - 1 - r}{u - d}. \tag{14.8}$$

To determine d and $u = \frac{1}{d}$, from Formula 14.7, we can multiply each side by $(u - d)$ to yield:

$$pu - pd = 1 + r - d$$
$$pu - (p - 1)d = 1 + r$$
$$pu + (1 - p)d = 1 + r$$
$$\frac{p}{d} + qd = 1 + r$$
$$\frac{.535}{d} + .465d = 1.00052425,$$

which can be solved as $d = .9929$ and $u = 1.007151$.

Figure 14.6 shows the updated binomial tree in the high interest rate environment. The amounts up and down in dollars are much greater than in prior trees in this chapter. The prevailing interest rate, r, determines the probability of the price going up p. Just by holding the stock each day we have a positive probability of it going up each day due to the risk-neutral pricing assumption forcing the risk interest rates to be applied to the

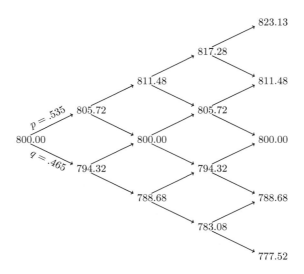

Figure 14.6   Binomial tree recalculated with high interest rates.

overall stock market. Risk-neutral probabilities say that we have a 53.5 percent chance of the stock going up each day. The expected value at the end of the week is $801.79. The expected value projected out to one year is $906.25.

14.4   Convergence of Binomial Model for Option Data

Now that we have looked at the Binomial Model intuitively, let us examine it as a practical method to calculate traded option values. Although the Black–Scholes formula has become the primary way to value European options, following the discrete Binomial Model with a more robust number of iterations can tell us whether this intuitive method is accurate enough to price real options in the market.

Following (Haug, 1998), a very handy reference book for anyone performing quantitative analysis of the various flavors of options, we use a set of formulas which generalized the Binomial Model to be usable as a pricing algorithm. Focusing on the simpler European options, which must be held until expiry, we know from Figure 14.2 that the model assumes the asset price at each node in the tree with n steps and maturity T in years is

$$Su^i d^{j-i}, \ i \in \{0, 1, \ldots, j\},$$

where u and d we know are our factors for up and down which are above and below 1 and in the range $0 < d < (1 + r) < u$ just like in Figure 14.1. More precisely,

$$u = \exp(\sigma \sqrt{\Delta t}), \ d = \exp(-\sigma \sqrt{\Delta t}) \ where \ \Delta t = T/n.$$

Our probability of a stock price increase at each step, p is defined:

$$p = \frac{\exp(b \Delta t) - d}{u - d} \ and \ q = 1 - p.$$

Now we can state the formula which simulates evaluation on the entire binomial tree to price call options and put options on stocks for initial price S and strike price K:

$$c = \exp(-rT) \sum_{i=a}^{n} \frac{n!}{i!(n-i)!} p^i q^{n-i} (Su^i d^{n-i} - K) \tag{14.9}$$

$$p = \exp(-rT) \sum_{i=0}^{a-1} \frac{n!}{i!(n-i)!} p^i q^{n-i} (K - Su^i d^{n-i}). \tag{14.10}$$

These are expected value formulas which sum the probability of each possible outcome and its payoff. If we convert the formulas into R code, we have two cases, call and put, and a **for**-loop to sum the probability-weighted outcomes. *binomial()* is the function name. When considering the call case, for $n = 4$ steps, the limits on the summation are 2:4. The

$$\frac{n!}{i!(n-i)!}$$

term evaluates to 6, 4, and 1 for $i = 2$, 3, and 4, respectively, and this corresponds to the numbers of paths to the rightmost nodes of the tree: S, Su^2, and Su^4. Below is the *binomial()* code.

```
#Binomial option pricing adapted from E.G.Haug book.
r = .08
b = r
sigma = .30
S = 100
K = 95
T = .5

binomial <- function(type,S,K,sigma,t,r,n) {
  deltat = T/n
  u = exp(sigma*sqrt(deltat))
  d = exp(-sigma*sqrt(deltat))
  p = (exp(b*deltat)-d)/(u-d)

  a = ceiling(log(K/(S*d^n))/log(u/d))
  val = 0
  if(type=='call') {
    for(i in a:n) {
      val = val +
        (factorial(n)/(factorial(i)*factorial(n-i)))*
        p^i*(1-p)^(n-i)*(S*u^i*d^(n-i)-K)
    }
  } else if(type=='put') {
    for(i in 0:(a-1))
      val  = val  +
        (factorial(n)/(factorial(i)*factorial(n-i)))*
        p^i*(1-p)^(n-i)*(K-S*u^i*d^(n-i))
  }
  exp(-r*T)*val
}
```

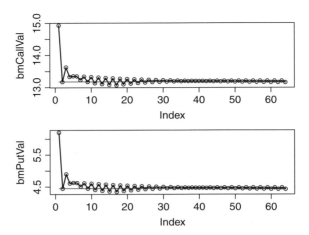

Figure 14.7 Convergence of binomial tree: the number of steps is on the horizontal axis and premium value is on the vertical axis. Top: call; Bottom: put.

The iterative *binomial()* method above can be compared to the classic Black–Scholes formula when valuing European options, below.

```
bs<-function(type,S,K,sigma,t,r){
  d1 <- (log(S/K) + (r+(sigma^2)/2)*t) / (sigma*sqrt(t))
  d2 <- (log(S/K) + (r-(sigma^2)/2)*t) / (sigma*sqrt(t))
  if (type=='call') val <- pnorm(d1)*S - pnorm(d2)*K*exp(-r*t)
  else if (type=='put') val <- pnorm(-d2)*K*exp(-r*t) -
        pnorm(-d1)*S
  val
}
```

Now we can see how well the values converge for the Binomial Model. The *plot()* code below shows us the calculated value on the *y*-axis for each *n* value, where *n* is the number of tree steps. Surprisingly, the calculated premiums start off not far off and converge fairly quickly. Figure 14.7 shows the call on top and the put on the bottom. The stock price, *S* stays at 100 and strike price, *K* is 95, meaning that the call is in-the-money (ITM) and the put is out-of-the-money (OTM).

```
#Invoke Binomial Method varying n:
N = 64
par(mfrow=c(1,2))
bmCallVal <- rep(0,length(1:N))
for(n in 1:N)
  bmCallVal[n] <- binomial('call',S,K,sigma,T,r,n)
plot(bmCallVal)
lines(bmCallVal,col=4)
bsCallVal <- bs('call',S,K,sigma,T,r)
lines(rep(bsCallVal,N),col=4)
bmPutVal <- rep(0,length(1:N))
for(n in 1:N)
  bmPutVal[n] <- binomial('put',S,K,sigma,T,r,n)
```

```
plot(bmPutVal)
lines(bmPutVal,col=4)
bsPutVal <- bs('put',S,K,sigma,T,r)
lines(rep(bsPutVal,N),col=4)
```

The best estimates of the Binomial Model ($N = 64$) and Black–Scholes values are shown in the output below.

```
> bmCallVal[N]
[1] 13.1524944608
> bsCallVal
[1] 13.174384319
> bmCallVal[N]/bsCallVal
[1] 0.998338453044
> bmPutVal[N]
[1] 4.42749118031
> bsPutVal
[1] 4.44938103847
> bmPutVal[N]/bsPutVal
[1] 0.99508024645
```

They are within one half of 1 percent as seen from the ratios of .995 and .998 above.

14.5   Put–Call Parity

The two major types of European options are related in price by a principle known as *Put–Call Parity*:

$$p = c - (S - K\exp(-rT)). \tag{14.11}$$

When the option is *at-the-money* (ATM) then the stock price, S, is equal to the present value of the strike price, $K\exp(-rT)$, so $p = c$. When the stock price is greater than the present value of the strike price, then the call is in the money, but the put is *out-of-the-money* (OTM) so the call price gets reduced by the amount $S - K\exp(-rT)$ to make them equal. Similarly, when the stock price is less than the present value of the strike price, then the put is *in-the-money* (ITM) and the call is OTM so the amount $S - K\exp(-rT)$ is negative and increases the right-hand side of Formula 14.11 to make the two sides equal. To see this more graphically, we have some R code below to plot it. The output is plotted in Figure 14.8.

```
#Visualizing Put-Call Parity:
S <- 75:125
M = length(S)
bmCallVal <- vector(length=M)
bmPutVal  <- vector(length=M)
n = 64
for(i in 1:M) {
  bmCallVal[i] <- binomial('call',S[i],K,sigma,T,r,n)
```

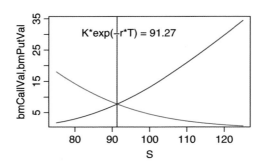

Figure 14.8   Put–call parity is most obvious at the present value of the strike price, $K \exp(-rT)$, where the call and put premium values are identical. Everywhere else for varying S and for fixed strike price $K = 95$, they are related by Formula 14.11.

```
    bmPutVal[i]   <- binomial('put',S[i],K,sigma,T,r,n)
}
par(mfrow=c(1,1))
plot(S,bmCallVal,type='l',col=4,
     ylab="bmCallVal,bmPutVal")
lines(S,bmPutVal,col=5)
#At the present value of the strike, K*exp(-r*T),
#the call and put have the same value (ATM).
pvK <- K*exp(-r*T)
abline(v = pvK)
text(c(pvK),c(30),paste("K*exp(-r*T) =",
          round(pvK,2)),cex=.75)
```

Now we consider the results of checking put–call parity:

```
> #Let's check Put-Call Parity:
> #S=100
> l = ceiling(M/2) #Find the middle price S[l]
> S[l]
[1] 100
> round(bmCallVal[l],4)
[1] 13.1525
> round(bmCallVal[l],4) ==
+    round(bmPutVal[l] + S[l] - pvK,4)
[1] TRUE
```

We see from the assertation of the last line of code, above, that put–call parity is met with rounding at four digits when the number of steps $N = 64$ and at S[26] = 100.

14.6   From Binomial to Log-Normal

The transition from the illustrative discrete-time binomial case and the more realistic continuous-time case involves going from the binomial distribution of stock prices to the familiar log-normal distribution. The binomial trees are used as an approximation to the case of continuous time in order to:

- illustrate the dynamic nature of the market with a small number of discrete random variables;
- calculate the value of American options in the case of early exercise.

The connection between the discrete and continuous-time models can be explained in detail (Shreve, 2004b). Returning back to the zero-risk free rate environment, $r = 0$, in the Binomial Model, we can choose any u and d such that:

$$0 < d < (1 + r) < u. \tag{14.12}$$

If we choose

$$u_n = 1 + \frac{\sigma}{\sqrt{n}}, d_n = 1 - \frac{\sigma}{\sqrt{n}} \tag{14.13}$$

for step n of the tree, we know that when $\sigma > 0$ then constraint (13.12) is met. Using (13.7) and (13.8),

$$p = \frac{1 + r + d_n}{u_n - d_n} = \frac{\sigma/\sqrt{n}}{2\sigma/\sqrt{n}} = \frac{1}{2}, q = \frac{u_n - 1 - r}{u_n - d_n} = \frac{\sigma/\sqrt{n}}{2\sigma/\sqrt{n}} = \frac{1}{2},$$

and we are, once again, back to symmetric probabilities of Section 14.1 above.

First of all, intuitively, since $u > 0$ and $d > 0$ and our initial stock price $S(0) > 0$ then, in the extension of an n-step binomial tree, $S(0)d^n$ can never reach or go below zero even though it can become infinitely close. This matches the behavior of stock prices as log-normal. In the log-normal distribution, the values of the random variable are positive. Secondly, if we use two random variables to indicate the number of heads, H_n, and tails, T_n at step n, then we know that

$$n = H_n + T_n, \tag{14.14}$$

because each outcome is either a head or a tail. We can also define a derived random variable

$$M_n = H_n - T_n, \tag{14.15}$$

as the number of heads minus the number of tails. If we add Equations 13.14 and 13.15 and divide by 2, we obtain

$$H_n = \frac{1}{2}(n + M_n), \tag{14.16}$$

and, if we subtract Equations 13.14 and 13.15 and divide by 2, we also can obtain

$$T_n = \frac{1}{2}(n - M_n). \tag{14.17}$$

So, if we have n up and down movements applied to $S(0)$, these can be tracked as

$$S_n(t) = S(0)u_n^{H_n}d_n^{T_n}, \tag{14.18}$$

and, by Equations 13.13 and 13.16 and 13.17,

$$S_n(t) = S(0) \left(1 + \frac{\sigma}{\sqrt{n}}\right)^{\frac{1}{2}(n+M_N)} \left(1 - \frac{\sigma}{\sqrt{n}}\right)^{\frac{1}{2}(n-M_N)}. \qquad (14.19)$$

As $n \to \infty$, the distribution of this random variable $S_n(t)$ converges to the distribution of

$$S(t) = S(0) \exp\left[\sigma W(t) - \frac{1}{2}\sigma^2 t\right], \qquad (14.20)$$

where $W(t)$ is a $N(0, t)$ random variable with variance t, although proving this is outside our scope. We now know that the distribution of $S(t)$ is log-normal because it is of the form Ce^K where C is a constant and K is normal.

14.7   Exercises

14.1. Asset Appreciation

Risk-neutral valuation of options assume that the prevailing interest rate, signified by r, is the basic rate of appreciation of equity securities, despite the fact that they are risky assets. To make this point more tangible, we can think about treasury bonds and real estate as have a similar rate r.

Assume you own a home in a market where real estate appreciates at a rate of 7 percent per year. If the home costs 100,000 initially and the rate is constant, what would we expect the home to be worth at the end of a decade?

14.2. Binomial Tree Accuracy

Determine the percentage increase in accuracy when going from $N = 32$ steps to $N = 64$ steps for the binomial tree for one put and one call option where $r = 0.08; b = r; sigma = 0.30; S = 100; K = 95; T = 0.5$. Use the Black–Scholes value as computed by the function $bsCallVal()$ as a reference.

15 Black–Scholes Model and Option-Implied Volatility

When traveling across the agricultural American Midwest, one can hear AM radio stations broadcast the futures prices of corn, soybeans, wheat, and other commodities every weekday at various times of the day. Iowa and Illinois lead the nation in corn production. Kansas leads the nation in wheat production. Listening to these farm reports is entertaining. Included in the broadcasts are very detailed weather reports. Weather is critical to many producers' livelihoods. After a few weeks of listening to these broadcasts, we learn that nobody truly knows for sure whether the agricultural market prices will go up or down on a trading day. Hedging the production chain price risk, especially for the farmers, who seasonally grow the crops, is achieved with futures and option securities. Producers very often want to lock in a price for delivering corn at the end of the season, or want to be compensated for a significant reduction in the agricultural price in order to guarantee recovering their fixed costs over the upcoming days and months.

From Chapter 14, we have gained more familiarity with the random walk processes assumed by the option models. We continue the option theme from the prior chapter and examine a very popular model for pricing European options. The most famous and widely accepted model of option valuation model is known as the Black–Scholes model of 1973 (Black and Myron, 1973). It revolutionized the pricing and trading of options which, prior to this, were priced in rather arbitrary ways. Black and Scholes relied upon the stochastic calculus. Stochastic calculus was invented by Itô in 1951 to address the need for a calculus for random variables as functions over time, like our stock market prices (Ito, 1951). Together with Merton, Black and Scholes were awarded the 1997 Nobel Prize in Economic Sciences for this invention. We discuss the Black–Scholes model here in order to complete our tour of financial analytics. We will try to make minimal use of stochastic calculus.

We saved this more mathematical material for the end of the book because it involves the more complex type of security: options. As mentioned in Chapter 14, options are derivative securities. Many people working in finance and investors in the market may never encounter options because they are considered too complex or risky for their risk appetite or they may be restricted from trading them if they work for a bank or securities firm, again, due to their risky nature. But discussing them provides a more complete financial analytics framework.

While we discussed mixture models as a way to more accurately represent true market distributions, most of the option literature and models in practice involve normal and log-normal distribution assumptions, so we will revert to that convention in order to discuss the industry standard option valuation model.

15.1   Geometric Brownian Motion

Geometric Brownian Motion (GBM) is a stochastic process and the assumption of market price movements for the Black–Scholes formula for finding the price of options in current market conditions. We begin where we left off in the prior chapter with GBM, which is also a log-normal process as in Formula 14.20. Introducing a *drift* term μ and taking the log of each side, we have $\sigma W(t) + (\mu - \sigma^2/2)t$. Since $W(t) \sim N(0, t)$, multiplying it by σ, a standard deviation term, makes the variance $\sigma^2 t$ and adding the term $(\mu - \sigma^2/2)t$ moves the mean from zero to $(\mu - \sigma^2/2)t$. So we have the well-known assumption of our stochastic process,

$$\ln\frac{S(t)}{S(0)} \sim Normal\left(\left(\mu - \frac{\sigma^2}{2}\right)t, \sigma^2 t\right). \tag{15.1}$$

Now let's look at GBM in its differential form. In stochastic calculus for finance, a stock price is described as having two components:

1. "trend" or deterministic behavior;
2. "random" or stochastic behavior.

In order to model this, we use

$$dS = S\mu dt + S\sigma dB,$$

where μ is the drift or instantaneous growth rate, σ is the standard deviation of returns, and $dB \sim N(0, 1)$. This description is satisfying because both the trend growth and the random component are proportional to the stocks price. We can rewrite this as

$$\frac{dS}{S} = \mu t + \sigma dB.$$

In ordinary calculus, if

$$y = g(x)$$

then

$$dy = g'(x)dx.$$

But in stochastic calculus, the calculus created for random variables, if X is a random variable:

$$Y = g(X)$$

then

$$dY = g'(X)dX + \frac{1}{2}g''(X)(dX)^2,$$

with the extra term due to the fact that $(dX)^2$ "accumulates."

Now consider again the stock model

$$\frac{dS}{S} = \mu t + \sigma dB$$

with a new random variable defined as

$$Y = \ln S,$$

which is the log of the stock price. Using the Itô's formula for the stochastic derivative we have

$$dY = d \ln S$$
$$= \left(S^{-1}\right) dS + \frac{1}{2}\left(-S^{-2}\right)(dS)^2$$
$$= \left(\frac{1}{S}\right) dS - \frac{1}{2}\left(\frac{dS}{S}\right)^2.$$

Using Itô's formula for the stochastic derivative we have

$$dY = d \ln S$$
$$= \left(\frac{1}{S}\right) dS - \frac{1}{2}\left(\frac{dS}{S}\right)^2$$
$$= (\mu dt + \sigma dB) - \frac{1}{2}(\mu dt + \sigma dB)^2$$
$$= (\mu dt + \sigma dB) - \frac{1}{2}(\mu^2 dt^2 + 2\mu dt dB + \sigma^2 dB^2)$$
$$= (\mu dt + \sigma dB) - \frac{1}{2}\sigma^2 t$$
$$= \left(\mu - \frac{1}{2}\sigma^2\right) dt + \sigma dB,$$

where the equality from line 4 to line 5 is true since $dt\dot{d}t \approx 0$, $dt\dot{d}B \approx 0$, and $dB\dot{d}B \approx dt$ as well in stochastic calculus. And since

$$d \ln S = \left(\mu - \frac{1}{2}\sigma^2\right) dt + \sigma dB,$$

we can integrate both sides over the interval $[0, T]$ to get

$$\ln S(T) - \ln S(0) = \left(\mu - \frac{1}{2}\sigma^2\right) T + \sigma B(T)$$

and take the exponential of both sides to get

$$S(T) = S(0)e^{\left(\mu - \frac{1}{2}\sigma^2\right)T + \sigma B(T)}, \tag{15.2}$$

which is the expression for geometric Brownian motion.

15.2   Monte Carlo Simulation of Geometric Brownian Motion

This stochastic process can be described without using differential equation notation simply as:

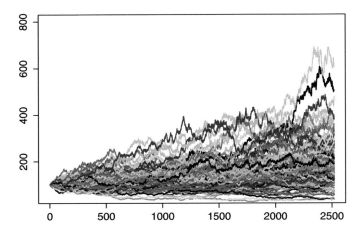

Figure 15.1   A 100-path Monte Carlo simulation of a typical stock using Geometric Brownian Motion. The price begins at 100 and goes as low as 25.04 and as high as 689.58 depending on the simulated path taken.

$$S(t) = S(0) \exp\left[\left(\mu - \frac{\sigma^2}{2}\right)t + \sigma z\sqrt{t}\right] \quad where \quad z \sim N(0,1). \quad (15.3)$$

In Figure 15.1 is a 100-path simulation of GBM process with $\mu = 0.07$ and $\sigma = 0.20$. The upward bias is caused by the drift parameter, μ. We can imagine a higher priced stock like IBM beginning a ten-year time horizon at \$100 per share and having 100 possible paths over that time horizon.

The R code for this one-year simulation appears below, inspired by the work of Carmona (Carmona, 2004). The paths are colored by the numeric path number to try to get as many unique colors as are available.

```
Npaths = 100
Nyears = 10
NdaysPerYr = 252
Ndays = NdaysPerYr*Nyears
muA = .07
muD = (1+muA)^(1/Ndays)-1      #daily ROR avg.
muD = exp(muA)^(1/Ndays)-1
sigmaA = .20
sigmaD = sigmaA/sqrt(Ndays) #daily volatility
rA = (muA - sigmaA^2/2)
rA
set.seed(2009)

#simulate:

sim <- function(init,Npaths,Ndays,muD,sigmaD,rD,isGBM) {
  X <- matrix(rep(0,Npaths*Ndays), nrow=Npaths, ncol=Ndays)
  X[,1] <- init #initial stock price
  for(t in 1:(Ndays-1)) {
    print(t)
    deltat = 1/NdaysPerYr
```

```
   tA = t/NdaysPerYr
   #Geometric Brownian motion model:
   X[,t+1] <- X[,t]*exp( rA*deltat + sigmaA *
           sqrt(deltat) * rnorm(Npaths) )
 }
 return(X)
}
```

The following function displays the simulation paths.

```
display <- function(X,Npaths,xlab,ylab) {
  #now go path by path:
  for(p in 1:Npaths)
    if(p==1) {
      plot(X[p,],col=p,type='l',ylim=c(50,100*8),
          xlab=xlab,ylab=ylab)
    } else {z
      lines(X[p,],col=p)
    }
}
```

The following runs the simulation.

```
par(mfrow=c(1,1))
par(mar=c(2,2,1,1))
X <- sim(100.0,Npaths,Ndays,muD,sigmaD,rD,isGBM=TRUE)
display(X,Npaths,xlab="Days",ylab="Price")
min(X)
max(X)
```

15.3 Black–Scholes Derivation

The Black–Scholes formula is the industry standard for valuing European options, and its derivation is an interesting process to witness. Here, it is being performed using ordinary calculus. The discount expected payoff of a call option:

$$c(S,0) = e^{-rT} E\left[(S_T - K)_+\right], \tag{15.4}$$

where $(x)_+$ means $max(0, x)$ and $S(T)$ follows geometric Brownian motion:

$$S(T) = S(0)e^{\left(r - \frac{\sigma^2}{2}\right)T + \sigma\sqrt{T}z} \tag{15.5}$$

and $Z \sim N(0, 1)$, where we substitute r for μ and $\sigma\sqrt{T}z$ in for $\sigma B(T)$ in Equation 15.2 to obtain Equation 15.5. Now,

$$\begin{aligned}
c(S,0) &= e^{-rT} E\left[(S_T - K)_+\right] \\
&= e^{-rT} \int_{-\infty}^{\infty} \left(S_0 e^{\left(r - \frac{\sigma^2}{2}\right)T + \sigma\sqrt{T}z} - K\right) f(z)dz \\
&= e^{-rT} \int_{-\infty}^{\infty} \left(S_0 e^{\left(r - \frac{\sigma^2}{2}\right)T + \sigma\sqrt{T}z} - K\right) \frac{1}{\sqrt{2\pi}} e^{-\frac{z^2}{2}} dz,
\end{aligned}$$

where $f(z)$ is the p.d.f. for z. Given the definition of Geometric Brownian Motion in Equation 15.3, we begin by solving for the lower bound of the above integral. Since the call option only pays when the terminal value of the security is greater than the strike, it must be that:

$$S(0)e^{\left(r-\frac{\sigma^2}{2}\right)T+\sigma\sqrt{T}z} - K \geq 0, \tag{15.6}$$

so we can look for the lower limit of the integration,

$$S(0)e^{\left(r-\frac{\sigma^2}{2}\right)T+\sigma\sqrt{T}z} - K \geq 0$$

$$e^{\left(r-\frac{\sigma^2}{2}\right)T}e^{\sigma\sqrt{T}z} \geq \frac{K}{S_0}$$

$$e^{\sigma\sqrt{T}z} \geq \frac{K}{S_0}e^{-\left(r-\frac{\sigma^2}{2}\right)T}$$

$$\sigma\sqrt{T}z \geq \ln\left(\frac{K}{S_0}\right) - \left(r-\frac{\sigma^2}{2}\right)T$$

$$z \geq \frac{1}{\sigma\sqrt{T}}\left[\ln\left(\frac{K}{S_0}\right) - \left(r-\frac{\sigma^2}{2}\right)T\right].$$

Let this lower limit be:

$$L = \frac{1}{\sigma\sqrt{T}}\left[\ln\left(\frac{K}{S_0}\right) - (r-\frac{\sigma^2}{2})T\right], \tag{15.7}$$

so that the call option's discounted expected payoff is now

$$c(S,0) = e^{-rT}\int_L^\infty \left(S_0 e^{\left(r-\frac{\sigma^2}{2}\right)T+\sigma\sqrt{T}z} - K\right)\frac{1}{\sqrt{2\pi}}e^{-\frac{z^2}{2}}dz.$$

Separating the exponential gives us:

$$c(S,0) = e^{-rT}\int_L^\infty \left(S_0 e^{rT}e^{-\frac{\sigma^2}{2}T}e^{\sigma\sqrt{T}z} - K\right)\frac{1}{\sqrt{2\pi}}e^{-\frac{z^2}{2}}dz.$$

Distributing the density through gives us

$$c(S,0) = \frac{e^{-rT}}{\sqrt{2\pi}}\left(\int_L^\infty S_0 e^{rT}e^{-\frac{\sigma^2}{2}T}e^{\sigma\sqrt{T}z}e^{-\frac{z^2}{2}}dz - \int_L^\infty Ke^{-\frac{z^2}{2}}dz\right)$$

and

$$c(S,0) = \frac{e^{-rT}}{\sqrt{2\pi}}\int_L^\infty S_0 e^{rT}e^{-\frac{\sigma^2}{2}T}e^{\sigma\sqrt{T}z}e^{-\frac{z^2}{2}}dz - \frac{e^{-rT}}{\sqrt{2\pi}}\int_L^\infty Ke^{-\frac{z^2}{2}}dz$$

$$= \frac{S_0}{\sqrt{2\pi}}\int_L^\infty e^{-\frac{\sigma^2}{2}T+\sigma\sqrt{T}z-\frac{z^2}{2}}dz - Ke^{-rT}\int_L^\infty \frac{1}{\sqrt{2\pi}}e^{-\frac{z^2}{2}}dz$$

$$= \frac{S_0}{\sqrt{2\pi}}\int_L^\infty e^{-\frac{1}{2}(z-\sigma\sqrt{T})^2}dz - Ke^{-rT}(1 - N(L)).$$

Now substitute $y = z - \sigma\sqrt{T}$, which shifts the bounds of integration down to $L - \sigma\sqrt{T}$:

$$c(S, 0) = \frac{S_0}{\sqrt{2\pi}} \int_L^\infty e^{-\frac{1}{2}(z - \sigma\sqrt{T})^2} dz - Ke^{-rT}(1 - N(L))$$

$$= \frac{S_0}{\sqrt{2\pi}} \int_{L - \sigma\sqrt{T}}^\infty e^{-\frac{1}{2}y^2} dz - Ke^{-rT}(1 - N(L))$$

$$= S_0(1 - N(L - \sigma\sqrt{T})) - Ke^{-rT}(1 - N(L)),$$

where

$$P(X \leq x) = N(x) = \int_{-\infty}^x \frac{1}{\sqrt{2\pi}} e^{-\frac{z^2}{2}} dz \qquad (15.8)$$

is the cumulative standard normal distribution function. Now we are nearing the end of the derivation!

Now, recalling in Equation 15.7 the lower bound of the integration

$$L = \frac{1}{\sigma\sqrt{T}} \left[\ln\left(\frac{K}{S_0}\right) - (r - \frac{\sigma^2}{2})T \right].$$

Subtracting $\sigma\sqrt{T}$ from both sides yields

$$L - \sigma\sqrt{T} = \frac{1}{\sigma\sqrt{T}} \left[\ln\left(\frac{K}{S_0}\right) - (r - \frac{\sigma^2}{2})T \right] - \sigma\sqrt{T}$$

$$= \frac{1}{\sigma\sqrt{T}} \left[\ln\left(\frac{K}{S_0}\right) - (r - \frac{\sigma^2}{2})T - \sigma^2 T \right]$$

$$= \frac{1}{\sigma\sqrt{T}} \left[\ln\left(\frac{K}{S_0}\right) - (r + \frac{\sigma^2}{2})T \right].$$

Now, recalling Equation 15.8 for the function $N(x)$, the cumulative standard normal distribution function, and we know from probability theory that $N(-L) = 1 - N(L)$. So that if

$$L = \frac{1}{\sigma\sqrt{T}} \left[\ln\left(\frac{K}{S_0}\right) - (r - \frac{\sigma^2}{2})T \right]$$

then

$$-L = -\frac{1}{\sigma\sqrt{T}} \left[\ln\left(\frac{K}{S_0}\right) - (r - \frac{\sigma^2}{2})T \right]$$

$$= \frac{1}{\sigma\sqrt{T}} \left[\ln\left(\frac{S_0}{K}\right) + (r - \frac{\sigma^2}{2})T \right].$$

Since $1 - N(L - \sigma\sqrt{T}) = N(-(L - \sigma\sqrt{T}))$ we have

$$-(L - \sigma\sqrt{T}) = -\frac{1}{\sigma\sqrt{T}} \left[\ln\left(\frac{K}{S_0}\right) - (r + \frac{\sigma^2}{2})T \right]$$

$$= \frac{1}{\sigma\sqrt{T}} \left[\ln\left(\frac{S_0}{K}\right) + (r + \frac{\sigma^2}{2})T \right]$$

$$= d_1.$$

The price of a European call for a non-dividend-paying stock with current price S_0 with strike price X, term T, and interest rate r is:

$$C = S_0 N(d_1) - Xe^{-rt} N(d_2), \tag{15.9}$$

where

$$d_1 = \frac{\ln\left(\frac{S_0}{X}\right) + \left(r + \frac{\sigma^2}{2}\right)t}{\sigma\sqrt{t}}$$

$$d_2 = d_1 - \sigma\sqrt{t},$$

and $N(z) = P(Z \leq z)$ is the cumulative distribution of the standard Normal random variable from Equation 15.8. Note that we used X for the strike price this time.

The Black–Scholes option pricing formula allows us to calculate the price of a European call or put option, given the stocks current price, the option strike price, the risk-free rate over the options life, and volatility.

The price of a European put for a non-dividend-paying stock with current price S_0 with strike price X, term T, and interest rate r is:

$$P = Xe^{-rT}[N(-d_2)] - S_0[N(-d_1)], \tag{15.10}$$

where

$$d_1 = \frac{\ln\left(\frac{S_0}{X}\right) + \left(r + \frac{\sigma^2}{2}\right)T}{\sigma\sqrt{T}} \tag{15.11}$$

and

$$d_2 = d_1 - \sigma\sqrt{T}. \tag{15.12}$$

15.4   Algorithm for Implied Volatility

As derived previously, for a non-dividend-paying stock with current price S_0 with strike price K, term T, and interest rate r the Black–Scholes price of a European call and put are specified in Equations 15.9 and 15.10.

Often, Equations 15.9 and 15.10 are used to compute what is called the *implied volatility* of the option prices. The strike, option price, underlying asset price, term, and interest rate are all known, but volatility is not. We observe the options prices in the market and solve the volatility σ that gives us the observed prices. This is accomplished by root-finding algorithms (Bennett, 2009).

Before we can calculate volatility, we must extract the known information from some source. Options as a set are represented as a structure known as an *option chain*. Option databases are quite large, often over 100 GB, and require R to interface with database software. We will examine the option chain for TARO, which is around 10 MB. To aggregate the option data and then extract the chain for TARO, we will use the RSQLite package. We can use root-finding algorithms to solve for the volatility implied by the variables known. For this we will implement both the Newton–Raphson and secant algorithms. With volatility for a given option estimated, we can aggregate volatilities for TARO across strike prices and durations to construct what is known as the *volatility surface* and the *volatility smile*. We can also aggregate across estimated volatilities for a given day and plot the behavior of volatility in time. This we will do using the `ggplot2` package.

The Newton–Raphson method solves for $f(x) = 0$ when the below recursion converges sufficiently:

$$x_{n+1} = x_n - \frac{f(x_n)}{f'(x_n)}.$$

The secant method also solves for $f(x) = 0$ by approximating the derivative of the function:

$$f'(x_{n-1}) \approx \frac{f(x_{n-1}) - f(x_{n-2})}{x_{n-1} - x_{n-2}}.$$

Substituting the approximation into the Newton–Raphson recursion yields:

$$x_n = x_{n-1} - \frac{f(x_{n-1})}{\frac{f(x_{n-1}) - f(x_{n-2})}{x_{n-1} - x_{n-2}}}$$

$$= x_{n-1} - f(x_{n-1})\frac{x_{n-1} - x_{n-2}}{f(x_{n-1}) - f(x_{n-2})}.$$

15.5   Implementation of Implied Volatility

With the option chain in hand, we can read it into R and examine its structure. In our analysis we will be concerned with `DataDate`: the date on which the data was recorded, `UnderlyingPrice`: the price of TARO on `DataDate`, `Type`: whether the option is a call or a put, `Expiration`: date on which the option expires, `Strike`: strike price of the option, `Bid`: price being offered by a potential buyer of the option, and `Ask`: price being demanded by a potential seller of the option. We need to process the data frame so it can be more useful.

```
> setwd(paste(homeuser,"/FinAnalytics/ChapXV",sep=""))
> taro<-read.csv("TARO.csv")
> str(taro)

'data.frame':   27650 obs. of  17 variables:
 $ X.1             : int  1 2 3 4 5 6 7 8 9 10 ...
 $ X               : int  1 2 3 4 5 6 7 8 9 10 ...
 $ UnderlyingSymbol: Factor w/ 1 level "TARO": 1 1 1 1 1 1 1 1 1 1 ...
 $ UnderlyingPrice : num  32.7 32.7 32.7 32.7 32.7 32.7 32.7 32.7 ...
 $ Exchange        : Factor w/ 1 level "*": 1 1 1 1 1 1 1 1 1 1 ...
 $ OptionRoot      : Factor w/ 418 levels "QTT020420C00025000",..:
 $ OptionExt       : logi  NA NA NA NA NA NA ...
 $ Type            : Factor w/ 2 levels "call","put": 1 2 1 2 1 2 ...
 $ Expiration      : Factor w/ 25 levels "2002-04-20","2002-05-18",..:
 $ DataDate        : Factor w/ 435 levels "2002-03-22","2002-03-25",..:
```

```
$ Strike          : num   25 25 30 30 32.5 32.5 35 35 40 40 ...
$ Last            : num   7 0.95 3.3 1.2 1.7 2.4 0.85 3 0.2 9 ...
$ Bid             : num   7.2 0 2.9 0.45 1.5 1.25 0.5 2.6 0 6.7 ...
$ Ask             : num   8.4 0.5 3.9 0.95 2.15 1.9 0.95 3.4 0.4 7.9 ...
$ Volume          : int   0 0 1 0 4 0 10 4 2 0 ...
$ OpenInterest    : int   43 90 181 334 946 34 403 75 293 43 ...
$ T1OpenInterest  : int   43 90 181 334 948 34 413 79 293 43 ...
```

```
> taro$Spread<-taro$Ask-taro$Bid
```

We proceed and convert `DataDate` and `Expiration` from factors to R date objects so that we can do date arithmetic on them, and define option `Price` and `Maturity`. We define the `Price` of the option to be the mid-point or average between the `Bid` and the `Ask` prices. While we could incorporate other information such as outstanding contracts or volume, the simple average will serve as a reasonable approximation. The `Maturity` is defined as years to expiration of the option, and so is calculated as the difference between the `Expiration` date and the current `DataDate` date, divided by the number of days in a year. Lastly, we define an implied volatility `IV` component which will hold our calculated implied volatilities and initialize it to zero.

```
> taro$Expiration<-as.Date(taro$Expiration)
> taro$DataDate<-as.Date(taro$DataDate)
> taro$Price<-(taro$Bid+taro$Ask)/2
> taro$Maturity<-as.double(taro$Expiration-taro$DataDate)/365
> taro$IV<-0.0
```

To isolate the dates for our analysis, we use the R function *unique()* to return the set of all `DataDate` values in the data frame. We proceed to take the first 150 dates, and subset to return only the options that correspond to those dates.

```
> dates<-unique(taro$DataDate)
> dates<-dates[1:150]
> taro<-subset(taro,DataDate %in% dates)
```

We now define the implied volatility functions we need. Recall that for a non-dividend-paying stock with current price S_0, with strike price X, term T, and interest rate r, the Black–Scholes price of a European call option and put option are

$$C = S_0 N(d_1) - Xe^{-rt}N(d_2)$$
$$P = Xe^{-rt}N(-d_2) - S_0 N(-d_1),$$

where

$$d_1 = \frac{\ln\left(\frac{S_0}{X}\right) + \left(r + \frac{\sigma^2}{2}\right)T}{\sigma\sqrt{T}}$$

$$d_2 = \frac{\ln\left(\frac{S_0}{X}\right) + \left(r - \frac{\sigma^2}{2}\right)T}{\sigma\sqrt{T}},$$

and $N(z) = P(Z \le z)$ is the cumulative distribution of the standard Normal random variable. With this in mind we can define a function to calculate the value of either a call or a put option. We calculate the values of d_1 and d_2 then the value of the call or put, depending on whether call or put is specified. Note that the R function *pnorm(d1)* calculates the probability $N(d_1) = P(Z \le d_1)$.

```
> bs<-function(type,S,K,sigma,t,r){
+    d1 <- (log(S/K) + (r+(sigma^2)/2)*t) / (sigma*sqrt(t))
+    d2 <- (log(S/K) + (r-(sigma^2)/2)*t) / (sigma*sqrt(t))
+    if (type=='call') val <- pnorm(d1)*S - pnorm(d2)*K*exp(-r*t)
+    else if (type=='put') val <- pnorm(-d2)*K*exp(-r*t) - pnorm(-d1)*S
+    val
+ }
```

Finally, we implement the secant method. Recall the secant method recursion

$$x_n = x_{n-1} - f(x_{n-1})\frac{x_{n-1} - x_{n-2}}{f(x_{n-1}) - f(x_{n-2})}$$

and implement the secant function recursively, with the possibility of the approximate volatility in the case that the recursion diverges. We do this by testing if the estimate implied volatility gets large enough to be equal to R's representation of infinity.

```
> secantIV<-function(type,V,S,K,sigma0,sigma1,t,r){
+    newSigma <- sigma0 - (bs(type,S,K,sigma0,t,r)-V)*(sigma0-sigma1)/
+              (bs(type,S,K,sigma0,t,r) - bs(type,S,K,sigma1,t,r))
+    if( abs(newSigma)==Inf ) return(0.0)
+    if( abs(newSigma - sigma0) < .001 ) return(newSigma)
+    else return(secantIV(type,V,S,K,newSigma,sigma0,t,r))
+ }
```

We also define the Newton–Raphson algorithm, although we don't use it extensively because of instability. Recall the Newton–Raphson method solves for $f(x) = 0$ when the recursion below converges sufficiently:

$$x_{n+1} = x_n - \frac{f(x_n)}{f'(x_n)}.$$

The problem lies in dividing by the derivative of the option value. In the case of the call option, and using the chain rule of differentiation, the derivative of the option is given as

$$\frac{\partial C}{\partial \sigma} = S_0 \phi(d_1)\sqrt{T},$$

where $\phi(x)$ is the density of the standard normal random variable evaluated at x. When the underlying price is much greater than the strike price and the time until expiration is long, the value of the normal distribution at this level can be very small, resulting in division by near zero, and causing the iteration to get out of control. We define the value of the Black–Scholes below for a call option.

```
> Val<-function(V,S,K,sigma,t,r){
+    d1 <- (log(S/K) + (r+(sigma^2)/2)*t) / (sigma*sqrt(t))
+    d2 <- (log(S/K) + (r-(sigma^2)/2)*t) / (sigma*sqrt(t))
+      val<-pnorm(d1)*S - pnorm(d2)*K*exp(-r*t)
+      return(val-V)
+ }
```

The Newton–Raphson method uses the derivative of the call option in calculating the update. Keeping in mind the above formula for the derivative of the call option with respect to the volatility σ, we define below a function to compute the derivative for the call option:

```
> dVal<-function(V,S,K,sigma,t,r){
+    d1 <- (log(S/K) + (r+(sigma^2)/2)*t) / (sigma*sqrt(t))
+    val <- S*dnorm(d1)*sqrt(t)
+    return(val)
+ }
```

Putting the pieces together, we define a function to estimate the implied volatility via the Newton–Raphson method $x_{n+1} = x_n - \frac{f(x_n)}{f'(x_n)}$ and iterate recursively until convergence is achieved.

```
> impliedVol<-function(V,S,K,sigma,t,r){
+    newSigma <- sigma - Val(V,S,K,sigma,t,r) / dVal(V,S,K,sigma,t,r)
+      if( abs(newSigma - sigma) < .001 ) return(newSigma)
+      else return(impliedVol(V,S,K,newSigma,t,r))
+ }
```

We test Newton–Raphson and secant methods to ensure they give similar results for the implied volatility for a call option priced at 2.875 with an underlying price of 24, a strike price of 22, an interest rate of 5 percent, and a time until expiration of six months, i.e. half a year.

```
> impliedVol(2.875,24,22,0.2,.5,0.05)
[1] 0.1871222
> secantIV('call',2.875,24,22,0.5,1,.5,0.05)
[1] 0.1871232
```

Convinced that our implied volatility solvers are working correctly, we now step through the option chain by date variable DataDate and calculate the implied volatility for each option on a given day via the secant method. The secant method can also diverge, but rarely.

```
> for(date in dates){
+    sub<-subset(taro,DataDate==date)
+    IV<-rep(0,dim(sub)[1])
+    for(i in 1:dim(sub)[1]){
+      IV[i]<-secantIV(sub$Type[i],sub$Price[i],sub$UnderlyingPrice[i],
+        sub$Strike[i],0.4,1,sub$Maturity[i],0.05)
```

```
+   }
+   taro[taro$DataDate==date,]$IV<-IV
+ }
> taro<-subset(taro,IV!=0.0)
> hist(taro$IV,breaks=100,main="")
```

Two histograms and a plot of option implied volatility are contained in Figures 15.2, 15.3 and 15.4.

```
> hist(taro$Spread,main="")
> vol<-data.frame(date=dates)
> vol$IV<-0.0
> for(date in dates){
+   vol[vol$date==date,]$IV<-mean(taro[taro$DataDate==date,]$IV)
+ }
> plot(vol$date,vol$IV,type='l',col='blue')
> library(ggplot2)
> ggplot(vol,aes(x=date,y=IV)) + geom_line()
```

We turn now to construction of the volatility smile. To examine the volatility smile for a single day, we subset the dataset for a single date: March 25, 2002. We then subset for put and call options out of the money, then plot the implied volatilities corresponding to these strike prices.

```
> tarosub<-taro[taro$DataDate=='2002-03-25',]
> taroput<-subset(tarosub,Type=='put' & UnderlyingPrice > Strike)
> tarocall<-subset(tarosub,Type=='call' & UnderlyingPrice < Strike)
```

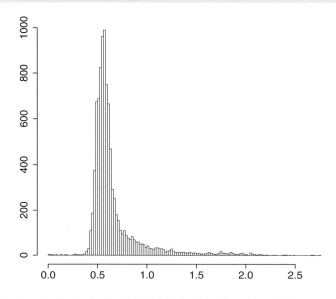

Figure 15.2   Histogram of option-implied volatility for TARO, April to November 2002.

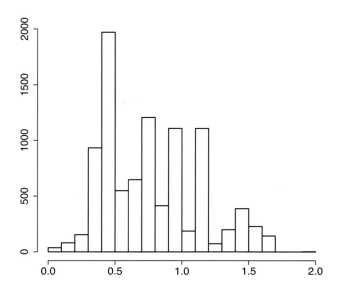

Figure 15.3   Histogram of Ask–Bid Spread of TARO options.

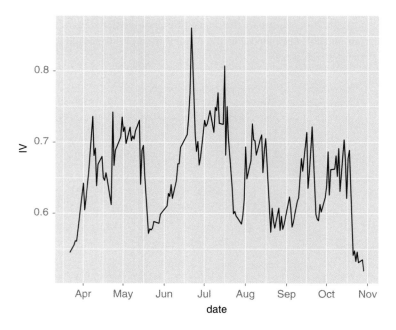

Figure 15.4   Time series plot of averaged implied volatility for calls and puts of various strikes and maturities for TARO from April 2002 to November 2002.

R's mesh-plotting functionality requires monotone values in the x and y directions. This is a problem since Strike prices are nested in Maturity. We can at least look at one "slice" of the volatility surface, i.e. for a single maturity to get a look at the volatility smile.

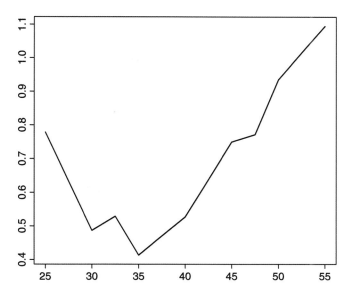

Figure 15.5   Volatility smile for TARO on March 25, 2002.

We observe in Figure 15.5 what has been documented in finance, specifically that implied volatilities for strike prices close to the underlying price are lower than implied volatilities for strike prices further away from the underlying price. And not only higher, but higher by a factor of two or three. This implies that investors are especially sensitive to large movements and "overpay" for options far from the current price.

```
> x<-append(taroput[1:3,]$Strike,tarocall[1:6,]$Strike)
> y<-append(taroput[1:3,]$IV,tarocall[1:6,]$IV)
> plot(x,y,type='l', xlab='Strike', ylab='Implied Volatility')
```

As an alternative to the mesh plot, we can use the R function plot3d() for a visualization of the volatility surface. We see the 3D object of which the volatility smile in Figure 15.6 is a single slice. We observe what has been documented in the options literature, that the steepness of the volatility smile decreases as maturity increases to the point that, for long maturity options, with maturity of say six months, the volatility smile is noticeable. This suggests that investors are less concerned with large price movements over long time frames than large price movements over shorter time frames.

15.6   The Rcpp Package

The Rcpp package, written by Dirk Eddelbuettel, allows the R developer to push down functions to the more efficient C++ language layer. Of course, C++, being a language for computer systems development, can be very efficient in terms of the generated code. To illustrate how R code can be sped up significantly using a C++ implementation of critical

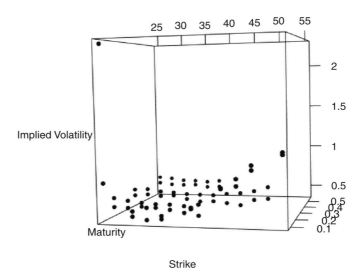

Figure 15.6   3D plot of implied volatility as a function of Maturity and Strike price.

functions, we begin with a simple Fibonacci number example (Eddelbuettel, 2013). The below C++ code is in a file called `fibonacci.cpp`.

```
#include <Rcpp.h>
using namespace Rcpp;

// [[Rcpp::export]]
int fibonacci(const int x){
if(x<2) return x;
else return(fibonacci(x-1)+fibonacci(x-2));
}
```

We integrate into R using the *sourceCpp()* function in Rcpp:

```
library(Rcpp)
sourceCpp(paste(homeuser","/FinAnalytics/ChapXV/fibonacci.cpp",sep=""))
```

and can now call the fibonacci function in R:

```
> fibonacci(20)

[1] 6765
```

Many times we need the function we are calling from R to itself call another function in C++. This is accomplished by defining the function above the function being exported to R.

Similarly, we can define and use the Black–Scholes formula in the secant algorithm. First, we define the file *secant.cpp* below.

```
#include <math.h>
#include <Rmath.h>
#include <R.h>
#include <Rcpp.h>
using namespace Rcpp;
double bs(int type, double S, double K, double sigma, double t, double r){
  double d1,d2,val;
  d1 = (log(S/K) + (r+pow(sigma,2)/2)*t) / (sigma*sqrt(t));
  d2 = (log(S/K) + (r-pow(sigma,2)/2)*t) / (sigma*sqrt(t));
  if(type==0) val = R::pnorm(d1,0.0,1.0,TRUE,FALSE)*S
  - R::pnorm(d2,0.0,1.0,TRUE,FALSE)*K*exp(-r*t);
  else if (type==1) val = R::pnorm(-d2,0.0,1.0,TRUE,FALSE)*K*exp(-r*t)
  - R::pnorm(-d1,0.0,1.0,TRUE,FALSE)*S;
  return val;
}
// [[Rcpp::export]]
double secant(int type, double V, double S, double K,
      double sigma0, double sigma1, double t, double r){
  if( fabs(sigma0-sigma1) < .001 ) return(sigma0);
  else{
    double newSigma = sigma0 - (bs(type,S,K,sigma0,t,r)-V)*
        (sigma0-sigma1)/
        (bs(type,S,K,sigma0,t,r) - bs(type,S,K,sigma1,t,r));
    return(secant(type,V,S,K,newSigma,sigma0,t,r));
  }
}
```

We compile the C++ code and link to R via the `Rcpp` function *sourceCpp()*.

```
sourceCpp(paste(homeuser,"/FinAnalytics/ChapXV/secant.cpp",sep=""))
```

We construct a wrapper for the secant function that reads whether an option is a call or put and then calls the secant function, coding call as 0 and put as 1:

```
CsecantIV<-function(type,V,S,K,sigma0,sigma1,t,r){
  if(type=='call') val<-secant(0,V,S,K,sigma0,sigma1,t,r)
  else if(type=='put') val<-secant(1,V,S,K,sigma0,sigma1,t,r)
  val
}
```

Now, we calculate the Black–Scholes implied volatility via the *secant()* function implemented in C++ and via the *secantIV()* function defined earlier in R and compare them to make sure they agree:

```
> secantIV('call',2.875,24,22,0.5,1,.1,0.05)
[1] 0.5553217
> CsecantIV('call',2.875,24,22,0.5,1,.1,0.05)
[1] 0.5553217
> dates<-dates[1:3]
> dates
[1] "2002-03-22" "2002-03-25" "2002-03-26"
```

We can now use the R *subset()* utility to select our dates of interest and calculate the implied volatilities.

```
> sub<-subset(taro,DataDate %in% dates)
> n<-dim(sub)[1]
> system.time(for(i in 1:n) sub$IV[i] <- secantIV(sub$Type[i],
+ sub$Price[i],
+ sub$UnderlyingPrice[i],
+ sub$Strike[i],
+ 0.4,
+ 1,
+ sub$Maturity[i],
+ 0.05)
+ )

   user  system elapsed
  0.203   0.001   0.272

> system.time(for(i in 1:n) sub$IV[i] <- CsecantIV(sub$Type[i],
+ sub$Price[i],
+ sub$UnderlyingPrice[i],
+ sub$Strike[i],
+ 0.4,
+ 1,
+ sub$Maturity[i],
+ 0.05)
+ )

   user  system elapsed
  0.082   0.001   0.084
```

According to the reported times, we sped up our time to compute the secant method implied volatilities, implemented by *secantIV()* and *CsecantIV()* from 272 milliseconds to 84 milliseconds. Depending upon the amount of branching and looping in the algorithm, results can vary.

15.7   Exercises

15.1. Working with Drift in the GBM Process

In the GBM model the upward trend which occurs when rates are positive is known as *drift*, denoted by μ. We can see the drift curve by running the *sim()* and *display()* functions with the annual vol *sigmaA* = 0.0. Run these functions.

(a) From the plot, what is the approximate total drift per year or net return just by looking at the plot?

(b) What is the formula for computing the expected future price $S(t)$ of simulation in terms of time in years t, initial stock price $S(0)$, drift μ, standard deviation, or volatility σ, when we use a normal variate z to generate the random future prices?

(c) If we begin with an initial market price of 100 for the simulated security, what is the expected future price in ten years? Use *sigmaA* = 0.0 again. You can perform this calculation with R or outside it.

15.2. Working with the Option Chain for TARO Pharmaceutical Industries

Run the code to produce the *subset()* and option values for TARO. Locate the price of the call option for expiration date 2002-07-20 upon the valuation date 2002-03-25 for the strike price of 35.0. What is the implied volatility at this price?

Appendix Probability Distributions and Statistical Analysis

For those who have not had a course in basic probability and statistics, or would like a refresher, here we review the important concepts. Chapter 3 provided a detailed discussion of the reasoning behind discrete probability, including the classic poker odds calculations. We will discuss both discrete and continuous probability because they are all important for financial analytics.

In discrete probability, there are three main distributions: the Bernoulli, the binomial, and the Poisson. We describe the situations where the binomial behaves as a Poisson, and the conditions under which both binomial and Poisson behave like a Normal. For discrete random variables in general, the *probability distribution function* or *p.d.f.* is defined as: $P(X = x)$, read as "the probability that random variable X takes on value x."

A.1 Distributions

Random variables are used to represent quantities that have random values. The x and y coordinates of a dart when landing on a dart board are a simple example of two random variables. As hard as we try to hit the center, there is always random variation with each attempt in the x and y directions. In statistics, traditionally an upper-case letter such as X is the random variable and x is a non-random variable representing a specific value it has. Once the dart is thrown we know that $X = x$ and $Y = y$, so we can measure the distance from the center as $\sqrt{x^2 + y^2}$.

We can also talk about the probability that $X = x$, written $P(X = x)$ or a range expression such as $P(x_1 < X < x_2)$. For example, we may want to know for the dart throw $P(\sqrt{X^2 + Y^2} \leq 2cm)$, to see if the throw was close to the center. These probabilities, P, can have values in the range $[0, 1]$. For example, you might have a probability of being within 2 cm of the center of .35 and I might have a probability of .15.

A series of random variables occurring successively is called a random or *stochastic* process. We can have a series of three dart throws by one individual person: $(X_1, Y_1), (X_2, Y_2), (X_3, Y_3)$.

A.2 Bernoulli Distribution

A Bernoulli random variable is an experiment with exactly two outcomes. A random variable has a Bernoulli distribution if it is distributed as below:

$$X = \begin{cases} 1 & \text{with probability } p \\ 0 & \text{with probability } 1-p \end{cases}. \tag{A.1}$$

The outcome $X = 1$ is called a "success" and occurs with probability p. The outcome $X = 0$ is called a "failure" and occurs with probability $1 - p$. We calculate the mean and variance of the Bernoulli random variable below:

$$E(X) = \sum xp(x) \tag{A.2}$$

$$= 1 \times p + 0 \times (1-p) = p \tag{A.3}$$

$$Var(X) = E(X^2) - E^2(X) \tag{A.4}$$

$$= \sum x^2 p(x) - \left(\sum xp(x)\right)^2 \tag{A.5}$$

$$= 1^2 \times p + 0^2 \times (1-p) - p^2 \tag{A.6}$$

$$= p - p^2 = p(1-p). \tag{A.7}$$

A.3   Binomial Distribution

The binomial distribution builds directly on the Bernoulli in that the binomial is the resulting distribution when we sum n independent and identically distributed (i.i.d) Bernoulli trials.

The p.d.f. for the Binomial distribution is:

$$P(X = x) = \binom{n}{x} p^x (1-p)^{n-x}, \tag{A.8}$$

where n is the number of trials, x is the number of successes and p is the probability of any given trial being successful. The number of successes ranges $x = 0, 1, 2, \cdots, n$ and the success probability p is such that $0 \le p \le 1$. The symbol $\binom{n}{x} = \frac{n!}{x!(n-x)!}$ is the binomial coefficient and is read "n choose x." The binomial distribution describes situations where we are concerned with the probability of the sum of some number of equivalent events, say the probability of there being six "heads" in the flipping of 10 coins. With this in mind, let us look at an example.

To calculate the mean of the binomial distribution we would by definition calculate

$$E(Y) = \sum yp(y) = \sum_{y=0}^{n} y \binom{n}{y} p^y (1-p)^{n-y}, \tag{A.9}$$

but solving for the expected value this way requires some messy algebra. An alternative is to look at the random variable Y as a sum of n Bernoulli random variables: $Y = X_1 + X_2 + \cdots + X_n$ and then use independence:

$$E(Y) = E\left(\sum_{i=0}^{n} X_i\right) = \sum_{i=0}^{n} E(X_i) = \sum_{i=0}^{n} p = np. \tag{A.10}$$

We can tackle calculation of the variance in a similar way. Since the variance of a sum of independent random variables is the sum of the variances, we can write:

$$Var(Y) = Var\left(\sum_{i=0}^{n} X_i\right) = \sum_{i=0}^{n} Var(X_i) = \sum_{i=0}^{n} p(1-p) = np(1-p). \tag{A.11}$$

Example

We flip a fair coin 100 times and want to calculate the probability of getting exactly 50 heads.

Solution

$$P(X = 50) = \binom{n}{x} p^x (1-p)^{n-x}$$

$$= \binom{100}{50}\left(\frac{1}{2}\right)^{50}\left(\frac{1}{2}\right)^{100-50}$$

We can calculate this in R as below.

```
> choose(100,50) * .5^50 * .5^(100-50)
[1] 0.07958924
```

A.4   Geometric Distribution

The geometric probability distribution is for finding the number, X_i, of Bernoulli trials needed to get one success, supported on the set $i = 1, 2, 3, \ldots$. The p.d.f. is stated as:

$$P(X = n) = p(x) = P(X_1 = 0, X_2 = 0, \cdots, X_{n-1} = 0, X_n = 1) \tag{A.12}$$

$$= P(X_1 = 0)P(X_2 = 0) \cdots P(X_{x-1} = 0)P(X_n = 1) \tag{A.13}$$

$$= (1-p)^{n-1}p. \tag{A.14}$$

The Expected Value is

$$E(N) = \frac{1}{p}. \tag{A.15}$$

The Variance is

$$Var(N) = \frac{1-p}{p^2}. \tag{A.16}$$

A.5   Poisson Distribution

We turn to the Poisson distribution. The Poisson distribution also describes the number of successes in a set of trials, but in the case where the number of trials is very large, but the probability of success for a given trial is very small. The Poisson distribution uses

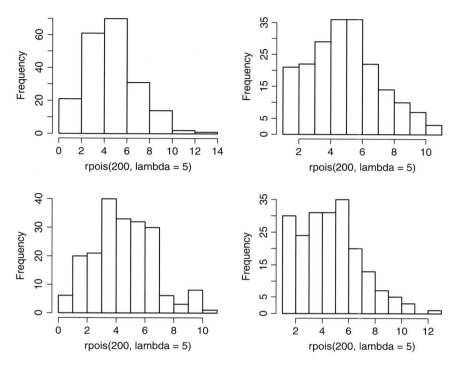

Figure A.1   Histograms of the Poisson distribution, 200 trials in each, $\lambda = 5$.

a discrete random variable N like X above. It is the number of arrivals, an event count, over a fixed period of time. One common use in finance is to simulate the arrival rate of jumps in a security price over time, for example, where λ is the mean number of arrivals in a given amount of time. The p.d.f. for the Poisson distribution is:

$$P(X = x) = \frac{e^{-\lambda}\lambda^x}{x!},$$

and is depicted in Figure A.1.

```
> library(ggplot2)
> par(mfrow=c(2,2))
> hist(rpois(200,lambda=5),main=""))
> hist(rpois(200,lambda=5),main=""))
> hist(rpois(200,lambda=5),main=""))
> hist(rpois(200,lambda=5),main=""))
```

To calculate the expected value of the Poisson random variable first recall $e^{\lambda} = \left(1 + \lambda + \frac{\lambda^2}{2!} + \frac{\lambda^3}{3!} + \cdots\right)$

$$E(X) = \sum_{x=0}^{\infty} xp(x) = \sum_{x=0}^{\infty} x\frac{e^{-\lambda}\lambda^x}{x!} \qquad (A.17)$$

$$= \lambda e^{-\lambda} \sum_{x=1}^{\infty} \frac{\lambda^{x-1}}{(x-1)!} = \lambda e^{-\lambda} \sum_{x=0}^{\infty} \frac{\lambda^x}{x!} \tag{A.18}$$

$$= \lambda e^{-\lambda} \left(1 + \lambda + \frac{\lambda^2}{2!} + \frac{\lambda^3}{3!} + \cdots \right) \tag{A.19}$$

$$= \lambda e^{-\lambda} e^{\lambda} = \lambda \tag{A.20}$$

A similar calculation yields the fact that for the Poisson $Var(X) = \lambda$.'

Example
Catching the Greedy Counterfeiter

Imagine the king's minter boxes coins n to a box. Each box contains m false coins. The king suspects this and randomly draws one coin from each of the n boxes and has these tested. What is the probability that the sample of n coins drawn contains exactly r false ones?

Solution
Since there are m counterfeits in each box of n coins, the probability of the drawn coin being counterfeit is m/n. The drawings are independent, so the probability of having r counterfeit coins is described as a binomial random variable. This yields:

$$P(r \text{ false coins}) = \binom{n}{r} \left(\frac{m}{n} \right)^r \left(1 - \frac{m}{n} \right)^{n-r}$$

$$= \frac{n!}{(n-r)!r!} \frac{m^r}{n^r} \left(1 - \frac{m}{n} \right)^n \left(1 - \frac{m}{n} \right)^{-r}$$

$$= \frac{1}{r!} \frac{n(n-1)\cdots(n-r+1)}{n^r} m^r \left(1 - \frac{m}{n} \right)^n \left(1 - \frac{m}{n} \right)^{-r}$$

$$\approx \frac{e^{-m} m^r}{r!},$$

because $\binom{n}{r} = \frac{n!}{(n-r)!r!}$ and recalling from calculus, if we hold m and r fixed while letting n become large, we see that $\frac{n(n-1)\cdots(n-r+1)}{n^r} \to 1$, $\left(1 - \frac{m}{n} \right)^n \to e^{-m}$, and $\left(1 - \frac{m}{n} \right)^r \to 1$. The approximation follows.

A.6   Functions for Continuous Distributions

In the case of a continuous distribution we have to be more careful in how we define the probability function. The core of the problem is that the quantity $P(X = x)$ is no longer defined in a useful way. Recall, the *cumulative distribution function* or *c.d.f.* of a random variable X is defined as

$$F_X(x) = P(X \le x); \tag{A.21}$$

probability density function or *p.d.f.* is defined as the function $f(x)$ that satisfies

$$F(x) = \int_{-\infty}^{x} f(u)du,$$

and the relationship to the p.d.f. is defined as

$$f(x) = \frac{d}{dx} F(x).$$

```
> ggplot(data.frame(x=c(-3,3)),aes(x=x)) +
+    stat_function(fun=dnorm, colour="blue") + +
stat_function(fun=pnorm,colour="red")
```

Since we have satisfied

$$\{X = x\} \subset \{x - \epsilon < X \le x\}, \tag{A.22}$$

we can take probabilities on both sides of the subset to arrive at

$$P(X = x) \le P(x - \epsilon < X \le x) = F_X(x) - F_X(x - \epsilon), \tag{A.23}$$

but since $F_X(x)$ is continuous for a continuous distribution we have

$$0 \le P(X = x) \le \lim_{\epsilon \to 0} [F_X(x) - F_X(x - \epsilon)] = 0, \tag{A.24}$$

which leaves us with the awkward fact that $P(X = x) = 0$ for all x when the random variable X has a continuous distribution function. However, looking at it twice, it must be this way. In the discrete case each segment of the histogram implies a jump in the c.d.f. $F_X(x)$. This means the rectangle of probability in the p.d.f. is of some nonzero width. In the continuous case, however, the width of this rectangle is zero, which means it can have no area. For continuous random variables, the meaningful probability to calculate is:

$$P(a \le X \le b) = F_X(b) - F_X(a) = \int_a^b f(u) du. \tag{A.25}$$

```
> dnorm1<-function(x) dnorm(x,mean=0,sd=.25)
> ggplot(data.frame(x=c(-3,3)),aes(x=x)) +
+    stat_function(fun=dnorm, colour="blue") +
+    stat_function(fun=dnorm1, colour="blue")
```

```
> dnorm(x=0,mean=0,sd=1)
[1] 0.3989423
> dnorm(x=0,mean=0,sd=.25)
[1] 1.595769
```

In Figure A.3 we can see how changing the parameter of the distribution from $\sigma = 1$ for the standard Normal and $\sigma = \frac{1}{4}$ compare.

```
> dnorm_limit<-function(x) {
+    y <- dnorm(x)
+    y[x<0|x>2]<-NA
+    y
+ }
```

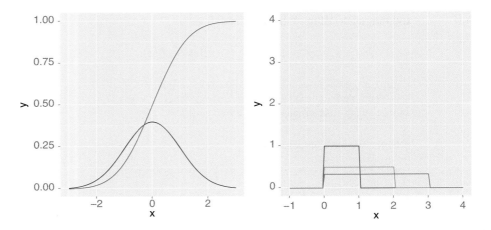

Figure A.2 On the left are two key functions of the Gaussian continuous distribution: the c.d.f. and the p.d.f. On the right are typical density functions (p.d.f.s) for uniform random variables.

```
> ggplot(data.frame(x=c(-3,3)),aes(x=x)) +
+    stat_function(fun=dnorm_limit,geom="area",fill="blue",alpha=0.2) +
+    stat_function(fun=dnorm)
```

A.7 The Uniform Distribution

This is probably the simplest continuous distribution. Early programming languages such as FORTRAN supplied this distribution and its variates as the only built-in distribution because of its versatility and the ability to transform the variates to variates of any other type. The uniform distribution is defined as

$$f(x) = \begin{cases} \frac{1}{b-a} & a \le x \le b \\ 0 & \text{otherwise,} \end{cases} \qquad (A.26)$$

with expected value $E(X) = \frac{a+b}{2}$ and variance $Var(X) = \frac{(b-a)^2}{12}$. When $a = 0$ and $b = 1$ the uniform distribution becomes a unit square. Figure A.2 depicts the square p.d.f.s for this distribution, generated by the code below.

```
> dunif1 <-function(x) dunif(x,max=1)
> dunif2 <-function(x) dunif(x,max=2)
> dunif3 <-function(x) dunif(x,max=3)
> ggplot(data.frame(x=c(-3,5)),aes(x=x)) +
+    stat_function(fun=dunif1, colour="blue") +
+    stat_function(fun=dunif2, colour="green") +
+    stat_function(fun=dunif3, colour="red")
```

A.8 Exponential Distribution

The exponential distribution has a p.d.f. defined as:

$$f(x) = \frac{1}{\beta} e^{-\frac{x}{\beta}} \tag{A.27}$$

and depicted in Figure A.3.

```
> dexp2<-function(x) dexp(x,2)
> dexp3<-function(x) dexp(x,3)
> ggplot(data.frame(x=c(0,4)),aes(x=x)) +
+    stat_function(fun=dexp, colour="blue") +
+    stat_function(fun=dexp2, colour="blue") +
+    stat_function(fun=dexp3, colour="blue") +
+    ylim(0,4)
```

To calculate the c.d.f. of the exponential distribution we calculate

$$F_X(x) = P(X \le x) = \int_0^x f(u)du = \int_0^x \frac{1}{\beta} e^{-\frac{u}{\beta}} du \tag{A.28}$$

$$= \frac{\beta}{\beta} \left(1 - e^{\frac{u}{\beta}} \right) = e^{\frac{x}{\beta}}. \tag{A.29}$$

In the context of the exponential distribution it is convenient to introduce the gamma function. The gamma function is useful in calculating the mean and variance of the exponential distribution and will be necessary for the introduction of the gamma distribution later. The gamma function $\Gamma(\alpha)$ as seen in advanced calculus is defined as

$$\Gamma(\alpha) = \int_0^\infty y^{\alpha-1} e^{-y} dy \tag{A.30}$$

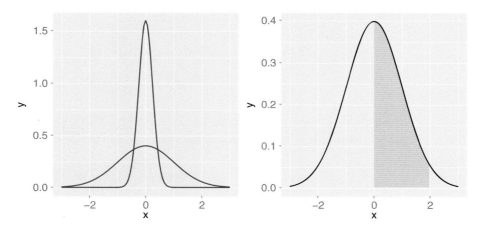

Figure A.3   The scale of the distribution is determined by the σ or standard deviation parameter on the left. Here we have $\sigma = 1$ for the standard Normal and $\sigma = \frac{1}{4}$. On the right, the region between $\sigma = 0$ and $\sigma = 2$ is depicted.

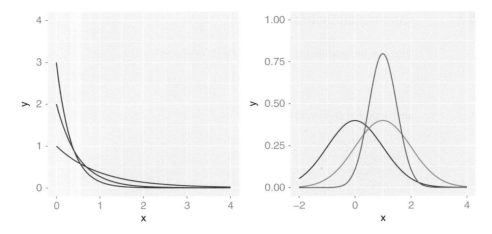

The p.d.f.s for the exponential and the Gaussian or normal distribution are depicted here.

If we let $y = x/\beta$ we arrive via the chain rule at

$$\Gamma(\alpha) = \int_0^\infty y^{\alpha-1} e^{-y} dy = \int_0^\infty \left(\frac{x}{\beta}\right)^{\alpha-1} e^{-x/\beta} \left(\frac{dx}{\beta}\right) = \frac{1}{\beta^\alpha} \int_0^\infty x^{\alpha-1} e^{-x/\beta} dx$$

(A.31)

while multiplying on both sides by β^α gives us

$$\Gamma(\alpha)\beta^\alpha = \int_0^\infty x^{\alpha-1} e^{-x/\beta} dx$$

which is our desired result.

This gamma equation provides (among other things) a short-cut to integrating by parts. Calculation of the expected value of the exponential distribution shows an illustration of this. In this case $\alpha = 2$ and we have:

$$E(X) = \int_{-\infty}^{+\infty} x f(x) dx = \int_0^\infty x \frac{1}{\beta} e^{-\frac{x}{\beta}} dx$$

(A.32)

$$= \frac{1}{\beta} \int_0^\infty x^{2-1} e^{-\frac{x}{\beta}} dx = \frac{1}{\beta} \Gamma(2)\beta^2 = \beta$$

(A.33)

In calculating variance we recall that $Var(X) = E(X^2) - E^2(X)$. Since we already know $E(X)$ we need only to calculate $E(X^2)$, and since $\alpha = 3$ in this case we have:

$$E(X^2) = \int_{-\infty}^{+\infty} x^2 f(x) dx = \int_0^\infty x^2 \frac{1}{\beta} e^{-\frac{x}{\beta}} dx$$

(A.34)

$$= \frac{1}{\beta} \int_0^\infty x^{3-2} e^{-\frac{x}{\beta}} dx = \frac{1}{\beta} \Gamma(3)\beta^3 = 2\beta^2$$

(A.35)

The variance of the exponential random variable is then

$$Var(X) = E(X^2) - E^2(X) = 2\beta^2 - \beta^2 = \beta^2$$

(A.36)

A.9   Normal Distribution

The p.d.f. for the Gaussian or Normal distribution is

$$f(x) = \frac{1}{\sigma\sqrt{2\pi}} e^{\frac{(x-\mu)^2}{2\sigma^2}},$$

(A.37)

and is depicted in Figure A.3 and A.4. Its c.d.f. and other properties are very well known.

$$E(X) = \mu$$

(A.38)

$$Var(X) = E(X^2) - E^2(X) = \sigma^2.$$

(A.39)

The following code will produce plots for this distribution:

```
> dnorm11<-function(x) dnorm(x,mean=1,sd=1)
> dnorm12<-function(x) dnorm(x,mean=1,sd=.5)
> ggplot(data.frame(x=c(-2,4)),aes(x=x)) +
+    stat_function(fun=dnorm, colour="blue") +
+    stat_function(fun=dnorm11, colour="green") +
+    stat_function(fun=dnorm12, colour="red") +
+    ylim(0,1)
```

A.10   Log-Normal Distribution

The log-normal distribution is used to model stocks, also known as equities, and commodity prices. The probability density function, depicted in Figure A.5, is defined as:

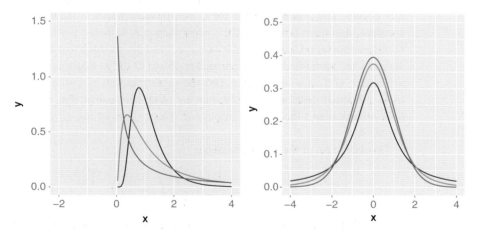

Figure A.5   The p.d.f.s for the log-normal and t-distribution are depicted here. On left are log-normal p.d.f. plots for $\sigma = \frac{1}{2}, 1$ and 2 where the log-normal distribution is characterized by the standard deviation parameter, σ. On the right are the p.d.f.s of the t_1 (blue), t_4 (green), and t_{25} (red) distributions.

$$f(x) = \frac{1}{x\sigma\sqrt{2\pi}} \exp\left(\frac{(\ln(x) - \mu)^2}{2\sigma^2}\right). \tag{A.40}$$

However, in practice, this p.d.f. is rarely used, because the prices are usually converted to log returns. At that point the normal p.d.f. can be used. The mean is:

$$E(X) = e^{\mu + \frac{1}{2}\sigma^2}. \tag{A.41}$$

The variance is:

$$Var(X) = \left(e^{\sigma^2} - 1\right)e^{2\mu + \sigma^2} = \left(e^{\sigma^2} - 1\right)E^2(X). \tag{A.42}$$

The following code will produce plots for this distribution:

```
> dlognorm <- function(x,sigma) { 1/x*dnorm(log(x),sd=sigma) }
> dlognorm1<-function(x) dlognorm(x,sigma=.5)
> dlognorm2<-function(x) dlognorm(x,sigma=1)
> dlognorm3<-function(x) dlognorm(x,sigma=2)
> ggplot(data.frame(x=c(-2,4)),aes(x=x)) +
+    stat_function(fun=dlognorm1, colour="blue") +
+    stat_function(fun=dlognorm2, colour="green") +
+    stat_function(fun=dlognorm3, colour="red") +
+    ylim(0,1.5)
```

A.11   The t_ν Distribution

The t_ν distribution is encountered often in statistics, and in financial statistics in particular. The reason for this is that, as the Central Limit Theorem kicks in and a sample average becomes normally distributed, the t_ν distribution is the mechanism by which this occurs. The ν parameter of the t_ν distribution, which is called the degrees of the freedom, describes how close the t_ν distribution is to being normal. With $\nu = 1$, the t_ν distribution is a Cauchy distribution, i.e. has tails so thick that both expectation and variance are undefined. As ν approaches 25 or 30 the t_ν distribution is close to being a Normal, and as ν approaches 100 the t_ν distribution is virtually indistinguishable from a Normal distribution. In finance we often see returns that are consistent with a t_4 distribution and this is very important. Three plots of the t_ν distribution appear in Figure A.5.

The definition of the t_ν distribution is:

$$f(x) = \frac{\Gamma\left(\frac{\nu+1}{2}\right)}{\sqrt{\pi\nu}\,\Gamma\left(\frac{\nu}{2}\right)}\left(1 + \frac{x^2}{\nu}\right)^{-\frac{\nu+1}{2}}, \tag{A.43}$$

with expected value of 0 (for $\nu > 1$) and variance of $\frac{\nu}{nu-2}$ (for $\nu > 2$). The skewness is 0 and excess kurtosis is $\frac{6}{\nu-4}$.

```
> t1<-function(x) dt(x,df=1)
> t4<-function(x) dt(x,df=4)
```

```
> t25<-function(x) dt(x,df=25)
> ggplot(data.frame(x=c(-4,4)),aes(x=x)) +
+   stat_function(fun=t1, colour="blue") +
+   stat_function(fun=t4, colour="green") +
+   stat_function(fun=t25, colour="red") +
+   ylim(0,.5)
```

A.12 Multivariate Normal Distribution

Another important distribution for securities is known as multivariate Gaussian or multivariate Normal distribution (MVN). It is useful when we have p stochastic random variables representing p stock securities in the p-dimensional vector, x. The p.d.f. formula is as follows:

$$f(x) = (2\pi)^{-\frac{k}{2}} |\Sigma|^{-\frac{1}{2}} \exp\left(-\frac{1}{2}(x-\mu)^T \Sigma^{-1}(x-\mu)\right), \tag{A.44}$$

where $\mu = (\mu_1, \mu_2, \cdots, \mu_p)^T$ is the mean vector, Σ is the covariance matrix, and $|\Sigma|$ is the determinant of Σ.

A.13 Gamma Distribution

The gamma distribution is defined by the p.d.f.:

$$f(x) = \begin{cases} \frac{1}{\Gamma(\alpha)\beta^\alpha} x^\alpha e^{-\frac{x}{\beta}} & \text{for } x > 0 \\ 0 & \text{elsewhere} \end{cases}. \tag{A.45}$$

Calculating expected value gives us:

$$E(X) = \int_{-\infty}^{+\infty} x f(x) dx = \int_0^\infty \frac{1}{\Gamma(\alpha)\beta^\alpha} x^\alpha e^{-\frac{x}{\beta}} dx \tag{A.46}$$

$$= \frac{1}{\Gamma(\alpha)\beta^\alpha} \int_0^\infty x^\alpha e^{-\frac{x}{\beta}} dx \tag{A.47}$$

$$= \frac{1}{\Gamma(\alpha)\beta^\alpha} \Gamma(\alpha+1)\beta^{\alpha+1} \tag{A.48}$$

$$= \frac{1}{(\alpha-1)!\beta^\alpha} \alpha! \beta^\alpha \beta = \alpha\beta. \tag{A.49}$$

Similar calculations yield the second moment $E(X^2) = \alpha(\alpha+1)\beta^2$ from which we can calculate the variance:

$$Var(X) = E(X^2) - E^2(X) \tag{A.50}$$

$$= \alpha(\alpha+1)\beta^2 - (\alpha\beta)^2 \tag{A.51}$$

$$= \alpha^2\beta^2 + \alpha\beta^2 - \alpha^2\beta^2 \tag{A.52}$$

$$= \alpha\beta^2. \tag{A.53}$$

A.14   Estimation via Maximum Likelihood

These parameters are properties of the theoretical distributions. A very important result in probability and statistics takes us from the theoretical distributions to the sample distributions of our datasets using a concept known as the *maximum likelihood estimator* (MLE). If we have a set of parameters like μ, σ^2, *Skew*, or *Kurt*, we want to estimate any of them for a sample which we believe is distributed according to their theoretical distribution. If we have a set of parameters $\theta = \{\theta_1, \ldots, \theta_N\}$, for example $\theta = \{\mu, \sigma\}$, and a joint distribution function $g(X|\theta)$ where $X = (X_1, \ldots, X_N)$, we can think about the likelihood function $L(\theta|X)$ as a function of the parameters themselves. Then we can also think about maximizing the likelihood of a parameter being equal to a given value. Since the log function is monotonically increasing, maximizing the log of a function is the same as maximizing the function itself. We can find the maximum by taking the first derivative, setting it equal to zero and solving for the independent variable, θ in this case (Hogg and Craig, 1978).

Let us begin with the classic Gaussian or Normal distribution. We know that the density function or p.d.f. for the normal distribution, $N(\mu, \sigma^2)$, for example, is:

$$f(x) = \frac{1}{\sigma\sqrt{2\pi}} \exp\left(-\frac{(x-\mu)^2}{2\sigma^2}\right). \tag{A.54}$$

If we have a sample of size N denoted by these random variables, X_i we can form the joint distribution, g, of these by multiplying N density functions together:

$$f(x_1, \ldots, x_N | \{\mu, \sigma\}) = \left(\frac{1}{\sigma\sqrt{2\pi}}\right)^N \prod_{i=1}^N \exp\left(-\frac{(x_i-\mu)^2}{2\sigma^2}\right). \tag{A.55}$$

If we already know σ^2 then this can be simplified and also serve as our likelihood function, L of μ:

$$= L(\mu|X) = \left(\sigma\sqrt{2\pi}\right)^{-N} \exp\left(-\sum_{i=1}^N \frac{(x_i-\mu)^2}{2\sigma^2}\right) \tag{A.56}$$

$$= \left(\sigma\sqrt{2\pi}\right)^{-N} \exp\left(-\sum_{i=1}^N \frac{(x_i-\mu)^2}{2\sigma^2}\right). \tag{A.57}$$

Now we can take the log of L:

$$\log L(\mu|X) = -N\log\left(\sigma\sqrt{2\pi}\right) + \left(\sum_{i=1}^N -\frac{(x_i-\mu)^2}{2\sigma^2}\right). \tag{A.58}$$

Now, taking the derivative with respect to μ and setting it equal to zero and solving will find the optimal μ:

$$\frac{\partial}{\partial\mu} \log L(\mu|X) = \frac{-2}{2\sigma^2} \sum_{i=1}^N (x_i-\mu) = 0. \tag{A.59}$$

After multiplying each side by $-2\sigma^2/2$, now we are left with

$$\sum_{i=1}^{N}(x_i - \mu) = 0 \iff \sum_{i=1}^{N}(x_i) - N\mu = 0 \iff \mu = \frac{1}{N}\sum_{i=1}^{N}x_i. \tag{A.60}$$

This classic derivation is a great illustration of a closed-form maximum likelihood estimator. Unfortunately for many distributions, this type of derivation is not possible, and so numerical techniques are required.

For the Poisson distribution, the MLE derivation goes as follows:

$$L(x|\lambda) = f(x_1, x_2, \cdots, x_n|p) = \prod_{i=1}^{n} f(x_i) \tag{A.61}$$

$$= \prod_{i=1}^{n} e^{-\lambda}\frac{\lambda^{x_i}}{x_i!} = e^{-n\lambda}\frac{\lambda^{\sum_{i=1}^{n} x_i}}{x_1!x_2!\cdots x_n!}. \tag{A.62}$$

Taking log yields:

$$l(x|\lambda) = -n\lambda + \left(\sum_{i=1}^{n} x_i\right)\log\lambda - \log(x_1!x_2!\cdots x_n!). \tag{A.63}$$

Taking the derivative and setting equal to zero yields

$$\frac{\partial}{\partial\lambda}l(x|\lambda) = -n + \sum_{i=1}^{n} x_i\frac{1}{\lambda} = 0. \iff \lambda = \frac{1}{n}\sum_{i=1}^{n} x_i. \tag{A.64}$$

And for the geometric distribution, the MLE derivation goes as follows:

$$L(x|p) = f(x_1, x_2, \cdots, x_n|p) = \prod_{i=1}^{n} f(x_i) \tag{A.65}$$

$$= \prod_{i=1}^{n} p(1-p)^{x_i} = p^n(1-p)^{\sum_{i=1}^{n} x_i}. \tag{A.66}$$

Taking log yields

$$l(x|p) = \log L(x|p) \tag{A.67}$$

$$= \log\left(p^n(1-p)^{\sum_{i=1}^{n} x_i}\right) \tag{A.68}$$

$$= \log p^n + \log(1-p)^{\sum_{i=1}^{n} x_i} \tag{A.69}$$

$$= n\log p + \left(\sum_{i=1}^{n} x_i\right)\log(1-p). \tag{A.70}$$

Recall that $\int\frac{1}{x}dx = \ln x$ and that $\frac{d}{dx}\ln x = \frac{1}{x}$, and taking the derivative and setting equal to zero gives us

$$\frac{\partial}{\partial p}l(x|p) = n\frac{1}{p} - \sum_{i=1}^{n} x_i\frac{1}{1-p} = 0 \tag{A.71}$$

$$\frac{n}{p} = \frac{\sum_{i=1}^{n} x_i}{1 - p}. \tag{A.72}$$

Cross-multiplying and distributing lets us solve for the maximum likelihood estimate $\hat{p}$:

$$n(1 - p) = p \sum_{i=1}^{n} x_i \tag{A.73}$$

$$n - np = p \sum_{i=1}^{n} x_i \tag{A.74}$$

$$n = p \sum_{i=1}^{n} x_i + np \tag{A.75}$$

$$n = p \left(\sum_{i=1}^{n} x_i + n \right) \tag{A.76}$$

$$p = \frac{n}{\sum_{i=1}^{n} x_i + n} \tag{A.77}$$

$$= \frac{1}{\bar{X} + 1}. \tag{A.78}$$

A.15   Central Limit Theorem

Now that we have derived optimal estimators of statistical parameters, we would like to know some properties of these estimators. What are the mean and variance of an estimator? How is an estimator distributed? The Central Limit Theorem states that a sum of more than 25 or 30 random variables is Normally distributed. The individual random variables might be all from the same distribution, or they can each be from a different distribution. This is an astonishing fact and is the reason why the Normal distribution is observed so often. Take, for example, the Scholastic Aptitude Test, or SAT. The distribution of scores on the SAT is nearly perfectly Normal. This is because a score on the SAT results from an accumulation of a multitude of factors: parental involvement in the student's education, innate ability, work ethic, diet, exercise habits, and so on. The same type of reasoning leads us to believe that market returns should be highly Normal. If individual investors make buy and sell decisions largely independently of each other, and based on varied information, then it should follow that the cumulative effect of these independently acting investors results in a return distribution that is close to being Normal. And indeed this is frequently the case. However, there are also many times when it is not the case. Sometimes investors do not buy and sell independently of each other. Sometimes they buy or sell all at the same time, resulting in a cumulative effect that is no longer Normal. We will illustrate this later.

Before we can formally define the Central Limit Theorem, we need to know some facts about sample averages. Let $X \sim (\mu, \sigma^2)$ be taken from an arbitrary distribution.

The sample average $\bar{X}$ is defined as:

$$\bar{X} = \frac{1}{n} \sum_{i=1}^{n} X_i$$
$$= \frac{X_1 + X_2 + X_3 + \cdots + X_n}{n}.$$

What are the properties of $E(\bar{X})$ and $Var(\bar{X})$?

$$E(\bar{X}) = E\left(\frac{1}{n} \sum_{i=1}^{n} X_i\right)$$
$$= \frac{1}{n} E\left(\sum_{i=1}^{n} X_i\right)$$
$$= \frac{1}{n} E(X_1 + X_2 + X_3 + \cdots + X_n)$$
$$= \frac{1}{n} [E(X_1) + E(X_2) + E(X_3) + \cdots + E(X_n)]$$
$$= \frac{nE(X)}{n}$$
$$= E(X).$$

$$Var(\bar{X}) = Var\left(\frac{1}{n} \sum_{i=1}^{n} X_i\right) = \left(\frac{1}{n}\right)^2 Var\left(\sum_{i=1}^{n} X_i\right)$$
$$= \frac{1}{n^2} Var(X_1 + X_2 + X_3 + \cdots + X_n)$$
$$= \frac{1}{n^2} [Var(X_1) + Var(X_2) + Var(X_3) + \cdots + Var(X_n)]$$
$$= \frac{n \cdot Var(X)}{n^2}$$
$$= \frac{Var(X)}{n}.$$

For $n \geq 25$ and any probability distribution for the X_is, we assume that $\bar{X}$ is Normally distributed. Due to the Central Limit Theorem, we can find the probability that a sample average is in an interval. This amazing convergence is illustrated in statistics books (Hogg and Craig, 1978).

$$P(a \leq \bar{X} \leq b) = P\left(\frac{a - \mu}{\frac{\sigma}{\sqrt{n}}} \leq \frac{\bar{X} - \mu}{\frac{\sigma}{\sqrt{n}}} \leq \frac{b - \mu}{\frac{\sigma}{\sqrt{n}}}\right)$$
$$= P\left(\frac{a - \mu}{\frac{\sigma}{\sqrt{n}}} \leq Z \leq \frac{b - \mu}{\frac{\sigma}{\sqrt{n}}}\right)$$
$$= P\left(Z \leq \frac{b - \mu}{\frac{\sigma}{\sqrt{n}}}\right) - P\left(Z \leq \frac{a - \mu}{\frac{\sigma}{\sqrt{n}}}\right)$$

where $Z \sim N(0, 1)$ is the standard normal random variable.

A.16   Confidence Intervals

We now discuss confidence intervals for the mean, variance, and sample proportion. When we have a large enough sample, we can find the Large-Sample Confidence Interval for μ.

$$P\left(-z_{\alpha/2} \leq Z \leq z_{\alpha/2}\right) = 1 - \alpha. \tag{A.79}$$

Due to Central Limit Theorem we can rewrite:

$$1 - \alpha = P\left(-z_{\alpha/2} \leq \frac{\bar{X} - \mu}{\sigma/n} \leq z_{\alpha/2}\right) \tag{A.80}$$

$$= P\left(-z_{\alpha/2}\frac{\sigma}{n} \leq \bar{X} - \mu \leq z_{\alpha/2}\frac{\sigma}{n}\right) \tag{A.81}$$

$$= P\left(\bar{X} - z_{\alpha/2}\frac{\sigma}{n} \leq \mu \leq \bar{X} + z_{\alpha/2}\frac{\sigma}{n}\right). \tag{A.82}$$

The Large-Sample Confidence Interval for probability parameter p:

$$1 - \alpha = P\left(-z_{\alpha/2} \leq \frac{\hat{p} - p}{\sqrt{\frac{\hat{p}(1-\hat{p})}{n}}} \leq z_{\alpha/2}\right) \tag{A.83}$$

$$= P\left(-z_{\alpha/2}\sqrt{\frac{\hat{p}(1 - \hat{p})}{n}} \leq \hat{p} - p \leq z_{\alpha/2}\sqrt{\frac{\hat{p}(1 - \hat{p})}{n}}\right) \tag{A.84}$$

$$= P\left(\hat{p} - z_{\alpha/2}\sqrt{\frac{\hat{p}(1 - \hat{p})}{n}} \leq p \leq \hat{p} + z_{\alpha/2}\sqrt{\frac{\hat{p}(1 - \hat{p})}{n}}\right). \tag{A.85}$$

A.17   Hypothesis Testing

The basic goal of hypothesis testing is to make a decision between two states of the world. Many times an analyst or researcher wants to answer a simple yes/no question. Does a drug produce an effect or not? Does smoking damage overall health or not? Is a given coin I am flipping fair or not? Are two stocks correlated or not? Are market returns normally distributed or not?

A good place to begin with is the coin-flipping example. Say we are in Las Vegas and flipping a coin provided by the house. We get the impression heads is showing up more than tails, but it is hard to gauge how much more, if there is even a difference at all. This raises an important question: How many flips of our mystery coin do we need, to conclude beyond reasonable doubt that the coin is not fair?

```
> flip<-rbinom(50,1,.55)
> flip
 [1] 0 1 0 1 1 1 1 0 1 0 1 1 1 1 0 0 1 0 1 1 0 1 0 1 1 1 1 1 0 1 0 1 1 0 1
[36] 1 1 0 1 1 1 1 1 1 1 0 1 1 1
> prop.test(sum(flip), 50, p=0.5, correct=FALSE)

1-sample proportions test without continuity correction
```

```
data:  sum(flip) out of 50, null probability 0.5
X-squared = 9.68, df = 1, p-value = 0.001863
alternative hypothesis: true p is not equal to 0.5
95 percent confidence interval:
 0.5833488 0.8252583
sample estimates:
  p
0.72
```

The code above illustrates hypothesis testing applied to a flipped coin. We have sampled from a slightly biased coin a total of 50 flips, where the coin is slightly biased in that the probability of getting 'heads' on a single flip is 0.55 or 55%. Now if we were to 'eyeball' such a scenario and guess whether the coin were fair or not, it would in most cases be difficult to say. However, if we apply our statistical machinery to the problem the answer is unabiguous. We observe `sum(flip)` heads and we wish to test whether this number of heads could have been produced from 50 flips of a coin with success probability of 0.5 or 50%. We observe a p val of 0.001863 and conclude that the observe number of heads would be highly unlikely to be produced by a fair coin. We therefore reject the claim that the coin is fair.

A.18   Regression

In regression, we are given vectors $x = (x_1, \ldots, x_p)$ and known ys that correspond to the xs. We try to determine a set of weights, β_0 and also $\beta_1, \ldots \beta_p$ to multiply $x_1, \ldots, x_n$ by and a sum to try to approximate ys. The equation for this is

$$\hat{y} = \beta_0 + \sum_{i=1}^{n} \beta_i x_i. \tag{A.86}$$

$\hat{y}$ is only an estimate while y is the actual observed value.

We can limit ourselves to the two-dimensional case when $p = 1$. The error between $\hat{y} = \beta_0 + \beta_1 x_1$ and y can be found.

We can write the sum of the squared errors, also known as a *Residual Sum of Squares* or RSS, as

$$RSS = S(\beta_0, \beta_1) = \sum_{i=1}^{p} \epsilon_i^2 = \sum_{i=1}^{p} (y_i - \mu_i)^2 \tag{A.87}$$

$$= \sum_{i=1}^{n} (y_i - \beta_0 - \beta_1 x_i)^2. \tag{A.88}$$

The goal now is to minimize this sum with respect to the model coefficients: the slope of the regression line β_1 and the y-intercept of the regression line β_0.

We take the derivative of the above equation with respect to β_0 and β_1, and set the derivatives equal to zero:

$$\frac{\partial S(\beta_0, \beta_1)}{\partial \beta_0} = -2 \sum_{i=1}^{p} (y_i - \beta_0 - \beta_1 x_i) = 0 \tag{A.89}$$

$$\frac{\partial S(\beta_0, \beta_1)}{\partial \beta_1} = -2 \sum_{i=1}^{p} (y_i - \beta_0 - \beta_1 x_i) x_i = 0. \tag{A.90}$$

Distribution through the summation leads to

$$n\beta_0 + \beta_1 \sum_{i=1}^{p} x_i = \sum_{i=1}^{p} y_i \tag{A.91}$$

$$\beta_0 \sum_{i=1}^{p} x_i + \beta_1 \sum_{i=1}^{p} x_i^2 = \sum_{i=1}^{p} x_i y_i \tag{A.92}$$

$$\beta_1 = \frac{\sum x_i y_i - \frac{\sum x_i \sum x_i}{p}}{\sum x_i^2 - \frac{(\sum x_i)^2}{n}} = \frac{\sum (x_i - \bar{x})(y_i - \bar{y})}{\sum (x_i - \bar{x})^2} = \frac{S_{xy}}{S_{xx}} \tag{A.93}$$

and

$$\beta_0 = \bar{y} - \beta_1 \bar{x}, \tag{A.94}$$

where $\bar{x} = \frac{1}{p} \sum x_i$ and $\bar{y} = \frac{1}{p} \sum y_i$.

Example

Fuel Efficiency For the classic case of fuel efficiency, we can use our equations for prediction:

```
> library(datasets)
> data(mtcars)
> x<-mtcars$mpg
> y<-mtcars$wt
> Sxy<-sum((x-mean(x))*(y-mean(y)))
> Sxx <- sum((x-mean(x))^2)
> beta1 <- Sxy/Sxx
> beta1
```

Now we have β_1.

```
[1] -0.140862
> beta0 <- mean(y) - beta1*mean(x)
> beta0
```

Now we have β_0.

```
[1] 6.047255
```

Below is the simple regression prediction formula which can be used once we have β_0 and β_1.

```
> yhat <- beta0 + beta1*x
> length(x)
[1] 32
```

We can use R to determine our β_0 and β_1 and compare these values to those computed above. Linear model or *lm()* is the way to access R's regression algorithm.

```
> m1<-lm(data=mtcars,wt~mpg+1)
> summary(m1)
> m1$coeff
(Intercept)              mpg
  6.047255      -0.140862
```

Indeed, they match. We should now look at the regression report from the *lm()* function.

```
Call:
lm(formula = wt ~ mpg + 1, data = mtcars)

Residuals:
    Min      1Q  Median      3Q     Max
-0.6516 -0.3490 -0.1381  0.3190  1.3684

Coefficients:
            Estimate Std. Error t value Pr(>|t|)
(Intercept)  6.04726    0.30869  19.590  < 2e-16 ***
mpg         -0.14086    0.01474  -9.559 1.29e-10 ***
---
Signif. codes:  0 '***' 0.001 '**' 0.01 '*' 0.05 '.' 0.1 ' ' 1

Residual standard error: 0.4945 on 30 degrees of freedom
Multiple R-squared:  0.7528,    Adjusted R-squared:  0.7446
F-statistic: 91.38 on 1 and 30 DF,  p-value: 1.294e-10

> yhat = m1$coeff[1]+m1$coeff[2]*x
> plot(x,y,col=4,xlab="x: weight",ylab="y: weight")
> points(x,yhat,col=2)
```

Figure A.6 depicts the regression line found by the R *lm()* function.

A.19   Model Selection Criteria

The Akaike Information Criterion or AIC is defined as

$$AIC_k = -2\log\left(\hat{L}\right) + 2k, \tag{A.95}$$

where $\hat{L}$ is the maximized likelihood, k is the number of parameters in the model and n is the sample size. The Bayesian Information Criteria or BIC is similar and is defined as

$$BIC = -2\log\left(\hat{L}\right) + 2k\log(n). \tag{A.96}$$

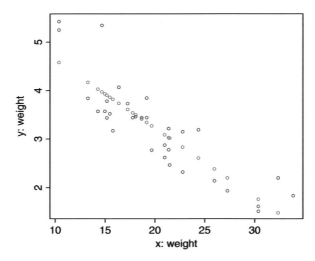

Figure A.6   Actual x and y values with the regression line found by calling *lm( )*.

The AIC and BIC are model selection criteria based on the idea that, while minimizing the log likelihood, there is a trade-off between the goodness of fit of the model and the complexity of the model. Model precision comes at a cost: model complexity. We want a model complex enough to be precise, but penalize the complexity at the rate $2k$ for the AIC and at a rate of $2k \log(n)$ for the BIC. The selected model is then the one that minimizes the sum of the negative log likelihood and penalization.

A.20   Required Packages

The following packages need to be downloaded to run the code in the various chapters:

```
library(DBI)
library(PerformanceAnalytics)
library(Quandl)
library(RSQLite)
library(Rcpp)
library(TSA)
library(corrplot)
library(datasets)
library(e1071)
library(foreign)
library(ggplot2)
library(huge)
library(igraph)
library(leaps)
library(moments)
library(party)
library(quadprog)
```

```
library(quantmod)
library(randomForest)
library(reshape2)
library(sbgcop)
library(stats)
library(tseries)
```

References

Ang, A., Bekaert, G. (2003). How Do Regimes Affect Asset Allocation? *NBER Working Paper* No. 10080, November. www.nber.org/papers/w10080.pdf

Ang, A., Bekaert, G. (2004). How Regimes Affect Asset Allocation. *Financial Analysts Journal* 60 (2).

Becker, R., Chambers, J., Wilks, A. (1988). *The New S Language: A Programming Environment for Data Analysis and Graphics*. Pacific Grove, CA, USA: Wadsworth and Brooks/Cole. ISBN 0-534-09192-X.

Benedict, N., Brewer, J., Haddad, A. (2015). *Mean-Variance Optimization for Equity Portfolios*, MSc capstone project, Graduate Program in Analytics, University of Chicago, June.

Bennett, M. J. (1986). *Proving Correctness of Asynchronous Circuits Using Temporal Logic*, UCLA Computer Science Department, Ph.D. Thesis. http://ftp.cs.ucla.edu/tech-report/198_-reports/860089.pdf

Bennett, M. (2009). Accelerated Root Finding for Computational Finance. *Symposium on Application Accelerators in High-Performance Computing* (SAAHPC'09), July 28–30, Urbana, Illinois, http://saahpc.ncsa.illinois.edu/09/papers/Bennett_paper.pdf

Bennett, M. J. (2014). *Data Mining with Markowitz Portfolio Optimization in Higher Dimensions*, May 21, http://ssrn.com/abstract=2439051.

Black, F., Myron, S. (1973). The Pricing of Options and Corporate Liabilities. *Journal of Political Economy* 81 (3): pp. 637–54.

Bodie, Z., Kane, A., Marcus, A. (2013). *Investments*, Tenth Edition. McGraw-Hill, September.

Box, G. E. P., Cox D. R. (1964). An Analysis of Transformations. *Journal of the Royal Statistical Society*. Series B (Methodological) 26 (2): pp. 211–52.

Breiman, L., Friedman, J. H., Olshen, R. A., Stone, C. J. (1984). *Classification and Regression Trees*. Belmont, CA: Wadsworth.

Brin, S., Page, L. (1998). Anatomy of a Large-Scale Hypertextual Web Search Engine, *Proceedings of the Intl. World-Wide-Web Conference*, pp. 107–17.

Bruder, B., Gaussel, N., Richard, J-C., Roncalli, T. (2013). *Regularization of Portfolio Allocation*. Lyxor Research, June.

Bystrom, H. (2013). *Movie Recommendations from User Ratings*, http://cs229.stanford.edu/proj2013/Bystrom-MovieRecommendationsFromUserRatings.pdf, Stanford University.

Carmona, R. (2004). *Statistical Analysis of Financial Data in S-Plus*, Springer Texts in Statistics. New York: Springer, ISBN 0387-20286-2.

Chamberlin, D. D., Boyce, R. F. *SEQUEL: A Structured English Query Language*. Proc. ACM SIGMOD Workshop on Data Description, Access and Control, Ann Arbor, Michigan (May 1974), pp. 249–64.

ACE and Chubb Are Now One, `http://new.chubb.com/en/us/?utm_source=bra nd_announcement&utm_medium=Q1&utm_term=SEM&utm_content=Google&utm_campa ign=Brand_Announce_US_EN_2016`

Clarke, E. M., Emerson, E. A. (1981). Design and Synthesis of Synchronization Skeletons Using Branching Time Temporal Logic, *Proceedings of Workshop on Logic of Programs*, pp. 52–71.

Colmerauer, A., Roussel, P. (1983). The Birth of Prolog. *ACM SIGPLAN Notices* 28 (3): p. 37.

Cryer, J. D., Chan, K. S. (2010). *Time Series Analysis with Applications in R*. Springer.

Damodaran, A. Notes from New York University Stern School of Business, `http://pages. stern.nyu.edu/~adamodar/New_Home_Page/invfables/pricepatterns.htm`

Eddelbuettel, D. (2013). *Seamless R and C++ Integration with Rcpp*. New York: Springer, 2013, ISBN 978-1461468677.

Eddelbuettel, D., Sanderson, C. (2014). RcppArmadillo: Accelerating R with High-Performance C++ Linear Algebra. *Computational Statistics and Data Analysis*, Volume 71, March 2014: pp. 1054–63.

Fairchild, G., Fries, J. (2012). *Lecture Notes: Social Networks: Models, Algorithms, and Applications* Lecture 3: January 24, `http://homepage.cs.uiowa.edu/~sriram/196/spring12/ lectureNotes/Lecture3.pdf`

Fama, E. F., French, K. R. (1995). Size and Book-to-Market Factors in Earnings and Returns. *Journal of Finance*, 50: pp. 131–55.

Fama, E. F., French, K. R. (1996). Multifactor Explanations of Asset Pricing Anomalies. *Journal of Finance*, 51: pp. 55–84.

Fletcher, T., Hussain, Z., Shawe-Taylor, J. (2010). Multiple Kernel Learning on the Limit Order Book. *JMLR Proceedings*, 11: pp. 167–74. `http://jmlr.org/proceedings/papers/v11/ fletcher10a/fletcher10a.pdf`

Fletcher, T. (2012). *Machine Learning for Financial Market Prediction,* Ph.D. Thesis, University College of London, `http://discovery.ucl.ac.uk/1338146/1/1338146.pdf`

Floyd, R. W. (1967). Assigning Meanings to Programs. *Proceedings of the American Mathematical Society Symposia on Applied Mathematics*, 19: pp. 19–31.

Forbes.com (2013). *Tenet to Buy Vanguard Health Amid "Obamacare" M&A Frenzy*, June 24.

Friedman, J., Hastie, T., Tibshirani, R. (2008). Sparse Inverse Covariance Estimation with the Graphical Lasso. *Biostatistics* 9: pp. 432–41.

Gareth, J., Witten, D., Hastie, T., Tibshirani, R. (2013). *An Introduction to Statistical Learning*. Springer.

GoogleFinance.com, *Titanium Metals Corp (NYSE:TIE)*, December 7, 2014. `www.google.com/ finance?cid=660449`

Goldfarb, D., Idnani, A. (1982). Dual and Primal-Dual Methods for Solving Strictly Convex Quadratic Programs. In J. P. Hennart (ed.), *Numerical Analysis*. Berlin: Springer-Verlag, pp. 226–39.

Goldfarb, D., Idnani, A. (1983). A Numerically Stable Dual Method for Solving Strictly Convex Quadratic Programs. *Mathematical Programming*. 27: pp. 1–33.

Greenblatt, J. (2006). *The Little Book That Beats the Market*, ISBN 0-471-73306-7.

Hamilton, J. D. (1994). *Time Series Analysis*, Princeton University Press.

Hartigan, J. A., Wong, M. A. (1979). Algorithm AS 136: A k-Means Clustering Algorithm. *Journal of the Royal Statistical Society*, Series C 28 (1): pp. 100–8. JSTOR 2346830.

Hastie, T., Tibshirani, R., Friedman, J. (2009). *The Elements of Statistical Learning: Data Mining, Inference, and Prediction*, Second Edition. Springer, February 2009.

Haug, E. G. (1998). *The Complete Guide to Option Pricing Formulas*. McGraw-Hill, ISBN 0-7863-1240-8.

Hoare, C. A. R. (1969). An Axiomatic Basis for Computer Programming. *Communications of the ACM* 12 (10): pp. 576–80, October.

Hogg, R. T., Craig, A. T. (1978). *Introduction to Mathematical Statistics*, Fourth Edition. Macmillan.

Hothorn, T., Hornik, K., Strobl, C., Zeileis, A. (2015). *Party: A Laboratory for Recursive Partytioning*. http://cran.r-project.org/web/packages/party/vignettes/party.pdf

Hull, J. (2006). *Options, Futures, and Other Derivatives*. Pearson/Prentice Hall.

Ihaka, R. (1998). R: *Past and Future History* (PDF) (Technical report). Statistics Department, The University of Auckland, Auckland, New Zealand.

Ito, K. (1951). On Stochastic Differential Equations. Memoirs, *American Mathematical Society* 4: pp. 1–51.

www.jdsu.com/News-and-Events/news-releases/Pages/jdsu-announces-1-for-8-reverse-stock-split.aspx

Karoui, N. E. (2009). *On the Realized Risk of High-Dimensional Markowitz Portfolios*. Department of Statistics, UC Berkeley, October.

Kinlay, J. (2011). *Can Machine Learning Techniques Be Used to Predict Market Direction? The 1,000,000 Model Test*. Posted on web site March 17, www.trade2win.com/boards/attachments/metatrader/130540d1330423251-build-neural-network-indicator-mt4-using-neuroshell-million-model-test.pdf

Laber, E.B., Zhou, H. Notes for ST 810 Advanced Computing, Department of Statistics, North Carolina State University, February, 25, 2013, www.stat.ncsu.edu/people/zhou/courses/st810/notes/lect09QP.pdf.

Ledolter, J. (2013). *Data Mining and Business Analytics with R*. John Wiley, May. ISBN: 978-1-118-44714-7, 368 pages.

MacQueen, J. B. (1967). Some Methods for Classification and Analysis of Multivariate Observations. *Proceedings of the 5th Berkeley Symposium on Mathematical Statistics and Probability* 1, University of California Press, pp. 281–97.

Markowitz, H. M. (1952). Portfolio Selection. *Journal of Finance* 7 (1): pp. 77–91.

Markowitz, H. M. (1959). *Portfolio Selection: Efficient Diversification of Investments*. New York: John Wiley & Sons. (Reprinted by Yale University Press, 1970, ISBN 978-0-300-01372-6.)

Morandat, F., Hill, B., Osvald, L., Vitek, J. (2012). *Evaluating the Design of the R Language*, ECOOP 2012-Object-Oriented Programming, 104-131, Lecture Notes in Computer Science 7313, Springer.

Oracle Unveils the Oracle Big Data Appliance: New Engineered System Helps Customers Maximize the Value of Enterprise Big Data. Oracle Openworld, San Francisco, October 3, 2011. www.oracle.com/us/corporate/press/512001

Pearl, J. (1988). *Probabilistic Reasoning in Intelligent Systems*. San Francisco: Morgan Kaufmann.

Pennacchi, G. (2007). *Theory of Asset Pricing*. Prentice Hall.

Perlin, M. (2006). *fMarkovSwitching: An R Package for Markov Regime Switching*.

Pnueli, A. (1977). *The Temporal Logic of Programs*. 18th Annual Symposium on Foundations of Computer Science (SFCS 1977), IEEE, pp. 46–57.

R Development Core Team. (2011). *R: A Language and Environment for Statistical Computing*. R Foundation for Statistical Computing.

Ruppert, D. (2011). *Statistics and Data Analysis for Financial Engineering*, Springer Texts in Statistics. New York: Springer, ISBN 9781441977861.

Sharpe, W. F. (1964). Capital Asset Prices: A Theory of Market Equilibrium under Conditions of Risk. *Journal of Finance* 19 (3), September 1964: pp. 425–42.

Sharpe, W. F., Alexander, G. J., Bailey, J. V. (1999). *Investments*, 6th Edition. Upper Saddle River, NJ: Prentice-Hall.

Shreve, S. (2004). *Stochastic Calculus for Finance I, The Binomial Asset Pricing Model*. New York: Springer.

Shreve, S. (2004). *Stochastic Calculus for Finance II, Continuous Time Models*. New York: Springer.

Shumway, R. H., Stoffer, D. S. (2006). *Time Series Analysis, and Its Applications with R Examples*. Springer.

Spechler, L. (2011). *Reverse Stock Splits Are Usually Good for Investors: Report*, Tuesday, March 22. `www.cnbc.com/id/42212417jdsu-announces-1-for-8-reverse-stock-split.aspx`

Swiss Move Roils Global Markets. *The Wall Street Journal*, January 16, 2015.

Tibshirani, R. (1996). Regression Shrinkage and Selection via the Lasso. *Journal of the Royal Statistical Society*, Series B 58: pp. 267–88.

Ullrich, C., Seese, D., Chalup, S. (2007). Foreign Exchange Trading with Support Vector Machines. In *Advances in Data Analysis*. Heidelberg, Berlin: Springer, pp. 539–46.

Venables, W. N., Ripley, B. D. (2002). *Modern Applied Statistics with S*, Fourth edition. Springer.

Whittaker, J. (1990). *Graphical Models in Applied Multivariate Statistics*. John Wiley, January, ISBN: 978-0-471-91750-2, 466 pages.

Zhao, T., Liu, H., Roeder, K., Lafferty, J., Wasserman, L. (2012). The Huge Package for High-Dimensional Undirected Graph Estimation in R. *Journal of Machine Learning Research* 13: pp. 1059–62, April.

Index